SHAKESPEARE'S LIBRARY.
VOL. V.

THE COMEDY OF ERRORS.

KING RICHARD III.

KING JOHN.

KING HENRY V.

THE SECOND PART OF
KING HENRY VI.

Shakespeare's Library

A COLLECTION OF THE

PLAYS ROMANCES NOVELS POEMS AND HISTORIES

EMPLOYED BY

SHAKESPEARE

IN THE COMPOSITION OF HIS WORKS

With Introductions and Notes

W. C. HAZLITT

SECOND EDITION

CAREFULLY REVISED AND GREATLY ENLARGED

The Text now First formed
from a New Collation of the Original Copies

VOLUME THE FIFTH
(Section II, Vol. I)

AMS PRESS INC.
New York
1965

822.33
Z H 431S

108372

AMS PRESS INC.
NEW YORK, N. Y. 10003

MANUFACTURED IN THE UNITED STATES OF AMERICA
ARNO PRESS, INC.

PREFACE.

———o———

THE Fifth and Sixth Volumes of "Shakespeare's Library," forming the second and concluding division of the present publication, contain eleven dramas, from which Shakespeare is supposed, with good reason, to have derived assistance, in greater or smaller measure, in the preparation of his own plays on the same subject.

These foundation-dramas stand, however, on a very unequal footing ; for, as elsewhere explained, the poet, in some cases, merely revised the existing texts ; in .rs, his obligation was scarcely more than nominal ; and in the rest, with one exception, the original piece supplied nothing beyond the outline and general suggestion.

The " Merry Wives of Windsor," as here reprinted from the 4to of 1602, exhibits, on the contrary, Shakespeare's own first sketch, afterwards completed and matured by himself, as we find it in the folio of 1623, and in the modern editions.

Almost all the dramatic compositions which are assembled in these two volumes are of the highest rarity ; but such is especially the case with the " Famous Victories of Henry V., 1598," " The Troublesome

Reign of King John, 1591," "The First Part of the Contention, 1594," the "True Tragedy of Richard, Duke of York, 1595," and the "True Tragedy of Richard III., 1594," all of which, with the exception of the last, are supposed to be *unique.* But three or four copies at most exist of any of them.

To bring them all together, therefore, in a convenient shape for reference appeared to be desirable. Of the whole number, four have never been collected before, and as regards three of the others, the "Taming of a Shrew," the "Famous Victories," and "King John," the editions employed in "Six Old Plays, 1779," were late reprints, instead of the *editiones principes*, which are generally purer, and (in inquiries of this kind) always more satisfactory and authoritative. But where the Editor of 1779, professing not to "depart from the original copies," chose the right texts, he failed altogether to observe that accuracy which in such cases is indispensable.

W. C. H.

THE COMEDY OF ERRORS.

THE PRINTER TO THE READERS.

———o———

THE writer hereof (loving Readers) having diverse
of this Poettes Comedies Englished, for the use
and delight of his private friends, who in Plautus
owne words are not able to understand them : I have
prevailed so far with him as to let this one go farther
abroad, for a publike recreation and delight to all
those, that affect the diverse sorts of bookes compiled
in this kind, wherof (in my judgment) in harmelesse
mirth and quicknesse of fine conceit, the most of
them come far short of this. And although I found
him very loath and unwilling to hazard this to the
curious view of envious detraction, (being as he tels
mee) neither so exactly written, as it may carry any
name of a Translation, nor such libertie therin used,
as that he would notoriously varie from the Poets
owne order : yet sith it is onely a matter of meri-
ment, and the litle alteration therof, can breede no
detriment of importance, I have over-rulde him so
farre, as to let this be offred to your curteous acceptance, and if you shall applaude his litle labour
heerein, I doubt not but he will endevour to gratifie
you with some of the rest better laboured, and more
curiously pollished.

Farewell.

* *Where you finde this marke, the Poets conceit is somewhat*
altred, by occasion either of the time, the country, or the phrase.

THE ARGUMENT.

———o———

* Two Twinborne sonnes, a Sicill marchant had,
Menechmus one, and Sosicles the other :
The first his Father lost a litle Lad,
The Grandsire namde the latter like his brother.
This (growne a man) long travell tooke to seeke
His Brother, and to Epidamnum came,
Where th' other dwelt inricht, and him so like,
That Citizens there take him for the same :
Father, wife, neighbours, each mistaking either,
Much pleasant error, ere they meete togither.

A PLEASANT AND FINE CONCEITED

C O M Æ D I E,

CALLED

M E N E C H M U S,

TAKEN OUT OF THE MOST EXCELLENT·

P O E T   P L A U T U S.

——*o*——

ACT I. SCENE I.

Enter PENICULUS, *a Parasite.*

PENICULUS was given mee for my name when I
was yong, bicause like a broome I swept all
cleane away, where so ere I become : Namely all the
vittels which are set before mee.   Now in my judgement, men that clap iron bolts on such captives as
they would keepe safe, and tie those servants in
chaines who they thinke will run away, they commit
an exceeding great folly : my reason is, these poore
wretches enduring one miserie upon an other, never
cease devising how by wrenching asunder their gives,
or by some subtiltie or other they may escape such
cursed bands.   If then ye would keep a man without

all suspition of running away from ye, the surest way
is to tie him with meate, drinke and ease :   Let him
ever be idle, eate his belly full, and carouse while
his skin will hold, and he shall never, I warrant ye,
stir a foote.   These strings to tie one by the teeth,
passe all the bands of iron, steele, or what metall so
ever, for the more slack and easie ye make them, the
faster still they tie the partie which is in them.   I
speake this upon experience of my selfe, who am
now going for Menechmus, there willingly to be tied
to his good cheare : he is commonly so exceeding
bountifull and liberall in his fare, as no marveyle
though such guestes as my selfe be drawne to his
Table, and tyed there in his dishes.   Now because I
have lately bene a straunger there, I meane to visite
him at dinner : for my stomacke mee-thinkes even
thrusts me into the fetters of his daintie fare.   But
yonder I see his doore open, and himselfe readie to
come foorth.

SCENE II.

Enter MENECHMUS *talking backe to his wife within.*

If ye were not such a brabling foole and mad-
braine scold as yee are, yee would never thus crosse
your husbande in all his actions.   'Tis no matter, let
her serve me thus once more, Ile send her home to
her dad with a vengeance.   I can never go foorth a
doores, but shee asketh mee whither I go ? what I
do ? what busines ? what I fetch ? what I carry ?
* As though she were a Constable or a toll-gatherer,
I have pamperd her too much : she hath servants
about her, wooll, flax, and all things necessary to
busie her withall, yet she watcheth and wondreth
whither I go.   Well sith it is so, she shall now have

some cause, I mean to dine this day abroad with a sweet friend of mine.

Pen. Yea mary now comes hee to the point that prickes me : this last speech gaules mee as much as it would doo his wife ; If he dine not at home, I am drest.

Men. We that have Loves abroad, and wives at home, are miserably hampred, yet would every man could tame his shrewe as well as I doo mine. I have now filcht away a fine ryding cloake of my wives, which I meane to bestow upon one that I love better. Nay, if she be so warie and watchfull over me, I count it an almes deed to deceive her.

Pen. Come, what share have I in that same?

Men. Out alas, I am taken.

Pen. True, but by your friend.

Men. What, mine owne Peniculus?

Pen. Yours (ifaith) bodie and goods if I had any.

Men. Why thou hast a bodie.

Pen. Yea, but neither goods nor good bodie.

Men. Thou couldst never come fitter in all thy life.

Pen. Tush, I ever do so to my friends, I know how to come alwaies in the nicke. Where dine ye to-day?

Men. Ile tell thee of a notable pranke.

Pen. What, did the Cooke marre your meate in the dressing? Would I might see the reversion.

Men. Tell me didst thou see a picture, how Jupiters Eagle snatcht away Ganimede, or how Venus stole away Adonis?

Pen. Often, but what care I for shadowes, I want substance.

Men. Looke thee here, looke not I like such a picture?

Pen. O ho, what cloake have ye got here?

Men. Prethee say I am now a brave fellow.

Pen. But hearke ye, where shall we dine?

Men. Tush, say as I bid thee man.

Pen. Out of doubt ye are a fine man.

Men. What? canst adde nothing of thine owne?

Pen. Ye are a most pleasant gentleman.

Men. On yet.

Pen. Nay not a word more, unlesse ye tell mee how you and your wife be fallen out.

Men. Nay I have a greater secret then that to impart to thee.

Pen. Say your minde.

Men. Come farther this way from my house.

Pen. So, let me heare.

Men. Nay farther yet.

Pen. I warrant ye man.

* *Men.* Nay yet farther.

Pen. Tis pittie ye were not made a water-man to row in a wherry.

Men. Why?

Pen. Because ye go one way, and looke an other, stil least your wife should follow ye. But what's the matter, Ist not almost dinner time?

Men. Seest thou this cloake?

Pen. Not yet. Well what of it?

Men. This same I meane to give to Erotium.

Pen. That's well, but what of all this?

Men. There I meane to have a delicious dinner prepard for her and me.

Pen. And me.

Men. And thee.

Pen. O sweet word. What, shall I knock presently at her doore?

Men. I knocke. But staie too Peniculus, let's not be too rash. Oh see shee is in good time comming forth.

Pen. Ah, he now lookes against the Sun, how her beames dazell his eyes.

Enter EROTIUM.

Ero. What mine owne Menechmus, welcome sweete heart.

Pen. And what am I, welcome too ?

Ero. You Sir ? ye are out of the number of my welcome guests.

* *Pen.* I am like a voluntary souldier, out of paie.

Men. Erotium, I have determined that here shal be pitcht a field this day ; we meane to drinke for the heavens : And which of us performes the bravest service at his weopon the wine boll, yourselfe as Captaine shall paie him his wages according to his deserts.

Ero. Agreed.

Pen. I would we had the weapons, for my valour pricks me to the battaile.

Men. Shall I tell thee sweete mouse ? I never looke upon thee, but I am quite out of love with my wife.

Ero. Yet yee cannot chuse, but yee must still weare something of hers : whats this same ?

Men. This ? such a spoyle (sweete heart) as I tooke from her to put on thee.

Ero. Mine owne Menechmus, well woorthie to bee my deare, of all dearest.

Pen. Now she showes her selfe in her likenesse, when shee findes him in the giving vaine, she drawes close to him.

Men. I thinke Hercules got not the garter from Hypolita so hardly, as I got this from my wife. Take this, and with the same, take my heart.

Pen. Thus they must do that are right Lovers : especially if they mean to [be] beggers with any speed.

Men. I bought this same of late for my wife, it stood mee (I thinke) in some ten pound.

Pen. There's tenne pounde bestowed verie thriftily.

Men. But knowe yee what I woulde have yee doo?

Ero. It shall bee done, your dinner shall be readie.

* *Men.* Let a good dinner be made for us three.

Harke ye, some oysters, a mary-bone pie or two,
some artichockes, and potato rootes, let our other
be as you please.

Ero. You shall Sir.

Men. I have a little businesse in this Cittie, by that
time dinner will be prepared.   Farewell till then,
sweete Erotium : Come Peniculus.

Pen. Nay I meane to follow yee : I will sooner
leese my life, then sight of you till this dinner be done.
[*Exeunt.*

Ero. Who's there ?   Call me Cylindrus the Cooke
hither.

Enter CYLINDRUS.

Cylindrus, take the Hand-basket, and heere, there's
ten shillings is there not ?

Cyl. Tis so mistresse.

Ero. Buy mee of all the daintiest meates ye can
get, ye know what I meane : so as three may dine
passing well, and yet no more then inough.

Cyl. What guests have ye to-day mistresse ?

Ero. Here will be Menechmus and his Parasite,
and myselfe.

Cyl. That's ten persons in all.

Ero. How many ?

Cyl. Ten, for I warrant you, that Parasite may
stand for eight at his vittels.

Ero. Go dispatch as I bid you, and looke ye returne with all speed.

Cyl. I will have all readie with a trice.   [*Exeunt.*

ACT II. SCENE I.

Enter MENECHMUS, SOSICLES. MESSENIO *his servant,*
and some Saylers.

Men. Surely Messenio, I thinke Sea-fairers never
take so comfortable a joy in any thing, as when they

have bene long tost and turmoyld in the wide seas, they hap at last to ken land.

Mes. Ile be sworn, I shuld not be gladder to see a whole Country of mine owne, then I have bene at such a sight. But I pray, wherfore are we now come to Epidamnum? must we needs go to see everie Towne that we heare off?

Men. Till I finde my brother, all Townes are alike to me : I must trie in all places.

Mes. Why then let's even as long as wee live seeke your brother : six yeares now have roamde about thus, Istria, Hispania, Massylia, Ilyria, all the upper sea, all high Greece, all Haven Towns in Italy. I think if we had sought a needle all this time, we must needs have found it, had it bene above ground. It cannot be that he is alive ; and to seek a dead man thus among the living, what folly is it?

Men. Yea, could I but once find any man that could certainly enforme me of his death, I were satisfied ; otherwise I can never desist seeking : Litle knowest thou Messenio how neare my heart it goes.

Mes. This is washing of a Blackamore. Faith let's goe home, unlesse ye meane we should write a storie of our travaile.

Men. Sirra, no more of these sawcie speeches, I perceive I must teach ye how to serve me, not to rule me.

Mes. I, so, now it appeares what it is to be a servant. Wel yet I must speake my conscience. Do ye heare sir? Faith I must tell ye one thing, when I looke into the leane estate of your purse, and consider advisedly of your decaying stocke, I hold it verie needful to be drawing homeward, lest in looking your brother, we quite lose ourselves. For this assure your selfe, this Towne Epidamnum, is a place of outragious expences, exceeding in all ryot and lasciviousnesse : and (I heare) as full of Ribaulds, Parasites,

Drunkards, Catchpoles, Cony-catchers, and Syco-
phants, as it can hold : then for Curtizans, why here's
the currantest stamp of them in the world.   Ye must
not thinke here to scape with as light cost as in other
places.   The verie name shews the nature, no man
comes hither *sine damno.*

Men. Yee say very well indeed : give mee my purse
into mine owne keeping, because I will so be the
safer, *sine damno.*

Mes. Why Sir?

Men. Because I feare you wil be busie among the
Curtizans, and so be cosened of it : then should I
take great paines in belabouring your shoulders, so to
avoid both these harms, Ile keep it my selfe.

Men. I pray do so sir, all the better.

Enter CYLINDRUS.

* I have tickling geare here yfaith for their dinners :
It grieves me to the heart to think how that cormor-
ant knave Peniculus must have his share in these
daintie morsels.   But what?   Is Menechmus come
alreadie, before I could come from the Market?
Menechmus, how do ye sir? how haps it ye come so
soone?

Men. God a mercy my good friend, doest thou
know mee?

Cyl. Know ye? no not I.   Where's mouldi-
chappes that must dine with ye?   A murrin on his
manners.

Men. Whom meanest thou good fellow?

Cyl. Why Peniculus worship, that whorson lick-
trencher, your Parasiticall attendant.

Men. What Peniculus? what attendant?   My attendant?   Surely this fellow is mad.

Mes. Did I not tell ye what cony-catching villaines
you should finde here?

Cyl. Menechmus, harke ye sir, ye come too soone backe again to dinner, I am but returned from the Market.

Men. Fellow, here thou shalt have money of me, goe get the priest to sacrifice for thee. I know thou art mad, els thou wouldst never use a straunger thus.

Cyl. Alas sir, Cylindrus was wont to be no stranger to you. Know ye not Cylindrus?

Men. Cylindrus, or Coliendrus, or what the divell thou art, I know not, neither do I care to know.

Cyl. I know you to be Menechmus.

Men. Thou shouldst be in thy wits, in that thou namest me so right, but tell me, where hast thou knowne me?

Cyl. Where? even heere, where ye first fell in love with my mistresse Erotium.

Men. I neither have Lover, neither knowe I who thou art.

Cyl. Know ye not who I am? who fils your cup and dresses your meate at our house?

Mes. What a slave is this? that I had somewhat to breake the Rascals pate withall.

Men. At your house, when as I never came in Epidamnum till this day.

Cyl. Oh thats true. Do ye not dwell in yonder house?

Men. Foule shame light upon them that dwell there, for my part.

Cyl. Questionlesse, hee is mad indeede, to curse himselfe thus. Harke ye Menechmus.

Men. What saist thou?

Cyl. If I may advise ye, ye shall bestow this money which ye offred me, upon a sacrifice for your selfe: for out of doubt you are mad that curse your selfe.

Mes. What a verlet art thou to trouble us thus?

Cyl. Tush he wil many times jest with me thus. Yet when his wife is not by, tis a ridiculous jest.

Men. Whats that?

Cyl. This I say, Thinke ye I have brought meate inough for three of you? If not, ile fetche more for you and your wench, and snatchcrust your Parasite.

Men. What wenches? what Parasites?

Mes. Villaine, Ile make thee tell me what thou meanest by all this talke?

Cyl. Away Jack Napes, I say nothing to thee, for I know thee not, I speake to him that I know.

Men. Out drunken foole, without doubt thou art out of thy wits.

Cyl. That you shall see by the dressing of your meat. Go, go, ye were better to go in and finde somewhat to do there, whiles your dinner is making readie. Ile tell my mistresse ye be here.

Men. Is he gone? Messenio I thinke uppon thy words alreadie.

Mes. Tush marke I pray, Ile laie fortie pound here dwels some Curtizan to whom this fellow belong.

Men. But I wonder how he knowes my name.

Mes. Oh ile tell yee. These Courtizans as soone as anie straunge shippe arriveth at the Haven, they sende a boye or a wench to enquire what they be, what their names be, whence they come, wherefore they come, &c. If they can by any meanes strike acquaintance with him, or allure him to their houses, he is their owne. We are here in a tickle place maister, tis best to be circumspect.

Men. I mislike not thy counsaile Messenio.

Mes. I, but follow it then. Soft, here comes somebodie forth. Here sirs, Marriners, keep this same amongst you.

Enter Erotium.

Let the doore stand so, away, it shall not be shut. Make hast within there ho : maydes looke that all things be readie. Cover the boord, put fire under

the perfuming pannes, let all things be very handsome.
Where is hee, that Cylindrus sayd stood without here?
Oh, what meane you sweet heart, that ye come not in?
I trust you thinke yourselfe more welcome to this
house then to your owne, and great reason why you
should do so. Your dinner and all things are readie
as you willed. Will ye go sit downe?

Men. Whom doth this woman speake to?

Ero. Even to you sir, to whom else should I speake?

Men. Gentlewoman ye are a straunger to me, and I
marvell at your speeches.

Ero. Yea sir, but such a straunger, as I acknowledge
ye for my best and dearest friend, and well you have
deserved it.

Men. Surely Messenio, this woman is also mad or
drunke, that useth all this kindnesse to mee uppon so
small acquaintance.

Mes. Tush, did not I tell ye right? these be but
leaves which fall upon you now, in comparison of the
trees that wil tumble on your necke shortly. I tolde
ye, here were silver tong'de hacsters. But let me talke
with her a litle. Gentlewoman what acquaintance
have you with this man? where have you seene him?

Ero. Where he saw me, here in Epidamnum.

Mes. In Epidamnum? who never till this day set
his foote within the Towne?

Ero. Go, go, flowting Jack. Menechmus what need
al this? I pray go in.

Men. She also calls me by my name.

Mes. She smels your purse.

Men. Messenio come hither, here take my purse.
Ile know whether she aime at me or my purse, ere I go.

Ero. Will ye go in to dinner, sir?

Men. A good motion, yea and thanks with all my
heart.

Ero. Never thanke me for that which you commaunded to be provided for yourselfe.

Men. That I commaunded?

Ero. Yea, for you and your Parasite.

Men. My Parasite?

Ero. Peniculus, who came with you this morning when you brought me the cloake which you got from your wife.

Men. A cloake that I brought you, which I got from my wife?

Ero. Tush what needeth all this jesting? Pray leave off.

Men. Jest or earnest, this I tell ye for a truth. I never had wife, neither have I, nor never was in this place till this instant; for only thus farre am I come, since I brake my fast in the ship.

Ero. What ship do ye tell me off?

* *Mes.* Marry ile tell ye, an old rotten weather-beaten ship, that we have saild up and downe in this sixe yeares, Ist not time to be going homewards thinke ye?

Ero. Come, come, Menechmus, I pray leave this sporting and go in.

Men. Well Gentlewoman, the truth is, you mistake my person, it is some other that you looke for.

Ero. Why, thinke ye I know ye not to be Menechmus, the sonne of Moschus, and have heard ye say, ye were borne at Siracusis where Agathocles did raigne, then Pythia, then Liparo, and now Hiero.

Men. All this is true.

Mes. Either shee is a witch, or else shee hath dwelt there and knew ye there.

Men. Ile go in with her, Messenio, Ile see further of this matter.

Mes. Ye are cast away then.

Men. Why so? I warrant thee, I can loose nothing, somwhat I shall gaine, perhaps a good lodging during my abode heere. Ile dissemble with her an other while. Nowe when you please let us go in, I made straunge with you, because of this fellow here, least he should tell my wife of the cloake which I gave you.

Ero. Will ye staie any longer for your Peniculus your Parasite?

Men. Not I, Ile neither staie for him, nor have him let come in, if he do come.

Ero. All the better. But sir, will ye doo one thing for me?

Men. What is that?

Ero. To beare that cloake which you gave me to the Diars, to have it new trimd and altred.

Men. Yea that will be well, so my wife shall not know it. Let mee have it with mee after dinner. I will but speake a word or two with this fellowe, then ile follow yee in. Hoe Messenio come aside: goe and provide for thyselfe, and these ship boyes in some Inne, then looke that after dinner you come hither for me. ◆

Mes. Ah maister, will yee be conycatcht thus wilfully?

Men. Peace foolish knave seest thou not what a sot she is, I shall coozen her I warrant thee.

Mes. Ay maister.

Men. Wilt thou be gone?

Mes. See, see, she hath him safe inough now. Thus he hath escaped a hundreth Pyrates hands at sea; and now one land-rover hath bourded him at first encounter. Come away fellowes.

ACT III.

Enter PENICULUS.

Twentie yeares I thinke and more, have I playde the knave, yet never playd I the foolish knave as I have done this morning. I follow Menechmus, and he goes to the Hall where now the Sessions are holden ; there trusting our selves into the prease of people, when I was in midst of all the throng, he gave me the slip, that I could never more set eye on him, and I dare sweare, came directly to dinner. That I would he that first devised these Sessions were hang'd, and all that ever came ot him : tis such a hinderance to men that have belly businesses in hand. If a man be not there at nis call, they amearce him with a vengeance. Men that have nothing else to do, that do neither bid anie man, nor are themselves bidden to dinner, such should come to Sessions, not we that have these matters to looke too. If it were so, I had not thus lost my dinner this day ; which I think in my conscience he did even purposely couzen me off. Yet I meane to go see : if I can but light uppon the reversion, I may perhaps get my peny-worthes. But how now ? is this Menechmus comming away from thence ? dinner done, and all dispatcht ? What execrable lucke have I ?

Enter MENECHMUS *the travailer.*

Tush I warrant ye, it shall be done as ye would wish. Ile have it so altered and trimd anew, that it shall by no meanes be knowne againe.

Pen. He carries the cloake to the dyars, dinner done, the wine drunke up, the Parasite shut out of doores. Well, let me live no longer, but ile revenge this injurious mockerie. But first ile harken awhile what he saith.

Men. Good goddes, who ever had such lucke as I ? Such cheare, such a dinner, such kinde entertainment ? And for a farewell, this cloake which I meane shall go with me.

Pen. He speakes so softly, I cannot heare what hee

saith. I am sure he is now flowting at me for the losse of my dinner.

Men. She tels me how I gave it her, and stole it from my wife. When I perceived she was in an error, though I knew not how, I began to sooth her, and to say every thing as she said. Meane while I far'd well, and that a' free cost.

Pen. Wel, I'le go talke with him.

Men. Who is this same that comes to me?

Pen. O well met fickle-braine, false and treacherous dealer, craftie and unjust promise-breaker. How have I deserved, you should so give me the slip, come before and dispatch the dinner, deale so badly with him that hath reverenst ye like a sonne?

Men. Good fellow, what meanest thou by these speeches? Raile not on mee, unlesse thou intendst to receive a railers hire.

Pen. I have received the injury (sure I am) alreadie.

Men. Prethee tell me, what is thy name?

Pen. Well, well, mock on sir, mock on; doo ye not know my name?

Men. In troth I never sawe thee in all my life, much lesse do I know thee.

Pen. Fie, awake Menechmus, awake; ye oversleepe your selfe.

Men. I am awake, I know what I say.

Pen. Know you not Peniculus?

Men. Peniculus, or Pediculus, I know thee not.

Pen. Did ye filch a cloake from your wife this morning, and bring it hither to Erotium?

Men. Neither have I wife, neither gave I any cloake to Erotium, neither filcht I any from any bodie.

Pen. Will ye denie that which you did in my company?

Men. Wilt thou say I have done this in thy company?

Pen. Will I say it? yea, I will stand to it.

Men. Away filthie mad drivell away; I will talke
no longer with thee.

Pen. Not a world of men shall staie me, but ile go
tell his wife of all the whole matter, sith he is at this
point with me. I will make this same as unblest a
dinner as ever he eate.

Men. It makes mee wonder, to see how every one
that meetes me cavils thus with me. Wherefore comes
foorth the mayd now?

Enter ANCILLA, EROTIUMS *mayd.*

Menechmus, my mistresse commends her hartily to
you, and seeing you goe that way to the Dyars, shee
also desireth you to take this chaine with you, and
put it to mending at the Goldsmythes, shee would
have two or three ounces of gold more in it, and the
fashion amended.

Men. Either this or any thing else within my power,
tell her, I am readie to accomplish.

Anc. Do ye know this chaine sir?

Men. Yea I know it to be gold.

Anc. This is the same you once tooke out of your
wives Casket.

Men. Who, did I?

Anc. Have you forgotten?

Men. I never did it.

Anc. Give it me againe then.

Men. Tarry, yes I remember it : tis it I gave your
mistres.

Anc. Oh, are ye advised?

Men. Where are the bracelets that I gave her likewise?

Anc. I never knew of anie.

Men. Faith, when I gave this, I gave them too.

Anc. Well sir, ile tell her this shall be done?

Men. I, I, tell her so, shee shall have the cloake and this both togither.

Anc. I pray Menechmus put a litle jewell for my eare to making for me : ye know I am alwaies readie to pleasure you.

Men. I will, give me the golde, ile paie for the workemanship.

Anc. Laie out for me, ile paie it ye againe.

Men. Alas I have none now.

Anc. When you have, will ye ?

Men. I will. Goe bid your mistresse make no doubt of these. I warrant her, ile make the best hand I can of them. Is she gone? Doo not all the gods conspire to loade mee with good lucke? well I see tis high time to get mee out of these coasts, least all these matters should be lewd devises to draw me into some snare. There shall my garland lie, because if they seeke me, they may think that I am gone that way. *I wil now goe see if I can finde my man Messenio, that I may tell him how I have sped.

ACT IV.

Enter MULIER, *the wife of* MENECHMUS *the Citizen, and* PENICULUS.

Mul. Thinkes he I will be made such a sot, and to be still his drudge, while he prowles and purloynes all that I have to give his Trulles?

Pen. Nay hold your peace, wee'll catch him in the nicke. This way he came, in his garland forsooth, bearing the cloak to the Dyars. And see I pray where the garland lyes, this way he is gone. See, see, where he comes againe without the cloake.

Mul. What shall I now do?

Pen. What? that which ye ever do ; bayt him for life.

Mul. Surely I thinke it best so.

Pen. Stay, wee will stand aside a little, ye shall catch him unawares.

Enter MENECHMUS *the Citizen.*

Men. It would make a man at his wittes end, to see how brabbling causes are handled yonder at the Court. If a poore man never so honest, have a matter come to be scand, there is hee outfaste, and overlaide with countenance : If a rich man never so vile a wretch, come to speake, there they are all readie to favour his cause. What with facing out bad causes for the oppressors, and patronizing some just actions for the wronged, the Lawyers they pocket up all the gaines. For mine own part, I come not away emptie, though I have bene kept long against my will : For taking in hand to dispatch a matter this morning for one of my acquaintaunce, I was no sooner entered into it, but his adversaries laide so hard unto his charge, and brought such matter against him, that do what I could, I could not winde my selfe out til now. I am sore afrayed Erotium thinks much unkindnes in me that I staid so long, yet she will not be angry considering the gift I gave her to day.

Pen. How thinke ye by that?

Mul. I thinke him a most vile wretch thus to abuse me.

Men. I will hie me thither.

Mul. Yea go pilferer, goe with shame inough, no bodie sees your lewd dealings and vile theevery.

Men. How now wife, what ail yee? what is the matter?

Mul. Aske yee mee whats the matter? Fye uppon thee.

Pen. Are ye not in a fit of an ague, your pulses beate so sore? to him I say.

Men. Pray wife why are ye so angry with me.

Mul. Oh you know not?

Pen. He knowes, but he would dissemble it.

Men. What is it?

Mul. My cloake.

Men. Your cloake.

Mul. My cloake man, why do ye blush?

Pen. He cannot cloake his blushing. Nay I might not go to dinner with you, do ye remember? to him I say.

Men. Hold thy peace Peniculus.

Pen. Ha hold my peace, looke ye, he beckons on mee to hold my peace.

Men. I neither becken nor winke on him.

Mul. Out, out, what a wretched life is this that I live.

Men. Why what aile ye woman?

Mul. Are ye not ashamed to deny so confidently, that which is apparant?

Men. I protest unto before all the goddes (is not this inough) that I beckond not on him.

Pen. Oh sir, this is another matter, touch him in the former cause.

Men. What former cause?

Pen. The cloake man, the cloake, fetch the cloake againe from the dyars.

Men. What cloake?

Mul. Nay ile say no more, sithe ye know nothing of your owne doings.

Men. Tell me wife, hath any of your servants abused you? Let me know.

Mul. Tush, tush.

Men. I would not have you to be thus disquietted.

Mul. Tush, tush.

Men. You are fallen out with some of your friends.

Mul. Tush, tush.

Men. Sure I am, I have not offended you.

Mul. No, you have dealt verie honestly.

Men. Indeed wife, I have deserved· none of these words, tell me, are ye not well?

Pen. What shall he flatter ye now?

Men. I speak not to thee knave. Good wife come hither.

Mul. Away, away, keep your hands off.

Pen. So, bid me to dinner with you againe, then slip away from me, when you have done, come forth bravely in your garland, to flout me: alas you know not me, even now.

Men. Why Asse, I neither have yet dined, nor came I there, since we were there togither.

Pen. Who ever heard one so impudent? Did yee not meete me here even now, and would make me beleeve I was mad, and said ye were a straunger, and ye knew me not?

Men. Of a truth since wee went togither to the Sessions Hall, I never returned till this very instant, as you two met me.

Pen. Go too, go too, I know ye well inough. Did ye think I would not cry quittance with you, yes faith, I have tolde your wife all.

Men. What hast thou told her?

Pen. I cannot tell, aske her?

Men. Tell me wife, what hath he told ye of me? Tell me I say, what was it?

Mul. As though you knew not, my cloake is stolne from me?

Men. Is your cloake stolne from ye?

Mul. Do ye aske me?

Men. If I knew, I would not aske.

Pen. O craftie companion, how he would shift the matter, come, come, deny it not, I tell ye, I have bewrayd all.

Men. What hast thou bewrayd;

Mul. Seeing ye will yeeld to nothing, be it never

so manifest, Heare mee, and ye shall know in fewe words both the cause of my griefe, and what he hath told me. I say my cloake is stolne from me.

Men. My cloake is stolne from me?

Pen. Looke how he cavils, she saith it is stolne from her.

Men. I have nothing to say to thee : I say wife tell me.

Mul. I tell ye, my cloake is stolne out of my house.

Men. Who stole it?

Mul. He knowes best that carried it away.

Men. Who was that?

Mul. Menechmus.

Men. T'was very ill done of him. What Menechmus was that?

Mul. You.

Men. I, who will say so ?

Mul. I will.

Pen. And I : that you gave it to Erotium.

Men. I gave it?

Mul. You.

Pen. You, you, you, shall we fetch a kennel of Beagles that may cry nothing but you, you, you. For we are wearie of it.

Men. Heare me one word wife, I protest unto you by all the gods, I gave it her not, indeed I lent it her to use a while.

Mul. Faith sir, I never give nor lend your apparell out of doores, mee thinkes ye might let mee dispose of mine own garments, as you do of yours. I pray then fetch it mee home againe.

Men. You shall have it againe without faile.

Mul. 'Tis best for you that I have : otherwise thinke not to roost within these doores againe.

Pen. Harke ye, what say ye to me now, for bringing these matters to your knowledge ?

Men. I say, when thou hast anie thing stolne from

thee, come to me, and I will helpe thee to seek it.
And so farewell.

Pen. God a mercy for nothing, that can never be,
for I have nothing in the world worth the stealing.
So now with husband wife and all, I am cleane out of
favour. A mischiefe on ye all.   [*Exit.*

Men. My wife thinks she is notably reveng'd on me,
now she shuttes me out of doores, as though I had
not a better place to be welcome too. If she shut
me out, I know who will shut me in. Now will I
entreate Erotium to let me have the cloake againe to
stop my wifes mouth withall, and then will I provide
a better for her. Ho who is within there? Some
bodie tell Erotium I must.speake with her.

Enter EROTIUM.

Ero. Who calls?

Men. Your friend, more then his owne.

Ero. O Menechmus, why stand ye here? pray come
in.

Men. Tarry, I must speake with ye here.

Ero. Say your minde.

Men. Wot ye what? my wife knowes all the matter
now, and my comming is, to request you, that I may
have againe the cloake which I brought you, that so
I may appease her : and I promise you, ile give ye an
other worth two of it.

Ero. Why I gave it you to carry to your dyars, and
my chaine likewise, to have it altered.

Men. Gave mee the cloake and your chaine? In
truth I never sawe ye since I left it heere with you,
and so went to the Sessions, from whence I am but
now returned.

Ero. Ah then sir, I see you wrought a device to
defraude mee of them both, did I therefore put yee in
trust ? Well, well.

Men. To defraud ye ?   No, but I say, my wife hath intelligence of the matter.

Ero. Why sir, I asked them not, ye brought them me of your owne free motion.   Now ye require them againe, take them, make sops of them : you and your wife together, think ye I esteeme them or you either. Goe, come to mee againe when I send for you.

Men. What so angry with mee, sweete Erotium ? Staie, I pray staie.

* *Ero.* Staie ?   Faith sir no : thinke ye I will staie at your request ?

Men. What gone in chafing, and clapt to the doores? now I am everie way shut out for a very benchwhistler : neither shall I have entertainment heere nor at home.   I were best go trie some other friends, and aske counsaile what to do.

ACT V.

Enter MENECHMUS *the traveller*, MULIER.

Men. Most foolishly was I overseene in giving my purse and money to Messenio, whom I can no where find, I feare he is fallen into some lewd companie.

Mul. I marvaile that my husband comes not yet, but see where he is now, and brings my cloake with him.

Men. I muse where the knave should be.

Mul. I will go ring a peale through both his eares for this dishonest behaviour.   Oh sir, ye are welcome home with your theeverie on your shoulders, are ye not ashamde to let all the world see and speake of your lewdnesse ?

Men. How now? what lackes this woman ?

Mul. Impudent beast, stand ye to question about it ?   For shame hold thy peace.

Men. What offence have I done woman, that I
should not speake to you?

Mul. Askest thou what offence? O shamelesse
boldnesse!

Men. Good woman, did ye never heare why the
Grecians termed Hecuba to be a bitch?

Mul. Never.

Men. Because she did as you do now, on whom
soever she met withall, she railed, and therefore well
deserved that dogged name.

Mul. These foule abuses and contumelies, I can
never endure, nay rather will I live a widowes life to
my dying day.

Men. What care I whether thou livest as a widow
or as a wife? This passeth, that I meet with none
but thus they vexe me with straunge speeches.

Mul. What straunge speeches? I say I will surely
live a widowes life, rather than suffer thy vile
dealings.

Men. Prethee for my part, live a widow till the
worldes end, if thou wilt.

Mul. Even now thou deniedst that thou stolest it
from me, and now thou bringest it home openly in
my sight. Art not ashamde?

Men. Woman, you are greatly to blame to charge
mee with stealing of this cloakè, which this day an
other gave me to carry to be trimde.

Mul. Well, I will first complaine to my father. Ho
boy, who is within there? Vecio go runne quickly
to my father, desire him of all love to come over
quickly to my house. Ile tell him first of your
prankes, I hope he will not see me thus handled.

Men. What a Gods name meaneth this mad woman
thus to vexe me?

Mul. I am mad because I tell ye of your vile
actions and lewde pilfring away my apparell and my
Jewels, to carry to your filthie drabbes.

Men. For whome this woman taketh mee I knowe
not, I know her as much as I know Hercules wives
father.

Mul. Do ye not know me? That's well, I hope
ye know my father, here he comes. Looke, do ye
know him?

Men. As much as I knew Calcas of Troy. Even
him and thee I know both alike.

Mul. Doest know neither of us both, me nor my
father?

Men. Faith nor thy grandfather neither.

Mul. This is like the rest of your behaviour.

Enter SENEX.

Sen. * Though bearing so great a burthen, as olde
age, I can make no great haste, yet as I can, I will
goe to my daughter, who I know hath some earnest
businesse with me, that shee sends in such haste, not
telling the cause why I should come. But I durst
laie a wager, I can gesse neare the matter: I suppose
it is some brabble between her husband and her.
These yoong women that bring great dowries to their
husbands, are so masterfull and obstinate, that they
will have their own wils in everie thing, and make
men servants to their weake affections. And yoong
men too, I must needs say, be naught now a dayes,
Well ile go see, but yonder mee thinks stands my
daughter, and her husband too. Oh tis even as I
gessed.

Mul. Father ye are welcome.

Sen. How now daughter? What? is all well? why
is your husband so sad? have ye bin chiding? tell
me, which of you is in the fault?

Mul. First father know, that I have not any way
misbehaved my selfe; but the truth is, I can by no

meanes endure this bad man to die for it : and therefore desire you to take me home to you againe.

Sen. What is the matter ?

Mul. He makes me a stale and a laughing stocke to all the world.

Sen. Who doth ?

Mul. This good husband here, to whom you married me.

Sen. See, see, how oft have I warned you of falling out with your husband ?

Mul. I cannot avoid it, if he doth so fowly abuse me.

Sen. I alwaies told ye, you must beare with him, ye must let him alone, ye must not watch him, nor dog him, nor meddle with his courses in any sort.

Mul. Hee hauntes naughtie harlottes under my nose.

Sen. Hee is the wiser, because hee cannot bee quiet at home.

Mul. There hee feastes and bancquets, and spendes and spoiles.

Sen. Wold ye have your husband serve ye as your drudge ? Ye will not let him make merry, nor entertaine his friendes at home.

Mul. Father, will ye take his part in these abuses, and forsake me ?

Sen. Not so, daughter ; but if I see cause, I wil as well tel him of his dutie.

Men. I would I were gone from this prating father and daughter.

Sen. Hitherto I see not but hee keepes ye well, ye want nothing, apparell, mony, servants, meate, drinke, all thinges necessarie : I feare there is fault in you.

Mul. But he filcheth away my apparell and my jewels, to give to his Trulles.

Sen. If he doth so, tis verie ill done, if not, you doo ill to say so.

Mul. You may beleeve me father, for there you may see my cloake which now he hath fetcht home againe, and my chaine which he stole from me.

Sen. Now will I goe talke with him to knowe the truth. Tell me Menechmus, how is it, that I heare such disorder in your life? Why are ye so sad man? wherein hath your wife offended you?

Men. Old man (what to call ye I know not) by high Jove, and by all the Gods I sweare unto you, whatsoever this woman here accuseth mee to have stolne from her, it is utterly false and untrue, and if I ever set foote within her doores, I wishe the greatest miserie in the worlde to light uppon me.

Sen. Why fond man, art thou mad to deny that thou ever setst foote within thine owne house where thou dwellest?

Men. Do I dwell in that house?

Sen. Doest thou denie it?

Men. I do.

Sen. Harke yee daughter, are ye remooved out of your house?

Mul. Father, he useth you as he doth me, this life I have with him.

Sen. Menechmus, I pray leave this fondnesse, ye jest too perversly with your friends.

Men. Good old father, what I pray have you to do with me? or why should this woman thus trouble me, with whom I have no dealings in the world?

Mul. Father, marke I pray how his eies sparkle, they rowle in his head, his colour goes and comes, he lookes wildly. See, see.

Men. What? they say now I am mad, the best way for me is to faine my selfe mad indeed, so I shall be rid of them.

Mul. Looke how he stares about, how he gapes.

Sen. Come away daughter, come from him.

Men. Bachus, Appollo, Phœbus, do ye call mee to

come hunt in the woods with you? I see, I heare, I come, I flie, but I cannot get out of these fields. Here is an old mastiffe bitch stands barking at mee, and by her stands an old goate that beares false witnesse against many a poore man.

Sen. Out upon him Bedlam foole.

Men. Harke, Appollo commaunds me that I shoulde rende out hir eyes with a burning lampe.

Mul. O father, he threatens to pull out mine eyes.

Men. Good gods, these folke say I am mad, and doubtlesse they are mad themselves.

Sen. Daughter.

Mul. Here father, what shall we do?

Sen. What if I fetch my folkes hither, and have him carried in before he do any harme.

Men. How now? they will carry mee in if I look not to my selfe : I were best to skare them better yet. Doest thou bid me, Phœbus, to teare this dog in peeces with my nayles? If I laie hold on him, I will do thy commandment.

Sen. Get thee into thy house daughter, away quickly.

Men. She is gone : yea Appollo I will sacrifice this olde beast unto thee : and if thou commandest mee, I will cut his throate with that dagger that hangs at his girdle.

Sen. Come not neare me, sirra.

Men. Yea I will quarter him, and pull all the bones out of his flesh, then will I barrell up his bowels.

Sen. Sure I am sore afraid he will do some hurt.

Men. Many things thou commandest me Appollo, wouldst thou have me harnesse up these wilde horses, and then clime up into the Chariot, and so over-ride this old stincking toothlesse Lyon. So now I am in the Chariot, and I have hold on the raines, here is my whip, hait, come ye wilde Jades make a hideous noyse with your stamping : hait I say, will ye not go?

Sen. What? doth he threaten me with his horses?

Men. Harke, now Appollo bids mee ride over him that stands there, and kill him. How now? who pulles mee downe from my Chariot by the haires of my head. Oh shall I not fulfill Appolloes command-ment?

Sen. See, see, what a sharpe disease this is, and how well he was even now. I will fetch a Physitian strait, before hee grow too farre into this rage. [*Exit.*

Men. Are they both gone now? Ile then hie me away to my ship, 'tis time to be gone from hence.
[*Exit.*

Enter Senex *and* Medicus.

Sen. My loines ake with sitting, and mine eies with looking, while I staie for yonder laizie Phisitian : see now where the creeping drawlatch comes.

Med. What disease hath hee said you? Is it a letarge or a lunacie, or melancholie, or dropsie?

Sen. Wherfore I pray do I bring you, but that you shuld tell me what it is? and cure him of it.

Med. Fie, make no question of that. Ile cure him I warrant ye. Oh here he comes, staie, let us marke what he doth.

Enter Menechmus *the Citizen.*

Men. Never in my life had I more overthwart for-tune in one day, and all by the villanie of this false knave the Parasite, my Ulisses that workes such mis-chiefs against mee his king. But let me live no longer but ile be revengde uppon the life of him : his life? nay tis my life, for hee lives by my meate and drinke. Ile utterly withdraw the slaves life from him. And Erotium shee sheweth plainly what she is; who because I require the cloake againe to carrie to my wife, saith I gave it her, and flatly falles out with me. How unfortunate am I?

Sen. Do ye heare him ?

Med. He complaines of his fortune.

Sen. Go to him.

Med. Menechmus, how do ye man? why keepe you not your cloake over your arme? It is verie hurtfull to your disease. Keepe ye warme I pray.

Men. Why hang thyself, what carest thou?

Med. Sir can you smell anie thing?

Men. I smell a prating dolt of thee.

Med. Oh I will have your head throughly purged. Pray tell me Menechmus, what use you to drinke? white wine or claret?

Men. What the divell carest thou?

Sen. Looke, his fit now begins.

Men. Why doest not as well aske mee whether I eate bread, or cheese, or beefe, or porredge, or birdes that beare feathers, or fishes that have finnes?

Sen. See what idle talke he falleth into.

Med. Tarry, I will aske him further. Menechmus, tell me, be not your eyes heavie and dull sometimes?

Men. What doest thinke I am an Owle?

Med. Doo not your guttes gripe ye, and croake in your belly?

Men. When I am hungrie they do, else not.

Med. He speakes not like a mad man in that. Sleepe ye soundly all night?

Men. When I have paid my debts I do. The mischiefe light on thee, with all thy frivolous questions.

Med. Oh now he rageth upon those words, take heed.

Sen. Oh this is nothing to the rage he was in even now. He called his wife bitch, and all to nought.

Men. Did I?

Sen. Thou didst, mad fellow, and threatenedst to ryde over me here with a Chariot and horses, and to kill mee, and teare me in peeces. This thou didst, I know what I say.

Men. I say, thou stolest Jupiters Crowne from his head, and thou wert whipt through the Towne for it, and that thou hast kild thy father, and beaten thy mother. Doo ye thinke I am so mad that I cannot devise as notable lyes of you, as you do of me?

Sen. Maister Doctor, pray heartily make speede to cure him, see ye not how mad he waxeth?

Med. Ile tell ye, hee shall be brought over to my house, and there will I cure him.

Sen. Is that best?

Med. What else? there I can order him as I list.

Sen. Well, it shall be so.

Med. Oh sir, I will make yee take neesing powder this twentie dayes.

Men. Ile beate yee first with a bastanado, this thirtie dayes.

Med. Fetch men to carry him to my house.

Sen. How many will serve the turne?

Med. Being no madder than hee is now, foure will serve.

Sen. Ile fetch them, staie you with him maister Doctor.

Med. No by my faith, Ile goe home to make readie all things needfull. Let your men bring him hither.

Sen. I go.   [*Exeunt.*

Men. Are they both gone? Good Gods what meaneth this? These men say I am mad, who without doubt are mad themselves. I stirre not, I fight not, I am not sicke. I speake to them, I know them. Well what were I now best to do? I would goe home, but my wife shuttes me foorth a doores. Erotium is as farre out with me too. Even here I will rest me till the evening, I hope by that time, they will take pittie on me.

Enter MESSENIO *the Travellers servant.*

*Mes. The proofe of a good servant, is to regard

his maisters businesse as well in his absence, as in his presence : and I thinke him a verie foole that is not carefull as well for his ribbes and shoulders, as for his belly and throate. When I think upon the rewards of a sluggard, I am ever pricked with a carefull regard of my backe and shoulders : for in truth I have no fancie to these blows, as many a one hath : methinks it is no pleasure to a man to be basted with a ropes end two or three houres togither. I have provided yonder in the Towne, for all our marriners, and safely bestowed all my masters Trunkes and fardels : and am now comming to see if he be yet got forth of this daungerous gulfe, where I feare me [he] is overplunged, pray God he be not overwhelmed and past helpe ere I come.

Enter SENEX, *with foure Lorarii, porters.*

Sen. Before Gods and men, I charge and commaund you sirs, to execute with great care that which I appoint you : if yee love the safetie of your owne ribbes and shoulders, then goe take me up my sonne in lawe, laie all hands upon him, why stand ye stil ? what do ye doubt ? I saie, care not for his threatnings, nor for anie of his words. Take him up and bring him to the Phisitians house : I will go thither before. [*Exit.*

Men. What newes ? how now masters ? what will ye do with me ? why do ye thus beset me ? whither carrie ye mee ? Helpe, helpe, neighbors, friends, Citizens !

Mes. O Jupiter, what do I see ? my maister abused by a companie of varlets.

Men. Is there no good man will helpe me ?

Mes. Helpe ye maister ? yes the villaines shall have my life before they shall thus wrong ye. Tis more fit I should be kild, then you thus handled.

Pull out that rascals eye that holds ye about the necke there. I'le clout these peasants, out ye rogue, let go ye varlet.

Men. I have hold of this villaines eie.

Mes. Pull it out, and let the place appeare in his head. Away ye cutthroat theeves, ye murtherers.

Lo. Omnes. O, O, ay, ay, crie pittifullie.

Mes. Away, get ye hence, ye mongrels, ye dogs. Will ye be gone? Thou raskal behind there, ile give thee somewhat more, take that. It was time to come maister, you had bene in good case if I had not bene heere now, I tolde you what would come of it.

Men. Now as the gods love me, my good friend I thank thee : thou hast done that for me which I shall never be able to requite.

Mes. I'le tell ye how sir, give me my freedome.

Men. Should I give it thee?

Mes. Seeing you cannot requite my good turne.

Men. Thou art deceived man.

Mes. Wherein?

Men. On mine honestie, I am none of thy maister, I had never yet anie servant would do so much for me.

Mes. Why then bid me be free : will you?

Men. Yea surelie, be free, for my part.

Mes. O sweetly spoken, thanks my good maister.

Servus alius. Messenio, we are all glad of your good fortune.

Mes. O maister, ile call you maister still, I praie use me in anie service as ye did before, ile dwell with you still, and when ye go home, ile wait upon you.

Men. Nay, nay, it shall not need.

Mes. Ile go strait to the Inne and deliver up my accounts and all your stuffe : your purse is lockt up safely sealed in the casket, as you gave it mee. I will goe fetch it to you.

Men. Do, fetch it.

Mes. I will.

Men. I was never thus perplext. Some deny me to be him that I am, and shut me out of their doores. This fellow saith he is my bondman, and of me he begs his freedome : he will fetch my purse and monie : well if he bring it, I will receive it, and set him free. I would he would so go his way. My old father in lawe and the Doctor saie I am mad, who ever sawe such straunge demeanors? well though Erotium be never so angrie, yet once againe ile go see if by intreatie I can get the cloake on her to carrie to my wife.   [*Exit.*

Enter MENECHMUS *the Traveller, and* MESSENIO.

Men. Impudent knave, wilt thou say that I ever saw thee since I sent thee away to day, and bad thee come for mee after dinner?

Mes. Ye make me starke mad : I tooke ye away and reskued ye from foure great bigboand villaines, that were carrying ye away even heere in this place. Heere they had ye up, you cried, Helpe, helpe. I came running to you : you and I togither beate them away by maine force. Then for my good turne and faithfull service, ye gave mee my freedome : I tolde ye I would go fetch your Casket, now in the mean time you ranne some other way to get before me, and so you denie it all againe.

Men. I gave thee thy freedome?

Mes. You did.

Men. When I give thee thy freedome, Ile be a bondman my selfe : go thy wayes.

Mes. Whewe, marry I thanke ye for nothing.

Enter MENECHMUS *the Citizen.*

Men. Forsworne Queanes, sweare till your hearts

ake, and your eyes fall out, ye shall never make me
beleeve that I carried hence either cloake or chaine.

Mes. O heavens, maister what do I see?

Men. Tra. What?

Mes. Your ghoast.

Men. Tra. What ghoast?

Mes. Your Image, as like you as can be possible.

Men. Tra. Surely not much unlike me as I thinke.

Men. Cit. O my good friend and helper, well met:
thanks for thy late good helpe.

Mes. Sir, may I crave to know your name?

Men. Cit. I were too blame if I should not tell thee
anie thing, my name is Menechmus.

Men. Tra. Nay my friend, that is my name.

Men. Cit. I am of Syracuse in Sicilia.

Men. Tra. So am I.

Mes. Are you a Syracusan?

Men. Cit. I am.

Mes. O, ho, I know ye: this is my maister, I
thought hee there had bene my maister, and was
proffering my service to him, pray pardon me sir, if
I said any thing I should not.

Men. Tra. Why doating patch, didst thou not
come with me this morning from the ship?

Mes. My faith he saies true, this is my maister, you
may go looke ye a man: God save ye maister: you
sir farewell. This is Menechmus.

Men. Cit. I say that I am Menechmus.

Mes. What a jest is this? Are you Menechmus?

Men. Cit. Even Menechmus the sonne of Moschus.

Men. Tra. My fathers sonne?

Men. Cit. Friend, I go about neither to take your
father nor your country from you.

Mes. O immortal Gods, let it fall out as I hope, and
for my life these are the two Twinnes, all things agree
so jump togither. I will speake to my maister. Menechmus.

Both. What wilt thou?

Mes. I call ye not both, but which of you came with me from the ship?

Men. Cit. Not I.

Men. Tra. I did.

Mes. Then I call you. Come hither.

Men. Tra. What's the matter?

Mes. This same is either some notable cousening Jugler, or else it is your brother whom we seeke. I never sawe one man so like an other, water to water, nor milke to milke, is not liker then he is to you.

Men. Tra. Indeed I thinke thou saiest true. Finde it that he is my brother, and I here promise thee thy freedom.

Mes. Well, let me about it. Heare ye sir, you say your name is Menechmus.

Men. Cit. I do.

Mes. So is this mans. You are of Syracusis?

Men. Cit. True.

Mes. So is he. Moscus was your father?

Men. Cit. He was.

Mes. So was he his. What will you say, if I find that ye are brethren and twins?

Men. Cit. I would thinke it happie newes.

Mes. Nay staie maisters both, I meane to have the honor of this exploit. Answere me : your name is Menechmus?

Men. Cit. Yea.

Mes. And yours?

Men. Tra. And mine.

Mes. You are of Syracusis ?

Men. Cit. I am.

Men. Tra. And I.

Mes. Well, this goeth right thus farre. What is the farthest thing that you remember there?

Men. Cit. How I went with my father to Tarentum, to a great mart, and there in the preasse I was stolne from him.

Men. Tra. O Jupiter !

Mes. Peace, what exclaiming is this? How old were ye then?

Men. Cit. About seven yeare old, for even then I shedde teeth, and since that time, I never heard of anie of my kindred.

Mes. Had ye never a brother?

Men. Cit. Yes, as I remember, I heard them say, we were two twinnes.

Men. Tra. O fortune!

Mes. Tush, can ye not be quiet? Were ye both of one name?

Men. Cit. Nay (as I think) they cald my brother, Sosicles.

Men. Tra. It is he, what need farther proofe? O Brother, Brother, let me embrace thee.

Men. Cit. Sir, if this be true, I am wonderfully glad, but how is it, that ye are called Menechmus?

Men. Tra. When it was tolde us that you and our father were both dead, our Graundsire (in memorie of my fathers name) chaungde mine to Menechmus.

Men. Cit. Tis verie like he would do so indeed. But let me aske ye one question more, what was our mothers name?

Men. Tra. Theusimarche.

Men. Cit. Brother, the most welcome man to mee, that the world holdeth.

Men. Tra. I joy, and ten thousand joyes the more, having taken so long travaile and huge paines to seeke you.

Mes. See now, how all this matter comes about. This it was, that the Gentlewoman had ye in to dinner, thinking it had bene he.

Men. Cit. True it is I, willed a dinner to be provided for me heere this morning, and I also brought hither closely a cloake of my wives, and gave it to this woman.

Men. Tra. Is not this the same, brother?

Men. Cit. How came you by this?

Men. Tra. This woman met me, had me in to dinner, enterteined me most kindly, and gave me this cloake, and this chaine.

Men. Cit. Indeed she tooke ye for mee: and I beleeve I have bene as straungely handled by occasion of your comming.

Mes. You shall have time inough to laugh at all these matters hereafter. Do ye remember maister, what ye promised me?

Men. Cit. Brother, I will intreate you to performe your promise to Messenio, he is worthie of it.

Men. Tra. I am content.

Mes. Io Tryumphe.

Men. Tra. Brother, will ye now go with me to Syracusis?

Men. Cit. So soone as I can sell away such goods as I possesse here in Epidamnum, I will go with you.

Men. Tra. Thanks my good brother.

Men. Cit. Messenio, plaie thou the Crier for me, and make a proclamation.

Mes. A fit office. Come on. O yes. What day shall your sale be?

Men. Cit. This day sennight.

Mes. All men, women and children in Epidamnum, or elsewhere, that will repaire to Menechmus house this day sennight, shall there finde all maner of things to sell: servaunts, household stuffe, house, ground and all: so they bring readie money. Will ye sell your wife too sir?

Men. Cit. Yea, but I thinke no bodie will bid money for her.

Mes. Thus Gentlemen we take our leaves, and if we have pleasde, we require a Plaudite.

FINIS.

KING RICHARD III.

The True Tragedie of Richard the Third : Wherein is showne the death of Edward the fourth, with the smothering of the two yoong Princes in the Tower : With a lamentable ende of Shores wife, an example for all wicked women. And lastly the coniunction and ioyning of the two noble Houses, Lancaster and Yorke. As it was playd by the Queenes Maiesties Players. London Printed by Thomas Creede, and are to be sold by William Barley, at his shop in Newgate Market, neare Christ Church doore. 1594. 4°.

It may be said that there is nothing in common between Shakespeare's play, as printed in 1597, and the "True Tragedy," as printed in 1594; but to a certain extent it seemed to be desirable to make the earlier and inferior drama part of the series, inasmuch as it serves to show the extraordinary mastery of Shakespeare and the poverty of the material with which he had to deal. Here, as elsewhere, he has gone a good deal to his favourite Holinshed, whom he has sometimes copied verbally. See Douce's "Illustrations," ii. 40-1.[1] Legge's "Richardus Tertius," of which three or four MSS. are known, is annexed much for the same reason. At the same time, it is gravely to be doubted whether it ever formed part of "Shakespeare's Library," or whether the great bard ever set eyes on it. It is the performance mentioned by Harington in the "Brief Apology of Poetry," attached to his version of Ariosto, 1591.

In connection with the play of "Richard III.," it would be as well for readers to have before them, or at least to peruse, the "Song of Lady Bessy," printed in the Percy Society's Series, in Halliwell's "Palatine Anthology," 1850, and by Mr Heywood separately, 8°, 1809; and also Giles Fletcher the elder's remarkable poem, published, or at least printed, in 1593, entitled "The Rising to the Crown of Richard the Third," which is inserted in Grosart's edition of Fletcher's works.

Christopher Brooke's powerful production, "The Ghost of Richard the Third," 4°, 1614, reprinted for the Shakespeare Society, is only noticeable as a striking outgrowth or outcome from the play, by which it was almost unquestionably suggested.

---

[1] Another Latin play on the subject, grounded more or less on Legge's, by Henry Lacy, of Trinity College, Cambridge, was performed there in 1586. It was never printed, but MSS. copies of it are in Harl. 2412 and 6926.

BARRON FIELD'S INTRODUCTION.[1]

—o—

MALONE commences his History of the English Stage by saying that "Dryden has truly observed that Shakespeare 'found not, but created first, the stage;'"[2] and the critic then proceeds to produce evidence which shows that this observation is not true, as most certainly it is not. "It was in truth (as Mr Collier more judiciously says) created by no one man, and in no one age; and, whatever improvements Shakespeare introduced, it will be seen that when he began to write for the theatre, our drama was completely formed and firmly established."[3] Bad as the following play is, it is a drama, completely formed, and was regularly acted. If Dryden had said that Shakespeare found the stage of brick, and left it of marble, it would have answered his purpose as well, and would have been nearer to the truth.

Of the propriety of making this reprint one of the Society's publications there can be no doubt. Architects tell us that when a gigantic object is of just and natural proportions, the only way to make it look large is to place a smaller natural object close to it; and they instance the dome of St Peter's Church at

---

1 To the Shakespeare Society's edition, 8°, 1844.
2 Prologue to an alteration of "Troilus and Cressida."
3 Preface to "History of English Dramatic Poetry," p. ix.

Rome. Were either the height or the breadth of that
monument exaggerated, and the building thus dis-
proportioned, it would look large without any such
comparison. So it is with our gigantic Shakespeare.
The best way to measure him is to place such an
ordinary contemporary work as the following in
juxtaposition with his " Richard the Third." The
author of the " True Tragedy" may perhaps, by
making a long arm, reach to the knee of the Colossus.
Massinger and Marlowe could walk under his huge
legs; Ben Jonson might touch his waist, by mounting
an antique; Beaumont and Fletcher could stand
under each of his arms. He could take up Ford and
Webster in the hollow of either hand; and so on.

Antiquity and priority to Shakespeare constituting
the only interest of the following piece, I have re-
frained from enforcing the metre [1] and modernising
the orthography of it, as I did in Heywood's " Edward the Fourth," and have made it, with the exception of palpable errors of the press, a *facsimile* of the
old edition, now reprinted through the liberality of
His Grace the Duke of Devonshire, the owner of the
copy.

The best introduction to this history will be found
in Mr Collier's edition of Shakespeare, vol. v., pp.
342–5. But I agree with Mr Boswell that our great

---

[1] In one instance, in Heywood's " Histories," I stretched the
word *canst*, to fill up the measure of the line, unnecessarily.
Page 37.
        " *Chub.* Thou cannest bear me witness, I had ta'en."

My brother, the Rev. F. Field, on reading the work, discovered
that the word " Chub " should be part of the line, and not the
name of the speaker. All the four old editions have the same
error. The members of the Society will therefore please to
correct the line as follows—

        Chub, thou canst bear me witness I had ta'en.

poet must be seen this humble work of his predecessor. Mr Collier says that "we cannot trace
any resemblances but such as were probably purely
accidental, and are merely trivial." The reader will
judge for himself. I have in the notes pointed out
several parallel ideas. The following line in the
Battle-scene is, in my opinion, quite enough to show
that Shakespeare considered Nature, as Molière said
of Wit, as his property, and that he had a right to
seize it wherever he found it—

> *King.* A horse, a horse, a fresh horse.

Mr Collier adds that "the portion of the story in
which the two plays make the nearest approach to
each other, is just before the murder of the Princes,
where Richard strangely takes a page into his con-
fidence respecting the fittest agent for the purpose."
This should hardly be called strange in our dramatist,
since it is authorised in the history by Sir Thomas
More—

> The same night King Richard said to a secret page of his, Ah,
> whom shall a man trust? they that I have brought up myself,
> they that I weened would have most surely served me, even
> those fail me, and at my commandment will do nothing for me.
> Sir, quoth the page, there lieth one in the pallet chamber with-
> out, that I dare well say, to do your grace pleasure, the thing
> were right hard that he would refuse, meaning by this James
> Tyrrell.

It is impossible to say who was the author of this
work. Mr Boswell, in reprinting the incorrect *torso*
of it in his edition of Shakespeare, inclined to think
it was the same person who wrote "The lamentable
Tragedie of Locrine," 1595, from the resemblance of
the style of the passage at page 117 to the two extracts
which he makes from that old play, in one of which
the word *revenge* is harped upon three times, and in
the other the word *Guendoline* six. But this is one of

the commonest artifices of rhetoric, and has been beautifully employed by Shakespeare himself—

> "If you did know to whom I gave the ring,
> If you did know for whom I gave the ring,
> And would conceive for what I gave the ring,
> And how unwillingly I left the ring,
> When nought would be accepted but the ring,
> You would abate the strength of your displeasure." [1]

It seems to have been a recommendation to our early historical plays (as the present is perhaps the very earliest printed one), to entitle them *true*—

> "So sad, so tender, and so *true*." [2]

So we have the "True Tragedy of Richard Duke of York," the precursor of Shakespeare's "Henry the Sixth;" and I have no doubt, from the manner in which the prologue to his "Henry the Eighth" dwells upon the words *truth* and *true*, that one of its titles was "All is true," and that it is the same play as is referred to by Sir Henry Wotton in 1613, under that name, as "representing some principal pieces of the raign of Henry 8," [3] and that by the words "a new play," which Shakespeare's "Henry the Eighth" could not have been in that year, Sir Henry meant only a revival.

The explanatory notes that are necessary to this reprint are so few and brief, that I have placed them at the foot of the page ; and the reader will remember, *passim*, that the letter *A* is used for the exclamation *Ah !* and *I* for the affirmation *Ay*, except where the latter is obviously the pronoun.

---

[1] "Merchant of Venice," act v.   [2] Shenstone.
[3] "Reliquiæ Wottonianæ, 3d ed. p. 425.

The Trve Tragedie of Richard the Third.

—o—

Enters TRUTH *and* POETRIE. *To them the Ghoast of
George Duke of Clarence.*

Ghost. CRESCE, cruor: sanguis satietur sanguine:
    cresce,
    Quod spero citò. O citò, citò, vendicta.[1]
                                                    [*Exit.*

---

[1] [Old copy, *cresse—sanguinis*, &c. Latin is almost always
misprinted in early plays.] "Increase, blood! Let blood be
satisfied with blood! Which I hope it quickly will. O, quickly,
quickly, revenge!" *Vindicta*, in our old plays, seems to have
constituted the knot, worthy of a Ghost's intervention to avenge.
In the "Battle of Alcazar," 1594, we have, "Enter three Ghosts
crying *Vindicta;*" and the word occurs in several other plays,
cited by Mr Gifford (Jonson, ii. 457) and Dyce (Peele, ii. 17),
insomuch that it exposed itself to ridicule; and our readers will
remember the passage in Lodge's "Wit's Miserie, or the World's
Madness," 1596, in which one of the devils is said to be "a foule
lubber, and looks as pale as the vizard of the ghost, who cried
so miserably at the theatre, "*Hamlet, revenge;*" and the anxiety
of the commentators, to discover whether this alluded to Shakespeare's "Hamlet," or to an older play upon that subject: an
anxiety just and natural as it respects the date of the great poet's
work, but worthless as to the question whether his play, at first
entitled "The Revenge of Hamlet," were meant to be ridiculed
or not.

Poetrie. Truth well met.

Truth. Thankes Poetrie, what makes thou vpon a
    stage?

Poet. Shadowes.

Truth. Then will I adde bodies to the shadowes,
Therefore depart and giue Truth leaue
To shew her pageant.

Poet. Why will Truth be a Player?

Truth. No, but Tragedia like for to present
A Tragedie in England done but late,
That will reuiue the hearts of drooping mindes.

Poet. Whereof?

Truth. Marry thus.
Richard Platagenet of the House of Yorke,
Claiming the Crowne by warres, not by dissent,
Had as the Chronicles make manifest,
In the two and twentith yeare of Henry the sixth,
By act of Parliament intailed to him
The Crowne and titles to that dignitie,
And to his ofspring lawfully begotten,
After the decease of that forenamed King,
Yet not contented for to staie the time,
Made warres vpon King Henry then the sixth,
And by outrage suppressed that vertuous King,
And wonne the Crowne of England to himselfe,
But since at Wakefield in a battell pitcht,
Outragious Richard breathed his latest breath,
Leauing behind three branches of that line,
Three sonnes: the first was Edward now the King,
George of Clarence, and Richard Glosters Duke,
Then Henry claiming after his decease
His stile, his Crowne and former dignitie
Was quite suppressed, till this Edward the fourth.

Poet. But tell me truth, of Henry what ensued?

Truth. Imprisoned he, in the Tower of London lies
By strict command, from Edward Englands King,
Since cruelly murthered, by Richard Glosters Duke.

Poet. Whose Ghoast was that did appear to vs?

Truth. It was the ghost of George the duke of
   Clarence,
Who was attected in King Edwards raigne,
Falsly of Treason to his royaltie,
Imprisoned in the Tower was most vnnaturally,
By his owne brother, shame to parents stocke,
By Glosters Duke drowned in a but of wine.

  Poet. What shield was that he let fall?

  Truth. A shield conteining this, in full effect,
Blood sprinkled, springs: blood spilt, craues due
   reuenge:
Whereupon he writes, *Cresce, cruor :*
Sanguis satietur sanguine : cresce,
Quod spero citò. O citò, citò, vendicta!

  Poet. What maner of man was this Richard Duke
   of Gloster?

  Truth. A man ill shaped, crooked backed, lame
   armed, withall,
Valiantly minded, but tyrannous in authoritie,
So during the minoritie of the yoong Prince,
He is made Lord Protector ouer the Realme.
Gentiles suppose that Edward now hath raigned
Full two and twentie yeares, and now like to die,
Hath summond all his Nobles to the Court,
To sweare alleageance with the Duke his brother,
For truth vnto his sonne the tender Prince,
Whose fathers soule is now neare flight to God,
Leauing behind two sonnes of tender age,
Fiue daughters to comfort the haplesse Queene,
All vnder the protection of the Duke of Gloster:
Thus gentles, excuse the length by the matter,
And here begins Truthes Pageant, Poetrie
Wend with me.   *[Exeunt.*

Enter EDWARD THE FOURTH, LORD HASTINGS, LORD
    MARCUS, *and* ELIZABETH.   *To them* RICHARD.

Hast. Long liue my soueraigne, in all happinesse.
Mar. An honourable age with Cresuss wealth,
Hourely attend the person of the King.
King. And welcome you Peeres of England vnto
    your King.
Hast. For our vnthankfulnesse the heauens hath
    throwne thee downe.
Mar. I feare for our ingratitude, our angry God
    doth frowne.
King. Why Nobles, he that laie me here
Can raise me at his pleasuré.
But my deare friends and kinsmen,
In what estate I now lie it is seene to you all,
And I feel myselfe neare the dreadfull stroke of death.
And the cause that I haue requested you in friendly
    wise
To meete togither in this,
That where malice & enuy sowing sedition in the
    harts of men
So would I haue that admonished and friendly
    fauours,
Ouercome in the heart of you Lord Marcus and
    Lord Hastings
Both, for how I haue gouerned these two and twentie
    yeares,
I leaue it to your discretions.
The malice hath still bene an enemy to you both,
That in my life time I could neuer get any lege of
    amity betwixt you,
Yet at my death let me intreate you to imbrace each
    other,
That at my last departure you may send my soule
To the ioyes celestiall :
For leauing behinde me my yoong sonne,

Your lawfull King after my decease,
May be by your wise and graue counsell so gouerned,
Which no doubt may bring comfort
To his famous realme of England.
But (what saith Lord Marcus and Lord Hastings)
What not one word ? nay then I see it will not be,
For they are resolute in their ambition.

   Eliz. Ah yeeld Lord Hastings,
And submit your selues to each other :
And you Lord Marcus, submit your selfe,
See here the aged King my father,
How he sues for peace betwixt you both :
Consider Lord Marcus, you are son to my mother the
     Queene,
And therefore let me intreat you to mittigate your
     wrath,
And in friendly sort, imbrace each other.

   King. Nay cease thy speech Elizabeth,
It is but folly to speake to them,
For they are resolute in their ambitious mindes,
Therefore Elizabeth, I feele my selfe at the last instant
     of death,
And now must die being thus tormented in minde.

   Hast. May it be that thou Lord Marcus,
That neither by intreatie of the Prince,
Nor curtuous word of Elizabeth his daughter,
May withdraw thy ambition from me.

   Mar. May it be that thou Lord Hastings,
Canst not perceiue the mark his grace aimes at.

   Hast. No I am resolute, except thou submit.

   Mar. If thou beest resolute giue vp the vpshot,
And perhaps thy head may paie for the losses.

   King. Ah Gods, sith at my death you iarre,
What will you do to the yoong Prince after my de-
     cease?
For shame I say, depart from my presence, and leaue
     me to my self,

For these words strikes a second dying to my soule :
Ah my Lords I thought I could haue commanded
A greater thing then this at your hands,
But sith I cannot, I take my leaue of you both,
And so depart and trouble me no more.

    Hast. With shame and like your Maiestie I submit
      therfore,
Crauing humble pardon on my knees,
And would rather that my body shal be a pray to
    mine enemy,
Rather then I will offend my Lord at the houre
And instance of his death.

    King. Ah thankes Lord Hastings.

    Eliz. Ah yeeld Lord Marcus, sith Lord Hastings
Is contented to be vnited.

    King. Ah yeeld Lord Marcus, thou art too ob-
      stinate.

    Mar. My gracious Lord, I am content,
And humbly craue your graces pardon on my knee,
For my foule offence,
And see my Lord my brest opened to mine aduersary,
That he may take reuenge, then[1] once it shall be said,
I will offend my gratious suffereinge.

    King. Now let me see you friendly giue one an other
      your hands.

    Hast. With a good will ant like your grace,
Therefore Lord Marcus take here my hand,
Which was once vowde and sworne to be thy death,
But now through intretie of my Prince,
I knit a league of amitie for euer.

    Mar. Well Lord Hastings, not in show but in deed,
Take thou here my hand, which was once vowed
To a[2] shiuered thy bodie in peecemeales,
That the foules of the ayre should haue fed
Their yoong withall,

---

    [1] Than, for "rather than."   [2] Have.

But now vpon aleageance to my Prince, I vow perfect
    loue,
And liue friendship for euer.

    King. Now for confirming of it, here take your
    oathes.

    Hast. If I Lord Hastings falcifie my league of
    friendship
Vowde to Lord Marcus, I craue confusion.

    Mar. Like oath take I, and craue confusion.

    King. Confusion.
Now, my Lords, for your yoong King, that lieth now
    at Ludlo,
Attended with Earle Riuers, Lord Gray, his two
    vnkles,
And the rest of the Queenes kindred,
I hope you will be vnto him as you haue bene to me,
His yeares are but yoong, thirteene at the most,
Vnto whose gouernment, I commit to my brother the
    Protector,
But to thee Elizabeth my daughter,
I leaue thee in a world of trouble,
And commend me to thy mother, to all thy sisters,
And especially I giue thee this in charge vpon & at
    my death,
Be loyall to thy brother during his authoritie,
As thy selfe art vertuous, let thy praiers be modest,
Still be bountifull in deuotion.
And thus leauing thee with a kisse, I take my last
    farwell,
For I am so sleepie, that I must now make an ende,
And here before you all, I commit my soule to
    almighty God,
My sauiour, and sweet redeemer, my bodie to the
    earth,
My Scepter and Crowne to the yoong Prince my
    sonne :
And now Nobles, draw the Curtaines and depart,

He that made me saue me,
Vnto whose hands I commit my spirit.
                    [*The King dies in his bed.*

   Enter SHORES WIFE, *and* HURSLY *her mayde.*

   Shor. O Fortune, wherefore wert thou called For-
      tune?
But that thou àrt fortunate?
Those whom thou fauourest be famous,
Meriting mere mercie,
And fraught with mirrors of magnanimitie,
And Fortune I would thou hadst neuer fauoured
   me.
   Hurs. Why mistresse, if you exclaime against For-
      tune,
You condemne your selfe,
For who hath aduanced you but Fortune?
   Shor. I as she hath aduanced me,
So may she throw me downe :
Bnt Hursly, doest not heare the King is sicke?
   Hurs. Yes mistresse, but neuer heard that euerie
      sicke man died.
   Shor. Ah Hursly, my minde presageth
Some great mishaps vnto me,
For last time I saw the King, me thought
Gastly death approached in his face,
For thou knowest this Hursly, I haue bene good to
   all,
And still readie to preferre my friends,
To what preferment I could,
For what was it his grace would deny Shores wife?
Of any thing, yea were it halfe his reuenewes,
I know his grace would not see me want,
And if his grace should die,
As heauens forfend it should be so,
I haue left me nothing now to comfort me withall,

And then those that are my foes will triumph at my
  fall,
And if the King scape, as I hope he will,
Then will I feather my neast,
That blow the stormie winter neuer so cold,
I will be throughly prouided for one :
But here comes Lodwicke, seruant to Lord Hastings.
How now Lodwicke, what newes?

Enters LODWICKE.

   Lod. Mistresse Shore, my Lord would request you,
To come and speake with him.
   Shor. I will Lodwicke.
But tell me what newes, is the King recouered?
   Lod. I mistresse Shore, he hath recouered,
That he long lookt for.
   Shor. Lodwicke, how long is it since
He began to mend?
   Lod. Euen when the greatest of his torments had
   left him.
   Shor. But are the nobles agreed to the content-
   ment of the Prince?
   Lod. The Nobles and Peeres are agreed as the
   King would wish them.
   Shor. Lodwicke thou reuiuest me.
   Lod. I but few thought that the agreement and his
   life would haue ended togither.
   Shor. Why Lodwicke is he dead?
   Lod. In briefe mistresse Shore, he hath changed
   his life.
   Shor. His life, ah me vnhappie woman,
Now is misery at hand,
Now will my foes tryumph at this my fall,
Those whom I haue done most good, will now forsake
  me.
Ah Hursly, when I enterteined thee first,

I was farre from change, so was I Lodwicke,
When I restored thee thy lands.
Ah sweete Edward, farwell my gracious Lord and
    souereigne,
For now shall Shores wife be a mirrour and looking
    glasse,
To all her enemies.
Thus shall I finde Lodwicke, and haue cause to say,
That all men are vnconstant.

 Lod. Why mistresse Shore, for the losse of one
    friend,
Will you abandon the rest that wish you well?

 Shor. Ah Lodwicke I must, for when the tree
    decaies
Whose fruitfull branch haue flourished many a yeare,
Then farewell those ioyfull dayes and ofspring of my
    heart,
But say Lodwicke, who hath the King made Protector,
During the innormitie [1] of the yoong Prince.

 Lod. He hath made his brother Duke of Gloster
    Protector.

 Shor. Ah me, then comes my ruine and decaie,
For he could neuer abide me to the death,
No he alwaies hated me whom his brother loued so
    well,
Thus must I lament and say, all the world is vncon-
    stant.

 Lod. But mistresse Shore, comfort your selfe,
And thinke well of my Lord,
Who hath alway bene a helper vnto you.

 Shor. Indeed Lodwicke to condemne his honour I
    cannot,
For he hath alway bene my good Lord,
For as the world is fickle, so changeth the minds of
    men.

---

[1] Not within legal age to reign.

Lod. Why mistresse Shore, rather then want should
    oppresse
You, that litle land which you beg'd for me of the
    King,
Shall be at your dispose.
    Shor. Thanks good Lodwicke.

Enter a CITIZEN *and* MORTON *a seruing man.*

    Cit. O maister Morton, you are very welcome met,
I hope you think on me for my mony.
    Mor. I pray sir beare with me, and you shall haue
    it,
With thankes too.
    Cit. Nay, I pray sir let me haue my money,
For I haue had thankes and too much more then I
    lookt for.
    Mor. In faith sir you shall haue it,
But you must beare with me a litle,
But sir, I marvell how you can be so greedie for your
    mony,
When you see sir, we are so vncertaine of our owne.
    Cit. How so vncertaine of mine owne?
Why doest thou know any bodie wil come to rob me?
    Mor. Why no.
    Cit. Wilt thou come in the night and cut my
    throate?
    Mor. No.
    Cit. Wilt thou and the rest of thy companions,
Come and set my house on fire?
    Mor. Why no, I tell thee.
    Cit. Why how should I then be vncertaine of mine
    owne?
    Mor. Why sir by reason the King is dead.
    Cit. O sir! is the King dead?
I hope he hath giuen you no quittance for my debt.

Mor. No sir, but I pray staie a while, and you shall
 haue it
Assoone as I can.
 Cit. Well I must be content, where nothing is to be
 had,
The King looseth his right they say,
But who is this?
 Mor. Marry sir it is mistresse Shore,
To whom I am more beholding too for my seruice,
Than the deerest friend that euer I had.
 Cit. And I for my sonnes pardon.
 Mor. Now mistresse Shore, how fare you?
 Shor. Well Morton, but not so well as thou hast
 known me,
For I thinke I shal be driuen to try my friends one
 day.
 Mor. God forfend mistresse Shore,
And happie be that Sunne shall shine vpon thee,
For preseruing the life of my sonne.
 Shor. Gramercies good father,
But how doth thy sonne, is he well?
 Cit. The better that thou liues, doth he.
 Shor. Thankes father, but I am glad of it,
But come maister Lodwicke shall we go?
And you Morton, youle bear vs company.
 Lod. I mistresse Shore,
For my Lord thinkes long for our comming.
         [*Exit omnes.*
 Cit. There there, huffer, but by your leaue,
The Kings death is a maime to her credit,
But they say, there is my Lord Hastings in the Court,
He is as good as the Ase of hearts at maw,[1]
Well euen as they brew, so let them bake for me:
But I must about the streets, to see and I can meete

---

[1] A game at cards. See the Shakespeare Society's edit. of
"Patient Grissil," p. 67.

With such cold customers as they I met withall euen
    now,
Masse if I meete with no better,
I am like to keepe a bad hoshold of it.   *[Exit.*

Enters RICHARD, Sir WILLIAM CASBIE, *Page of his
Chamber, and his traine.*

  Rich. My friends depart,
The houre commands your absence.
Leaue me and euery man look to his charge.
                   [Exit traine.
  Cas. Renowned and right worthie Protector,
Whose excelency far deserues the name of king then
    protector,
Sir William Casbie wisheth my Lord,
That your grace may so gouerne the yoong Prince,
That the Crowne of England may flourish in all hap-
    pinesse.   *[Exit Casbie.*
  Rich. Ah yoong Prince, and why not I?
Or who shall inherit Plantagines but his sonne?
And who the King deceased, but the brother?
Shall law bridle nature, or authoritie hinder inherit-
    ance?
No, I say no : Principalitie brooks no equalitie,
Much less superioritie,
And the title of a King, is next vnder the degree of a
    God,
For if he be worthie to be called valiant,
That in his life winnes honour, and by his sword
    winnes riches,
Why now I with renowne of a souldier, which is neuer
    sold but
By waight, nor changed but by losse of life,
I reapt not the gaine but the glorie, and since it be-
    commeth
A sonne to maintaine the honour of his deceased father,

Why should I not hazard his dignitie by my brothers
    sonnes?
To be baser than a King I disdaine,
And to be more then Protector, the law deny,
Why my father got the Crowne, my brother won the
    Crowne,
And I will wear the Crowne,
Or ile make them hop without their crownes that de-
    nies me :
Haue I remoued such logs out of my sight as my
    brother Clarēce
And king Henry the sixt, to suffer a child to shadow
    me,
Nay more, my nephew to disinherit me,
Yet most of all, to be released from the yoke of my
    brother
As I terme it, to become subiect to his sonne,
No death nor hell shall not withhold me, but as I rule
    I will raign,
And so raign that the proudest enemy shall not
    abide
The sharpest shoure. Why what are the babes but
    a puffe of
Gun-pouder? a marke for the soldiers, food for fishes,
Or lining for beds, deuices enough to make them
    away,
Wherein I am resolute, and determining needs no
    counsell,
Ho, whose within?

Enters PAGE *and* PERCIUALL.

Per. May it please your Maiestie.
Rich. Ha villaine, Maiestie.
Per. I speake but vpon that which shal be my
    good Lord.
Rich. But whats he with thee ?

Page. A Messenger with a letter from the right
honourable

The Duke of Buckingham.   [*Exit* PAGE.

Rich. Sirra giue place.

Ah how this title of Maiestie, animates me to my
purpose,

Rise man, regard no fall, haply this letter brings good
lucke,

May it be, or is it possible,

Doth Fortune so much fauour my happinesse

That I no sooner deuise, but she sets abroach ?

Or doth she but to trie me, that raising me aloft,

My fall may be the greater, well laugh on sweete
change,

Be as be may, I will neuer feare colours nor regard
ruth,

Valour brings fame, and fame conquers death.

Perciuall.

Per. My Lord.

Rich. For though thy letter declares thy name,

Thy trust to thy Lord, is a sufficient warrant

That I vtter my minde fully vnto thee,

And seeing thy Lord and I haue bene long foes,

And haue found now so fit opportunitie to ioyne
league,

To alaie the proude enemy, tell him thus as a friend,

I do accept of his grace, and will be as readie to put
in practise

To the vttermost of my power, what ere he shalbe to
deuise ;

But wheareas he hath writ that the remouing of the
yoong

Prince from the Queenes friends might do well,

Tell him thus, it is the only way to our purpose,

For he shall shortly come vp to London to his Coronation,

At which instant, we will be both present,

And where by the helpe of thy Lord, I will so plaie
  my part,
That ile be more than I am, and not much lesse then
  I looke for,
No nor a haire bredth from that I am,
Aiudge thou what it is Perciuall.

Per. God send it my Lord, but my Lord willed me
to satisfie you, and to tell you by word of mouth that
he hath in readinesse a braue company of men.

Rich. What power hath he?

Per. A braue band of his owne.

Rich. What number?

Per. My Lord, to the number of five hundreth
footmen.
And horsmen ayders vnto him, is my Lord Chamberlaine, and my Lord Hastings.

Rich. Sounes, dares he trust the Lord Hastings?

Per. I my Lord as his owne life, he is secret I
warrant you.

Rich. Well Perciuall, this matter is waightie and
must not be slipt, therefore return this answere to thy
Lord, that to morrow I will meet him, for to day I
cannot, for now the funerall is past I must set a
screene before the fire for feare of suspition : again,
I am now to strengthen my selfe by the controuersie
that is betwixt the kindred of the King deceast, and
the Queene thats liuing, the yoong Prince is yet in
hucsters handling, and they not throughly friendes,
now must I so worke, that the water that driues the
mill may drowne it. I climbe Perciuall, I regard
more the glorie then the gaine, for the very name of
a King redouble a mans life with fame, when death
hath done his worst, and so commend me to thy
Lord, and take thou this for thy paines.

Per. I thanke your grace, I humbly take my leaue.
                                    [*Exit* PERCIUALL.

Rich. Why so, now Fortune make me a King,

Fortune giue me a kingdome, let the world report the Duke of Gloster was a King, therefore Fortune make me King, if I be but King for a yeare, nay but halfe a yeare, nay a moneth, a weeke, three dayes, one daye, or halfe a day, nay an houre, swounes half an houre, nay sweete Fortune, clap but the Crowne on my head, that the vassals may but once say, God saue King Richards life, it is inough. Sirrha, who is there?

Enter PAGE.

Page. My Lord.

Rich. What hearest thou about the Court?

Page. Ioy my Lord for your Protectorship for the most part. Some murmure, but my Lord they be of the baser sort.

Rich. A mightie arme wil sway the baser sort, authority doth terrifie.

But what other newes hearest thou?

Page. This my Lord, they say the yong king is comming vp to his coronation, attended on by his two vncles, Earle Rivers & Lord Gray, and the rest of the Queenes kindred.

Rich. A parlous[1] bone to ground vpon, and a rush stifly knit,[2] which if I could finde a knot, I would giue one halfe to the dogs and set fire on the other.

Page. It is reported my Lord, but I know not whether it be true or no, that the Duke of Buckingham

---

[1] Perilous.

[2] This looks like a proverbial expression; but I have not been able to find an instance of the last of the phrase. *Nodum in scirpo quærere* was the Roman proverb for *to stumble on plain ground*, and in Sir Philip Sidney's Sonnets there is an allusion to it :—

"O, this it is : the knotted straw is found."

is vp in the Marches of Wales with a band of men, and as they say, hee aims at the Crowne.

Rich. Tush a shadow without a substance, and a feare without a cause : but yet if my neighbours house bee on fire, let me seek to saue mine owne, in trust is treason, time slippth, it is ill iesting with edge tooles, or dallying with Princes matters, Ile strike whillst the yron is hote, and Ile trust neuer a Duke of Buckingham, no neuer a Duke in the world, further then I see him. And sirrha, so follow me.

[*Exit* RICHARD.

Page. I see my Lord is fully resolued to climbe, but how hee climbes ile leaue that to your iudgements, but what his fall will be thats hard to say : But I maruell that the Duke of Buckingham and he are now become such great friends, who had wont to love one another so well as the spider doth the flie : but this I haue noted, since he hath had the charge of Protector, how may noble men hath fled the realme, first the Lord Marcus sonne to the Queene, the Earl of Westmorland and Northumberland, are secretly fled : how this geare will cotten[1] I know not. But what do I medling in such matters, that should medle with the vntying of my Lordes points, faith do euen as a great many do beside, medle with Princes matters so long, til they proue themselues beggars in the end. Therefore I for feare I should be taken napping with any words, Ile set a locke on my lips, for feare my tongue grow too wide for my mouth.   [*Exit* PAGE.

---

[1] To *cotton* is to succeed, to prosper.   *Gear* is any business or matter.

> " Come on, sir frier, picke the locke,
> This gere doth cotton hansome,
> That covetousnesse so cunningly
> Must pay the lechers ransome. "

—" Troublesome Raigne of King John," part I.

Enter the yoong PRINCE, *his brother,* DUKE OF YORKE, EARLE RIUERS, LORD GRAY, SIR HAPCE, SIR THOMAS VAUGHAN.

King. Right louing vnckles, and the rest of this company, my mother hath written, and thinks it conuenient that we dismisse our traine, for feare the towne of Northampton is not able to receiue vs : and againe my vnckle of Gloster may rather think we come of malice against him and his blood : therefore my Lords, let me here your opinions, for my words and her letters are all one : and besides I myselfe giue consent.

Riu. Then thus may it please your grace, I will shewe my opinion. First note the two houses of Lancaster and Yorke, the league of friendship is yet but greene betwixt them, and little cause of variance may cause it breake, and thereby I think it not requisite to discharge the cōpany because of this. The Duke of Buckingham is up in the Marches of Wales with a great power, and with him is ioyned the Protector, for what cause I know not, therefore my Lords, I haue spoken my mind boldly, but do as your honours shall thinke good.

Vaugh. Why my Lord Riuers, wherefore is he Protector but for the Kings safetie ?

Riu. I Sir Thomas Vaughan, and therefore a traitor, because he is Protector.

Gray. We haue the Prince in charge, therefore we neede not care.

Riu. We haue the Prince, but they the authoritie.

Gray. Why take you not the Duke of Buckingham for the Kings friend ?

Riu. Yes, and yet we may misdoubt the Duke of Gloster as a foe.

Gray. Why then my Lord Riuers, I thinke it is

conuenient that we leaue you here behind vs at Northamton, for conference with them, and if you heare their pretence be good towards the King, you may in Gods name make returne & come with them, but if not, leaue them and come to vs with speed. For my sister the Queene hath willcd that we should dismisse our companie, and the King himselfe hath agreed to it, therefore we must needs obey.

Riu. If it please your grace I am content, and humbly take my leaue of you all.   [*Exit.*

King. Farewell good vnckle, ah gods, if I do live my fathers yeares as God forbid but I may, I will so roote out this malice & enuie sowne among the nobilitie, that I will make them weary that were the first beginners of these mischiefes.

Gray. Worthily well spoken of your princely Maiestie,
Which no doubt sheweth a king-like resolution.

Vaugh. A toward yoong Prince, and no doubt forward to all vertue, whose raigne God long prosper among vs.

King. But come vnckle, let vs forward of our iourny towards London.

Riu. We will attend vpon your Maiestie.
                         [*Exit omnes.*

Enters an old Inne-keeper, and RICHARDS *Page.*

Page. Come on mine Oste, what doest thou vnderstand my tale or no?

Oste. I faith my guest you haue amazed mee alreadie, and to heare it again, it wil mad me altogither, but because I may think vpon it the better, I pray you let me heare it once more.

Page. Why then thus, I serue the right honourable the Lord Protector.

Oste. I, I know that too well.

Page. Then this is his graces pleasure, that this nigh the will be lodged in thy house, thy fare must be sumptuous, thy lodgings cleanly, his men vsed friendly and with great curtesie, and that he may haue his lodging prepared as neare Lord Riuers as possible may be.

Oste. Why sir if this be all, this is done alreadie.

Page. Nay more.

Oste. Nay sir, & you loue me no more, heres too much already.

Page. Nay, my Lords graccs pleasure is further, that when all thy guesse [1] have tane their chambers, that thou conuey into my Lords hands the keyes of euery seuerall chamber, and what my Lords pleasure is further, thou shalt know in the morning.

Oste. How locke in my guesse like prisoners, why doe you heare my guesse ? mee thinkes there should be little better then treason in these words you haue vttered.

Page. Treason villaine, how darest thou haue a thought of treason against [2] my Lord, therefore you were best be briefe, and tell me whether you will do it or no ?

Oste. Alasse what shall I do ? who were I best to offend ? shall I betrai that good olde Earle that hath laine at my house this fortie yeares ? why and I doe hee will hang me : nay then on the other side, if I should not do as my Lord Protector commands, he will chop off my head, but is there no remedie ?

Page. Come sir be briefe, there is no remedie. therefore be briefe, and tell me straight.

Oste. Why, then sir heres my hand, tell my Lord Protector he shall haue it, I will do as he commands mee, but euen against my will, God is my witnesse.

---

[1] *Guesse* is the old plural for *guests.*
[2] *I.e.*, have a thought, against my lord, of treason.

Page. Why then farewell mine Oste.

Osie. Farewell euen the woorst guest that ever came
to my house.   A maisters, maisters, what a troublesome vocation am I crept into, you thinke we that be
In-keepers get all the world; but I thinke I shall get
a faire halter to my necke, but I must go see all things
done to my great griefe.   [*Exit.*

Enters the mother QUEENE, *and her daughter, and her
sonne, to sanctuary.*

Earle *Riuers* speakes out of his chamber.

Ho mine Oste, Chamberlaine wheres my key?
What pend vp like a prisoner?   But staie, I feare I
      am betraid,
The sodain sight of Glosters Duke, doth make me
      sore afraid :
He speake to him, and gently him salute,
Tho in my heart I enuie [1] much the man,
God morrow my Lord Protector to your grace,
And Duke of Buckingham God morrow too,
Thankes noble Dukes for our good cheare, & for your
      cõpany.

Here enters BUCKINGHAM *and* GLOSTER, *and their
traine.*

Rich. Thou wretched Earle, whose aged head
      imagins nought but treacherie,
Like Iudas thou admitted wast to sup with vs last
      night
But heauens preuented thee our ils, and left thee in
      this plight :

---

[1] Envy for "hate."

Greeu'st thou that I the Gloster Duke, shuld as Pro-
    tector sway?
And were you he was left behind, to make vs both
    away?
Wilt thou be ringleader to wrŏng, & must you guide
    the realme?
Nay ouer boord al such mates I hurl, whilst I do
    guid the helm :
He weed you out by one and one, Ile burne you vp
    like chaffe,
Ile rend your stock vp by the rootes, that yet in
    triumphs laffe.
    Riu. Alas good Dukes for ought I know, I neuer
    did offend,
Except vnto my Prince vnloyall I have bene,
Then shew iust cause, why you exclaime so rashly in
    this sort,
So falsely thus me to condemne, vpon some false
    report :
But am I here as prisoner kept, imprisoned here by
    you?
Then know, I am as true to my Prince, as the proudest
    in thy crue.
    Buc. A[1] brauely spokē good old Earle, who tho his
    lims be num.
He hath his tongue as much at vse, as tho his yeares
    were yong.
    Rich. Speakest y^u the truth, how durst y^u speak, for
    iustice to apeale?
When as thy packing with thy Prince, thy falshood do
    reueale.
A Riuers blush, for shame to speake, like traitor as
    thou art.

---

[1] Ah!

Riu. A brayd[1] you me as traitor to your grace :
No altho a prisoner, I returne defiance in thy face.
The Chronicles I record, talk of my fidelitie, & of my
    progeny,
Wher, as in a glas y^u maist behold, thy ancestors &
    their trechery.
The wars in France, Irish cŏflicts, & Scotland knowes
    my trust,
When thou hast kept thy skin vnscard, and let thine
    armor rust :
How thou vniustly here exclaim'st,
Yea far from loue or kin,
Was this the oath which at our princes death,
With vs thou didst combine ?
But time permits[2] not now, to tell thee all my
    minde :
For well tis known that but for fear, you neuer wold
    have clind.[3]
Let Commons now haue it in hand, the matter is
    begun,
Of whom I feare the lesser sort, vpon thy part will
    run.
My Lords, I cannot breath it out in words like to
    you : but this,
My honor, I will set to sale,[4] let any comman man
    come in,
And say Earle Riuers faith vnto his Prince did
    quaile,
Then will I lose my lands and life, but if none so can
    doo,

---

[1] Braid for upbraid. See Huloet's Dict. The word is used
by Shakespeare :—

    " 'Twould braid yourself too near for me to tell it."

—" Pericles," Scene I.
[2] Old copy omits *not*.   [3] Climb'd.   [4] Pledge?

Then thou Protector iniur'st me, and thy copartner
    too :
But since as Iudges here you are, and taking no
    remorce,
Spare me not, let me haue law, in iustice do your
    worst.
    Buc. My Lord, lay down a cooling card,[1] this
    game is gone too far,
You haue him fast, now cut him off, for feare of ciuill
    war,
Iniurious Earle I hardly brooke, this portion thou
    hast giuen,
Thus with my honor me to touch, but thy ruth shall
    begin.
    Riu. But as thou art I leaue thee here,
Vnto the officers custody,
First bare him to Pomphret Castle,
Charge them to keep him secretly :
And as you heare from me so deale,
Let it be done immediatly :
Take from our Garrison one whole band,
To guard him thither safely.
    Riu. And send'st thou me to common Iayle?
Nay then I know thy minde :
God bless these yoong and tender babes,
That I do leaue behinde.
And God aboue protect them day and night,
Those are the marks thou aim'st at, to rid them from
    their right.
Farewell sweet England and my country men,
Earle Riuers leades the way :
Yet would my life might rid you from this thrall,

---

[1] A card so decisive as to cool the courage of the adversary—

    " There all is marr'd ; there lies a cooling card."

—" First Part of Henry VI.," v. 4.

But for my stock and kindred to the Queen, I greatly
feare thē all.
And thus disloyall Duke farewell, when euer this is
knowne,
The shame and infamy thereof, be sure will be thine
owne.[1]   [*Exit.*

Rich. So now my Lord of Buckingham, let us
hoyst vp saile while the winde serues, this hot beginning must haue a quicke dispatch, therefore I charge
and command straightly,[2] that euerie high way be
laid close, that none may be suffered to carrie this
newes before we our selues come, for if word come
before vs, then is our pretence bewraid, and all we
haue done to no effect. If any aske the cause why
they may not passe, vse my authoritie, and if he resist
shoote him through. Now my Lord of Buckingham,
let vs take post horse to Stony Stratford, where hap-
pily ile say grace to the Princes dinner, that I will
make the devoutest of them forget what meat they
eate, and yet all for the best I hope.   [*Exit.*

Enter the yoong PRINCE, LORD GRAY, SIR THOMAS
VAUGHON, SIR RICHARD HAPC, *and their traine.*

Hap. Lord Gray, you do discomfort the King by
reason of your heauinesse.
Gray. Alasse sir Richard, how can I be merry
when we haue so great a charge of his grace : and
again this makes me to greeue the more, because wee
cannot heare from Earle Riuers, which makes me
think the Protector and he haue bene at some words.
King. Why good vnkle comfort your selfe, no doubt

---

[1] Part of the old play of "King John," which preceded
Shakespeare's drama, is also in ballad measure.   And see
Reed's "Shakespeare," xx. 462.
[2] Strictly.

my vnkle Earle Riuers is well, & is comming no doubt
with my vnkle of Gloster to meete vs, else we should
haue heard to the contrarie.   If any haue cause to
feare, it is my selfe, therefore good vnkle comfort
your selfe and be not sad.

Gray. The sweete ioyce of such a grape would
comfort a man where he halfe dead, and the sweete
words of such a Prince would make men carlesse of
mishaps, how dangerous soeuer.

Hap. Lord Gray, we heare now by all likelihoods
the Protector not to be farre, therefore wee are to
entertaine him and the Duke of Buckingham with
curtesie, both for the Princes behalfe and for our
owne.

Gray. Sir Richard Hapc, I shall hardly shew the
Protector or the Duke of Buckingham any mery countenance, considering how hardly I haue been vsed by
them both, but yet for love to my prince I will bridle
my affectiõ, but in good time they come.

Enters RICHARD, DUKE OF BUCKINGHAM, *and their
traine.*

Rich. Long liue my Princely Nephew in all happinesse.

King. Thankes vnckle of Gloster for your curtesie,
yet you haue made hast, for we lookt not for you as
yet.

Rich. Therein I shew my humble dutie to your
grace, whose life I wish to redouble your deceased
fathers dayes.

King. Thankes good vnckle.

Buc. Long liue my gratious Prince.

King. Thankes Buckingham, but vnckle you will
beare vs company towards London ?

Rich. For that cause we came.

Buc. Gentlemen on afore keep your roomes, how

now Lord Gray doo you iustle in the presence of the King? This is more then needs.

Gray. My Lord, I scarce touched you, I hope it be no offence.

Rich. Sir no great offence, but inward enuy will burst out. No Lord Gray, you cannot hide your malice to vs of the Kings blood.

King. Why good vnckle let me know the cause of your suddaine quarrell?

Rich. Marry thus noble Nephew, the old wound of enuy, being rubbed by Lord Grayes venomous rashnesse, is growne to such a venomous sore that it is incurable, without remooue of dead flesh.

Buc. Lord Gray, I do so much dislike thy abuse, that were it not in presence of the Prince, I would bid thee combate: but thus and it shal like your grace, I arest, & atache this Lord Gray, Sir Thomas Vaughon, and Richard Hapce, of high treason to your grace. And that Lord Gray hath conueyed money out of the Tower to relieue our enemies the Scots, and now by currying favor with your Maiestie, he thinkes it to be hid.

Rich. Only this I adde, you gouerne the Prince without my authoritie, allowing me no more then the bare name of Protector, which I wil haue in the despight of you, and therefore as your competitor Earle Riuers is alreadie imprisoned, so shall you be, till time affoord the law to take place.

Gray. But whereas we are atacht as traytors to his grace, and gouerne him without your authoritie, why we have authority from the mother Queene. And for the deliuery of the mony to the Scots, it was done by a generall consent of you all, and that I haue your hands to shew for my discharge, therfore your arest & atachment is not lawfull: & yet as lawful as your quarrell is right.

Rich. Thy presumption condemnes thee Lord

Gray, thy arest is lawfull. Therefore see them speedily and secretly imprisoned, and after the coronation they shall answer it by law, meane while, Officers looke to your charge.

King. A Gods, and is it iustice without my consent? Am I a King and beare no authoritie? My louing kindred committed to prison as traytors in my presence, and I stand to giue aime at them.[1] A Edward, would thou laist by thy fathers side, or else he had liued till thou hadst bin better able to rule. If my ncere kindred be committed to prison, what remaines for me, a crowne? A but how? so beset with sorrows, that the care & grief wil kil me ere I shall enioy my kingdome. Well since I cannot command, I wil intreat. Good vnkle of Gloster, for all I can say little, but for my vnkle Lord Gray, what need he be a theef or conuey money out of the Tower, when he hath sufficient of his own? But good vnkle let me baile them all: If not, I will baile my vncle Lord Gray if I may.

Rich. Your grace vndertakes you know not what, the matters are perillous, especially against the Lord Gray.

King. What perilous matters, considering he is a friend to vs?

Rich. He may be a friend to win fauour, & so climbe to promotion in respect of his equals. His equals, nay his betters.

King. I know my vnkle will conceale no treason, or dangerous secresie from vs.

Rich. Yes secrets that are too subtil for babes. Alasse my Lord you are a child, and they vse you as a child: but they consult and conclude of such mat-

---

[1] To give *aim* was to stand within a convenient distance from the butts, to inform the archers how near their arrows fell to the mark.

ters, as were we not carefull, would proue preiudiciall
to your Maiesties person. Therefore let not your
grace feare any thing by our determination, for as my
authoritie is onely vnder your grace, so shall my
loyaltie deserue hereafter the iust recompence of a
true subiect, therefore I hauing charge frõ my brother
your father, & our late deceased king, during the
minoritie of your grace, I will vse my authoritie as I
see good.

King. Ay me vnhappie king.

Gray. Nay let not your grace be dismaid for our
imprisonmēt, but I would we could warrant your grace
from harme, & so we humbly take our leaues of your
grace, hoping that ere long we shall answer by law to
the shame & disgrace of you all.   [*Exit.*

Rich. Go, you shall answere it by law.

King. But come vnkle shal we to Lon. to our
vntimely coranatiõ ?

Rich. What else and please your maiestie, where
by the way I will appoint trustie Officers about you.

Buc. Sound Trumpet in this parley, God saue the
King.

Rich. Richard.[1]

Enter the mother QUEENE, *and her yoong sonne the*
DUKE OF YORKE, *and* ELIZABETH.

Yorke. May it please your grace to shew to your
children the cause of your heavines, that we knowing
it, may be copartners of your sorrowes.

Queen. Ay me poore husbandles queene, and you
poor fatherlesse princes.

Eliz. Good mother expect the liuing, and forget

---

[1] There is character in still making Gloucester try the sound
of his greatness.

the dead. What tho our Father be dead, yet behold his children, the image of himselfe.

Queen. Ay poore Princes, my mourning is for you and for your brother, who is gone vp to an vntimely crownation.

Eliz. Why mother he is a Prince, and in handes of our two vnkles, Earle Riuers & Lord Gray, who wil no doubt be carefull of his estate.

Queen. I know they will, but kings haue mortall enemies, as well as friends that esteeme and regard them. A sweet children, when I am at rest my nightly dreames are dreadful. Me thinks as I lie in my bed, I see the league broken which was sworne at the deathe of your kingly father, tis this my children and many other causes of like importance, that makes your aged mother to lament as she doth.

Yorke. May it please your grace.

Queen. A my son, no more grace, for I am so sore disgraced, that without Gods grace, I fall into dispaire with myself, but who is this?

Enter a MESSENGER.

Yorke. What art thou that with thy gastly lookes preaseth into sanctuary, to affright our mother Queene.

Mess. A sweet Princes, doth my counteance bewray me?
My newes is doubtfull and heauie.

Eliz. Then utter it to vs, that our mother may not heare it.

Queen. A yes my friend, speake what ere it be.

Mess. Then thus may it please your grace, The yong prince comming vp to his coronation, attended on by his two vnckles, Earle Riuers and Lord Gray, and the rest of your kindred, was by the Duke of Buckingham and the Protector, met at stonie Stratford, where on a suddaine grew malice betweene the

Duke of Buckingham and the Lord Gray, but in the end, the Duke of Buckinghams malice grew so great, that he arested and attached all those of your kindred of high treason, whereupon the Protector being too rash in iudgement, hath committed them all to Pomphret Castle.

Queen. Where I feare he will butcher them all, but where is the Prince my sonne?

Mess. He remains at London in the Bishops palace, in the hands of the Protector.

Queen. A traitors, will they laie hands on their Prince, and imprison his Peeres, which no doubt meanes well towards him : But tell me, art not thou seruant to the Arch-Bishop of Yorke?

Mess. Yes and it please your grace, for himselfe is here at hand with Letters from the Councell, and here he comes.

Enter Cardinall.

Queen. But here my friend, griefe had almost made me forget thy reward. A come my Lord, thou bringest the heauie newes, come shoote thine arrow, and hit this heart that is almost dead with griefe alreadie.

Car. What ere my newes be, haue patience, the Duke of Gloster greets your grace.

Queen. Draw home my Lord, for now you hit the marke.

Car. The Prince your sonne doth greete your grace.

Queen. A happie gale that blew that arrow by, A let me see the Letter that he sent, perhaps it may prolong my life awhile.

Yorke. How doth my brother, is he in health my Lord?

Car. In health sweete Prince, but longes to haue thy companie.

Yorke. I am content, if my mother will let me go.

Car. Content or not, sweete Prince it must be so.

Queen. Hold, and haue they persuaded thee my sonne to haue thy brother too away from me, nay first I will know what shall become of thee, before I send my other sonne to them.

Car. Looke on this Letter and aduise yourselfe, for thus the Councell hath determined.

Queen. And haue they chosen thee among the rest, for to persuade me to this enterprise? No my Lord, and thus persuade your selfe, I will not send him to be butchered.

Car. Your grace misdoubts the worst, they send for him only to haue him bedfellow to the King, and there to staie & keep him company. And if your sonne miscary, then let his blood be laid vnto my charge: I know their drifts and what they do pretend, for they shall both this night sleepe in the Tower, and to morrow they shall both come forth to his happie coronation. Vpon my honour this is the full effect, for see the ambusht nobles are at hand to take the Prince away from you by force, if you will not by faire meanes let him go.

Queen. Why my Lord will you breake Sanctuary, and bring in rebels to affright vs thus? No, you shall rather take away my life before you get my boy away from me.

Car. Why Madame haue you taken Sanctuary?

Queen. I my Lord, and high time too I trow.

Card. A heauie case when Princes flie for aide, where cut-throates, rebels, and bankerouts should be. But Madame what answere do you returne, if I could persuade you, twere best to let him go.

Queen. But for I see you counsell for the best, I am content that you shall haue my son, in hope that you will send him safe to me, here I deliuer him into you hands. Farewell my boy, commend me to thy brother.

Yorke. Mother farewell, and farewell sister too, I
will but see my brother and returne to you.

Queen. Teares stops my speech.   Come let vs in
my Lord.   [*Exit.*

Car. I will attend vpon your grace.   Hold take
the Prince, the Queen & I hauc done, Ile take my
leaue, and after you ile come.   [*Exit* CAR.

Yorke. How now my friend, shall I go to my
brother?

Cat. What else sweete Prince, and for that cause
wee are come to beare you company.   [*Exit omnes.*

Enter foure watchmen.   Enter RICHARDS *Page.*

Page. Why thus by keeping company, am I become
like vnto those with whom I keepe company.   As my
Lorde hopes to weare the Crown, so I hope by that
means to haue preferment, but in steed of the Crowne,
the blood of the headles light vpon his head : he hath
made but a wrong match, for blood is a threatner
and will haue reuenge.   He makes hauocke of all to
bring his purpose to passe : all those of the Queens
kinred that were committed to Pomphret Castle, hee
hath caused them to be secretly put to death without
iudgemēt : the like was neuer seen in England.   He
spares none whom he but mistrusteth to be a hinderer
to his proceedings, he is straight chopt vp in prison.
The valiant Earle of Oxford being but mistrusted, is
kept close prisoner in Hames Castle.   Againe, how
well Doctor Shaw hath pleased my Lord, that preached
at Paules Crosse yesterday, that proued the two
Princes to be bastards, whereupon in the after noone
came downe my Lord Mayor and the Aldermen to
Baynards Castle, and offered my Lord the whole
estate vpon him, and offered to make him King,
which he refused so faintly, that if it had bene offered

once more, I know he would haue taken it, the Duke
of Buckingham is gone about it, and is now in the
Guild Hall making his Oration. But here comes my
Lord.

Enter RICHARD *and* CATESBY.

Rich. Catesby content thee, I haue warned the
Lord Hastings to this Court, and since he is so hard
to be wonne, tis better to cut him off then suffer him,
he hath bene all this while partaker to our secrets,
and if he should but by some mislike vtter it, then
were we all cast away.

Cat. Nay my Lord do as you will, yet I haue
spoken what I can in my friends cause.

Rich. Go to, no more ado Catesby, they say I haue
bin a long sleeper to day, but ile be awake anon to
some of their costs. But sirrha are those men in
readinesse that I appointed you to get?

Page. I my Lord, & giue diligent attendance vpon
your grace.

Rich. Go to, looke to it then Catesby, get thee thy
weapons readie, for I will enter the Court.

Cat. I will my Lord. [*Exit.*[1]

Page. Doth my Lord say he hath bene a long
sleeper to day? There are those of the Court
that are of another opinion, that thinks his grace
lieth neuer lõg inough a bed. Now there is court
held to day by diuerse of the Councell, which I feare
me wil cost the Lord Hastings and the Lord Standley their best cappes: for my Lord hath willed
mee to get halfe a dozen ruffians in readinesse, and
when he knocks with his fist vpon the boord, they
to rush in, and to crie, treason, treason, and to
laie hands vpon the Lord Hastings, and the Lord

---

[1] For *Exit* with *Richard.*

Stannley, which for feare I should let slip, I will giue
my diligent attendance.

Enter RICHARD, CATESBY, *and others, pulling* LORD
HASTINGS.

Rich. Come bring him away, let this suffice, thou
and that accursed sorceresse the mother Queene hath
bewitched me, with assistance of that famous strumpet
of my brothers, Shores wife : my withered arme is a
sufficient testimony, deny it if thou canst : laie not
Shores wife with thee last night ?

Hast. That she was in my house my Lord I cannot
deny, but not for any such matter.   If.

Rich. If, villain, feedest thou me with Ifs & ands,
go fetch me a Priest, make a short shrift, and dispatch
him quickly.   For by the blessed Saint Paule I
sweare, I will not dine till I see the traytors head,
away Sir Thomas, suffer him not to speak, see him
executed straight & let his copartner the Lord Standly
be carried to prison also, tis not his broke head I
haue giuen him, shall excues him.

[*Exit with* HASTINGS.[1]

Catesbie goe you and see it presently proclaimed
throughout the Citie of London by a Herald of Armes,
that the cause of his death and the rest, were for
conspiring by Witchcraft the death of me and the
Duke of Buckingham, that so they might gouern the
King and rule the realme, I thinke the proclamation
be almost done.

Cat. I my good Lord, and finished too.

Rich. Well then about it.   But hearst thou Catesbie,
meane while I will listen after successe of the Duke
of Buckingham, who is labouring all this while
with the Citizens of London to make me King,

---

[1] Compare Shakespeare's play, act iii. sc. 4.

which I hope will be shortly, for thou seest our foes now are fewer, and we neerer the mark then before, and when I haue it, looke thou for the place of thy friend the Lord Hastings, meane while about thy businesse.

Cat. I thanke your grace.　　　[*Exit* CATESBIE.

Rich. Now sirrha to thee, there is one thing more vndone, which grieues me more then all the rest, and to say the truth, it is of more importance then all the rest.

Page. Ah that my Lord would vtter it to his Page, then should I count my selfe a happie man, if I could ease my Lord of that great doubt.

Rich. I commend thy willingnesse, but it is too mightie, and reacheth the starres.

Page. The more waightie it is, the sooner shall I by doing it increase your honours good liking toward me.

Rich. Be assured of that, but the matter is of waight & great importance, and doth concerne the state.

Page. Why my Lord, I will choake them with gifts that shall performe it, therefore good my Lord, trust me in this cause.

Rich. Indeed thy trust I know to be so true, that I care not to vtter it vnto thee. Come hither, & yet the matter is too waightie for so meane a man.

Page. Yet good my Lord, vtter it.

Rich. Why thus it is, I would haue my two Nephewes the yoong Prince and his brother secretly murthered, Sownes villaine tis out, wilt thou do it? or wilt thou betray me?

Page. My Lord you shall see my forwardnesse herein, I am acquainted with one Iames Terrell, that lodgeth hard by your honors chamber, with him my Lord will I so worke, that soone at night you shall speake with him.

Rich. Of what reputation or calling is that Terrell, may we trust him with that which once knowne, were the vtter confusion of me and my friends for euer ?

Page. For his trust my Lord, I dare be bounde, onely this, a poore gentleman he is, hoping for preferment by your grace and vpon my credit my Lord, he will see it done.

Rich. Well in this be verie circumspect and sure with thy diligence, be liberall, and looke for a day to make thee blesse thy self, wherein thou seruedst so good a Lord. And now that Shores wifes goods be confiscate, goe from me to the Bishop of London, and see that she receiue her open penance, let her be turned out of prison, but so bare as a wretch that worthily hath deserued that plague : and let there be straight proclamation made by my Lord the Mayor, that none shall releeue her nor pittie her, and priuie spies set in euerie corner of the Citie, that they may take notice of them that releeues her : for as her beginning was most famous aboue all, so will I haue her end most infamous aboue all. Haue care now my boy, and win thy maisters heart for euer.

Enter Shores *wife.*

Shor. Ah unfortunate Shores wife, dishonour to the King, a shame to thy countrey, and the onely blot of defame to all thy kindred. Ay why was I made faire that a King should fauour me ? But my friends should haue preferd discipline before affection : for they know of my folly, yea my owne husband knew of my breach of disloyaltie, and yet suffered me, by reason hee knew it bootlesse to kicke against the pricke. A sweet King Edward, little didst thou thinke Shores wife should haue bene so hardly vsed, thy vnnaturall brother not concent with my goods which are yet confiscate in his custodie, but yet more to adde to my present miserie, hath proclaimed vpon great penaltie, that none whatsoeuer shall either aide or succour me, but here being comfortlesse to die in the streets with hunger. I am constrained to beg, but I feare tis in vaine, for none will pittie me. Yet here come one to whom I have done good, in restoring his lands that were lost, now will I trie him to see if he will giue mee any thing.

Enters LODOWICKE.

Lod. A time how thou suffrest fortune to alter estates, & changest the mindes of the good for the worst. How many headlesse Peeres sleepe in their graues, whose places are furnish with their inferiours? Such as are neither nobly borne, nor vertuously minded. My heart hardly bewailes the losse of the yoong King, by the outrage of the Protector, who hath proclaimed himselfe King, by the name of Richard the third. The Commons murmure at it greatly, that the yoong King and his brother should be imprisoned, but to what end tis hard to say, but many thinks they shall neuer come forth againe. But God do all for the best, and that the right heires may not be vtterly ouerthrowne.

Shor. A gods what a griefe is it for me to aske, where I haue giuen.

Lod. A my good Lord Hastings, how innocently thou diedst the heauens beare witnesse.

Shor. Good sir, take pittie vppon mee, and releeue mee.

Lod. Indeed tis pittie to see so faire a face to aske for almes,
But tell me, has thou no friends?

Shor. Yes sir I had many frends, but when my chiefest friend of all died, the rest then forsooke me.

Lod. Belike then thy fact was notorious, that thy

friends leauing thee would let thee go as a spoyle for villaines. But heerst thou I prethie tell me the truth, and as I am a gentleman, I will pittie thee.

Shor. A Lodowick, tell thee the truth, why halfe this intreatie serued thee, when thy lands had bene cleane gone had it not bene for Shores wife, and doest thou make me so long to begge for a litle.

Lod. Indeed my lands I had restored me by mistresse Shore, but may this be she?

Shor. I Lodowicke, I am she that begged thy lands of King Edward the fourth, therefore I pray thee bestow something on me,

Lod. A gods what is this world, and how vncertaine are riches? Is this she that was in such credit with the King? Nay more that could command a King indeed? I cannot deny but my lands she restored me, but shall I by releeuing of her hurt myselfe, no: for straight proclamation is made that none shall succour her, therefore for feare I should be seene talke with her, I will shun her company and get me to my chamber, and there set downe in heroicall verse, the shamefull end of a Kings Concubin, which is no doubt as wonderfull as the desolation of a kingdome.   [*Exit.*

Shor. A Lodowick if thou wilt giue me nothing, yet staie and talke with me. A no he shuns my company, all my friends now forsake mee: In prosperitie I had many, but in aduersitie none. A gods have I this for my good I haue done, for when I was in my cheefest pomp, I thought that day wel spent wherein I might pleasure my friend by sutes to the King, for if I had spoken, he would not haue said nay. For tho he was King, yet Shores wife swayd the swoord. I where neede was, there was I bountifull, and mindfull I was still vppon the poore to releeue them, and now none will know me nor succour me: therefore here shall I die for want of sustenance. Yet here comes another whom I haue done good vnto in sauing the life of his sonne, wel I will trie him, to see if he will giue me any thing.

Enter a CITIZEN *and another.*

Cit. No men no lawes, no Prince no orders, alls husht neighbour now hees king, but before he was king how was the tems [1] thwackt with ruffians? what fraies had we in the streets? Now he hath proclaimed peace betweene Scotland and England for sixe yeares, to what end I know not, vsurpers had need to be wise.

Shor. A good sir releeue me, and bestow something vpon me.

Cit. A neighbour, hedges haue eyes, and highwayes hauc cares, but who ist a beggar-woman? the streets are full of them, Ifaith. But heeres thou, hast thou no friendes that thou goest a begging so?

Shor. Yes sir I had friendes, but they are all dead as you are.

Cit. Why am I dead neighbour? why thou arrant queane what meanst thou by that?

Shor. I meane they are dead in charitie. But I pray sir, had not you the life of your sonne saued in the time of king Edward thc fourth by one Shores wife?

Cit. Yes marry had I, but art thou a sprig of the same bough? I promise you neighbor I thoght so, that so idle a huswife could not be without the acquaintance of so noble a strumpet: well for her sake ile giue thee somewhat.

Shor. Nay then know, that I am shee that saued the life of thy condemned sonne.

Cit. Who art thou Shores wife? Lye still purse,

---

[1] Thames?

neighbour I would not for twentie pounds haue giuen her one farthing, the proclamation is so hard by king Richard. Why minion are you she that was the dishonour to the King? the shame to her husband, the discredit to the Citie? Heare you, laie your fingers to worke, and get thereby somewhat to maintaine you. O neighbour I grow verie choloricke, and thou didst saue the life of my sonne, why if thou hadst not, another would : and for my part, I would he had bene hangd seuen yeeres ago, it had saued me a great deale of mony then. But come let vs go in, & let the quean alone.   [*Exeunt.*

Shor. Alasse thus am I become an open shame to the world, here shall I die in the streets for want of sustenance, alasse is my fact so heinous that none will pitie me? Yet heere comes another to whom I haue done good, who is least able to pleasure me, yet I will trie him, to see if he will giue me any thing.

Enter Morton *a Seruing man.*

Mor. Now sir, who but king Richard beares sway, and hath proclaimed Iohn Earle of Linclone, heire aparant to the Crown, the yoong Princes they are in the Tower, nay some saies more, they are murthered. But this makes me to muse, the Duke of Buckingham and the King is at such variance, that did all in all to helpe him to the Crowne, but the Duke of Buckingham is rid downe to Breaknock-Castle in Wales, and there he meanes to raise vp a power to pull down the vsurper : but let them agree as they will, for the next faire winde ile ouer seas.

Shor. A Shores Wife, so neere driuen, to beg of a seruing man, I, necessitie hath no law, I must needs. Good sir releeue me, and giue me something.

Ser. Why what art thou?

Shor. In briefe Morton, I am Shores wife, that haue done good to all.

Ser. A foole, and euer thy owne enemy. In troth mistresse Shore, my store is but small, yet as it is, weele part stakes, but soft I cannot do what I would, I am watcht.

Enters PAGE.

Shor. Good Morton releeue me.

Ser. What should I releeue my Kings enemy?

Shor. Why thou promist thou wouldst.

Ser. I tell thee I wil not, & so be answered. Sownes I would with all my heart, but for yonder villaine, a plague on him. [*Exit.*

Page. An honest fellow I warrant him. How now Shores wife will none releeue thee?

Shor. No one will releeue her, that hath bene good to all.

Page. Why twere pitie to do thee good, but me thinkes she is fulsome and stinkes.

Shor. If I be fulsome shun my company, for none but thy Lord sought my miserie, and he hath vndone me.

Page. Why hath he vndone thee? nay thy wicked and naughtie life hath vndone thee, but if thou wantest maintenance, why doest thou not fall to thy old trade againe?

Shor. Nay villaine, I haue done open penance, and am sorie for my sinnes that are past.

Page. Sownes is Shores wife become an holie whoore, nay then we shall neuer haue done.

Shor. Why hang thee, if thy faults were so written in thy forehead as mine is, it would be as wrong with thee. But I prethie leaue me, and get thee from me.

Page. And cannot you keepe the Citie but you must runne gadding to the Court, and you staie here a litle longer, ile make you be set away, and for my part, would all whoores were so serued, then there would be fewer in England then there be.   And so farewell good mistresse Shore.   [*Exit.*

Shor. And all such vsurping kings as thy Lord is, may come to a shamefull end, which no doubt I may liue yet to see.   Therefore sweet God forgiue all my foule offence :
And though I haue done wickedly in this world,
Into hell fire, let not my soule be hurld.   [*Exit.*

Enter MAISTER TERRILL, *and* SIR ROBERT BROKEN-
BERY.

Bro. Maister Terrell, the King hath written, that for one night I should deliuer you the keyes, and put you in full possession.   But good M. Terrell, may I be so bold to demand a question without offence ?

Ter. Else God forbid, say on what ere it be.

Bro. Then this maister Terrell, for your comming I partly know the cause, for the king oftentimes hath sent to me to haue them both dispatcht, but because I was a seruant to their father being Edward the fourth, my heart would neuer giue me to do the deed.

Ter. Why sir Robert you are beside the matter, what neede you vse such speeches what matters are betweene the King and me, I pray you leaue it, and deliuer me the keyes.

Bro. A here with teares I deliuer you the keyes, and so farwell maister Terrell.   [*Exit.*

Ter. Alasse good sir Robert, hee is kind hearted, but it must not preuaile, what I haue promised the King I must performe.   But ho Myles Forest.

For. Here sir.

Ter. Myles Forest, haue you got those men I spake of, they must be resolute and pittilesse.

For. I warrant you sir, they are such pittilesse villaines, that all London cannot match them for their villanie, one of their names is Will Sluter, yet the most part calles him blacke Will, the other is Iack Denten, two murtherous villaines that are resolute.

Ter. I prethie call them in that I may see them, and speake with them.

For. Ho Will and Iack.

Will. Here sir, we are at hand.

For. These be they that I told you of.

Ter. Come hither sirs, to make a long discourse were but a folly, you seeme to be resolute in this cause that Myles Forest hath deliuered to you, therefore you must cast away pitie, & not so much as thinke upon fauour, for the more stearne that you are, the more shall you please the King.

Will. Zownes sir, nere talke to vs of fauour, tis not the first that Iack and I haue gone about.

Ter. Well said, but the Kings pleasure is this, that he wil haue no blood shcad in the deed doing, therefore let me heare your aduises ?

For. Why then I thinke this maister Terrell, that as they sit at supper there should be two dags [1] readie charged, and so suddeinly to shoote them through.

Ter. No, I like not that so well, what saiest thou Will, what is thy opinion ?

Will. Tush, heeres more adoo then needes, I pray bring mee where they are, and ile take them by the heeles and beate their braines against the walles.

Ter. Nay that I like not, for tis too tyrannous.

Dout. Then heare me maister Terrell, let Will take one, and ile take another, and by the life of Iack Douton weele cut both their throates.

Ter. Nay sirs, then heare me, I will haue it done

---

[1] Pistols.

in this order, when they be both a bed at rest, Myles Forest thou shalt bring them vp both, and betweene two feather beds smother them both.

For. Why this is verie good, but stand aside, for here comes the Princes, ile bring you word when the deed is done. [*Exit* TERRILL.

Enter the PRINCES.

Yorke. How fares my noble Lord and louing brother?

King. A worthie brother, Richard Duke of Yorke, my cause of sorrow is not for my selfe, but this is it that addes my sorrow more, to see our vnckle whom our father left as our Protector in minoritie, should so digresse from dutie, loue and zeale, so vnkindly thus to keepe vs vp prisoners, and know no sufficient cause for it.

Yorke. Why brother comfort your selfe, for tho he detaine vs a while, he will not keepe vs long, but at last he will send vs to our louing mother againe: whither if it please God to send vs, I doubt not but that our mother would keepe vs so safe, that all the Prelates in the worlde should not depriue her of vs againe: so much I assure myselfe of. But here comes Myles Forest, I prethy Myles tell my kingly brother some mery storie to passe away the time, for thou seest he is melancholy.

King. No Myles, tell me no mery storie, but answere me to one question, what was he that walked with thee in the Gardeine, me thought he had the keyes?

For. My Lord, it was one that was appointed by the King to be an ayde to sir Thomas Brokenbury.

King. Did the King, why Myles Forest, am not I King?

For. I would have said my Lord your vnckle the Protector.[1]

King. Nay my kingly vnckle I know he is now, but let him enioye both Crowne and kingdome, so my brother and I may but enjoy our liues and libertie. But tell me, is sir Robert Brokenbery cleane discharged?

For. No my Lord, he hath but charge for a night or two.

King. Nay then, new officers, new lawes, would we had kept the old still. But who are they whose gastly lookes doth present a dying feare to my liuing bodie. I prethee tell me Myles what are they?

For. One my Lord is called Iack Denten, the other is called Will Slawter. But why starts your grace?

King. Slawter, I pray God he come not to slaughter my brother and me, for from murther and slaughter, good Lord deliver vs. But tell me Myles is our lodging prepared?

For. I my Lord, if it please your brother & you to walke vp.

King. Then come brother, we will go to bed.

For. I will attend vpon your grace.

Yorke. Come Myles Forest beare vs company.

For. Sirs staie you two here, and when they are a sleep ile call you vp. [*Exit.*

Den. I promise thee Will, it greues mee to see what mone these yoong Princes make, I had rather then fortie pounds I had nere tane it in hand, tis a dangerous matter to kill innocent princes, I like it not.

Will. Why you base slaue, are you faint hearted, a little thing would make me strike thee, I promise thee.

Den. Nay go forward, for now I am resolute : but come, lets too it.

---

[1] See Shakespeare, act iv. sc. i.

Will. I prethee staie, heele call vs vp anon.   But
sirrha Iacke, didst thou mark how the King started
when he heard my name ?   What will he do when he
feeles me ?

For. But ho sirs, come softly, for now they are at
rest.

Will. Come we are readie, by the masse they are
a sleepe indeed.

For. I heare they sleepe, and sleepe sweet Princes,
neuer wake no more, for you haue seene the last
light in this world.

Iack. Come presse them downe, it bootes not to
cry againe, Iack vpon them so lustily.   But maister
Forest now they are dead what shall we do with
them ?

For. Why goe and bury them at the heape of
stones at the staire foote, while I goe and tell maister
Terrell that the deed is done.

Will. Well we will, farewell maister Forest.

Enter TERRELL.

Ter. How now Myles Forest, is this deed dispatcht ?

For. I sir, a bloodie deed we haue performed.

Ter. But tell me, what hast thou done with them ?

For. I haue conueyd them to the staires foote
among a heape of stones, and anon ile carry them
where they shall be no more founde againe, nor all
the cronicles shall nere make mentiō what shall
become of them : yet good maister Terrell, tell the
King my name, that he may but reward me with a
kingly thanks.

Ter. I will go certifie the King with speed, that
Myles Forest, Will Slawter, and Iack Denten, they
three haue done the deed.   And so farewell.

[*Exeunt omnes.*

Enter the DUKE OF BUCKINGHAM *with his dagger drawne.*

Ban.[1] Ah good my Lord, saue my life.

Buc. Ah villaine, how canst thou aske for mercie, when thou hast so vniustly betraied me?

Ban. I desire your grace but giue me leaue to speake.

Buc. I speake thy last villain, that those that heare it, may see how vniustly thou hast betraied me.

Ban. Then thus my Lord. First, the proclamation was death to him that harboured your grace.

Buc. Ah villaine, and a thousand crownes to him that could betraie me.

Ban. Ah my Lord, my obeysance to my Prince is more.

Buc. Ah villain, thou betraiedst me for lucre, and not for dutie to thy Prince, why Banister, a good seruant thinkes his life well spent, that spends it in the quarrel of his maister. But villain make thyselfe readie, and here receiue thy death. *10 8372*

Enter a HERALD.

Her. Henry Duke of Buckingham, I arest thee in King Richards name as a traytor.

Buc. Well Herald, I will obey thy rest. But am I arrested in King Richardes name, vsurping Richard, that insatiate blood succour, that traitor to God & man. Ah Richard, did I in Guild Hall pleade the Orator for thee, and held thee in all thy slie and wicked practices, and for my reward doest thou alot me death? Ah Buckingham, thou plaidst thy part and made him King, and put the lawfull heires be-sides: why then is Buckingham guiltie now of his

---

death? yet had not the Bishop of Ely fled, I had escaped.

Enters sixe others to rescue the DUKE.

All. Come, the Duke of Buckingham shall not die : We will take him away by force.

Her. Why villaines, will you bee Traytours to your Prince?

Buc. Nay good my friends giue me leaue to speake, and let me intreate you to laie your weapons by. Then know this countrey men, the cause I am arested this, Is for bringing in your lawfull King, which is Henry Earle of Richmond now in Brittaine,[1] and meanes ere long to land at Milford Hauen in Wales, where I doo know hee shall haue ayde of the cheefest of the Welch, hee is your lawfull King, and this a wrongfull vsurper. When you shall heare of him landed in that place, then take vp weapons and amaine to him, hee is the man must reaue you of this yoake, and send the vsurper headlesse to his home, and poore Buckingham praies vpon his knees, to blesse good Richmond in his enterprise, and when the conquest shall be giuen to him, graunt he may match with Ladie Elizabeth, as promise hath to fore by him bene past, while[2] then my friendes, leaue mee alone to death, and let me take this punishment in peace. Ah Buckingham was not thy meaning good in displacing the usurper, to raise a lawfull king? Ah Buckingham it was too late, the lawfull heires were smothered in the Tower, sweet Edward and thy brother, I nere slept quiet thinking of their deaths. But vaunt Buckingham, thou wast altogither innocent of their deaths. But thou vilain, whom of a child I nurst thee vp, and hast so vniustly betraid thy Lorde?

---

[1] Bretagne.   [2] Till.

Let the curse of Buckingham nere depart from thee.
Let vengeance, mischiefes, tortures, light on thee and
thine. And after death thou maist more torture feele,
then when Exeon turnes the restlesse wheele. And
banne thy soule were ere thou seeme to rest. But
come my friends, let me away.

 Her. My Lord, we are sorie. But come laie handes
on Banister.   *[Exeunt.*

 Enter KING RICHARD, SIR WILLIAM CATESBIE, *and*
       others.

 King. The goale is got, and golden Crowne is
   wonne,
And well deseruest thou to weare the same,
That ventured hast thy bodie and thy soule,
But what bootes Richard, now the Diademe
Or kingdome got, by murther of his friends,
My fearefull shadow that still followes me,
Hath summond me before the seuere iudge,
My conscience witnesse of the blood I spilt,
Accuseth me as guiltie of the fact,
The fact a damned iudgement craues,
Whereas impartiall iustice hath condemned.
Meethinkes the Crowne which I before did weare,
Inchast with Pearle and costly Diamonds,
It turned now into a fatall wreathe,
Of fiery flames, and euer burning starres,
And raging fiends hath past ther vgly shapes,
In Stygian [1] lakes, adrest to tend on me,
If it be thus, what wilt thou do in this extremitie ?
Nay what canst thou do to purge thee of thy guilt ?
Euen repent, craue mercie for thy damned fact,
Appeale for mercy to thy righteous God,
Ha repent, not I, craue mercy they that list.

---

[1] Old copy, *studient.* Boswell's correction.

My God, is none of mine.   Then Richard be thus
    resolu'd,
To place thy soule in ballance with their blood,[1]
Soule for soule, and bodie for bodie, yea mary
    Richard,
That's good, Catesbie.

    Cat. You cald my Lorde, I thinke?

    King. It may be so.   But what thinkst thou
      Catesbie?

    Cat. Of what my Lord?

    King. Why of all these troubles.

    Cat. Why my Lord, I hope to see them happily
      ouercom'd.[2]

    King. How villain, doest thou hope to see me hap-
      pily ouercom'd?

    Cat. Who you my Lord?

    King. Ay villaine, thou points at me, thou hopest
      to see me ouercom'd.

    Cat. No my good Lord, your enemies or else noɩ.

    King. Ha, ha, good Catesbie, but what hearest thou
of the Duke of Buckingham?

    Cat. Why he is dead my Lord, he was executed at
Salisbury yesterday.

    King. Why tis impossible, his friends hopes that he
shall outliue me, to be my head.

    Cat. Out-liue you, Lord thats straunge.

---

[1] This line seems corrupt.   Archdeacon Nares interprets *to
valance*, to adorn with drapery, and quotes from " Hamlet "—

    " Thy face is valanc'd [bearded] since I saw thee last."

Perhaps we should read, *To place thy soul in balance?*   Old
copy, *Pace—vallence.*   Field's suggestion.

[2] The ancient particle of *come* was *comed* or *comen.*   Daniel
has the latter, and the former is vulgar with the Scotch to this
day—
    " He would have well becom'd this place."

—"Cymbeline," act v. sc. i.

King. No Catesbie, if a do, it must be in fames,[1]
And since they hope he shall out liue me, to be my
    head,
He hops without his head, & rests among his fellow
    rebels.

Cat. Mary no force[2] my Lord.

King. But Catesbie, what hearest thou of Henry
Earle of Richmond?

Cat. Not a word my Lord.

King. No : hearest thou not he liues in Brittaine,[3]
In fauour with the Duke.
Nay more, Lady Margaret his mother conspires against
    vs,
And perswades him that hee is lineally descended
    from Henry
The fourth, and that he hath right to the Crowne,
Therefore tell me what thinkst thou of the Earle?

Cat. My Lord, I thinke of the Earle as he doth
    deserue,
A most famous gentleman.

King. Villaine doest thou praise my foe, and commend him to my face?

Cat. Nay my Lord, I wish he were as good a friend
as he is a foe, else the due deserts of a traytor.

King. Whats that?

Cat. Why my Lord, to loose his head.

King. Yea mary, I would twere off quickly, then.
But more to the strengthening of his title,
She goes about to marry him to the Queenes eldest
    daughter,
Ladie Elizabeth.

Cat. Indeed my Lord that I heard was concluded,
By all the nobilitie of Brittaine.

King. Why then there it goes,
The great diuell of hell go with all.

---

[1] Flames.   [2] No matter.   [3] Bretagne.

A marriage begun in mischiefe, shall end in blood :
I thinke that accursed sorceresse the mother Queene,
Doth nothing but bewitch me, and hatcheth con-
  spiracies,
And brings out perillous birds to wound
Their Countries weale,
The Earle is vp in Armes,
And with him many of the Nobilitie,
He hath ayde in France,
He is rescued in Brittaine,
And meaneth shortly to arriue in England :
But all this spites me not so much,
As his escape from Landoyse the Dukes Treasuror,
Who if he had bene prickt foorth for reuenge,
He had ended all by apprehending of our foe,
But now he is in disgrace with the Duke,
And we farther off our purpose then to fore,
But the Earle hath not so many byting dogs abroad,
As we haue sleeping curres at home here,
Readie for rescue.
 Cat. But my Lord, I maruell how he should get aide
  there,
Considering he is no friend to Brittaine.
 King. Ay so thou maist maruell how the Duke of
  Brittaine,
Durst wake such a foe as England against him,
But euill fare makes open warre.
But who comes there Catsbie ?
Ha one of our spurres to reuenge :
The Lord Standley, father in law to Ladie Margaret,
His comming is to vs Catsbie,
Wert not that his life might serue,
For apprehension against our foe,
He should haue neither Iudge nor Iury,
But guiltie death without any more ado.
Now Lord Standley, what newes ?
Haue you receiued any letters of your late embassage
  into

Brittaine? What answere have you receiued of your
   letters?

Enter-LORD STANDLEY, *and his sonne* GEORGE.

Stan. Why my Lord, for that I sent, I haue receiued.
King. And how doth your sonne then, is he in
   health?
Stan. For his health my Lord, I do not mistrust.
King. Faith tell vs, when meanes he to arriue in
   England?
And how many of our Nobilitie is with him?
And what power is with him?
Stan. And please your grace,
His power is vnknowne to me,
Nor willingly would not I be priuy to such causes.
King. Oh good wordes Lord Standley, but giue
me leaue to gleane out of your golden field of elo-
quence, how braue you pleade ignorance, as though
you knew not of your sonnes departure into Brittaine
out of England.
Stan. Not I my Lord.
King. Why is not his mother thy wife, & dares he
passe ouer without the blessing of his mother, whose
husband thou art?
Stan. I desire your maiestie but giue me leaue to
speake?
King. Yea speak Standley, no doubt some fine
coloured tale.
Stan. And like your grace, wheras you mistrust
that I knew of my sonnes departure, out of England
into Brittaine, God I take to record it was vnknowne
to me, nor know not yet what his pretence is: for at
his departure, was I one of the priuy councell to your
brother King Edward the fourth, and that she was
able to relieue him without my helpe : I hope her suf-

ficiencie is knowne to your grace. Therefore I
humbly craue pardon.

King. Well Standley, I feare it will be proued to
the contrarie, that thou didst furnish him both with
mony and munition, which if it be, then looke for no
fauour at my hands, but the due deserts of a traitor:
but let this passe. Whats your repaire to our presence?

Stan. Only this my Lord, that I may repaire from
the court, to my house in the country.

King. Ay sir, that you might be in Cheshire and
Lancashire, then should your Postes passe inuisible
into Brittaine, and you to depart the realme at your
pleasure, or else I to suffer an intollerable foe vnder
me, which I will not. But Standley to be brief, thou
shalt not go. But soft Richard, but that it were better
to be alone than to haue noysome company, hee shall
goe, leauing for his loyaltie a sufficient pledge. Come
hither Standley, thou shalt goe, leauing me here thy
sonne and heire George Standley for a pledge, that
hee may perish for thy fault if neede should be, if
thou likest this, goe, if not, answere me briefly, and
say quickly no.[1]

Stan. I am to aduise my selfe vppon a secret cause,
and of a matter that concernes me neare: say that I
leaue my sonne vnto the King, and that I should but
aide Earle Richmond, my sonne George Standley dies,
but if my faith be kept unto my Prince George Standley liues. Well I will except the King's proffer.
And please your grace I am content, and will leaue
my sonne to pledge.

King. Here come hither, and with thee take this
    lesson.
Thou art set free for our defence,
Thou shalt vpon thy pledge make this promise,
Not only to staie the hinderance of the Earle,

---

[1] See Shakespeare, act iv. sc. 4.

But to preuent his purpose with thy power.
Thou shalt not seeke by any meanes to aide or rescue
    him.
This done, of my life thy sonne doth liue :
But otherwise thy sonne dies and thou too, if I catch
    thee :
And it shall go hard but I will catch thee.
   Stan. And you shall go apace, and yet go without me.
But I humbly take my leaue of your grace. ⸱ Farewell
    George.
   King. How now, what do you giue him letters ?
   Stan. No my Lord I haue done :
The second sight is sweet, of such a sonne.   [*Exit.*
   King. Carry George Standley to prison.
   Geo. Alasse my Lord, shall I go to prison ?
   King. Shall you go to prison, what a questions that ?
So pricke the lambe, and wound the damme.
How likest thou this Catesbie ?
   Cat. Oh my Lord so excellent that you haue im-
prisoned his sonne.
   King. Nay now will we looke to the rest,
But I sent the Lord Louell to the mother Queene,
Concerning my sute to her daughter Elizabeth,
But see in good time here he is.
   How now Louell, what newes ?
What saith the mother Queene to my sute ?

        Enters LOUELL.

   Lou. My Lord very strange she was at the first,
But when I had told her the cause, she gaue concent :
Desiring your maiestie to make the nobilitie priuie to it.
   King. God haue mercy Louell, but what saith Lady
Elizabeth ?
   Lou. Why my Lord, straunge, as women will be at
the first, But through intreatie of her mother, she
quicklie gaue consent.   And the Queene wild me to

tel your grace, that she meanes to leaue Sanctuary, and to come to the court with al her daughters.

King. I marry Louell let not that opportunitie slippe, looke to it Catesbie, be carefull for it Louell, for thereby hangs such a chance, that may inrich vs and our heires for euer.   But sirs hard ye nothing of the Scottish Nobles that met at Nottingham, to conferre about the marriage of my Neece.

Cat. Not a word my Lord.

Enters MESSENGER.

King. Gogs wounds who is that? search the villaine, has he any dags about him?

Mess. No my Lord I haue none.

King. From whence comes thou?

Mess. From the Peeres at Nottingham and Scotland, & they greete your Maiestie.

Lou. Sirrha is the marriage concluded betweene the Scottish Earle and the faire Lady Rosa ?

Cat. Prethie tell vs, is it concluded?

Page. How saies thou, is it concluded?

King. Nay will you giue me leaue to tell you that? Why you villaines will you know the secrets of my letter by interrupting messengers that are sent to me? Away I say, begone, it is time to looke about : away I say, what here yet villaines?

Mess. My Lord, I haue some what to say besides?

King. Then speake it, what hast thou to say?

Mess. This my Lord, when the Peeres of England and Scotland met at Nottingham togither, to confer about the marriage of your Neese, it was straight determined that she shuld be married with the Scottish Earle.   And further my Lord, the Councel commanded me to deliuer vnto your grace the treasons of Captain Blunt, who had the Earle of Oxford in charge in Hames castle, now are they both

fled, and purposeth to ayde the Earle of Richmond
against your grace. Now my Lord I take my leaue.

King. Messenger staie, hath Blunt betraied, doth
Oxford rebell and aide the Earle Richmond, may
this be true, what is our prison so weake, our friends
so fickle, our Ports so ill lookt to, that they may
passe and repasse the seas at their pleasures, then
euerie one conspires, spoyles our Conflex, conqueres
our Castles, and Armes themselues with their owne
weapons vnresisted? O villaines, rebels, fugetives,
theeues, how are we betrayd, when our owne swoordes
shall beate vs, and our owne subiects seekes the sub-
uertion of the state, the fall of their Prince, and sack of
their country, of his,[1] nay neither must nor shall, for
I will Army with my friends, and cut off my enemies,
& heard them to their face that dares me, and but
one, I one, beyond the seas that troubles me : wel
his power is weake, & we are strong, therefore I wil
meet him with such melodie, that the singing of a
bullet shal send him merily to his lõgest home.
Come follow me.

Enter EARLE RICH.[2] EARLE OXFORD, P. LANDOYS, &
CAPTAIN BLUNT.

Rich. Welcome deare friends and louing country-
men,
Welcome I say to Englands blisfull Ile,
Whose forwardnesse I cannot but commend,
That thus do aide vs in our enterprise,
My right it is, and sole inheritance,
And Richard but vsurps in my authoritie,
For in his tyrannie he slaughtered those
That would not succour him in his attempts,
Whose guiltlesse blood craues daily at Gods hands,

---

[1] There seems to be some corruption here.   [2] Richmond.

Reuenge for outrage done to their harmlesse liues :
Then courage countrymen, and neuer be dismay'd,
Our quarels good, and God will helpe the right,
For we may know by dangers we haue past,
That God no doubt will giue vs victorie.
    Ox. If loue of gold, or feare of many foes,
Could once haue danted vs in our attempts,
Thy foote had neuer toucht the English shoare,
And here Earle Oxford plites his faith to thee,
Neuer to leaue in what we haue vndertane,
But follow still with resolution,
Till thou be crownd as conquerer in the field,
Or lose thy life in following of thy right :
Thy right braue Richmond, which we wil maintaine
Maugre the proudest bird of Richards brood.
Then cousin Richmond being resolued thus,
Let vs straight to Arms, & God and S. George for vs.
    Blunt. As this braue Earle haue said, so say we all,
We will not leaue thee till the field be wonne,
Which if with fortunate successe we can performe,
Thinke then Earle Richmond that I followed thee,
And that shall be honour inough for mee.
    Lan. So saith Landoyse that honors Richmond so
With loue vnfeined for his valure past,
That if your honour leade the way to death,
Peeter Landoys hath sworne to follow thee.
For if Queen mother do but keepe her word,
And what the Peeres haue promised be performed,
Touching the marriage with Elizabeth,
Daughter to our King Edward the fourth,
And by this marriage ioyne in vnitie
Those famous Houses Lancashire and Yorke,
Then England shall no doubt haue cause to say,
Edwards coronation was a ioyfull day.
And this is all Landoys desires to see.
    Rich. Thanks Landoys, and here Earle Richmond
        vows,

If their kinde promises take but effect,
That as they haue promised I be made King,
I will so deale in gouerning the state,
Which now lies like a sauage shultred groue,
Where brambles, briars, and thornes, ouer-grow those
    sprigs,
Which if they might but spring to their effect,
And not be crost so by their contraries,
Making them subiect to these outrages,
Would proue such members of the Common-weale,
That England should in them be honoured,
As much as euer was the Romane state,
When it was gouernd by the Councels rule,
And I will draw my swoord braue country-men,
And neuer leaue to follow my resolue,
Till I haue mowed those brambles, briars and thornes
That hinder those that long to do vs good.
    Ox. Why we have scapt the dangeroust brunt of all,
Which was his garrison at Milford Hauen,
Shall we dismay, or dant our friends to come?
Because he tooke the Duke of Buckingham?
No worthie friends, and louing country-men,
Oxford did neuer beare so base a minde,
He will not winke at murthers secretly put vp,
Nor suffer vpstarts to enioy our rightes,
Nor liue in England vnder an vsurping king,
And this is Oxfords resolution.
    Rich. But Blunt, looke whose that knocks.
    Blunt. My Lord, tis a messenger from the mother
      Queene,
And the Ladie Standley your mother, with letters.
    Rich. Admit him straight, now shall we heare some
    newes.

Enters MESSENGER.

    Mess. Long liue Earle Richmond.
The mother Queene doth greet your honour.

Rich. Welcome my friend, how fares our mother & the rest?

Mess. In health my Lord, and glad to hear of your ariual safe.

Rich. My friend, my mother hath written to me of certaine that are comming in our aide, the report of whose names are referd to thee to deliuer.

Mess. First, theirs the Lord Talbut, the Earle of Shreuesbury sonne and heire, with a braue band of his owne.

There is also the Lord Fitz Harbart, the Earle of Pembrookes sonne and heire.

Of the Gentlemen of the Welch, there is sir Prise vp Thomas and Sir Thomas vp Richard, and sir Owen Williams, braue gentlemen my Lord. These are the chiefe.

Rich. Are these the full number of all that come?

Mess. Only two more my Lord, which I haue left vnnamed, the one is sir Thomas Denis a Westerne gentleman, and ioynd with him one Arnoll Butler, a great many are willing, but dares not as yet.

Rich. Doth Arnoll Butler come, I can hardly brooke his trecherie, for hee it was that wrought my disgrace with the King.

Ox. Well my Lord, wee are now to strengthen our selues with friends, and not to reape vp olde quarrels, say that Arnoll Butler did iniurie you in the time of peace, the mendes is twise made, if he stand with you in the time of warres.

Rich. Well my friend, take this for thy good newes, And commend me to our mother and the rest.
Thus my Lords, you see God still prouides for vs:
But now my Lords touching the placing of our battell[1] best,
And how we may be least indangered,

---

[1] Army.

Because I will be foremost in this fight,
To incounter with that bloodie murtherer,
My selfe wil lead the vaward of our troope,
My Lord of Oxford, you as our second selfe,
Shall haue the happie leading of the reare,
A place I know which you will well deserue,
And Captaine Blunt, Peter Landoyse and you,
Shall by[1] in quarters as our battels scowtes,
Prouided, thus your bow-men Captaine Blunt,
Must scatter here and there to gaull their horse,
As also when that our promised friends do come,
Then must you hold hard skirmish with our foes,
Till I by cast of a counter march,
Haue ioynd our power with those that come to vs,
Then casting close, as wings on either side,
We will giue a new prauado on the foe,
Therefore let vs towards Aderstoe amaine,
Where we this night God-willing will incampe,
From thence towards Lichfield, we will march next
     day,
And neerer London, bid King Richard play.   [*Exit.*

Enters the PAGE.

Page. Where shall I finde a place to sigh my fill,
And waile the griefe of our sore troubled King?
For now he hath obtaind the Diademe,
But with such great discomfort to his minde,
That he had better liued a priuate man, his lookes
     are gastly,
Hidious to behold, and from the priuie sentire of his
     heart,
There comes such deepe fetcht sighes and fearefull
     cries,
That being with him in his chamber oft,

---

[1] Bide.

He mooues me weepe and sigh for company,
For if he heare one stirre he riseth vp,
And claps his hand vpon his dagger straight,
Readie to stab him, what so ere he be,
But he must thinke this is the iust reuenge,
The heauens haue powred vpon him for his sinnes,
Those Peeres which he vnkindly murthered,
Doth crie for iustice at the hands of God,
And he in iustice sends continuall feare,
For to afright him both at bed and boord,
But staie, what noyse is this, who haue we here?

Enters men to go to RICHMOND.

How now sirs, whither are you going so fast?
   Men. Why to Earle Richmonds Camp to serue
    with him,
For we haue left to serue King Richard now.
   Page. Why comes there any more?
   Men. A number more.   [*Exit.*
   Page. Why these are the villaines my Lord would
haue put his life into their hands. A Richard, now
do my eyes witnesse that thy end is at hand, For thy
commons make no more account of thee then of a
priuate man, yet will I as dutie bindes, giue thee
aduertisements of their vniust proceedings. My
maister hath lifted out many, and yet hath left one to
lift him out of all, not onely of his Crowne, but also
of his life. But I will in, to tell my Lord of what is
happened.

Enters RICHMOND, *and* OXFORD.

   Rich. Good my Lord depart, and leaue me to my-
selfe.
   Ox. I pray my Lord, let me go along with you.
   Rich. My Lord it may not be, for I haue promised

my father that none shall come but my selfe, therfore good my Lord depart.

Ox. Good my Lord haue a care of your self, I like not these night walkes and scouting abroad in the euenings so disguised, for you must not now that you are in the vsurpers dominions, and you are the onely marke he aimes at, and your last nightes absence bred such amazement in our souldiers, that they like men wanting the power to follow Armes, were on a sodaine more liker to flie then to fight: therefore good my Lorde, if I may not stand neare, let me stand aloofe off.

Rich. Content thee good Oxford, and tho I confesse myself bound to thee for thy especiall care, yet at this time I pray thee hold me excused. But farewell my Lord, here comes my Lord and father.

Enters STANDLEY *and another.*

Stan. Captaine I pray thee bring me word when thou doest discrie the enemy. And so farewell, and leaue me for a while.

Rich. How fares my gratious Lord and father?

Stan. In good health my sonne, & the better to see thee thus foreward in this laudable enterprise, but omitting vain circumstances, and to come briefly to the purpose, I am now in fewe words to deliuer much matter. For know this, when I came to craue leaue of the King to depart from the court, the king verie furiously began to charge me that I was both acquainted with thy practises and drifts, and that I knew of thy landing, and by no meanes would grant me leaue to go, till as pledge of my loyaltie and true dealing with the king, I should leaue my yoong sonne George Standley. Thus haue I left my son in the hands of a tyrant, onely of purpose to come and speake with thee.

Rich. But omitting this, I pray tell me, shall I looke for your helpe in the battell?

Stan. Sonne I cannot, for as I will not go to the vsurper, no more I will not come to thee.

Rich. Why then it is bootlesse for us to staie, for all we presumed vpon, was on your aide.

Stan. Why sonne, George Standlyes death would doo you no pleasure.

Rich. Why the time is too troublesome, for him to tend to follow execution.

Stan. O sonne, tyrants expect no time, and George Standley being yoong and a grissell, is the more easie to be made away.

Rich. This newes goes to my heart, but tis in vaine for mee to looke for victorie, when with a mole-hill, we shall encounter with a mountaine.

Stan. Why sonne, see how contrarie you are, for I assure you, the chiefest of his company are liker to flie to thee, then to fight against thee: and for me, thinke me not so simple but that I can at my pleasure flie to thee, or being with them, fight so faintly, that the battell shall be wonne on thy part with small incountring. And note this besides, that the King is now come to Lester, and means to morrow to bid thee battel in Bosworth.

Enters Messenger.

Mess. Come my Lord, I do discry the enemy.

Stan. Why then sonne farewell, I can staie no
    longer.

Rich. Yet good father, one word more ere you
    depart,
What number do you thinke the kings power to be?

Stan. Mary some twentie thousand. And so fare-
    well.

Rich. And we hardly fiue thousand, being beset

with many enemies, hoping vpon a few friends, yet
dispair not Richmond, but remember thou fightest in
right, to defende thy countrey from the tyrannie of an
vsurping tyrant, therefore Richmond goe forward, the
more dangerous the battell is in atteining, it prooues
the more honourable being obteined.   Then forward
Richmond, God and Saint George, for me.

Quisquam regno gaudet, ô fallax bonum.[1]

Enters the KING, *and the* LORD LOUELL.

King. The hell of life that hangs vpon the Crowne,
The daily cares, the nightly dreames,
The wretched crewes, the treason of the foe,
And horror of my bloodie practise past,
Strikes such a terror to my wounded conscience,
That sleep I, wake I, or whatsoeuer I do,
Meethinkes their ghoasts comes gaping for reuenge,
Whom I haue slaine in reaching for a Crowne.
Clarence complaines, and crieth for reuenge.
My Nephues bloods, Reuenge, reuenge, doth crie.
The headlesse Peeres come preasing for reuenge.
And euery one cries, let the tyrant die.
The Sunne by day shines hotely for reuenge.
The Moone by night eclipseth for reuenge.
The Stars are turnd to Comets for reuenge.
The Planets chaunge their courses for reuenge.
The birds sing not, but sorrow for reuenge.
The silly lambes sits bleating for reuenge.
The screeking Rauen sits croking for reuenge.
Whole heads of beasts comes bellowing for reuenge.
And all, yea all the world I thinke,
Cries for reuenge, and nothing but reuenge.
But to conclude, I haue deserued reuenge.

---

[1] Old copy, *regna gaudit—fallex.*

In company I dare not trust my friend,
Being alone, I dread the secret foe :
I doubt my foode, least poyson lurke therein.
My bed is vncoth, rest refraines my head.
Then such a life I count far worse to be,
Then thousand deaths vnto a damned death :
How wast death I said? who dare attempt my
    death?
Nay who dare so much as once to thinke my death?
Though enemies there be that would my body kill,
Yet shall they leaue a neuer dying minde.
But you villaines, rebels, traitors as you are
How came the foe in, preasing so neare?
Where, where, slept the garrison that should a beat
    them back ?
Where was our friends to intercept the foe?
All gone, quite fled, his loyaltie quite laid a bed?
Then vengeance, mischiefe, horror, with mischance,
Wilde-fire, with whirlewinds, light upon your heads,
That thus betrayd your Prince by your vntruth.
    King.[1] Frantike man, what meanst thou by this
    mood?
Now he is come more need to beate him backe.
    Lou. Sowre is his sweete that sauours thy delight,
great is his power that threats thy ouerthrow.
    King. The bad rebellion of my foe is not so much,
as for to see my friends do flie in flocks from me.
    Lou. May it please your grace to rest your selfe
content, for you haue power inough to defend your
land.
    King. Dares Richmond set his foote on land with
such a small power of stragling fugatiues?

---

[1] This seems to be a continuation of the King's speech, but a
change of his mood, from delirium to reason. Compare Richard's
dream in Shakespeare, and the whole of our poet's act v. sc. 3,
with this scene.

Lou. May it please your grace to participate the cause that thus doth trouble you?

King. The cause Buzard, what cause should I participate to thee? My friends are gone away, and fled from me, keep silence villaine, least I by poste do send thy soule to hell, not one word more, if thou doest loue thy life.

Enter CATESBIE.

Cat. My Lord.

King. Yet againe villaine, ô Catesbie is it thou? What comes the Lord Standley or no?

Cat. My Lord, he answeres no.

King. Why didst not tell him then, I would send his sonne George Standleys head to him.

Cat. My Lord I did so, & he answered, he had another sonne left to make Lord Standley.

King. O vilaine vilde, and breaker of his oath, the bartardes ghoast shall hant him at the heeles, and crie reuenge for his vild fathers wrongs, go Louell, Catsbie, fetch George Standly forth, him with these handes will I butcher for the dead, and send his headlesse bodie to his sire.

Cat. Leaue off executions now the foe is heere that threatens vs most cruelly of our liues.

King. Zownes, foe mee no foes, the fathers fact condemnes the sonne to die.

Lou. But guiltlesse blood will for reuengement crie.

King. Why was not he left for fathers loyaltie?

Lou. Therein his father greatly iniured him.

King. Did not your selues in presence, see the bondes sealde and assignde?

Lou. What tho my Lord the vardit own, the titles doth resign.[1]

---

[1] *i.e.,* What, though my Lord the verdict recognize, and the titles resign?

King. The bond is broke and I will sue the fine,
except you will hinder me, what will you haue it
so ?

Lou. In doing true iustice, else we answere no.

King. His trecherous father hath neglect his word
and done imparshall wast[1] by dint of sword, therefore
sirrah go fetch him. Zownes draw you cuts who shall
go, I bid you go Catesby.[2] A Richard, now maist
thou see thy end at hand, why sirs why fear you thus ?
why we are ten to one, if you seeke promotion, I am
Kinge alreadie in possession, better able to performe
then he. Louell, Catesby, lets ioyne louingly and
deuoutly togither, and I will diuide my whole kingdome amongst you.

Both. We will my Lord.

King. We will my Lord, a Catesbie, thou lookest
like a dog, and thou Louell too, but you will runne
away with them that be gone, and the diuel go with
you all, God I hope, God, what talke I of God, that
haue serued the diuell all this while. No, fortune
and courage for mee, and ioyne England against
mee with England, Ioyne Europe with Europe, come
Christendome, and with Christendome the whole
world, and yet I will neuer yeeld but by death onely.
By death, no die, part not childishly from thy Crowne,
but come the diuell to claime it, strike him down, & tho
that Fortune hath decreed, to set reuenge with triumphs
on my wretched head, yet death, sweete death, my
latest friend, hath sworne to make a bargaine for my
lasting fame, and this, I this verie day, I hope with
this lame hand of mine, to rake out that hatefull heart
of Richmond, and when I haue it, to eate it panting
hote with salt, and drinke his blood luke warme, tho
I be sure twil poyson me. Sirs you that be resolute
follow me, the rest go hang your selues. [*Exit.*

---

[1] [Old copy, *past.*]   [2] See Shakespeare, act iv. sc. 4.

The battell enters, RICHARD *wounded, with his* PAGE.

King. A horse, a horse, a fresh horse.

Page. A flie my Lord, and saue your life.

King. Flie villaine, looke I as tho I would flie,[1] no first shall this dull and sencelesse ball of earth receiue my body cold and void of sence, you watry heauens rowle on my gloomy day, and darksome cloudes close vp my cheerfull sownde, downe is thy sunne Richard, neuer to shine againe, the birdes whose feathers should adorne my head, houers aloft & dares not come in sight, yet faint not man, for this day if Fortune will, shall make thee King possest with quiet Crown, if Fates deny, this ground must be my graue, yet golden thoughts that reache for a Crowne, danted before by Fortunes cruell spight, are come as comforts to my drooping heart, and bids me keepe my Crowne and die a King. These are my last, what more I haue to say, ile make report among the damned soules.

[*Exit.*

Enters RICHMOND *to battell againe, and kils* RICHARD.

Enters REPORT *and the* PAGE.

Re. How may I know the certain true report of this victorious battell fought to day, my friend what ere thou beest, tel vnto mee the true report, which part hath wonne the victorie, whether the King or no?

Page. A no the King is slaine and he hath lost the day, and Richmond he hath wonne the field, and tryumphs like a valiant conquerer.

Re. But who is slaine besides our Lord and soueraigne?

Page. Slaine is the worthie duke of Northfolke he, & with him Sir Robart Brokenby, Lieftenant of the

---

[1] See Shakespeare, act v. sc. 4.

Tower, besides Louell, he made also a partner in this Tragedie.

Re. But wheres sir William Catsby?

Page. Hee is this day beheaded on a stage at Lester, because he tooke part with my Lord the King. But stay Report, & thou shalt heare me tell the briefe discourse. And how the battell fell, then knowe Report, that Richard came to fielde mounted on horsback, with as high resolue as fierce Achillis mongst the sturdie Greekes, whom to encounter worthie Richmond, came accompanied with many followers, and then my Lord displayde his colours straight, and with the charge of Trumpet, Drum and Fyfe, these braue batalians straight encountred, but in the skirmish which cõtinued long, my Lord gan faint, which Richmond straight perceiued, and presently did sound a fresh alarme, but worthie Richard that did neuer flie, but followed honour to the gates of death, straight spurd his horse to encounter with the Earle, in which encountry Richmond did preuaile, & taking Richard at aduantage, then he threw his horse and him both to the ground, and there was woorthie Richard wounded, so that after that he nere recouered strength. But to be briefe, my maister would not yeeld, but with his losse of life he lost the field. Report farewell.

Enter EARLE RICHMOND, EARLE OXFORD, L. STAND-
LEY, *and their traine, with the Crowne.*

Rich. Now noble Peeres and woorthie countrymen, since God has giuen vs fortune of the day, let vs first giue thankes vnto his Deitie, & next with honors fitting your deserts, I must be gratefull to my country men, and woorthie Oxford for thy seruice showne in hote encountring of the enemy, Earle Richmond bindes himselfe in lasting bondes of faithfull loue and perfect vnitie. Sory I am for those that I haue lost by our so dangerous encountring with the foe, but sorrow cannot bring the dead to life : and therefore are my sorrows spent in vaine. Onely to those that liue, thus much I say, I will maintain them with a manuall paie. And louing father, lastly to your selfe, tho not the least in our expected aide, we giue more thankes for your vnlooked for aide, then we haue power on sodaine to declare, but for your thanks I hope it shall suffise that I in nature loue & honor you.

L. Stan. Well spoken sonne, and like a man of worth, whose resolutiõ in this battell past, hath made thee famous mongst thy enemies. And thinke my son, I glory more to heare what praise the common people gaue of thee, then if the Peeres by general full consent had set me downe to weare the Diadem. Then liue my sonne thus loued of thy friends, and for thy foes prepare to combate them.

Ox. And Oxford vowes perpetuall loue to thee, wishing as many honours to Earle Richmond, as Cæsar had in conquering the world, & I doubt not but if faire fortune follow thee, to see thee honoured mongst thy country men, as Hector was among the Lords of Troy or Tulley mongst the Romane Senators.

Rich. How fares our louely mother Queene?

Enters mother QUEENE *and* ELIZABETH.

Queen. In health Earle Richmond, glad to heare the newes that God hath giuen thee fortune of the day. But tell me Lords, where is my sonne Lord Marquesse Dorset, that he is not here ? what was he murthered in this Tragedie?

Rich. No louely Queene your sonne doth liue in France, for being distrest and driuen by force of tempest to that shore, and many of our men being

sicke and dead, we were inforst to aske the King for
aide, as well for men as for munition, which then the
King did willingly supply, prouided, that as hostage
for those men, Lord Marquesse Dorset should be
pledge with thē.   But Madame now our troubled
warre is done, Lord Marquesse Dorset shall come
home againe.

Queen. Richmond, gramercies for thy kinde good
newes, which is no little comfort to thy friends, to see
how God hath beene thy happie guide in this late
conquest of our enemies.   And Richmond, as thou
art returned with victorie, so we will keepe our words
effectually.

Rich. Then Madame for our happie battelles victorie, first thankes to heauen, next to my foreward
country-men, but Madame pardon me tho I make bold
to charge you with a promise that you made, which
was confirmed by diuerse of the Peeres, touching the
marriage of Elizabeth, and hauing ended what I
promised you, Madam, I looke and hope to haue my
due.

Stan. Then know my sonne, the Peeres by full consent, in that thou hast freed them from a tyrants yoke,
haue by election chosen thee as King, first in regard
they account thee vertuous, next, for that they hope
all forraine broyles shall seace, and thou wilt guide
and gouerne them in peace, then sit thou downe my
sonne, and here receiue the Crowne of England as
thy proper owne, sit downe.

Ox.   Henry the seuenth, by the grace of God, King
of England, France, and Lord of Ireland, God saue
the King.

All. Long liue Henry the seuenth, King of England.

Rich. Thanks louing friends and my kind country-
men, and here I vow in presence of you all, to root
abuses from this common welth, which now flowes

faster then the furious tyde that ouerflowes beyond the bankes of Nile. And louing father, and my other friends, whose ready forwardnesse hath made me fortunate, Richmond will still in honourable loue count himselfe to be at your dispose, nor do I wish to enioy a longer life, then I shall liue to think vpon your loue. But what saith faire Elizabeth to vs ? for now wee haue welcommed our other friends, I must bid you welcome Ladie amongst the rest, and in my welcome craue to be resolued, how you resolue touching my profered loue vnto you, here your mother and the Peeres agree, and all is ended, if you condescend.

Eliz. Then know my Lord, that if my mother please, I must in dutie yeeld to her command, for when our aged father left his life, he willed vs honour still our mothers age : and therefore as my dutie doth command, I do commit my self to her dispose.

Queen. Then here my Lord, receiue thy royall spouse, vertuous Elizabeth, for both the Peeres and Commons do agree that this faire Princesse shall be wife to thee. And we pray all, that faire Elizabeth may liue for aye, and neuer yeeld to death.

Rich. And so say I, thanks to you all my Lords, that thus haue honoured Richmond with a Crowne, and if I liue, then make account my Lords I will deserue this with more than common loue.

Stan. And now were but my sonne George Standley here,
How happie were our present meeting then,
But he is dead, nor shall I euer more see my sweete
Boy whom do I loue so deare, for well I know the vsurper
In his rage hath made a slaughter of my aged ioy.

Rich. Take comfort gentle father, for I hope my brother George will turne in safe [1] to us.

---

[1] Return in safety.

Stan. A no my sonne, for he that ioyes in blood,
will worke his furie on the innocent.

Enters two MESSENGERS *with* GEORGE STANDLEY.

Stan. But how now what noyse in this?

Mess. Bchold Lord Standley we bring thy sonne,
thy sonne George Standley, whom with great danger
we haue saued from furie of a tyrants doome.

L. Stan. And liues George Standley? Then
happie that I am to see him freed thus from a
tyrants rage. Welcome my sonne, my sweete George
welcome home.

George Stan. Thanks my good father, and George
Standley ioyes to see you ioynd in this assembly.
And like a lambe kept by a greedie Woolfe within
the inclosed sentire of the earth, expecting death
without deliuerie, euen from this daunger is George
Standley come, to be a guest to Richmond & the
rest: for when the bloodie butcher heard your honour
did refuse to come to him, hee like a sauage tygre
then inraged, commanded straight I should be mur-
dered, & sent these two to execute the deed, but
they that knew how innocēt I was, did post him off
with many long delayes, alleaging reasons to alaie his
rage, but twas in vaine, for he like to a starued
Lionesse still called for blood, saying that I should
die. But to be briefe, when both the battels ioyned,
these two and others, shifted me away.

Rich. Now seeing that each thing turnes to our
content,   .
I will it be proclaimed presently, that traytrous Richard
Be by our command, drawne through the streets of
Lester,
Starke naked on a Colliers horse let him be laide,
For as of others paines he had no regard,
So let him haue a traytors due reward.

Now for our marriage and our nuptiall rytes,
Our pleasure is they be solemnized
In our Abby of Westminter, according to the ancient
    custom due,
The two and twentith day of August next,
Set forwards then my Lords towards London straight,
There to take further order for the state.
    Mess. Thus Gentles may you heere behold,
The ioyning of these Houses both in one,
By this braue Prince Henry the seauenth,
Who was for wit compared to Saloman,
His gouernment was vertuous euery way,
And God did wonderously increase his store,
He did subdue a proud rebellious Lord,
That did encounter him vpon blacke heath.
He died when he had raigned full three and twentie
    yeares
Eight moneths, and some odde dayes, and lies buried
In Westminster. He died & left behind a sonne.
    Mess. A sonne he left, a Harry of that name,
A worthie, valiant and victorious Prince,
For on the fifth yeare of his happie raigne,
Hee entered France, and to the Frenchmens costs,
Hee wonne Turwin and Turney.
The Emperor serued this King for common pay,
And as a mersonary prince did follow him.
Then after Morle and Morles, conquered he,
And still he keepe the French men at a bay.
And lastly in this Kings decreasing age he conquered
Bullen, and after when he was turned home he died,
When he had raigned full thirtie eight yeares,
Nine moneths and some odde dayes, and was buried
    in Windsore.
He died and left three famous sprigs behinde him.
    Edward the sixt:
He did restore the Gospell to his light,
And finished that his father left vndone.

A wise yoong Prince, giuen greatly to his booke.
He brought the English seruice first in vse,
And died when he had raigned six yeares, fiue
Moneths, & some odde dayes,
And lieth buried in Westminster.

Eliza.[1] Next after him a Mary did succeede,
Which married Philip King of Spaine,
She raigned fiue yeares, foure moneths and some
Odde dayes, and is buried in Westminster.
When she was dead, her sister did succed.

Queene.[1] Worthie Elizabeth, a mirrour in her age,
By whose wise life and ciuill gouernment,
Her country was defended from the crueltie
Of famine, fire and swoord, warres fearefull messengers.
This is that Queene as writers truly say,
That God had marked downe to liue for aye.
Then happie England mongst thy neighbor Iles,
For peace and plentie still attends on thee :
And all the fauourable Planets smiles
To see thee liue in such prosperitie.
She is that lampe that keepes faire Englands light,
And through her faith her country liues in peace :
And she hath put proud Antichrist to flight,
And bene the meanes that ciuill wars did cease.
Then England kneele upon thy hairy knee,
And thanke that God that still prouides for thee.
The Turke admires to heare her gouernment,
And babies in Iury sound her princely name,
All Christian Princes to that Prince hath sent,

---

[1] It is so absurd that the Queen and her daughter should take this Chorus out of the mouths of the two Messengers, that I at one time thought that the words *Eliza., Queene,* were misplaced from a marginal note in the manuscript, calling the attention of the reader that *Queen Elizabeth* was now the subject of the Chorus ; but that King Richard's two murderers should speak this Epilogue is perhaps equally preposterous.

Atter her rule was rumord foorth by fame.
The Turke hath sworne neuer to lift his hand,
To wrong the Princesse of this blessed land.
Twere vaine to tell the care this Queene hath had;
In helping those that were opprest by warre :
And how her Maiestie hath stil bene glad,
When she hath heard of peace proclaim'd from far.
Ieneua, France, and Flanders hath set downe,
The good she hath done, since she came to the
    Crowne.
For which, if ere her life be tane away,
God grant her soule may liue in heauen for aye.
For if her Graces dayes be brought to end,
Your hope is gone, on whom did peace depend.

APPENDIX.

—o—

[FOR permission to print the following Latin Play, the Members of the Shakespeare Society were indebted to the Rev. Dr Archdall, Master, and the Fellows of Emmanuel College, Cambridge, to the Library of which House belongs the manuscript. There is another copy in the University Library, and the existence of the piece has always been well known. The Emmanuel MS. is written in a tolerably fair engrossing hand of about the year 1640.[1]

The University Library copy is also a transcript from some common original, in a still fairer scrivener's hand, and has supplied me with the few blanks left in the Emmanuel copy, although the former has in return some blanks which are filled up in the latter. It was not considered worth while to make a complete collation of the two copies ; but the Emmanuel one is evidently transcribed by the better Latinist, though the inferior calligraphist. This manuscript also alone contains the names of the actors, the English marginal notes, and the orders of processions, the University manuscript having no English

---

[1] Two copies are in the British Museum, and at least one in private hands.

but the textual stage-directions in the last part.   But
the latter commences with the following title, which
is omitted in the former :

Thomæ Legge legum doctoris
Collegii Caio-goneviliensis in
Academia Cantabrigiensi
magistri ac Rectoris.

Richardus tertius Tragedia trivespa
habita Collegii Divi Johnis
Evangeliste
Comitii Bacchelaureorum
Anno Domini 1579
Tragedia in tres acciones devisa.

The work is alluded to by Sir John Harrington in
his "Apologie of Poetry," 1591, as follows : "For
tragedies, to omit other famous tragedies, that which
was played at St. John's in Cambridge, of Richard III,
would move, I think, Phalaris the tyrant, and terrefie
all tyrannous-minded men ; " and this observation is
quoted by Thomas Heywood in his "Apology for
Actors," 1612, at p. 55 of the Society's reprint of that
work.   The play is also alluded to in Nash's " Have
with you to Saffron Walden," 1596, as follows :—"or
his fellow codshead, that in the Latine tragedie of
King Richard cries *Ad urbs, ad urbs, ad urbs,* when
his whole part was no more than *Urbs, urbs, ad arma,
ad arma."*—Vid. post.

The author of this play was Dr. Thomas Legge,
who probably wrote it for the purpose of being performed before the Queen.   In the year 1592, he was
Vice Chancellor of the University, "and," says Mr.
Collier,[1] "in a communication to Lord Burghley, he
refers to some offence given to the Queen, probably

---

[1] " Hist. of Dram. Poet.," i. 296.

by requiring, in answer to her wishes to see a play at Cambridge, time and the use of the Latin tongue; and mentions that the University had sent some of its body to Oxford, to witness the entertainment there given to Her Majesty, in order to be better prepared hereafter to obey her directions." Besides the play of "Richardus Tertius," he wrote a tragedy called the "Destruction of Jerusalem," and to use Fuller's words,[1] "having at last refined it to the purity of the publique standard, some plageary filched it from him, just as it was to be acted." Fuller also informs us that Dr. Palmer, afterwards Dean of Peterborough, was the original performer of Richard, and very successful in Legge's other play. Dr. Legge died in 1607, and his monument and portrait are still existing at Caius College, of which he was appointed Master by the Founder.

Mr. Halliwell kindly informs me that, in 1586, Henry Lacey wrote a play under the same title, but that it is a poor imitation of Legge's. Of Lacey's play two copies will be found in the British Museum, MSS. Harl. 2412, 6926. That the "University Men" had acquired some reputation by their theatrical performances, is proved by the well-known dialogue in "The Return from Parnassus,"[2] in which Kemp and Burbage are seen in treaty with two of them, called *Philomusus* and *Studioso*, for engagements as actors, and in which one of them gives a taste of his quality, by reciting the opening speech of Shakespeare's "Richard the Third."]

---

[1] Fuller's "Worthies," ii. 156.
[2] Hazlitt's "Dodsley," vol. ix.

RICHARDUS TERTIUS.

—*o*—

D. SHEPHARD, Elizabetha Regina.
Mr FOX, Cardinalis, Archiepis : Cantu :
Mr WHALEY, Nuntius.
L. W. HOWARD, Eduardus Rex quindecem annorū.
Mr PALMAR, Richardus dux Glocest :
Mr STRINGER, dux Buckingh :
Mr WILKINSON, Riverius ⎫
Mr BOOTH, Hastingus ⎪
Mr HODSON, Stanleus ⎬ *Barones.*
Mr HILL, Sr. Hawardus postea dux Norfolciensis ⎪
Mr BAYLY, Lovellus ⎭
Mr STANTON, Episco : Eliensis.
Ds PILKINGTON, ancilla Reginæ.
Mr ROBINSON, Catsbeius, Juris peritus.
Mr HILL, Sr. Howardus, Equestris ordinis.[1]
Ds PUNTER, servus ducis Glocestriæ.
Mr KNOX, Hastingus, miles calligatus.
Ds FRAUNCE, civis Londinensis.
Ds HOWLAND ⎫
Ds IIENLOWE ⎬ *chorus tumultuantiū civiu Satelles Becke*
Mr KENDALL ⎭ *[Buckᵉ.]*
Ds REMER, Archiepisco : Eboracensis.

Serviens ad arma.

Prosecutor vulgo pursevant.

RHODES med : Richardus dux Eboracensis parvulus ⎫
Mr BOWES, Graius heros adolescens ⎪
⠀⠀⠀⠀⠀⠀⠀Vaghanus ⎪
WOODCOCKE.⠀Conjux Shori ⎬ *Muti.*
⠀⠀⠀⠀⠀⠀⠀Hawt ⎪
⠀⠀⠀⠀⠀⠀⠀Sacerdos ⎪
⠀⠀⠀⠀⠀⠀⠀Quinq filiæ Elizabethæ Reginæ. ⎭

---

[1] Inserted twice.

CHAPMAN, Argumentū primæ actionis.[1]

Eduardus quartus, rex Angloru mortem obiit

Hic duos reliquit filios. Eduardus maior princeps Walliæ annos habebat quindecem, alter Richardus dux Eborū undecimū vitæ annū egit. Richardus dux Glocestriæ, frater Eduardi defuncti, homo nimia ambitione elatus, cum nepotis adhuc tenerā ætatem videret, facile ad regnū aditū sibi patêre putat. Itaq primū reginæ p amicos psuadet ut Eduardus quintus iter nullo milite armaret, dum Londinū e Wallorū finib⁹ properaret. Interim ipse cum amicis clam comunicat, quantū inde periculū sibi crearetur si regis tenelli tutela solis reginæ propinquis demandaretur. Qui dū cæteris heroib⁹ inviderent, facile in eorum pniciem regis nomine abuti possent. Itaq Riveriū virū nobilem regis avunculū, et Grayū fratrem ejus uterinū á rege ipso avulsū in vincula conjicit. Qui nec ita multo post, Pontefracti capite plectuntur. Regem ipsū, tutor à senatu illustri declaratus, in suā tutelā accipit, porro a Regina, quæ tū ad asylum metu confugerat, Ducem Eborū parvulū, p Cardinalem Archiepiscopū Eboracensem, nihil tum suspicantem, abstulit. Ubi Regios pueros in Arce tanquā in Carcere conclusisset, primū Hastingū nobilem virū, quod nimis eū studere nepotibus suspicaretur, injustè damnatū morte afficit. Cardinalis, Episcopus Eliensis, Stanleus heros in carcerem detruduntur, ne quid inceptis suis obstarent, quod eorū fidem erga regulos pertimesceret. Postremò Shori conjux (quoniam morti eam damnare non poterat) tanquā meretrix infamiæ pœna afficitur.

---

[1] This line is written in red ink, and the name is perhaps that of the transcriber.

ACTUS PRIMUS.

Elizabetha Regina, Cardinalis,
Nuntius.

Regina.

Quicunq lætis credulus rebus nimis
confidit, et magna potens aula cupit
regnare, blandū quærit is malū, licet
magnū nihil sperare generosū genus
jubebat : Eduardi tamen Regis thoro
conjuncta sum, post quā tuos thalamos
    mihi,
generose Gray, triste fatū sustulit.
dulci veneno gustiebam credula,
et rapuit altis inclytus titulis honor
donec meū spernebat abjectū genus
cognatus heros Regis, et tristem meis
Inimicus affinis parabat exitū.
His cura major, filii quod traditur,
et Regiū curat Nepotum avunculus.
volui meos Regi propinquos jungere
comites, ut annis altiùs primus amor
hæreat, tenera dū surgit ætas grandior.
nec tristis hæc contenta peste sors fuit
prius malū majoris est gradus mali
Exhalat ægrotum maritus spiritū,
et fata rumpunt regis impia manu
sævæ sorores, invident virū mihi
mortale fatis luditur genus. sibi
spondere quicquā non potest tam
    stabile
fortuna quod non versit anceps. sor-
    dida
manet domus tantùm beata, dum timet
virtus ruinas magna. Postquā duplici
mater sobole ditata sum Regis domū
petebat hæredem remota Wallia :
nec principe libenter suo gens Cam-
    bria
carebat : hinc iter properat huc filius

Brevis ordo cōmitatuū meorū, ut
    cingerent
Regale diademate caput : Matrem
    licet
gaudere læta sceptra cogunt nlii :
At gaudiū sperare promissu sibi
mens avida non audet, timet adeptū
    bonū,
metūq pturit semel natus metus,
multisq curis pectus urit anxiū,
Sin filiis externa vis adhuc nihil
minetur infidū, nec extortū sibi
Regnū, domus Lancastria Eduardo
    incidet,
Et rapta quondam sceptra victrici
    manu
pati potest adhuc : tamen domesticus
premit timor, majusq formidat nefas
animus malis assuetus, et vario tremor
mentem tumultu, spesq laceram dis-
    trahit,
Infaustus ô Regni favor multis suā
conversus in pœnam ruit, postquā diu
falso viros splendore lusit credulos.

Cardinalis.

Regina præcellens Elizabetha caput,
curas cur anxio revolvis pectore?
et publicū luctu tuo oneras gaudiū?
quin sperne mentis turbidæ ludibria
Matrisq tristes læta deme spiritus,
dum filii caput corona cingitur.

Regina.

Sacrū caput præstans honore Cardinis,
insignis Archipræsul atq Cantii,
nescire quenquam miserias miserū
    magis.
Quod tempus unquā lachrymis caruit
    mihi?

Non Regis Eduardi gemo durā luem,
odiū ne triste plango demens heroū
vetus hoc malū. Cum Walliā linquens suā
stipato armatus rediret milite
ut regna patris jure possideat suo
Eduardus hæres: Sermo multorū frequens
aures fatigat, nec monere desinit,
nullis ut armis sepiat princeps iter,
se subditis committeret nudū suis.
sin clauderet milite suo Regis latus
stipata regem sola Graiorū domus
timere tum mali nihil princeps potest:
Mox in suā armari necem tot milites
Proceres putabunt: nuꝑ extinctæ minæ
facile fidem dabunt, et vulnera recrudescere
sanata malè mox suspicantur. Ergo dum
sese timent objicere inermes hostib⁹.
Ferro simul vitam tuentur illico,
Belli furore totū inundavit solū,
Calcante tellus equite terrendū gemit
belli tumultu ardebit insana Anglia
statimq amoris fœdus ictū frangitur.
Tum ꝑfidū mulctabit authorem scelus
pœnasꝑ pendet lapsa Graiorū domus.
Primū ꝑ artus gellidus excurrit metus
tandem suis temebunda monitis animo
mox litteris edere cuncta fratrib⁹
ut milite nullo cingant filii latus,
pompaq magna Regis exonerent iter.
ubi sola secreta sagax repeto metus,
nova cura mentem concutit formidine,
nec prædæ nudus offeratur hostibus,
Ingens domū nostram invidia premit, furit
ambitio, nullā cœca dum maculam timet
se modica non tuetur ætas filli.
fratri suo mortem intulit Glocestrius
Quomodo nepoti ambitio parcet potui.

Card.

Cesset timere matris infælicis amor,
Vanosꝑ desine falsa mentiri dolos.
Injustus est rerū æstimator dolor,
Nunquid juvat terrere vano pectora
tremore? pessimus augur in malis timor,
semperq sibi falsò minatur, et suā
vocat ruinā quamvis ignotā priùs.
Proceres sepultis morte Regis litibus
longam quitem consecrarunt: nec minas
veretur extinctas sanata Brittania.
Odia movebit nova rebellis qui timet
priora.

Nuntius.

Mediū Rex iter sospes tenet.

Regina.

Quæ filiū nunc detinet fessū via?

Nuntius.

Bis sera stellifero excidit cœlo dies
Northamptonū cum fessa membra tangerent.

Regina.

Et quanta turba Regiū claudit latus?

Nunt.

Ubi Wallia mutaret accellerans sedes,
frequens satelles sepiebat principem,
illiq multos junxit assiduus labor.
Postquā tuas Riverius literas
cepisset, omni milite corpus principis
nudabat, unus cōmigrat Riverius,
suoq junctus Graius heros patruo.

Regina.

Dux obviā Glocestrius Regi fuit?

Nunt.

Is literis Regi salutem nuntiat,
regno suo precatur æternū decus,

multaq præce cõmune gaudiũ beat.
Honore præstans dux Buckinghamiæ
affatur officiis iisdem Principem,
Regiq promittunt brevi comites fore
Scribit frequens Riverio Glocestrius,
Invisit et Graiũ nepotem literis
benigne pollicetur omnia nunciis
et pars fatigat magna nobiliũ simul.

Regina.

Postquã favor flatu secundo vexerit
ratem procul : reliquit idem languidus
alto mari, multisq jactat fluctibus.
Res prosperæ si quando lætari jubent,
rursus revolvor in metus, nec desinit
animus pavere læta quamvis cerneret.

Card.

Facilè sinistris credit auguriis timor.

Reg.

Nihil sapit, quisquis parũ doctus sapit.

Card.

Hoc facilè credunt, qui nimis miseri
timent.

Reg.

Quisquis cavet futura, torquetur minus.

Card.

Sperare virtus magna, nunquã desinit.

Reg.

Quò plura speras falsò, turbaris magis.

Card.

Terrent adhuc sopita nobiliũ mala ?

Reg.

Veterata non sanatur illico vulnera.

Card.

Sancivit ista morte princeps fœdera.

Reg.

Tum principe mori dubia quærunt
fœdera.

Card.

Privata vincit odia cõmunis salus.

Reg.

Privata publicã quietem destruit
ambitio.

Card.

Semp esse nũ miserã juvat.

Reg.

Timere didicit quisquis excelsus stetit.
rebusq magnis alta clauditur quies.
Auro venenũ bibitur ignotum casæ
humili malũ, ventisq cunctis cognita
superba sũmo, tecta nutant culmine.

ACTUS SECUNDUS;

RICH. DUX GLOC. HEN. DUX BUCK-
INCHAMIÆ, RIVERUS HEROS, HAS-
TINGUS HEROS.

Gloc.

Riverianæ splendor et decus domus,
custos pupilli regis, heros nobilis,
Qualis cruentæ matris eripiens minis
Electra fratrem servat in regnũ patris
Talis nepotem Wallicis tutans agris
reddis suæ incolumem fidelis patriæ.
Populus tam frequens fidem merito
  sonat
En gratus hic tibi labor Britaniæ
Et nos pares psolvimus grates tibi
castos labores Wallicæ norunt sedes
curam parem regis fatetur longum iter,
postquã suo Wallia carebat principe,
at ubi suũ mundo diem reparat coma
radiante Tytan, et leves umbras fugat,
cras principis jungemur et lateri simul

qua ducitur recta Stonistratfordiam.
Primo die celeri gradu properabimus,
quod nunc locus proceres tot unus non
    capit.

River.

O Claudiani Rector illustris soli,
dux inclyte et generis propago Regii
Præstare Regi jussit officiũ meũ
Fortuna quicquid nostra præclarũ
    dedit.
Pondenda bello est vita Regi debita,
Si modo aliter nequeunt minæ frangi
    hostiũ,
Vestræ quia mensæ patebant mihi
    dapes
hac nocte, vobis jure multũ debeo.
Jam laxat artus languidos gratus sopor
Lectoq fessa membra componi juvat,
placidam quietem noctis opto prox-
    imæ.

Gloc.

Præclare dux est stella Buckinghamiæ
cui servus olim nomen haud latens
    dedit,
Et orte claro Hastinge patru stemate
En sol vocato nocte frenos desernes
sudore fumantes juvas mersit salo,
Vacuũ q cælũ luna plustrat viris
silentiũ imperans, nitida simul cohors
comitatur, aspergens lumen vagũ polo
Porro locus omni liber arbitrio vacat
secretas aures nullus exhibet comes
Annon vides quam sit miser proceru
    status,
diuq spreta ut nobilis virtus jacet
Regi licet sanguine superbo jungimur,
clarisq lucet inclytũ titulis genus,
aditus tamen mihi nullus ad regem
    patet,
vetantq cum nepote patruũ vivere
Quò tanta matris cedit impudentia?
jam fœminæ succumbit Anglorũ decus
En nostra dubitatur fides, sepultus est
debitus, honor, spretusp sanguis no-
    bilis

sordescit : olim matris omnino suæ
tutela Regis sacra cognatis datur.
Illis quando honore tamen haud cedi-
    mus
et in nepotem æqualis elucet fides,
parũ decebat matris abjectũ genus,
Regni thoros amor nisi quod impulit
claros negare patruos Regi suos
minusq nobili comite circundare
Parum decorũ principi aut nobis erit
comes magis potentior tuebitur
quod nos malũ manet, si qui male
nobis precantur, Regiũq claudant
    latus
primosq prævenient amores principis,
et illius favore consenescerent,
quorũ mens tenella flectetur statim,
atq pueros fucata demulcent leves
seris nec annis respuũt quicquid prius
placet.   In amores deliciasq pristinas
ætas probat decursa, nec se corrigit
Eduardus olim quartus (ætas plenior
quamvis fuit, temqusp longũ plurima
seræ noverca disciplina evasserat)
hem multa quondam facta damnavit
    sua
lapsũ priorem nec resuesit tardior
sensus : Quod heros sensit heu Clar-
    entius
Ille, ille novit (heu nimis) frater meus
quam conjugi rex cessit olim credulus
nimis, heu nimis tum nostra suade-
    bant mala
quòd uxor horreat maritus quem colit
quòd dura nostras sors premebat res
    diu
Regina quantũ mihi creasset tum luem
perfida, malũ mens nisi sagax auertit?
nos ille cœlũ qui sua torquet manu,
dirisq flamis triste vindicat scelus,
fœlix potenti liberavit dextera.
Heu quot brevi frater furore concitus
dolis eorũ morte damnatos truci
perdidit, inani voce pulsantes Jovem?
Nunquã suo parcebat ira sanguini
stragi suorũ una propinquos addidit

Sed vetera plangimus : novū iminet
   malū.
Nam si tenello solus hæret principi
cōmunis hostis, atq stipabit thronū
ìnfesta nobis una Graiorū domus.
Mox hostiū vires caput nostrū luet,
dum principis sacrato abuti nomine
audebit ad nostrā ruinam atrox domus
Hoc Jupiter tam providus pater vetet
Quod morte sanxit sacra pacis fœdera
Eduardus, et veteri medetur vulneri
Quietis, atq dexteras nos invicem
conjunximus, simulata pacis pignora
valuit potestas sacra Regis tū magis
quam pace ficta dubia procerū fœdera
pactuq jussu principis percussimus
quemquamne tantus vexat insanū stupor ?
huic credat ut demens repente qui
   novus
Ex hoste tam vetusto amicus sumitur?
firmius inhærebit brevis animi favor,
quàm longa multis invidia lustris ma-
   nens ?
nunc ergo maturare conciliū decet,
quò longius serpit malū, fieri solet
rubustius, vires semper colligit.

Buckin.

O Claudiane rector, atq Regia
de stirpe princeps, turbido infœlix
   quia
visa est tumultu ardere rursus Anglia,
et bella cœperunt fremere civilia
tuæ ut secreto instillet auri murmure
concepta jussi verba servulū meū,
tua signa Buckinghamiū sequi ducem
miscere præsens verba presenti diu
quærebū, ut hæc tecū loqui possem
   simul
Regina nobis insolens abutitur
statim premi scelus decet, majus nefas
parit semel motū malū, et nescit modū
sanare te regni luem tantū decet
quidvis ferent potius potens procerū
   cohors

cruore quàm Regina nostro luderet,
Gnatūq caput armaret in nostrū ferox.

Gloc.

Te patriæ dux ergo vindicem voco
et selere materno labantis Angliæ.
Te, te poli qui jura pcipitis Regis
Et vos corruscū testor agmen cælitū
tantū Britonū pristinū quæro decus
Acris gravi medela confert vulneri
Regina nunc abest : suis afferre opem
captis nequit removere jam tutò
   licet
A Rege cunctas patriæ labes suæ
Quin dormientem comprimere Ri·
   veriū,
intraq tecta claudere hospitem decet
Sin fugerit, tū consciū probat metus
mox famulæ illius petas claves domus
qua nup hospes se Riverius abdidit
Sin abnuat, Regis imperiū urgeas
nec ullus inde servus erumpat foras,
sed sedulò claudantur intus singuli
nostrisq verbis advove clā servulos
(horreret admisso licet nondū die
nox atra) nostrū sepiant corpus tamen
quod luce prima nos nepotem adibi-
   mus.

Buck.

Regis propinquos si coerces vinculis
cæcoq captos claudis audax carcere,
Illico tumultū plebs ciebit mobilis
Juditia dum non recta sortiris : reis
et criminis parū nocentes arguas.

Gloc.

En dignitatem principis lædunt sui,
et nobilem violare sanguinem student
lacerare quærunt Angliā discordiis.
Longa Britonū classe sulcavit mare
Marchio Graiorū frater : in nostrā
   necem
tot milites armare crudelis potest ?
profundere atq principū longas opes.

Hasting.

At vinculis si patruū premi suū
Heros videbit Graius, is rapida manu
Stipabit Eduardū : tremens Britañia
parabit arma : seditio miseros trahet.
Ardore belli conflagrabunt omnia
nostraq populus strage purgabit scelus.

Glocest.

Aditus viarū munit assiduis vigil,
Irrumpat hinc ut nemo Northampto-
    niam,
nostrūq prius ad regem iter pverteret,
Post quā leves discussit umbras Luci-
    fer,
Nudamq jubebit fugam Phœbea fax,
nos statuimus Regem priores visere
ut grata principi fides sic luceat.

Buck.

Intende nervos viriū, vinci nequit
generosus ardor, mentis et nullus labor
curam fatigat anxiam sumī ducis
Nunquam fidem fallā.

Hast.

        Polus tristi priùs
jungetur orco, sydera natabunt aquis
amicus ignis fluctib[9] sævus erit
vincet diem nox : quam meam damnes
    fidem.

River.

Nescio quid animus triste presagat
    malū,
horrent timore membra : cor pavet
    metu
Demiror hi claves quid hospitii petant,
quæ tanta cecidit temporū mutatio
Ultro prioris noctis onerabant dapes
An jam retentū morte mulctant im-
    proba ?
Mihi sunt amici : non amet fucos fides
Vacillat animus, hæret, haud placet
    sibi.
Si fugio, nullus est fugæ tutus locus :

Si lateo, sceleris conscius demens ero
en animus ullos innocens negat metus,
manere certū est : quicquid evenit,
    feram.
Duces adibo : causa quæ sit audiam.

Glocest.

O Regis hostis, impiū atq audax ca-
    put !
tu nobiles mulctare suppliciis studes ?
et insolentes seminas discordias
tu principis nutum ad necem ūram
    vocas ?
tuisq demens regna misces litibus.
Præstabis istud credis nefandū nefas !

River.

Præclare princeps, tale de me nil
    putes,
hoc absit (oro) crimen a nostra fide.

Glocest.

Tace scelestū Regis exitiū tui
patiemur ultro sanguinem nostrū peti ?
perdes Britonū solus excelsū decus ?
at vos atro mulctate raptū carcere.
comitesq nostrū cæteri cingant latus.

River.

Quo me trahitis.   Quam jubet pœnà
    potens
fortuna ? quæ nunc me manent miserū
    mala ?
si morte mulctet, jure damnet publico
Nam quæ salutis spes relinquitur
    mihi ?

EDUARD : REX : DUX : BUCKING :
    DUX GLOCES : SERVUS REGIS.

Eduard :

Amore captus patriæ preceps iter
quamvis facio, dum Wallicas muto
    sedes
lubens tamen relinquo Stonistratfordiā

quod hoc ferunt properare nunc Glocestriū
quoniā tot unus non capit proceres
locus.

Buck.

Cinctus suis Eduardus huc confert
gradū,
generosa quos beant avorū stemata
præite, plebei sequantur ordines.

Gloc.

Rex vivat æternū Britanus inclytus.

Eduardus.

Gnatus mihi conspectus est mi patrue
postquā sedes modò barbaras mutavimus
habeoq tantis gratiā vobis parem.

Buck.

Tibi beatū firmet imperiū deus.

Ed. Rex.

Tuam simul laudo fidem, dux inclyte.

Gloc.

Natura me tuis fidelem jussibus
nescia resisti consecravit et dolos
genus struere Regale me regi vetat
cum cæteris comune psuadet fidem
officiū. Aquas inimicus ignis incolet.
sulcabit astra navis et sævo mari
ignota quercus surget, oblitū tui
si quando falsa corrumpat fides.
Vitā tuis ponā libens bellis, tuis
infestus hostib⁹ mori cupio diè
Quæ te supbe Graie, vel fratrem tuū
ambitio tenet, et Riveriū patruū
dum principem vobis studetis subdere
En pessimis miscetis Anglos litib⁹
Florensq deridetur ortus sanguinis,
Cur usq Dorsetti minatur Marchio
nobis, in arcem irrupit audax Belini

Prædatur inde Regis opes rapida
manu
Et classe longu oneravit ingenti salū.

Ed. Rex.

Quid Marchio patravit uterinus mihi
nescio : fides suspecta avunculi mei
Graiiq fratris (crede mihi) nunquā fuit.

Glo.

Immo tuas tanti latant aures doli,
Rex inclyte, secretū magis pugnat
scelus.
Te pduellionis esse aio reum
Sceleste Graie, teq sceleris consciū
Vahanne nuntio : proditorem patriæ
pfide voco Haute * simul : squalenti
carcere
abdite statim, patriæ graves penas
luant.

Servus.

Puerū misellum, lachrymis rigat genas
tristia videns ad vincula correptū
fratrem.

Gloc.

Te liberam⁹ serve famulato tuo
nec te vollumus hærere lateri principis
tu principi fidelis stabis comes
Regisq te ppetuus adjunget labor.

SERVUS REGIS, SERVUS DUCIS
GLOC.

Servus Regis.

Regni paterni pondus imbellis puer
Non sustinet, suisque victus virib⁹
tandem ruit : tuetur hostes intimos
Munita nomine sacra majestas suo
parare dum tristem luem clam cogitat
ambitioq Regni pva suspecti fides
nec principem sinit anxiū quiescere
Secreta solii pugna. qui loco stares

---

* Sir Thomas Vaughan and Sir Richard Hawte.

minore tutior. nec amissi premet
Sceptri metus, vel dissimilis avorū
    honor.
Qui clara torques sydera altitonans
    pater,
tuisq pingis ignibus cœli globos,
Britanniæ potens defende principem
ut jura verus reddat hæres Angliæ
Quis huc minister advolat celeri pede'?
Quo nunc adeo generose pcipitas
    gradū?

Ser. Glo.

Misit nepoti nobilis Riverius.

Ser. Reg.

Duci ne tu minister illi carceris.

Ser. Glo.

Ego Claudianæ fidus astabā comes.

Ser. Reg.

Quorsū nepoti nuntius patrui venis.

Ser. Glo.

Ubi mordet impransū fames Glo-
    cestriū
Ducis onerabant lauta mensam prandia
Oculis perrat sedulus cunctas dapes,
misitq selectos cibos Riverio,
animoq jussit æquo ferre singula,
nil rebus illius esse formidabile.

Ser. Reg.

Num respuit benigna demens munera.

Ser. Glo.

Quem longus usus ferre psuasit malū
Fortuna quoties cura tristis intonat,
Vitæ cupit solamen afflictæ minus,
ubi gratias pleno refundit pectore
Deferre Graio lauta jussit fercula
quem fregerat non cognitus priùs
    dolor
nec asperos dedicit minor casus pati

ut blanda fractū verba confirment
    ducis
et turbidā pmulceant mentem dapes,
At jussa me tanti viri decet exequi.

Ser. Reg.

An fronte simulatus latet blanda dolus
ut impitis alta figat vulnera ?
An sorte nos mutata felici beat
Fortuna, miseros carceris solvens
    metu ?
Faustus cadat tantis procellis exitus.

ACTUS TERTIUS.

ANCILLA REGINÆ, ARCHIEP. EBORᾰ
    REGINA.

Ancilla.

Qui vindices faces potens torques
    manu,
mitisq rebus collocas fessis opem,
miserere jactatæ Eboracensis domus.
Quis est malorū finis ? heu ! heu !
    quamdiù
Regina victa luctibus diris gravat ?
Quæ possidet ferox Erinnis Regiam.
Tortos vel angues Megara crudelis
    vibrans
Luctūq majorem prior luctus vocat
Et vix malis Regina tantus sufficit.
Quis me p auras turbo raptam devehet
ne tot misera tristes querelas audiam
mæstæ domus luctusq matris lugubres

Archiep. Ebor.

Lett his servants   Nondum fugata nocte
be about him   sol reparat diem,
wh hoods.   Nec deserit fatri vices
    Phœbi soror
vel pulsa cælo contrahit lumen vagū
nox sera : Quorsū noctis umbris par-
    cere
quæris, celere solamen, imensū malū

desiderat : æger non patitur animus moras

Lett yem bee knocking in the pallace as remooveinge. Mentem placare turbidam matris para. Sed quis tumultus? turba quanta Regia Effare tanti nocte, strepitus quid velint.

Ancilla.

Splendens honore antistes Eboracensiū
Diros tibi renovare me casus jubes
post quā Luna fessis suaserat,
et cæca nox horreret, amisso die
Increbuit aula, vinculis Riverium
duris premi et Graiū nepotem : tū locus
quis principem capiat, tenere neminem.
Postquā paterent tanta reginæ mala,
animus tremore concitus subito stupet,
Solvuntur (heu) labante membra spiritu
Postquā trementes misera vires colligit,
en, talibus mox astra pulsat vocibus
O dura fata, parcite : heu quod voluitis
Quantū scelus spiratis ? an pœnæ placent,
In hoc caput jaculare vindices faces
Irate pater : inocens quid admisit puer ?
quid meruit parvus quid infans pditur ?
una ruina concutis totā domum
Non sustinet labante mox collo caput
Largo madescunt imbre profusæ genæ
cor triste magnis æstuat dolorib.
cultū decorum regiæ vestis procul
removet, et eximii rubores muricis
Quieta nunquam constat, huc, illuc, fugit,
tolli jubet iterūq poni corpora.
Et semp impatiens sui status, citò

mutatur, et cœlū quærelis verberat
nunc filiū gemit, suorū nunc luem,
curamq serā, tanta sentiunt vulnera
dempti satellitis. [reclamat anxia] *
Mox illa asylo purpurā servos jubet
aurūq fulvū rapere, supellectilem
et quas habebat regia excelsas opes,
Et ne leves obsint moræ vehentib.
hinc brevior ut pateret ad templū via
interna jussit pforari mœnia
Regis, quàm asylū clauditur patiū
Charūq demens filiū tenens sinu,
et, quinq mater filias vocans fugit
sacras ad ædes. Interim tremens metu
qualis leonis faucibus vastis premi
fugiens timet, dum præda poscitor, fera.

Regina,

A curtaine being drawne, let the queene appeare in ye Sanctuary, her 5 daughters and maydes about her, sittinge on packs, fardells, chests, cofers. The queene sitting on ye ground wth fardells about her. Eboracensis urbis excellens pater. Ergo deese quid malis nostris potest ? aut fata vincere nostra quis potuit miser ? Frustra timemus jam videre quæ horruit magnæ domus (heu) reliquiæ parvæ sumus. tantuq miseros templa tutantur sacra
Durū parant funus propinqui sanguinis :
nec quis tenet regem locus, servi sciunt
An non perimus : ulla spes manet domus ?

Archiep. Ebor.

Metus remitte, pone curas anxias
Erroris istud omne quodcunq et malū
Quicquāne gravis animos levat miseros dolor ?

---

* All bracketed words are supplied from the University Library MS.

Quin mitiùs de reb[9] istis cogita.
Mihi nup ubi suadet soporem cæca nox
me suscitat somno sepultū nuntius
Hastingus heros misit, hic narrat mihi
traxisse Northamtoniæ moras duces,
ubi subditis stipatus hæret rex suis
Pectus mihi quisquā timore luderet,
nam cuncta tandem sorte 'fœlici
cadent.

Regina.

Ille, ille nostri durus hostis sanguinis
Hastingus, ille principi exitiū parat :
En, vindices mater deos supplex
precor,
Dirū caput flāmis nefandis obruant.

Archiep. Ebor.

Lax furentis turgidos animi motus,
et siste prudens impetus mentis graves
testor deorū numen, astra qui sua
torquent manu, si filiū præter tuū
quenquā coronant, proximo statim die
fratri huic suo decora regni insignia
trademus ; en magnū sygillu nunc
tibi,
quod mihi tuus quondam maritus detulit,
reddam tuo quem nunc tueris filio.

Archiep. solus.

Rector potens Olympi, et altitonans
pater
Ergo placidam sana quietem patriæ,
ut tractet hæres sceptra puerili manu
Ne dura regnū pœna victori cadet
belliq spem fingunt novā Lancastriæ,
dum cæde se litabat hostis impia.
Sed quid facis ? quæ mentis oblivio
capit ?
Cuiquamne te magnū sygillū tradere ?
cui detulisti ? fœminæ ? quin semp fuit
invisa, tum fidem duces ludent tuā,
dum magna Regni cure temere pro-
ditur
Num fœminæ credis ? facile resistitur

Et in tuū vis sæviet solū caput
Nunc ego mittā qui sygillū clam petat,
ut non meam duces levem damnent
fidem.

SERVUS GLOC.CHORUS PROCERŪ TU-
MULTUANTIŪ CIVES, HASTING[9]
HEROS, ARCHIEP. EBOR.

Servus Gloc.

Jam quamlibet defendit excubitor viā
totamq densæ Thamesim sulcant rates,
ut nemo prumpat ad asylū profuga.
Nil Claudiane dux sacrā metuas fidem
Quin matris ad templa surripiunt opes

Let artificers   Quos hic tumultus
come running   concitatis improbi?
out with clubs   Quo pellit insanos
and staves.   Elizabethæ furor ?

Prim[9] proc.

Urbs, urbs, Cives, ad arma, ad arma.

Servus.

En arma doliis vehuntur abdita
quib[9] necem ducibus rebelles clam
parant.

2[9] Procer.

Some armed with Quodnā malū tantus
privy coates   tumultus parturit ?
with gownes
throwne over.   3[9] Procer.
Some unarmed.

Onerata navigiis Tamesis horruit
aqua.

4[9] Procer.

Regina fugiens arma multa simul ve-
hit ?

5[9] Procer.

Quidnā parat regina crudelis malū ?

6[9] Procer.

At arma feriant, si minentur, non ve-
hant.

7⁹ *Procer.*

Dii feminæ tam triste vindicent nefas.

8⁹ *Procer.*

At te deus pusille princeps, muniat.

Archiep. Ebor.

Regni potentis nobilis procerū cohors.
An rumor audax credulos ludit, metus
Spargens novos ? vel crescit in luctus
   vetus
malū ? furensq repetit agnitu priùs
Ambitio thronū ? et poscit in prædā
   sibi ?
Præceps moras tumultus haud patitur,
   leves
Supplex ad aras sternitur mater tre-
   mens.
Regina regnū suspicatur filii
plures atro clauduntur heroes specu
Quorū fides regis tutelā meruit
Imbecillis regis ætas admittit nefas,
Scelusq facile concitat timidū licet,
Sanū statim expedire consiliū decet,
Donec quis errat qui dolos patat magis
sed clarus huc Hastingus heros advo-
   lat.

Hastingus.

Non vos latebat, chara civiū cohors,
Rex me quibus est amplexus amorib⁹.
Arctius ct cjus colere chara pignora
cogunt benigni tanta regis munera.
Quorū nisi vitam mea luerem nece,
ingrata fœdaret magis nulla nota
Lædi doleo rumore pacem futili,
varioq turbari Britannos murmure :
Hospes video tumultuari subditos
per tota raptare volantes mœniu.
Quorsū metu vexare vano pectora
juvat ? Ora quicquid mentiuntur garrula,
pspecta mihi fides Glocestria satis fuit,
En, ducit alacri Regulū pompa modo,
   ut
tenerū corona cingeret fulva caput.

At dura quos premit proceres custodia
Lacerare probris profidi Glocestriū
quærunt ducem : cæcoq frigent carcere
litem sacratus dū senatus poneret
Unū precor supplex (patres) sententia
ne nostra mentem posterā preverteret,
ne publico lites vigerent funere
Ad arma ne nos via rebellis concitet
Justissima licet bella suadere queant.
Horū feretur causa semp justior.
Armis suis quicunq claudant principem
dum mœnib⁹ Regalis adventat puer,
urbis principi pacata gratuletur suo.

REX EDUARDUS, PRÆTOR LONDIN-
   ENSIS.

Eduardus.'

Ubi barbaras sedes mutavimus feræ
gentis, revertor sospes ad patrios lares
Urbis supbæ clarus hic pollet nitor,
Regniq splendet majus inclyti decus.
Urbs chara, salve tanta : nunquā
   gaudia
post tot ruinas Asiæ Argivis nunquā
Optata patriæ regna et Argolicas opes
cum bella post tam longa primi vise-
   rent
Vix hospiti tot lustra tam lætū tibi
redditū licet tantis miser naufragiis
ereptus esses dux Cephalenius parant
Quam cressit amissæ voluptas patriæ
hospes diu postquā carebas, et suos
negant aspectus longam iter nihi.

Prætor Lond.

Illustre patriæ decus rex inclyte
en læta profudit cohors se civiū
ut gratuletur principi multū suo -
sol nostro ut alter luceas fœlix polo
hæresq patris jura Britannis dares
cives deū pulsabit anxius prece.

Dux Gloc.

The King goeing Eduardus en rex ves-
about the stage.   ter, o cives mei,[1]
honore fulgens regio, en potens puer
chare Britannis principem vides tuū,
virtute præstantem fidelis abdite.

ACTUS QUARTUS.

Hastingus Heros.

Regina inædibus squalens sacris sedet
Duris propinqui comprimuntur vin-
    culis
Tutorq declaratus Angliæ modo
suffragiis Glocestrius nostris fuit.
Magnū sygillū præsuli Eborū demitur
Hunc Claudianus jure potens vulnerat,
quod prodidit levi sigillū fœminæ
Fœlix beabit cuncta sors, hostes jacent
et Pontefracti, jam manent tristem
    necem
Properate fato, mox graves pœnas
    luant.
Sed quid cesso sacrū senatū visere.

DUX GLOCEST. DUX BUCK. CARD.
    EBOR. EPISC. ELIENS. STANLEIUS
    HASTING[9] HOWARDUS, LOVELLUS,
    BARONES.
        Glocest.

Illustris o procerū cohors, quos Anglia
gens nobilis peperit, nil tandem mo-
    vet
tam triste reginæ scelus ? tantam pati
infamiam generosa mens adhuc po-
    test ?
Malitia tam diu latebit fœminæ ?
En, gnatū asylo inimica captivū tenet,
ut querulo rebellis agitet murmure
proceres Britanniæ, atque duris vul-
    neret
verbis, tumultu turba conceito. Quasi
    fides

incerta tutorū sit, anxius quibus
senatus Eborū ducis curam dedit
Nec parvulū hostis amotus procul
solū tenetur, aut bene notatus cibus :
Trahunt magis moderata puerū ludi-
    cra
Aetas suis æquata deliciis placet.
Nunquā seni colludet imistus puer,
fratrisq ludo frater instabit magis.
Solere parvis magna sæpe crescere
Quis nescit ? ingens regis esset dede-
    cus
Nostramq damnet non levis fidem
    labes,
Dum fama Gallis profuga obgannit,
    sacras
quòd fugit ad aras principis frater
    metu.
Citiùs nihil volare maledicto potest :
Opinio firmata nec statim perit.
Ergo viri mittantur assensa sacro
quorū dubia nunquam fides regi fuit,
Matri minùs suspecta, cognita patriæ
    satis,
ut filiū sacro solutū carcere, fratri suo
restituat. At tuam fidem
tantū negotiū requirit (Cardinis
honore præstans Archipræsul inclyte)
Præstare si tua non gravetur sanctitas.
Hoc regis ingens flagitat solatiū,
salusq fratris, certa patriæ quies.
Sin detinet regina gnatū pertinax,
nec matris infœlix amor morem gerit :
Suprema regis jussa luctantem pre-
    mant
Malitia constabit, odiū, protervia
Quæ mentis est opinio nostræ, lubens
audi (favente namq spiritū deo)
Nunquā meos urgebo sensus pertinax,
sed facile flectet sævior sententia.

Dux Buckin.

Quem solitudo principis non comovet,
procerūq deflectens honor, aut patriæ
Salus diu jactata ? dū claustris sacris
gnatū premit vesana mater, dedecus

Ingens puer sejunctus affert principi
Nec tutū erit carere fratre parvulo,
Vulgus probris futile lacessit improbis,
quasi nulla regis cura magnates tenet,
Non solū prolis mater ortū vendicat
suisq tantùm stulta delitiis putet
nasci : vocat regni decus : patriam statim
curare dulcis matris oblitū jubet.
Quòd melius hæc suadere Cardinis pater
Antistes excellens potest, assentior
Sin pavida amoris mater ignorat modū,
vi filiū sibi jubebit eripi.

Hastin. Heros.

Quorsum sacris hæreret ulnis parvu-
lus ?
fratri triumphū Regis aut cur invidet ?
Sin filii tremebunda periculū tremit,
At hic paternū sepiet frequens genus
Hic à sacro jussus senatu tutor est,
Regisq curabunt amantes subditi.
Tum mutuū fratrū vocat solatiū
proterva mater sin recusat mittere
Cardinis illū præsul ereptū avehat.

Card.

Ut fratris aula frater oblectet simul,
aut gratus Angliæ meus prosit labor,
meisq recuso æquale viribus nihil.
Gnatū sacra sin mater æde continet,
solusq fratrem rex suū non impetrat :
promissa templo jura nunquā rumpere
tamen decet, sanxisse quem divū Pe-
trum
primū ferunt, mox prisca firmavit fides,
et longus ordo principū pepigit : bonis
multis sacra pepcisse pacta constitit,
nec ullus Isthei audet Alanis feris
præbens fugam violare, nec rigens nive
tellus perenni hircana, vel sparsus Scytha
Nemo sacrilegus diis datam rumpit fidem.

At Regulo fratrem dabit matris sinus,
nec filii invidet parens solatio
Sin fratris aula fratre ppetuò vacet,
et filiū mater sacro carcere tenet,
Nihil meus damnabiter castus labor,
solusq matris impediet cæcus amor.

Dux Buckin.

Quin matris impediet magis protervia
Audebo vitam pignori deponere
nullam timoris vel sibi causā putet,
vel filio, nemo lubens cum fœmina
pugnabit : optarem propinquis mulie-
brem
sexū simul : perturbat Angliā minus.
Quibus odiū peperit scelus tantū suū,
Non quod genus suo trahunt de sanguine,
Sin chara nec regina nobis, aut sui
essent propinqui : Regis at fratrem tamen
odisse quid juvat ? genus enim nobile
junxit propinquos : at nisi invisus sibi
Honor esset, et minetur infamem notam
Nolis, suū nunquā negaret filiū,
Suspecta enim nunquam fides procerū fuit
Suū sibi proceres relinquent filium,
Sibi si loco mater decoro [manserit]

[Dux Gloc.]

Nunc ergo vobis filiū si deneget,
quorū fides sibi satis est cognita :
Imanis hæc erit protervia fœminæ,
Non frigidæ mentis pavor. Sin adhuc timet
Infausta mater, quæ timere umbrā potest,
tantò magis cavere matris amor jubet
Suspecta ne furtū sacrū gnatū suū
ad exteros regina mittat. Millies
promissa templo jura præstat frangere,
tantū senatus dedecus quam perferat.
Aliiq nostrûm luderent pulcrū caput

spectare qui fratrem cadentem principis
possumus : ergo filiū matri suū
Templo solutum vi decebit eripi,
ne jure simus exteris ludibrio.
Nec ego fidem lubens asyli læderem,
cui robur ætas longa struxit plurimū;
Nec primus olim privilegiū suū
Templis dedissem, Arisve nunc paci-
ferer,
Si pertinax in debitores creditor
sæviet et illis vincula minetur horridus,
adversa quos fortuna damnavit sibi
oppressit ære aut prodigū alieno mare
ut corpus ereptū ara tueatur piū
sane impiis et civibus, vel furibus
quos nullus unquā continere metus
potest
Sicariisq parcere, an non impiū
Sin pacta asylo jura tansū protegunt
Iniqua quos fortuna vexat : furibus
cur sacra? cur sicariis? cur civibus
Nequā patent? abundat (heu) malis
sacrū
Nunquid deus patronus impiis erit?
Num jura Petrus ista pepigit furibus?
Aliena prodigos rapere pius locus
movet sibiq rapta furto credere
onusta spoliis deserit conjux virū :
Ludens maritū furta templo condidit
Erumpit hinc cædi frequens sicarius,
tutūq patrato locū sceleri putat
Ergo benigna sacra demi furibus
nec jus asyli violet, et gratū deo
Sanctūq erit, quod pontifex mitis
nimis
princeps ne pactus est misericors
nescio
quis, non satis prudens tamen, quod
læderent
nunquā supstitione ducti posteri,
Sed sua sacris promissa servemus,
nihil
Ducem tamen tuentur inclusū sacra
Injusta damna, jus vetat, natura, lex,
Nec principem moramur aut Episcopū

Contraq vim quisquis locus tutus satis
Indulta sǎcra leges impediunt minus
si dura veniam suaserit necessitas
At quæ premit tristis ducem necessitas?
Regi fidelem Regiū probat genus,
psuadet insontem mali ætas nescia.
Cur impetret dux innocens sacrā
fidem?
Alius sacrū infanti lavacrū postulat
At pacta sacris jura quisquis impetrat,
Imploret ipse mentis impulsu suæ
Quid innocens poscat puer? quid
meruit?
Matura nunquā ferret ætas carcerem :
Horreret aras illico iratus puer
Aliena si prædatus huc quis advolat,
corpus tuentur sacra si cedet bonis,
hæc pontifex transferre, vel princeps
nequit.

Episc. Eliens.

Ut pacta templo jura, creditorib[9]
erepta servent debitorū corpora
acerba quos latère forsan sors jubet,
divina lex psuasit : indulgent simul
decreta pontificū sacra miseris fugā
Aliena cedent æra creditoribus
tantū : labore rursus ut crescat suo,
curaq damnū reparet assidua prius
Carcere solutus debitor excussis bonis
In nuda quis sæviret atrox tergora?

Dux. Buckingh.

probabitur hæc sanc mihi sententia
Uxor virū linquens ad aras si fugeret:
non pace Petri hæc eripi templo Petri
potest? puer lascivus exosus scholæ
hæret sacris : hunc pedagogus nunc
sinet?
at is tremet virgam, timebat hic nihil.
Indulta novi sacra vires pueris nihil
sit ara consiliis patrona dum lubet.
huic sacra denegantur pacta, debile
quòd nescit ingeniū petere nec integra
merere vita patitur, aut tutus malis

princeps egere potuit, haud lædit sacra
Is quisquis ut prodesse possit, eximet.

Stanl. Heros.

Quòd expedit Regi, Britannis Angliæ,
ut fratris aula frater una luderet,
hærere posthac mens dubia non potest.
Mulcere mentem matris opto molliùs :
hunc fortè sano ducta consilio dabit,
Sin filiū proterva mater detinet,
sacrisq deneget parere jussibus,
suo ducem fratri satelles liberet,
ludoq puerū armata restituet manus.

Howard Heros.

Concessa matri filii incunabula
ætasq fluxit ludicra deliciis suis
Nunc chara reliquos poscit annos
    patria
questus graves Matris nihil moror
si filium negat solutū carcere
sacro, fratri illū liberabunt milites.

Dux Glocest.

Uno senatus ore matri nuntiū
te poscit antistes, sacrū jussū expedi
Te præsuli comitem dux Bucking-
    hamiæ
Jungas, et Howarde præstans stemate
Amoris at si mater haud ponit modū
natūq nobis surripere demens studet :
Mox eriment robusti asylo milites,
            frustraq prolem planget
After they bee   ereptam sibi
come downe   Nunc te negotiū grave
from the
seates.   antistes vocat
        Responsa matris prox-
        imi morabimur.

ELIZABETH REGINA, ARCH. EBOR.
HOWARDUS HEROS DUX.

Archiep. Ebor.

Mater potens illustre regina caput
nunc ore quamvis verba dicantur meo,

non esse credas nostra : decrevit fre-
    quens
procerū senatus, et Glocestrius simul
    Protector, ut suadente natura licet
hæreret uno matris amplevu puer,
ætasq prima cum parente promptius
versetur: haud sinit tamen regni decus
Maculas honorem filii demens tui
Denuo suis turbata sedibus pax ruit
Britannia falso dum metu pavida sedes
squalens asylo, si tenetur carcere
conclusus unà frater alter principis,
dulci sui fratris carens solatio.
Odium fratrū plebs suspicatur illicò,
Sacra ad ædes quod fugit metu puer.
Ergo tuū reddes solutū carcere
Gnatū, tuos e vinculis sic liberas
et principi magnū creas solatiū
et gestiet secura Nobiliū cohors.

Regina.

Summo galeri honore præcellens
    pater,
Quod fratris in domo simul fratrem
    decet
manere, non repugno : quamvis tutiùs
uterq dulci matris hæreret sinu,
Quorū tenera adhuc timere ætas jubet.
Et cum minus tuetur ætas junior,
tum morbus hunc premebat infestus diu
curamq matris grande periculū vocat
Tantò magis minatur ægroto tabes
recidiva, nec vulnus secundū fortiter
Natura priùs oppressa fert nec se satis
potest tueri.   Quam frequens operam
    dabit
Matrona scio, quæ filiū curet meū
sedulò, mihi tamen meū decet magis
Gnatum relinqui cùm melius illū scio
nutrire, cujus semp ulnis parvulus
hæsit, hec illū mollius quispiā potest
fovere, quā quæ ventre mater sustulit.

Archi. Ebor.

Negare demens nemo regina ah potest,

quin filius melius tuæ relinquitur
custodiæ nunc matris amplexu puer
ut vivat, hæroū inclyta optaret cohors
simul decoro si maneres in loco,
utriq̄ sin natura vitam consecras
sacris tuā, et posthac piæ studet preci
devota mens ; at fratris aula luderet
frater, puer, templo solutus, nec sacro
carcere piū matris suæ furtū hæreat.
Prudenter matris ulnis eripitur puer,
nec usq̄ matris garriet petulans sinu
Infans ut alat sæva regem Wallia,
et barbaros luceret inter filius
nup fuit contenta majestas tua.

Regina.

Contenta nunquam : cura non eadem
    tamen
tenebat utriusq̄ matrem filii
Jussit nihil timere regis tunc salus
Huic membra multo lassa morbo de-
    sident.
O vix labantis tollit artus corporis
Quæ tanta gnati cura patruū tenet ?
Si filiū iṁatura fata absorbeant,
et fila chara avidæ sorores amputent
Suspecta mors ducem tamen Gloces-
    triū
reum arguet, nec fraudis effugiet no-
    tam.
An lædi honorem regis aut suū putet,
hoc si loco morabitur tutissimo ?
Suspecta nulli fuit asyli fides.
hîc incolere cum matre filiū sinant.
latêre templo tuta decrevi magis,
quàm cum meis diri timere carceris
pœnas ; asylo quos latêre nunc malim,
quàm vinculis dedisse vestris dexterā.

Howard.

Hos aliquid ergo patrasse nosti con-
    scia ?

Regina.

Patrasse nec quicquā scio, nec vin-
    cula

quorsū premant : sed non levis timor
    fuit,
ut qui colorem non mirantur carceris
hi mortis omnem negligant causā
    simul.

Card.

Movetur ira : de suis posthac nihil.
Parcet tuis agitata causa judici,
nec tībi minatur aliquis heroū metus.

Regina.

Imò, timere quid vetat manus pius,
cum vita non tuetur inocens meas
An hostibus Regina chara sim magis,
tristis malorum causa quæ fui meis ?
Matrive parcet juncta Regi chara-
    stirps ?
Meos propinquū non minus laudat
    genus
cum frater hic sit Regis, ille avun-
    culus
Quin filius mecum morabitur simul,
Mens nisi aliud solertior psuaserit
Nam suspicor procerum magis tristem
    fidem
quod absq̄ causa filiū avidè flagitent.

Card.

Hoc suspicantur matris at sinū
    magis,
ne forte gelidus corda pstringens metus
ad exteros relegare cogat filiū.
Sin patruo negare filiū juvet,
Manus tibi violentas exprimet,
seroq̄ justis pulsa viribus dabis,
Non hunc asylo pacta jura muniunt,
quæ nec dedicit imbellis ætas poscere,
et vita nil timere jussit integra.
Lædi fidem promissam asylo non
    putant,
si filiū sacris solutū liberant,
sacramq̄ vim minatur vitæ tibi
Est talis amor erga nepotem patrui
ut principis turpem fugā tremesceret.

Regina.

Amore sic teneri nepotis patruus
ardebat amens, nil ut horreret magis,
quàm ne suas pusillus evadat manus
nepos. fugam suadere matrem filio
putat, tabes cui longa discessum negat.
Aut quis tueri filium locus magis
potest asylo? quod Caucasus nunquā
    ferox
Imanis aut violavit olim Thracia.
At sacra merere iñocens nescit puer
Nunc ergo frustra parvulus templū
    petit.
Præcląra Tutoris consulit carū caput
Furem tuentur sacra nequaquā piū
at parvulus non indiget puer sacris
Cuivis timere vita prohibet integra,
metūq vacuū jussit esse nescia
ætas mali : faxit deus tandem præcor
ut corde pellat jure conceptū metū
Hærere templo turpitur gnatū putat.
Protector (at protector horū sit pre-
    cor,
nec in suos crudelis hostis sæviat)
An frater unà fratris ut ludat domo ?
Lucisse morbus jam vetat tristis diu
pestisq languens : an deesse parvulo
possunt, quibuscū prima gestit ludere
ætas, pares honore nisi dentur modo
Regum supbo junctus atq sanguine ?
quorū minùs concors ea esse ætas
    solet,
falsò sibi promittit illustris cohors
Fratrum duorū mutuū solatiū
Ludit sui secura juris æmula
Natura dū fraterna fingeret odia
pueris lites magis placent domesticæ
binumq vulnus sentiunt statim fratrū
turbata pectora, atq se minus posti
possunt : magis lusore quovis gestiet
quam frater cognatus puer, et statim
admissa sordescit voluptas, nec diu
domesticæ placere delitiæ possunt
At sacra non poscebat nescius puer ?
Quis ista sibi secrata dixit nuntius ?

Tu quære, quærat Claudianus, audiet
At non negasse finge : sine parvulū
non posse, sine ardore asylū linquere
Manebit invitus tamen : templū mihi
si posco solū, bona tuebitur simul.
Nemo Caballū sacrilega sacris eripit ;
templo puer latêre securus nequit ?
Quin filiū matri pupillū detulit
Britania lex, posessa si nulli bona
accepta referat : jura matri suū
mandent pupillū : quæ suos vis sacris
Inimica tutrici pupillos auferet
cum matre virtus fugeret hostilis
    manus ?
Eduardus inimicis suis linquens miser
extorta manib[9] sceptra, ad aras mox
    sacras
fugi gravida, rex ortus in lucem ibi
    fuit
primosq natales sacros nactus puer.
Fuit timor non parvus hostibus patris,
Dubiāq fecit pacis incertæ fidem
utriq asylum præbuit tutā sedem,
donec patris gnatum reversi amplexi-
    bus
Templū relinquens læta traderem,
    fides
tam certa regiæ sit utinā suæ.
Quæ sit timoris causa nec quisquā
    roget
mecum sacris manebit ædibus puer
Quiqunq pacta jura asylo rumperet
precor sacra fruatur impius fuga
nec invidio duris opem hostib[9] sacra.

Card.

Quid agimus ? ira cæcā mentem velli-
    cat
et pungit interdū ferox Glocestriū
non flectitur preci pectus iratū levi
pugnare verbis non juvat, jussus sacros
sumi senatus differo, quibus times
parere frustra ; grande suspitionis est
tormentū : acriter errore torquetur suo
decepta. Si regina charū patruo

mandas nepotem, et ceteris quos Anglia
proceres suos gens nobilis jactat diu.
Charā mihi vitā tibi pro filio
Nunquā timebo pignori deponere
Sin filiū nobis tuum mater negas,
rursus tibi psuasor haud posthac ero,
et filiū coacta deseres tamen.
Tremescit anceps cogitationū: Vincin?

Regina.

Concussit artus nostros horridus timor,
torquetq vinctus frigido sanguis metu
Quid agimus, animū distrahit dubius
pavor
Hic natus urget, fortius illinc patruus
Testor deū verū atq quicquid possi-
dent
Cæli beatū conjugis manes mei,
Non aliud Eduarde in meo nata mihi
jam quæro, quam tua sceptra regali
potens
gestaret aula, jura Britannis daret,
Regisq lætū vivat æternū genus
Quid fluctuaris? ergo prodis filiū?
et sponte quæsitū neci mater dabis
An non tuorū injussa terrent vincula?
Sin cogitet protector Anglorū decus
En, possidet natū priorem principis,
contentus illo sit : non poscit istū
patria
Is quærit unū, utrunq mater postulo
unum dari rogo, duos cui debuit
At hujus horescis nihil demens minas?
procerūq vim tantū feris? natū tamen
amittis, et tuo perire vulnere
vides tuos, properare Cardinis pater
matris quærelæ, nec moras parvas
facit
statim vicinā vim minatur patruus
promissa asylo jura nec prolem tegunt
Nunquā fugæ miles viam celeri dabit
Armatus omnes occupat hostis locos.
Aut quæ capit fidelis amotū sedes?
Obscura Cardindlis haud fides fuit
sempq sancti authoritas erat patris

Huic filiū manda tuū, Quin eripi
sinu videre filiū mater potes?
patrisq funus ultimum regis domus.
Horrenda fulminet ferox Glocestrius
potius, feram, patiar, maneat gnatus
modo !
Erras, utrosq pditis et gnatū simul
tuosq ferre nec Glocestrensem potes.

Card.

Dum cæca vires ira colligit, in tuā
præceps ruinā armata infœlix amor.
Cur patruo charam nepotem denegas,
cui cura major Angliæ comittitur?
meritò nos inertiæ damnas simul,
et esse stultos arguis, quando nihil
horum timemus, quale tu demens
times.
Cùm nos tamen Glocestrio junxit
duci
assidua regni cura, nec magis fuit
pspecta cuiquā vita Richardi ducis.

Regina.

Tam stulta nunquā, mentis aut inops
fui,
vos, esse stultos ut reor cunctos,
fidem
vestràmq suspitione læderem mea.
Acumen ergo desidero simul et fidem
quorū alterum si desit, in nostrū caput
ruet luemq patria magnam parit,
nil sacra naturæ moratur fœdera
Regni cupido insana : nobilis furit
Ambitio fratrū cæde, nec maculā
timet?
Veterū parū mentita psuasit fides
Romana fraterno madebant sanguine
mœnia : suo sin regna fratri parcere
haud
veréntur ; an frustra nepos patruū
timet.
Si regii diversa fratres incolant,
erit salus utriq servemus alterū,
utrumq servabis : duos defendere
unius in vita potes : nec tutū erit

ædibus iisdem vivere ambobus simul
Merces non ponit una singulas
Mercator in navi, procella quem frequens
jubet timere, nec marari turbines
rabidi solent frustra : licet mihi consciæ
recti, loco servare sancto filiū
me posse sperem, dura quamvis in-
tonet
crudelis horrendūq patruus fulminet,
En filium vestris tamen manib⁹ simul
vobis in illo mando fratrem, quos pie
servare vos decebit. à vobis ego
tum mater illū denuo repetam, caro
quando omnis sūmi ante judicis thronu
posthac simul clangente sistetur tuba.
Tremebunda scio quæ vestra splen-
descit
fides, spatiosa quam sit dexteræ po-
tentia,
testata tot rebus simul prudentia,
Nihil ut meis deese tutandis queat.
suspecta sin vobis potestas vestra erit,
Illum mihi vos p deos relinquite
p regis Eduardi throni castam fidem
Quantoq me nimis timere dicitis
Tantū timere vos minùs, decet parū
O dulce pignus, alterū regni decus,
spes vana matris, cui patris laudes ego
demens precabar frustra, avi longas
dies
tibi patronus adsit tot procellis arbiter
mundi deus, tutoq portu collocet
impulsa vela, mæstæ matris accipe
infixa labris oscula infœlix tuis.
Is novit unus rerū habenas qui tenet,
quando dies lucebit altera, tuis denuo
cum nostra labris imprimentur oscula
Jam quod timebis id genus dedit tuū
Si vulnus haud statis miser, matris tuæ
imitare luctus : sin negat lachrymas
tibi
generosus animus ; at suos planct⁹
tamen
concede matri, flere novimus priùs

En, sume fletus matris, è misero patris
quicquid relictū funere : an quicquid
potest
flebilius esse regis Eduardi nece ?
at alter Eduardus tamen erat, dui
potens
supba regni sceptra gestaret patris,
hic finxit ora gnatus Eduardi minor
Dicendus at magis meo ex utero meus
Tum turma suffulsit meorū nobilis,
nec morte fatum fregit una singulos
Nunc dira fratrem Carceris cùstodia
avulsit : ipsum possidet regem fides
metuenda   Richardi : reliquias en
patris
solas : in hoc fuit una spes lapsæ
domus,
in quo simul nunc auferentur omnia.
Quis te manet fiti exitus tristis ? quib⁹
heu fluctib⁹ una iñocens exponitur ?
si dura parvū fata quærunt, ultimū
domus tuæ funus, petam mater simul
viventis occulos ad mea claudā manu,
et matris in sinu puer pereas. vale
fili vale, matris vale solatiū.
Qualis remota matre crudelis leo
prædam minorem morsibus vastis pre-
mens
raptavit ore ; talis sinu meo
crudelis avulsit nepotem patruus.

Howard.

En candidas profusa lachrymis genas
variis tenellos filii artus implicet,
amplexibus suprema spargens oscula,
nec plura singultus sinit anhelans
loqui.
Hæsitq medio rapta gutture egredi
vox jussa, nec reperit viam infœlix
amor.
Quid matris adeò chara vexas pectora ?
post terga discedens relinquit filiū.

Card.

Noli timere nobilis princeps, simul

cum fratre colludes tuo ; regis domū
nil suspicare matris orbatus sinu.

ACTUS QUINTUS.

Catesbeius, Dux Buck.

Cates.

Plagis tenêre lætus imbelles feras
Glocestrius triumphat : in manus suas
optata cæcidit præda ; tuta fraus loco
versatur ; obscuro tenetur carcere
nepos uterq decora regni jam libet
spondere sibi, soliumq fratris mortui.
Qualis feras odore longo sentiens
sagax canis, postquā vicinā præda
    pcipit,
cervice celeri pugnat, et presso vias,
scrutatur ore : tallis omnib[9] modis
optare dextris sceptra fratris dimicat,
regnoq sperato prope Britanniæ inhiat.
Regni futuri jacta jam sunt semina :
procerū cohors irata Reginæ nequit
pferre stirpem poscit ad pœnā ferox
dum lite pugnant anxii, clā pdere
dum cogitat, quicunq cœptis obstre-
    pant
Duce absq Buckinghamio, sed nectere
dolos sūos veretur, et fraudes timet.
Jussit ducis mentem supbā incendere
Et concitare prolis odiū regiæ,
ut sceptra parvis excidant infantib[9],
patruiq Buckinghamius fraudes juvet,
Regnumq dux incensus acquirat sibi.
Ut suspicentur interim proceres nihil,
hi de creando rege jussi consulunt.
Catesbei, quid cessas parere duci
    thronū
Huc ferre Buckinghamiū video gradū:
animo tumet supbus : huic nectam
    dolos.
Flos Angliæ, præclara progenies Jovis,
Et maximū quassæ Britaniæ decus ;
Quid otiū securus alis, im̄emor

propriæ salutis ? quale vulnus accipit
collapsus imperii status, si concitus
temere furor juvenilis opprimat insciū
Ætatis haud mnlcetur ira fervidæ.

Dux Bucking.

At si quis excelsa potens aula, levis
Im̄unis imperio deæ suæ potest
jactare fœlicem statū haud fragili loco,
Excelsus id Buckinghamus heros.
    potest
Quodnam sed omen istud ambiguus
    jacis
Dubio ore carceris nigri lecto specu
an hostis in nostrum caput frustra ruit.

Cates.

Locus sed omni liber arbitrio tacet.

Buck.

Nudate turba servuli vestra latus.

Cates.

Nil timet generosa magnanimi indoles,
Se posse vinci, magna virtus dum
    negat
præmia ferunt fastus sui Riverius
heros, Grausq primus hic gradul mali
Rex sceptra puerili manu quassans
    furit,
Minatur olim non multas fore suas
injurias, nec dura fratris vincula,
nec avunculi tulit sui ; mater comam
lacerata vindictam petit, minor genu
quicquid propinquus sit, sibi fieri putat
Nunc ergo prudens ista tecum cogita :
Nam si pepersit hostib[9] manus tuis,
et traxerunt matris propinqui spiritū,
Nunquā tuas cessabit in pœnas furor
At si timori spiritū evomant tuo,
iramq justam sanguine extinguant suo
Regem timebis, scelere dum vincet
    scelus
domusq cognatæ fremat diram luem.

Buck.

Furor brevis pueri statim restinguitur

Cates.

At ira præceps est magis pueri levis.

Buck.

Minuet dies, vehemens quod est ruet
    illico.

Cates.

Nunquam sinit parentis imensus dolor.
mori : incitant matrem suorū vincula
Et filiū matris quærelæ.

Buck.
            Criminis
pars istius Glocestrius fuit.

Cates.
            Furor
satiatur ultione. Sontem negligit
punit scelus.

Buck.
        Ducis potest authoritas
ferociam pueri minuere.

Cates.
           Dum puer
est.

Buck.

At suū scmp timebit patruum.

Cates.

Quenquam timere nescit imperii
    decus.

Buck.

Quod nos tueri salubre consilium
potcst.

Cates.

Quod principi necem vestram solum
    vetat.

Buck.

Pulsabit usq matris ira filium.

Cates.

Nocere mortuus nihil gnatus potest.

Buck.

Mali medela sola tollere principem.

Cates.

Vinci nisi scelere novo scelus nequit
Quoddam scelus honestum necessitas
    facit
Plagis tenetur capta dispositis fera
Quasi vinculis uterꝗ servatur nepos
levi peribunt Claudii nutu ducis
periere jam jam, si tibi nunc consulas
Glocestrium munit satelles clam ducere
mores notat secretos excubitor tuos
qualem tuorum minimè falsam putes,
adversus illum fortè si quicquam pares
Nihil timendū si vides, time tamen
incerta multorū fides : constans nihil :
Inimica crede cuncta : turbatus solet
simulare multa vultus, et finget dolos
Fratri Thyestes liberos credens suos,
mistum suorum sanguinem genitor
    bibit.

[*Buck.*]

Quid nunc, cur hæres quodne consiliū
    diu
Vesane torques : Carceri hæroas datos
an pœnitebit ? hoc inertis est viri.
Hinc regis ita terret : an puerū times ?
An fœminā ? nam fata cognatos pre-
    munt.
Versantur illinc odia splendidi Ducis
cujus potestas suma, quem cuncti tre-
    munt
Quæris salutem ? tutus hinc eris magis
confide sumis, et fidem præsta Duci

Cates.

Properata Regem fata si vita eximant
parabit hæres sceptra Richardus sibi
Tu sola jactatæ columnia patriæ
ambire regnū ope dux tua Glocestrius
facile potest : utriꝗ vitam munies.

Buck.

Nunqā meo ludet cruore regius puer
Cujus minas satiabit ereptū caput
Jactura parva principis, vitam suā
servare si posses. parum pueros de-
    cent
decora regni : matris hoc regnū in-
    vidæ
haud regis esset, cujus impulsu in
    necem
solū suorū armatur iratus puer.

Dux Buck. Dux Glocest. Cates-
    beius.

Buck.

O Claudiane rector, Ebori domus
spes una, nec non periculi consors
    mei
nobis gravem tuus parat necem nepos.
Casus suorū mæstus Eduardo satus
plangit, minasq fletib[9] miscet graves
Abdenda vinculis opaci carceris
infausta proles Regis, an n̄ra nece
suæ domus litabit ultrices deos.

Gloc.

Horrere vindicis potentiæ faces
cogunt trucesq regis irati minæ
salubre præcipitare consiliū jubet
Quò longius serpit malū robustius
fieri solet, brevisq consiliis mora
datur.

Buck.

    Medela tristis ingenti malo
paratur : en facilè scelus vinci nequit
Sempq minatur ira cæca principis :
vindicta sceptro armata pugnat ace-
    rimè.
Testor deum verū, sumumq cælorū
    decus,
quodcunq   consulas,   sequor   vitæ
    ducem.

Gloc.

Tremulos p artus horror excurrit vagus
Juvenile novi regis, ingeniū, ferox
indocile, flecti non potest ? frangi
    potest.
Si patiamur, exitiū parat nobis grave.
redimere vitam vinculis regis licet,
At heu pudet fraterna regna demere
undiq frequens ridet Lancastriū genus,
lapsamq gaudebit domu æmuli sui.
Consulere sed vitæ quia proprie juvat,
nec patriā decet onerare luctib[9] :
fraterna posco sceptra jure sanguinis,
vestræq fautores salutis vos voco.
Cœptis tuā si spondeas nostris fidem,
Juro supremos qui tonant cœlum
    deos,
natus meus solamen unicū, tuā
gnatam maritus uxorem ducet sïbi.
Quod vendicas Herfordiensis eris
    comes,
aquis carebit Thamesis, æquor pisci-
    bus
partes priùs quàm pfidus linquā tuas.

Cates.

Nunc ergo cœpta vota demens pfice,
primùmq Regulos ad arcem trans-
    feras
famulosq substituas novos nepotibus,
dicto tuo quos audientes autumas ;
Et nulla deinceps ad Regem pateat
    via
populi strepitū ad tuos transfer lares,
et subditorum averte regi lumina,
calcentq tua posthac clientes limina.

Gloc.

Quin Angliæ proceres latêre fraudem
    convenit
dum rapta nostris sceptra manib[9]
    caderent.

Cates.

Adhuc corona regiū cingi caput
non posse dimissi docebut nuntii

tuoq jussu confluat procerū cohors
ut magna celebrentur comitia Britanniæ.
dum cogitabundi suū capiunt iter,
et urbe undati manebunt virib⁹,
et arma meditantes priusquā jungerent,
Incerta cū sit invicem fides sibi,
erepta puero sceptra tutus posside.

Bucking.

At nobilem non fallet Hastingū dolos
Stanleius heros urbe quoq confidet,
Antistes Eliensis astum intelligent.
Si clam coire sepatim senserint.

Gloc.

De reb⁹ Angliæ gravissimis ut consulant
coire proceres singuli jussu meo,
ne nostra cœpta intentus anim occupet.

Bucking.

At quis tui simul comes consilii erit
Res magna paucis expediri non potest.

Gloc.

Quem non metu posessa sceptra com-
   priment
Deesse nostro authoritas voto nequit.

Buck.

Pervince multis præmiis vulgus leve
donisq cumula plurimis, qui partib⁹
ut hæreant tuis facilè duci queant.
vincere pecunia quos nequit, coget
   timor.

Cates.

Difficile procerū animos statim cog-
   noscere.

Gloc.

Quasi publicis de reb⁹ anxius nimis
quos suspicor solicitus usq consulā
dum multa ʳproponā dubius, et vol-
   vimus

secreta regni, mens patebit abdita
Hastingus unus principi palā studet,
et debitos differt honores regulis :
hic gratus Anglis et potens multū
   mea
juvare sceptra, vel mori priùs decet.

Cates.

Is principi favebat Eduardo nimis
nunquā potest promissa convelli fides.

Gloc.

Tentare pversam decet mentem magis
Forsan virū frangas reluctantem metu,
ego interim rebus Britanniis consulā.

Cates.

Quid nunc agis Catesbeie ? quin tibi
   consulas :
nunc avoca astus animi, nunc fraudes,
   dolos,
Totum Catsbeiū. Thronū si particeps
   fraudis Ducis procuret Hastingus :
   fidem
tibi derogas, minusq posthac creditur
si spiritū pemtus inimicus expuat,
quasi ptinax amor colat pueros minus :
præesse solus tu potes Lecestriæ
successor Hastingi : duces credent
   magis :
bene est : perat, ut nostra creseat
   gloria
Infausta dirus rumpat ensis viscera.
Studere fingam Regulis durū nimis,
flecti nec ulla ptinax posset prece.

STANLEIUS, HASTINGUS.

Stan.

Pectus stupet, dubiòq pculsū metu
agitatur, huc illuc rotatur, nec potest
se evolvere : ominatur aliquod mens
   malū
divulsa quid consilia sibi locis volunt ?
dum pars in arce, pars alia prætorio

deliberat : novit tonans pater ill quid
disjunctus heros mente versat callidè.
Nervos vel imperio inhiare, vel necem
nobis, vel insidias struere regi quæat,
Hoc quicquid est metuo nimis.

Hast.

Ponas metū
Illustre Stanlei genus, nec torqueat
suspitio mentem vana : nihil in nos
grave
patrare possunt, quamdiu meus simul
Catesbeius adsit (inde qui nunquam
solet
abesse) quod velut ore prolatum suo
absens licet non audio.

Stanl.

fides et adultera
non rarò tecta fronte blanda abscon-
ditur.
Virtutis umbra turpe pugnat vitiū
falsumq vultū haud exprimunt pauci
dies,

Hast.

Cumulata meritis firma constitit fides.
Jussu meo Lecestri sume colunt,
Multūq Northamtoniis potens valet.
rerū mearū sumā in illo colloco.

Stan.

Serū est cavendi tempus in mediis
malis,
libido regni cæca nullā vim timet,
Imbellis ætas regis obruitur statim,
In nosq secretū nefas post sæviet,
quoscunq participes timet sceleris sui,
in nuda præda pfidis sumus hostib⁹.
repetamus at patrios lares celeri gradu
ubi sepiat suis clientes viribus.
Incœpta fortè pfidus metuet furor.

Hast.

Frustra timemus prosperam sortem
satis

verbis benignis alloqui, blandi Duces
solent, mihiq plurimum semp student :
Et ipse populi vota, rumores, metus
comunicavi Catesbeio dudū meo
Torquebit alios cura magna principis
quærunt ducem cives, nepotem neg-
ligunt.
Quòd ista me celavit, haud æque fero
fugare lubet ? nos arguet reos fuga.
atq revocatos ira pderet magis.
Tutos manentes vita servat inocens.
Sin nos malū maneret, alterius velim
scelesta mens, non nostra damnaret
fuga.
Fraus ista (crede) nulla quam demens
times.
Rude priùs in cœlū chaos mutabitur.
prius astra terris hæreant, flamine
salū,
quam fallat astrinctam fidem Catsbeius.

Stan.

Mox exitus tantis malis fidem debit.

Dux Gloc. Catesbeius, Howard equestris ordinis.

Dux Gloc.

Spes concutit mentem metusq turbidā,
trepidumq gemino pectus eventu labat.
Imago regni semp errat ante oculos
mihi,
et usp dubium impellit ambitio gravis
turbatq pectus : flama regni concita
nescit quiescere : sceptra nunc tantū
placent.
Non desinā dum sumā votorū attigi
Multum exagitat incerta nobiliū fides
cui nostra certus consilia credam haud
scio :
Nec sunt loco tuto sitæ fraudes meæ.

Howard.

Quid pectus anxiū tumultu verberas?
nescit timere quisquis audet magna;
jam
regnū petis; fortuna fortes adjuvat.
ars prima regni posse te cives metu
retinere: qui cives timet, rebelles
excitat.
Audebit omnia quisquis imperio regit
et dura tractat sceptra regali manu.

Gloc.

Pectus nihil pturbat ignavus metus
Excede pietas, mente si nostra lates.
Tuetur ensis quicquid invitū tenes.
Aperire nunc ferro decet fraudi viā,
mactetur hostis, quisquis obstabat
mihi.

Howard.

Quid Pontefracti vinculis captos tenes
matris propinquos, nec mori tandem
jubes?
Indulta vita cæteris animos dabit,
et ultro pœnas mite supplitiū vocat
Ferro perempti spiritum infestū expuant
firmes amicos, cæteri metu labant.

Gloc.

Hostes simul perire præsentes volo,
obstare quos sceptris meis novi sagax,
et unus omnes occupet pariter metus.
Quorū dubia studio resistit meus levi.
Illos prement mox dura captos vincula.
Quo flectit Hastingus animū.

Catsb.

Tantū in tuū
caput.

Gloc.

Meis adjutor esse ptibus
renuit.

Catsb.

Priùs profundat arctus Ithicū

fretū et rapax consistet aqua Siculi
maris,
Noxq atra terris ante splendorem
dabit.
Fraudes abominatur ferox quassans
caput
Et semp Eduardi fidelem filiis
fore spondet, hostem regis hostiḷ⁹
gravē.

Gloc.

Quid arma possunt regis irati, sciet,
iramq nostram sanguine extinguet
suo.
Discant parere principi metu sui,
At qua via mactabo vesanū caput?

Catsb.

Conjugis amore captus insanit Shori,
Flamas libido nec furentes continet.
Hanc arguas capiti veneficiis tuo
mortem struere: causam suæ sin
pellicis
amore cæcus, et furore fervidus
tuetur infœlix patronus; consciū
sceleris nefandi suspiceris illico,
et proditorem patriæ incusa suæ:
mox amputet securis infaustum caput.

Gloc.

Proceres in arcem confluunt jussu
meo
statim favere quos Regi scio
palam opprimam, reumq criminis
arguā
satelles abscindet bipenni mox caput
nec sentiet senatus insidias stupens.

Catsb.

Sin abstinet sacris comitiis callidus
heros, novus quærendus est fraudi
modus.

Gloc.

At illico invise inclytum Howarde
caput,

blandisq vocibus morantem concita
sacris abesse comitiis noli pati.

Catsb.

Solumne poscis diræ Hastingū neci?

Gloc.

Stanleius heros, atq Cardincus pater,
Præsul Eliensis comprimentur vin-
    culis,
animum ut fidelem carceris donet
    specus.
Sin impotenti ptinax snimo abnuat
quisquam nec Hastingi monet tristes
    lues :
ferrū secabit triste noxiū caput :
Infida strictus ensis eruet viscera.
Res et profecto stulta nequitiæ mo-
    dus.

HASTINGUS HEROS, HOWARDUS
HASTING[9] MILES CALLIGATUS.

Hast. Heros.

Miror quid huc eunti equus humi tur-
    piter
prosternitur, deus omen avertet malū
sed vana sortis quid movent ludi-
    bria ?
Et dura Stanleius tremebat somnia.
visū sibi aprū nuntiat somno caput,
lacerare dente, mox fluit humeris
    cruor,
mihiq demens consulit, turpem fugam
Lasciva nos fortuna gestit ludere
ridetq turbatos levi casu viros,
quibus tamen nihil minatur invida.

Howard.

propera nobile Hastinge caput, celera
    gradū.

Hast. Hæ.

Fœlix ades tandem sacrate diis pater,
secretas aures accomoda paululū mihi.

Howard.

Omitte tandem : quid sacerdotem diu
affare ? confessore nil adhuc opus,
nihil sui securus infœlix videt
mox quàm sibi sacerdote damnato
    opus erit.

Hast. Her.

Hastinge, nunquā excidet menti dies
olim nefanda, tristes et nimis, istius
quando sub arcis mœnib[9] totus tre-
    mens
diræ metu necis, ultimò te viderim ?

Hast. Miles Calligatus.

O nominis decus unicū tibi, et genus
illustre, nunquā tam gravis casus
    mihi
aut tristis excidit : tibi nullū tamen
(Diis gratia) malū tum necis lucrū
    fuit
Æquata sors utrisq fuit.

Hast. Her.

                            Imo magis
hoc diceres, secreta mentis nostræ si
cognosces : quod singuli posthac
    scient,
At nemo adhuc. Oh Hastinge nun-
    quā quod sciem
vitæ magis dubius fui quam illo die
Nunc temporū mutata series. ad
    necem
hostes trahuntur Pontefracti isto die
nostram cruore suo quitem sanciunt.
Nunquā magis securus ex animo meo
Hastinge, vixi, nec metu magis vacat
jactata nullis fluctib[9] vita.

Hast. Miles.

                            Id deus
faxit.

Hast. Her.

Quid hæres.

Hast. Mi.

Id precor.

Hast. Her.
Scio satis.

Howard.

Quin rumpas heros nobilis segnes
  moras :
Nam te diu senatus expectat sagax.
De reb[9] ut tot consulant nobile caput.
Descescit : heu nescit miser tristem
  sibi
luem parari. Ah quid nimis pueris
  faves ?
Te te fefellit falsa Catsbei fides,
captuq plagis præda retineris miser.

Dux Gloc. Dux Buck. Hast. her.
Episc. Eliens. Satelles.

Dux Buck.

Quam magna regni cura tutorem pre-
  mit,
Ducemq vexat Claudianū, quis patres
Ignorat, hunc solum intuetur Anglia,
Suisq reb[9] poscit authorem ducem.
Vestrā seorsim selegit prudentiā
quorū fidele consultant canū caput
Et ut procuret anxius negotia
celebrare comitia regis anxius studet :
Quò regiū diademate caput cingeret,
ut gratus esse mortuo fratri queat,
cujus sepulti filiū exornat piè.

Gloc.

Veneranda o patrū cohors, et maximū
Potentis imperii decus : faustū deus
indulgeat nunc rebus istis exitū.
Nec somniator ego nimis tardus fui,
qui tam frequenti serus adsū curiæ,
Somnus negotiis consultor est gravis
  meis.
Tantumne mane lectulo elapsus senex

Eliensis antistes venis ? senem quies,
Juvenem labor decet : ferunt hortū
  tuū
decora fragra plurimū producere.

Episcop. Eliens.

Nil tibi claudetur, hortus quod meus
producit : esset lautius vellem mihi,
quò sim tibi gratus.

Gloc.

Quid imperii status,
Salusq regni poscat, et patriæ decus ;
vestris adhuc jactate consiliis patres ;
Abesse cogunt paululū negotia :
nec sit molestus fortè discessus, pcor.

Hast. Her.

Operam navare maximam, patres
  decet,
ut dum gerit rex sceptra puerili manu,
pellamus omnem fortiter discordiā,
quæ scissa nup regna diu exercuit,
Hoc flagitat secura patriæ salus,
clariq poscit mollis ætas principis,
et ultimo fides sacramento data
Regi sepulto : majus hoc nullū fuit
Regni satellitiū. Ergo proceres si
  invicē
consentiant, florebit hoc regnū diu :
Sin invicem dissentiant brevi ruet.
Purgare tandem patriam macula decet,
et scelere nosmet liberare pessimo.
Sed ecce retrò dux venit dubio gradu :
quassans caput torvo supcilio furit.
Duro labellū dente comprimit ferox,
et pectore irato tegit dirū malū.

Gloc.

Quas destinatis his patres pœnas, suis
Qui nunc veneficiis mihi exitū parant,
qui sum supbo regis ortus sanguine,
Tutorq declaratus hujus insulæ.

Hast. Her.

Quas patriæ pferre debet proditor
Nec moror honorem, nec excuso decus.

Gloc.

Sensus mihi omnes fratris uxor fas-
cinat.

Hast.

Verbis stupentes triste dimittunt
   caput
Justas luat regina pœnas pessima.
parū tamen placet, quod aures hæc
   meas
adhuc latebant : fraude captivi mea
erant propinqui matris : hodie jam
   meis
hi Pontefracti capite plectuntur dolis.

Gloc.

Comitata modò regina Shori conjuge
Suis venifica càntibus me prodidit ;
Fluit tabo corpus, occuli somnū neg-
   ant,
Stomacho invidet lentū tibi fastidiū,
Venas hiantes deserit pulsus cruor,
exangue brachiū exaruit, officiū negat.

Hast.

Heu, frigido cor palpitat tremulū
   metu.
Num pulcra destinatur morti pallaca ?
pereunt amores : concubinā conjugis
Regina nunquā consuleret usquā sui.
Timent loqui.   Securus alloquar
   ducem
Si fecerint gravissimas pœnas lunat.

Gloc.

Si fecerint ? itanae mihi ? si fecerint ?
quū dico factū : quod tuū luet caput,
Sceleste proditor.

Satell.

Let yᵉ Protec-
tor give a blow on
yᵉ counsel-table ;
and let one of yᵐ
of yᵉ gard break
in thereat with his
halbᵗ and strike yᵉ
L. Stanley on yᵉ
head.

proditi, proditio.

Gloc.

Te perduellionis esse
aio reū.

Episc. Eliens.

Percussit (hic) clarū Satelles Stanleū
An occidit, stillans rigat genas cruor.

Gloc.

Vos pduellem date neci, servi, statim,
Sacra morituro mox sacerdos finiet
Juro sacrū Paulū, priùs non prandeo,
Pœnas quàm mihi pendat abscissum
   caput.
Patremq Cardineū, Eliensem præsu-
   lem,
Dominum Stanleium coerce vinculis :
Sceleris pœnas Shora pellex impu-
   dens
damnata psolvet, jubente judice.

Hast.

Quis nostra digne conqueri potest
   mala ?
heu, quas miser voces dabo ? quæ
   lachrimis
nostris Aëdon exhibet luctus graves ?
O machinator fraudis et diri artifex
sceleris ; mearū prodidit fallax amor
blandaq tectū fronte secretū malū,
cur invident severa fata vitam : in
   mea
quid morte tam potens erit versutia ?
suūq cumulat gaudiū luctu meo ?
Sed parce demens lachrymis. Testor
   sacrū
heu numen adversum mihi : [simul
   voco
quocunq defugistis intus inferi
terris opacis iñocens morti trahor ;
Simplex fides non intrat aulā nec pie

Dedicit supba pompa vivere, in meā statim
Fortuna pœnā mutat inimicas dotes.

Gloc.

An luctus attonitos muliebris comovet?
tantas moras suadere lachrymæ queant?
non abripitis hunc? impio ferro caput
auferte. Quid cunctamini istū perdere.

Hast.

Gaudet dolor sua fata multis spargere
nec solus in pœnam placet: vestras colos
sævæ sorares impetrat: ludunt genus
mortale cæca fata: præmonstrant malū
vitare, quod vetant tamen. Perteriti 3
somno nihil Stanleus hæros comovet.
Heu visus est lacerare caput utriq aper
frendens cruento dente, longus defluit
cruor p humeros: insignia dederunt apri
nomen Glocestrio: ter lapsus insidenti equus
cecidit, senatū dum nefandū viserem.

Gloc.

Isti malū sibi quærunt satellites
qui dum moras faciunt inanes fletib⁹
demetere cessant impiū ferro caput.

Hast.

Hei mihi; salutis nulla spes? nunc ad necem
trahite, quib⁹ fortuna jus in nos dedit.
quid lachrimis miser moror? pio manus
cruore spargite. Ultimū solis vale

cœleste jubar proditum reparans diem.
Vale cohorte nobilis nitida soror
Phœbi quieta: longa jam nox obruet.

DUX GLOC. CIVES LONDINENS. NUNTIUS.

Gloc.

Cives properate: hic adestis prope licet,
Serò nimis nobis, in arce quos modo
Hastingus impiiq consortes sui
sceleris pmissent, Deus si non opem
tulisset idq licet diu celaverint
astu: ante decimā solis (ut sit) istius
pcepimus metuq subito pciti
quæcunq casus arma dedit (ut cernitis)
miseri induimus, ipsiq jam opprimuntur aut
Virtute nostra, gratia vel Cœlitū.
magis doli hujus principis in pessimos
ac sceleris authores redundabit malū.
Nunc ergo vos jussu vocati estis meo,
imane quia constaret omnibus nefas,
p vos ut inotesceret quærentib⁹.

Cives.

Jussus fideles exequemur sedulò
O ptinax scelus mendacio cædem tegens
blandaq tantū fronte contentū malū?
quis nescit imanes dolos sævi ducis,
dubitatq captū fraude nobilem virū?
suū scelus plerunq in authorem redit,
priùs in alios postquā crudelis sæviit.

Nunt.

Corurcus Hastingi hausit ensis spiritu.

Cives.

Ut gesta res est, quæso paucis expedi.

Nunt.

Postquā ad locū durus satelles trax-
erit,
ad astra tollit heros lumina :
Ex ore casto concipit Deo preces
Quæcunq nostra contumax supbia.
supplitia meruit (inquit) ô numen
sacrū,
utinam meo jaṁ jam luatur sanguine.
Vix ultimas moratur carnifex preces
quin solvit illico ense corporis obicem.

Cives.

Extinguit Hastingū suorū ingens
favor,
animusq lætis credulus rebus nimis,
nec triste suspicatur integer scelus,
authore donec miserè amico plectitur.
Sed hic gradum confert ad arma serviens,
Quid civib⁹ clamare quærit publicè.

Serviens ad Arma.

Cœptis nefandis hic scelestus prodi-
tor
Hastingus, horrendi caput primū
mali
Et turba pjuro gerens morem duci,
struxere tectos principis Glocestrii
vitæ dolos, altiq Buckinghamii,
Ultriq dum sacro senatu consident :
Ut sic ruinosæ pemptis Angliæ
Rectorib⁹, sedis supremæ culmina
Scandant supbi sumā, celso vertice.
quamvis inepti, qui ruentis maxima
Regni gubernarent Britanni pondera.
Quis nescit Hastingum parentem prin-
cipis
traxisse secū ? turpiter quis regiū
nescit malis fœdasse nomen morib⁹ ?
Splendore vel spoliasse regnū pristino
dictis suis, factis suis, turpem virū ?
Quis nescit Hastingi libido pdita
quot virginū passim pudorem pdidit ?
Lectiq rupit conjugalis fœdera,

amplexus infames adulter pellices.
Nam Shora pellex nota scortū nobile,
hujusq cædis pticeps et conscia,
Hunc nocte polluto suprema lectulo
accepit amplexu parū castè suo
Ut morte pœnas jure pendat maximas,
turpem gravi qui scelere vitam polluit.
Ne si diu dilata damnati foret
mors traditoris, marte funesto suā
jurata poscat turba demens principem
Quæ pœna festinata fallet singulis,
Dirosq in tantū tumultus comprimet.

Cives.

Præceps agendi magna pturbat modus
fœtumq festinans parit serū canis.

Civis alter.

Hæc scripta sunt alto prophetæ
spiritu
Nam tantulo quî tanta possent tem-
pore
vel cogitari dicta, vel sīc exprimi
Pulcræ mihi sanè videntur literæ,
pulcrèq depingi videtur chartula,
et pulcra postremò loquendi formula,
Illud tamen mirū videtur maximè,
tam pulchra tam pvo parari tempe.

Civis.

En Shora tremulū cereum gerens
manu,
Induta pœnas linteo infames luit,
Regum inclyta meretrix tyranno dat
duci
pœnas, pater descende Jupiter, et
thoro
tam grata pignora nunc tuo rape :
nam tuā
Lædam vel Europā, puta deserere
polū,
Oh misera, me miseret tui, piget,
pudet :
(Licet impudica mulier, et minus
proba)

Privare vita dum nequit Dux Claudius
spoliare fora quærit iratus tibi.

PROCESSIO SOLENNIS.

CHORUS.

Preces Deo fundamus ore supplices,
Ne sit nota polluta mens adultera.

1. Fidem tuere conjugū
   Lectum probro libera
   Defende privatos thoros.
   Furtiva ne lædat Venus.

2. Quemcunq facti pœnitet
   Purga solutum crimine

Exempla sanent posteros
Furtiva ne fœdet Venus.

EPILOGUS.

Quas dirus admovit Richardus machinas,
quantisq regnandi libido luctibus
affecit afflictam videtis patriam,
Ut celsa regni scandat altus culmina
Frendens aper, regni lues, Glocestrius,
Illustris Hastingi cruor defunditur,
quòd regulis vivus faverat pvulis
Regno repugnantes novo Riverius,
Vahanus et Graius repressi carceris
horrore, læthali præmuntur vulnere.

THE SHEWE OF THE PROCESSION.

A Tipstaffe
Shore's Wife in her petticote, haveinge a taper
   burninge in her hand
The Verger
Singinge men
Præbendaries
The Bishope of London
Citizens.

ACTIO SECUNDA.

DRAMATIS PERSONÆ.

Mr. PALMAR, Dux Glocestrensis
Mr. STRINGER, Dux Buckinghamiæ
Mr. BAYLY, Lovellus Heros
Mr. ALMY, Prætor Londinensis
Mr. WEBSTER, Fitz Williā, Recordor London, ut vulgo
        loquūtur, Civis amicus Shawi
Mr. CLAYTON, Doctor Shawe
Ds. MORRELL, Civis Primus
Ds. FRAUNCE, Civis secundus
Mr. SMITH, Hospes

Nobilis
Servus unus et alter Buck :
Foggs
Fagge
Ds. Remer
Ds. Methen   }   Duo Epis.   }   Muti.

ARGUMENTUM.

Postquā hos omnes in potestatem suā Richardus dux Glocestrensis rede-
gisset, quorū erga regem fidem metuebat : quorum Hastingū nobilem morte
affecit, cæteros in carcerem conjecisset, in id studiū sedulaò incumbit, ut
citò sui in Regni injustam possessionem veniat. Itaq ut Londinensis fraude
induceret, ut ultro cum cæteris nobilibus regnū sibi deferant, Regis ortū,
fratrisq sui ducis Eboracensis parvuli damnavit, Regem Eduardum fratrem,
non ita multò antè defunctū, adulterii p ducem Bucking : in Curia Prætoris
accusavit, neq sui ipsuis matri Ducissæ quondā Eboracensi pepercit. Tandem
delatam sibi Majestatem, quam tantopere inhiebat, ægre ut videbatur assu-
mens soleñibus comitiis coronatur.

ACTUS PRIMUS.

Dux Gloc. Dux Buck. Lovellus
Heros.

Gloc.

Illustris heroū propago, Ducū genus
insigne Buckinghamiorū, particeps
nostriq consilii Lovelle nobilis :
Quin rumpimus segnes moras strenuū
    decet
fore, magna quisquis cogitat, res nihil
    habet
Isthæc periculi : audire decet haud
    amplius
quis influentis dona sortis respuit ?
Regem potest creare Buckinghamius
donor ducis erat semp hic amplissimi :
virtute te natura firma roborat,
et corporis vestivit anxia dotibus.
Tibi rursus aciem inclusit ingenii pa-
    rem,

Nec te magis Minerva quinquā lumi-
    nat.
Sequi decet, natura quo præstans
    vocat :
tantū potest excelsa Buckinghamius
Tolluntur hostes ecce suspecti mihi,
omnesq diri carceris vincula premunt,
Regis favor quos armat in regnum
    meū
Jubere cunctos voce licet una mori
Hastingus interemptus heros occidit :
Stanleus heros continetur vinculis
Et Eliensem Episcopū carcer domat.
reliqui jacent, tetra specu clausi, meis
quicunq cœptis impii favent parū.

Buck.

Puerum levem regnare ? fortunæ jocus
lasciva ridens sceptra miscet litibus :
Virtus suo succumbet infans ponderi.
Tuo cogita quosnā struis regno dolos :

Nunquā tuos jussus relinquā ptinax.
res expedire magnas nescit illico.

Gloc.

En ipsa temporum jubet securitas
audacter aggredi prius quæ consulis,
animis oportet prævidere singula,
res arduas nec aggredi temere decet.
Quis exitus rerum futurus cogitat
·Sapiens prius. [Gerenda cuncta pro-
vidè.]

Lovel.

Quicquid timendū, juncta consilia ex-
plicent
En temporis nimium premunt angus-
tiæ,
quo regiū caput corona cingeret !
Nunc ergo cunctis impandū publicè,
Ut non sacris statim comĩtiis con-
fluant
Regni moras psuadet occasio gravis
ne cingat antè caput corona Reguli,
quam luceat secunda Novembris dies
Hic destinatus est dies solennibus
dum cogitant mora tarda quid velint
sibi
Patrios lares procul relinquentes suis.
dum viribus nudati adessent, Nobiles
Incerta dū dubios opinio torqueat,
mutuāq suspicentur incerti fidem,
agitata mente consilia nec digerant
suam priusquā vim rebelles jungerent:
tu rapta pueris sceptra tutus posside
Mox nomini devicta succumbet tuo
invidia, dū ferro repellat principem.

Buck.

Ferat licet decepta nobiliū cohors
animusq prudens ferro tentaret nihil :
ad arma junget ptinax populi foror,
motuq cæco rapitur, in præceps ruit,
quocunq fertur : verba convenient
feris
injustè factis : victanec cedet metu

concepta rabies temere, qualis
ferro Mæander funditur rapiens, pati
Neque scit resistentem sibi, et dirū
fremit.

Lovell.

Mulcere blandis plebis ingeniū ferox
decet, sequitur lubens, et ultro pellitur
At quem suorū civiu favor beat
inter suos, nec parva micat authoritas,
tractare molliùs rudem mentem potest,
tuū psuaderi regnū civibus,
Urbs Angliæ præclara Londinū tuis.
Inducta votis si faveret, vicimus :
errore capti cæteri cedent pari :
Possessa regna facilè ferro munies,
At quis color regni probetur civibus,
ne decepi captos ragaces senserint ?
irata se plebs graviter illudi feret.

Buck.

Infausta gens tot lassa vincitur malis :
stragemq majorem minantur parvuli
Lasciva regna : Anglia novas lites
timet :
et matris haud cessabit in pœnas furor.
Tua regna luctus auferent teterrimos,
qui natus es regū supbo sanguine,
tantamq regni sustines molem sagax.

Lovell.

Istum facile plebs sentiet callida dolū,
causamq regni credet injustam fore.

Gloc.

Quidni dolis facilis patet nostris via
Palā fratris damnentur infames thori
pudica sceptra non ferunt probrū :
spurios vetant regnare jura filios.
Amore postquam rex flagraret Luciæ
ætate tam calcante dum notas priùs
iterum Venus furtiva delicias petat
et libido sævis nec modū flamis dedit,
temere spospondit Luciæ regni thoros,
illāq participem sui regni vocat.

Experta sæpe Venus parit fastidiū
sordent amores Luciæ tū principi,
Nec furta lecto quærit obscuro impro-
bus.
Decepit animū conjugi obstrictū suæ,
et possidet Regina promissos thoros.
Tum Lucia locū pulsa pellici dedit,
adhuc rapaces nil timens fati minas
Hinc filios generi suo infames pater
genuit adulter (vulnus Angliæ grave)
Nec adhuc thronus maculā tulit solū
patris :
Lectū priorem lusit impudens amor.
Nostri parentis Eboracensis ducis
Thalamis ducissæ turpe mentiti viri
Vestigiū secretus invenit comes,
Coitus nefandos nec dolus tegere po-
test
Socium tædæ sciunt, pudetq criminis
fœdæq matris fœda proles rex fuit,
Eduardus, ignoto deceptus filio
incesta sceptra detulit falsus pater
Diversa fratris ora patrem denegant,
moresq degeneres fratri meus pater
vultus habebat, talis aspectu fuit,
Imago dissimilis fratris stuprū docet :
Amoris hæres turpis, haud regni fuit.

Buck.

Et jure vendicas : dolos quid quæri-
mus ?
fatetur æquitatis istud plurimū.
Iter patet cœptis : Quid utendū arti-
bus ?
quomodo ista turbæ verba constabunt
levi ?
aut cujus in tantis dolis sequêris
fidem ?

Gloc.

Nil frigidus cor torqueat tremulū metus.
Quæ non secreto vincitur prælio
fides ?
Civem potentem facile Londinū dabit,

Et qui dolos tegere sagax nostros potest,
animosq blandus comovere civiū,
Multisq vincere Londinenses premiis
Inter suos Prætor valet plurimùm
vanos honores ambit et fluxas opes,
multūq avaræ mentis instigat furor
Reddet fidelems pes honoris improba
et pellit usq longā numorū sitis :

Lovell.

Falsis sacris nihil fallacius fuit.
plebem facile mentita ludunt numina
Animus statim devotus impetum dabit.
Si præco scripturæ fidelis, dū sacra
insculpit aurib[9] piis oracula,
divina vel præcepta populo psonet,
Comemoret olim fraude deceptos
thronos
Lectiq probrū, vulnus et claræ domus.

Buck.

Vir literis insignis est Doctor Shaue
Prætori eadem matre conjunctus frater
Hunc laude ditarunt frequentes literæ:
Fucata cives sanctitas mirè allicit,
cujus tamen menti facilè labes sedet,
hoc munus exequi fidele qui potest.

Gloc.

Aliqui meorū accersat urbis Londini
Prætorem, honore inter suos magno
virū,
sumiq tinctū literis fratrem Shauiū.
Ubi Prætor animos civiū demulcerit,
Et nostra regna civib[9] psuaserit :
hos convenit pleno senatu te alloqui
Miratur illustrem ducē vulgus rude
Fulgore populus captus attonitus
stupet,
lapsūq cælitus deū putat sibi.
Vultu tuo plebs victa succumbit statim
dulci veneno mox stupentes opprime
ut filios pari insequantur et odio,

Promitte libertatis alta præmia,
urbem beabit lecta civiū quies,
et fine nullo crescet imensū decus,
si vindicent lecti stupro infamem
 domū,
et sceptra nobis jure reddant sanguinis.

Lovell.

Dum predicet coitus nefandos et
 fratris
novos amores, matris et probrū tuæ,
domusq regis dedecus sanctus pater,
donec tuarū præco laudum maximis
virtutib[9] decorat intentus Shaus
Quasi cælitus repente lapsus advola.
Te principem divinitus crearier
populus levis putabit, atq spiritu
ductū sacro, dictasse te Regē Shaū
credet levemq distrahet mentē stupor.

Dux Glog. Prætor Lond. Doct.
 Shaa.

Dux. Gloc.

Præclare prætor urbis illustrissimæ,
et sancte præco, diisq sacratū caput.
en, magna molimur futura comoda,
et maximā regno quietem quærim[9]
Hujusq laudis magna vobis pars erit
quos novimus regno precari prospera,
uterq votis anxius si pareat
Nunc ergo vestrā posco secretā fidem,
tam magna quib[9] arcana regni pandim[9]
Honorib[4] magnis fidem pensabim[0]
largisq fidos præmiis ditabimus.

Prætor.

Protector illustris, propago splendida
Regis, tibi lubens fidem conservo meā.
Quod impas, fidele munus exequar.

Gloc.

Contrita mutuis cædib[9] Britannia
heu terret, et majora suadent vulnera

infirma pueri sceptra, matris et furor.
sceleri mederi quis facile demens
 potest ?
deponat animo justa qui Regis timet,
et malè parebit regis imperio pudor,
viro potenti vera laus non contigit
Fortuna quos impellit, invitos malè
vetatq sæpe facere quod cupiunt piè,
Justus facile erit, cui vacat pectus
 metu.
Suadent mihi decora regni nobiles,
regnare quem regalia jubent stemata.
Vos civiū suadere mentib[9] velim
in urbe, quorum fama tanta splendidè
celebratur, ut mihi sceptra regni deferant.

Præt.

Quo jure tu Regnū nepotis vendicas ?
ne temere plebs irata turbas concitet,
ubi senserint spoliatū honore principem.

Gloc.

Talia tuis clam sparge Prætor civib[9].
Lecti stuprati natus incestus fuit
Eduardus olim frater, alienos thoros
dum matris amor avarus admisit, ducis
atq soboli falsos pepotes miscuit.
Facti probrū pudibundus invenit
 comes,
stuprūq secretū fatentur famuli
Imago dissimilis patris nothū vocant
moresq degeneres fratris : me filiū
legitimè imago nota psuasa ducis,
iidemq mores patris et voces pares
neq tulit hanc solū labem infœlix
 genus
Majore dedecore domū infamem
 gravat
matrem secutus frater Eduardus suā
Nam conjugali Luciæ junctus fide,
repudia sponsæ nunciat amator novus,
thalamisq primis ludit injunctā fidem
Elizabetha serò regali face
uxor secunda, juncta principi fuit.

Possidet iniqua mater alienos thoros,
fœdosq patri filios pellex tulit.
Dum populus ista cogitat secū, statim
in curia cives tum dux inclytus
corā docebit ista Buckinghamius
Procerūq quæ sit omniū sententia
Splendore populus raptus insignis
   viri,
me fortè principem suis suffragiis
clamabat, et regem vocabat Angliæ
Hæc cruce Pauli sacra fundens dog-
   mata
populò simul divine præco edissere
Sed turpe probrū matris invitus quosi
pstringe nostrā cautus offensā gravem
metuisse fingens ; laudib[9] ubi nos tuis
copiosus ornabis ; subito quasi cœlitus
Princeps datus Britanniæ, laudes meas
Stipante pompa intercipiā, miraculū
dum creduli meditantur, illico nominis
spes falsa seducit facilè, nunc exequi
vos expedit fideliter quod jussimus.

Dr. Shau.

Mox tua fidelis impata psequar.
hunquā meā damnabis incertā fidem.

ACTUS SECUNDUS.

CIVIS PRIMUS. CIVIS SECUNDUS.

Civis 1.

Quoùsne scinditur Britannia litib[9]
Luctusq cumulat luctib[9] fatum grave ?
dirum premit recens malū ? pene
   modū
severa fata nesciunt. Nunquā domus
Irata plena cædib[9] pacabitur ?
hæresve nullus sceptra impune geret ?
At jam nihil stirpem timent Lancastriā
Erepta ferro regna : jam novū scelus
infausta sibi domus parat, quantū
   luem

præsagit assuetis malis animus ? fides
Est nulla regni, nec suis parcere
   potest
ambitio domens. Glocestriū ducem
ambire regnū murmurat secreta plebs
Patrui nefas crudele, tetrū, parvuli
latent in obscuro nepotes carcere,
en Comĩtiis de cèrto ascriptus dies.
Glocestrii tantùm ducis frequens
   Cliens
attrìta pulsat limina : illic emicat
illustris aulæ splendor, istuc confluunt
mitiora quisquis supplici implorat
   prece.
Quicunq Regis nuda calcat limina
Et principis servus fidelis veseret
illū minùs edocta vulnerat cohors.

Civis 2.

Charū caput, duræq sortis pticeps
fidelis, heu, quā nos premūt casūs
   graves ?
fessam repetit en turbo sævus Angliā,
veresq triste reparat amissas malū.

Civis 1.

Effare quæ cives manent lasos mala.

Civis 2.

Brevi scelus complectar horrens
   impiū,
dum reb[9] otiosus intentus novis
vagarer, et comūne regni gaudiū
revolvo præceps ecce fertur impetu
insana plebs, cæco frequens cursu ruit
Denso statim miscebar agmini stupens :
Ad templa rapimur : dubias aures
   porrigo :
Expecto sacra : cogitabundus steti
Divinus ecce præco scandit pulpitū,
quem literis lucere clarū jactitant,
sordere fœdis moribus, doctor Shaa.
Mox è sacris sic orsus est oraculis.

SEMEN BEATUM THORUS ADULTER
   DENEGAT
PROLES NEC ALTAS SPURIA RADICES
   DABIT.

Postquā diu regni decus quàm vulnerat
Lecti probrū præmonstrat, et falsæ
   faces :
thori fidem quantū beabunt numina :
Lectiq decepti scelestos filios
peccata testantes patris quantū hor-
   reant :
bona falsus hæres quamvis occupat
   patris :
furtū tamen mox prodit ignotū deus,
Suoq restituit sua hæredi bona.
Qui posidebat regis infandos thoros
fidemq lusit conjugalē pelluca
Elizabetha falsa mater, impio
declamat ore quodq primū Luciæ
promissus olim lectus Eduardi fuit
Ergo thoros hæc possidebat Luciæ
Injusta mater Elizabetha, liberos
et polluit macula suos adultera.
nec filios mentita fædabat fides
solū regis patris ; polluta mater ar-
   guit
spureosq natales, suis dum liberis
adulteros furtiva miscuit Venus.
summi ducis, falsūq patris filiū
diversa suadent ora solus exprimit
Richardus effigiem patris : regem
   vocat
vultus ducis : Nunc ergo jure vendicat
amissa patris regna. Mox Glocestriū
ad astra laudibus ferebat : Regis
quod splendor hic lūcebat, hic verus
   nitet,
vultus patris, virtus frequens quantū
   beat
hunc intueri jussit, hunc solū coli
omnes stupent vultumq demittunt,
   fremunt,

mox intuentur invicem, venit Glocestrius
suas laudes serus amittit : comes
stipabat ingens.   Ubi ducem vidit
   Shaus,
Rex Angliæ, quasi lapsus esset cœlitus,
En (inquit) en chari Britanni, en
   principem
hunc intueri rursus, hunc coli jubet
Periisse quasi frustra blanditias pudet
jam tum priores, dux prius cū ab-
   fuit
hæc vera imago patris, hic vultus
   ducis,
Nescit mori pater Richardo sospitus.
Stipante pompa, spiritus altos gerens.
p densa pumpens virorū, civib[9]
spectanda præbet ora dux, alto sedet.

Civis 1m.

Quis hujus at sermonis eventus fuit.

Civis 2d.

Postquam Shaus periisse laudes cerneret,
populū nec acclamare lætis vocib[9]
Rex vivat æternū Richardus : (nam
   stupet
tum populus, admiratur infandū nefas)
cœpti pudet, scroq cognovit scelus :
reparare vires quærit amissus pudor
frustra priùs spretāq virtutem timet :
En civiū vultus miser fugiens, domū
subducit ipse se clam.   At hic quid
   vult sibi
in curia corona tanta civiū.

Civis 1.

Coire cives prætor hic jussit suos.
de rebus ut nos consulat gravissimis
Propago Buckinghamiorū nobilis.

Civis sec.

Avertet omen triste propitius Deus.

DUX BUCK. PRÆTOR LOND. NO-
BITIS, SERVUS UNUS ET ATTER
BUCKINGHAMII.

Dux Buck.

Amore vestso ductus (ô cives mei)
dc rcb[9] alloquar hodie gravissimis.
Sunt ista patriæ decora maximè
vobis nec auditu seorsim tristia,
Quos nunc beat fortuna lætos undiq
Quæ namq vestris expetita sæpiùs
votis, diup frustra defessis erant
sperata tempora, prætio quæ maximo
parasse, vel laborc sumo non piget,
oblata vobis gratis adsunt omnia !
Si tanta, tamq optata quæ sunt quæ-
ritis,
tranquilitas sæcuræ vitæ, liberū
dulcis tutela, salusq conjugū.
heu quis priùs tot explicatis sæculis
vos pculit metus gravis ? Nam p deos
cœlumq quicquid possidet, quis tot
dolis
tantisq tutò pfrui suis rebus
potuit ? quis esse liberis solatio ?
quis in suis regnare solus ædib[9] ?
Mens horret illam psequi tyrannidem,
p ima quæ grassata regni viscera
exhausit œdes neq pestis invida
insontibus novit pcere.   Quid expli-
cem
exacta quanta sunt tributa sæpius ?
extoriā vi, quanta visa luxui ?
Nec grande civis ferre vectigal potest
Exhaustus, mulcta crevit imensum
levis,
pœnaq gravis pcussit offensū brevem.
meminisse Burdetti ārbitror (cives
mei)
cui, quod jocatus est lepidè, demi
caput
Rex jussit indignè, nefas judex licet
horreret nefandū, locusq nobilis
urbis senator qui diu vestræ fuit,

heu quam graves ppessus est pœnas
miser,
viris quòd illis ipse multa debuit
quos intimè rex invidebat impius ?
Non est necesse ut psequāar
adesse pene neminem vestrū puto
qui tam cruenti tempis non sit me-
mor,
metusq non sit ipse conscius sui,
quem vel nefandus regis injeci̧t furor,
vel civiū tot improborū ingens favor.
Rex nāmq ferro nactus imperiū grave :
hunc victos iratus decora lædere
regni putabat impiè, qui sanguine
affinis esset aut amoris vinculo
conjunctus his princeps, prius quo\
oderat
At huic malo quem majus accessit
malū
vitæ dubius hærebat, haud belli exitus
Qui vexat lucertus modo : sed (quo\
fœdius)
urget tumultus civiū esse maximus
qui tum solet, cum nobiles odio invicem
tacito ardeant, nec optimates acriùs
se maximis exulcerabūt litib[9]
Quam, sceptra cùm gestaret infes\
manu
Eduardus, intestina tandem prælia
sic æstuabant undiq ? ut tristi nece
pars interiret maxima civiū,
hæc, hæc fuit tam fœda strage
omniū,
qualem vidit devicta nunquā Gallia
Hæc præpotens exhausit Angloru
genus
hæc pristinis spoliobat illos virib[9]
Sumant tot urbes tanta clades omniū
dubia minatur pax pares bello mina\
Numos luunt domini, atq agros quis
quis tenet
Mactatur, irā principis quisnā fugit ?
Jam nemo non timore languebat
miser,

nec ulla non plena periclis erant tempa
,At at quis illi charus esse creditur,
cui frater odio erat suus ? confidere
quib[9] potest, cui frater esse pfidus
videtur ? aut quib[9] pepercit mitior,
fratri suo qui toties damnū intulit ?
At quos colebat intimus, nihil moror :
honore vei quales decoro pinxerat.
]uis nescit uña plus potnisse pelli-
cem,
regni viros quàm totius primarios ?
Invitus ista sanè vobis affero :
Sed nota quæ singulis quid attinet
tacere, quo non impulit libidinis
mānis æstus, amoris et cæcus furor ?
Quæ virgo paulo pulchrior ? quæ
fœmina
plus cæteris decora, matris è sinu.
quam non mariti vel rapuit am-
plexib[9] ?
abivis at licet tyrannis ingruat :
hujus tamen quæ cæteris sensit minas
urbs nostra, cujus potius ornasset decus,
]uòd prima regni sedes est, et præmia
lefensus olim sæpe princeps debuit.
Majora benefacta vivus spreverat,
nec mortuus referre gratiā potest.
Alter en eodem restat ortus sanguine,
rex gratior suis futurus subditis,
quiq meritis refere vestris debita,
votisq respondere possit affatim.
Nec animus illa (credo) vestris excidant,
doctus sacrorū præco quæ sparsit
priùs.
Nunquam fidem fefellit interpres
dei :
patruū sacerdos fratris ad regnū vocat,
Glocestriū regnare quia jussit deus
nec sceptra patris tractat impurus
nepos,
aut polluat regni decus lecti probrū
Richardus hæres fratris unicus fuit :
huic civiū decrevit et procerū cohors

magnanima, supplex ut rogaret patruū,
Regni velit decus tueri principis,
sumeret onus pollentis hæres insulæ.
facturus est ægrè, scio : regni labor
deterret ingens, certat invidiæ rapax :
Ingrata pacem sceptra nequaquā colunt.
Quantis cietur fluctib[9] fallax decor ?
mihi crede (cives) non potest tantū
puer
onus tueri : pulsat aures vox sacra,
Infausta regna levis quib[9] puer præ-
.   est.
Fœlix acumen invidū decet thronū,
ætasq plena, patrā qualem vides,
Si chara vobis ergo civiū salus,
aut si juvent optata pacis fœdera ;
tam fausta procerū vota laudetis
simul.
uno creetur ore rex Glocestrius :
tantum laborem promptus assumet
magis,
Si vox fatiget vestra nolentem priùs,
mens ergo quæ sit vestra, palā dicite
Altū quid hoc silentiū ? plebs cur
tacet ?

Prætor.

Vix forte populus aure dicta concipit.

Buck.

affabor illos ergo rursus altiùs,
Elapsa sunt iniqua (cives) tempa :
pax alma tandem sorte fœlici viget,
Nisi suo demens quis invideat bono,
Aut nescit uti, dū premebat Angliā
Eduardus atrox sæviens vultu truci,
Insula quib[9] jactatur usq fluctib[9] ?
Non vita tuta civiū, nunquā bona
sunt clausa cuiq, dissipatq singula
luxus, nefandi tum libido principis
Quæ virgo fuit intacta ? Quæ conjux
labe
carebat injusta ? licet quicquid lubet,
misera fuit cunctis potestas civib[9]

sed Londinensib[9] longè miserrima,
illis licet benigna psuasit locus.
Sed unus est, pericula qui tot vindicet,
Dux ipse regio creatus stemate,
quem singuli colunt, Glocestriæ decus :
Regnare quem leges jubebant patriæ,
hœresq solus Rcgiæ manet domus.
furtiva proles matris injustæ, patris
frustra sibi vendicat thronos adulteri
Vir nup ista vos docebat optimus
dum sacra vobis præco fundit dog-
mata
divina nullus ora damnabit pius.
Hic nobilis comota Magnatū cohors
et magna civiū corona, supplices
Orare statuunt patruū, ut hæres suū
capessat imperiū, decus nec patriæ
falsus nepos corrumpat.   Id faciet
lubens
si sponte id vos exoptare senserit.
Clamore mentem publico ergo effun-
dite
Y**e** Mayor and Quid hoc ? adhuc tacet ?
others goeing   Mirū nimis.
to y**e** Duke.

Prætor.

Unus solebat ore jussus publico
De rebus alloqui cives magnis suos
Hinc forsitan responsa quærenti da-
but
Effare cives, urbis interpres tuæ.

Fitzwil. Recor.

Quàm sorie fœlici cadant magis
omnia
quàm fratre quondā rege, quis demens
negat ?
Mihi nec est necesse singula psequi
memoravit hæc dux omniū claris-
simus.
Estis duorū facile testes temporū.
Quautū prior premebat ætas, postera
quam grata lucet, quem latet ? cupit

magnanimus heros ergo nunc cognos-
cere,
regnare num Glocestriū placet ducem .
Quod singulos statuisse constat ordines,
Regemp proceres Angliæ verū vo
cant.
Vir ille quis, quantusve sit, quis ves
ciat ?
Quo jure poscat hæres imperii decus;
Admonuit omnes doctus interpres dei
et arte qui pandit polū, doctor Shaa :
Edatis ergo voce mentem Rounding the
publica.   Mayor in y**e**
                     eare.

Dux Buck.

Est ptinax nimis istud silentiū
de rebus his (amici) longè màximis
vos alloqui, non jure queror concitus.
Amor sed comotus, ignotū bonū
vobis adhuc referre quòd cupio lubens
Hoc singulis erit salubre civib°.
manifesta mentis signa precor edite
statim.

Servus unus et Alter.

Rex vivat æternū Richardus.

Prætor.

Aula levi tota susurrit murmure,
Cives tacent, spectant retro quæ vox
fuit
mirantur, acclamant nihil regnū duci

Dux. Buck.

Vox hercule læta, clamor atq maximus,
dum nemo voce contrà quicquā mur-
muret.
Vox ergo civiū una cum sit omniū
pariter mihi comites (precor) cras
jungite
Præcemur una supplices ducem, velit
Nomen deinde sustinere principis.

Nobilis.

Heu quid genas fletu rigas miser, dolos

Weeping behind ye Duke tourning his face towards ye wall. juvato nefandos plangere haud pcis tibi. Furtū piū si lachrymarū, sed tamen

læthale. Solus fata mundi qui vides tremende pater, insontib⁹ miseris necem averte, tristem sed sequor comes.ducē.

ACTUS TERTIUS.

DUX BUCK. CIVES.

Buck.

Let ye Mayor come first accompanied wᵗʰ citizens, then the Duke wᵗʰ other nobles: they assemble at Bernhardes Castle. Veneranda civiū cohors, quos affatim Urbs possidet præclara Londinū, en sua jam quisq sponte contulit faustū gradū, et quilibet confluxit

ordo civiū,
ut dempta sceptra Adulteris nepotib⁹
Glocestrio gerenda reddant patruo
Ne regiā mentita proles inquinet.
Sed tu priùs nostri ducem adventus mone
Ne tantus anxiū tumultus illico pturbet, Illū supplices cives petunt
quos Angliæ torquent graves casus, sui
dignetur aditū subditis fidelibus,
de rebus illū maximis dum consulunt
ngens onus regni labor, nec allicit
Statim bonos blandū venenū, quos favor
vexabit intestinus æternis minis
En delicatas eligunt fraudes domos,
et nulla cingunt tela principem satis,

cautuq licèt, at sermo popularis premit.
Sed ista quorsū psequor? Quod si piū
onus coronæ cura comendat gravis
nihilq suspectū facit illū fides
at illū metuo deterreat, nepotibᵃ
vivis adhuc, infame regnū patrui.
honore plenus est: latere dux cupit

His servant returneth and secretly reporteth to ye Duke whome he sendeth againe. a turbidus semotus invidiæ malis Aditum negat Protector (o cives mei)

Tantāq turba suspicatur, nisi priùs
Adventus hujus causa quæ sit, audiat.
Quod magna procerū turba supplex consulit
cinctusq multo cive prætor, nuncia.
Domesticū torquet malū, quod auribᵌ
tantū suis solicita mandabit cohors.
At nos Glocestriū rogemus supplices
Rogamus [inani] reluctantē prece
Ut sceptra regni justus hæres occupet.
Sed nunc duobᵌ cinctus esse Episcopis,
apparet in sumā domo princeps pius:
ah, sola dux divina fœlix cogitat.

Cives.

O fraude pugnas pjurax audacia
colore dum ludet alieno, nil timet
secura: nescire cæteros putat
tectum malum, sibiq blanditur nefas.

DUX BUCK. DUX GLOC. CHORUS CIVIUM.

Buck.

Te civiū profusa flagitat cohors
excelse præses, ut tua de re gravi
præsentiā alloqui liceret. Afferunt
ignota regno bona, decus magnū tibi
Non audet eloqui jūssus pios tamen,
Id nisi licere voce testaris tua.

Gloc.

Quicunq mens jussit, licebit dicere
publica juvat decreta scire civiū.

Buck.

Diu nimis ppessa plebs tyrannidē,
lætatur hæc luxisse tandem tempa,
se pristino quib⁹ timore solveret,
vitaq grata sit sua securitas.
De rebus ergo dū coiret publicis
statumq regni plena civium cohors
tractaret, hæres unicus, regni decus
ut vendices, sanxere sacris jussib⁹ :
nec sceptra prolem fratris impurā
    ferunt,
injusta quam matris Venus suæ pre-
    mit,
Nunc ergo turba civiū frequens adest,
ut voce supplex publica mutū petat,
ut pristino cives timore liberes,
regnum et sagaci debitū tractes manu.

Gloc.

Quàm vera cives sanxerint, licèt sciā;
fratris tamen manes veneror olim mei,
nec in meos ferox nepotes patruus
demens ero, verbisq nec populus feris
pulsabit iratus, thronū quod ambiā
Fratris mei, nec exteræ probris simul
gentes lacessent, si dolis patruus meis
Nepotib⁹ regnum scelestus auferā,
aut sceptra tollam dubia cognati laris
Potius latebo tutus invidiæ malis,
nec cæcus animū pulsat ambitus meū.
satis premunt sceptri propinqui mu-
    nera,
vos attamen mihi dixisse non piget.
Cogit potiùs amor referre gratiam
Nec vos nepotem obsecro colatis nunc
    minùs
cujus magis privatus imperiū ferā,
Regnare qui puer licet novit parū
Laborib⁹ meis adjutus is tamen,
Regni decus puer satis tuebitur :

Viguisse quod nup magis nemo nega
tutela postquā tanta regni traditur
veterata cessat ira, franguntur minæ
bonoq languent pulsa consilio odia
partim, Dei sed maximi nutu magis
Nil sceptaa damnes regis (ô civis
    probe)
debet mihi nomen placere subditi.

Buck.

Da pauca rursus alloqui (ô dux in-
    clyte)
regnare non sinant nepotes subditi :
summi vetant proceres : vetat vulgus
    rude
Regnū student purgare adultera labe
sin justa regni sceptra spernas ptinax.
At posse flecti nobilem sperant prece,
qui regio splendore cultu gaudeat.
de rebus hisce quid ergo statuas,
    audiant.

Gloc.

Quod invident regnū paternū liberis,
doleo, fratris qui honoro manes mortui
Utinam queant nepotis imperiū paṭi !
Sed regere populū nullus invisum po:.
    test
Hæc quia video statuisse consensu pari,
regnumq spuriis aurerunt nepotib⁹
Cum jura regni solus hæres vendicem
quod filius relictus unus sum patris,
cum sit necesse civibus cedere meis :.
Vota sequar : en, regna posco debita :
votis creari subditorū principem
Magis reor.   Curā Angliæ accipimus,
    simul
Et Galliæ rex gemina regna vendico
Sanctiùs habænas Angliæ princeps
    regā
Magis pacata civiū quies monet.
Tum nostra discet fræna victa Gallia :
hæc Angliæ subacta ditabit genus
Cujus miser si gloriā non quærerem
utinam sorores filum rumpant pfidæ.

Chorus.

The Duke and noblemen go in to the Kinge, the Maior and Citizens departe away.

Richardus rex, Richardus rex, Richardus rex.

Cives.

Quærit colorem triste virtutis scelus
pudet sui deforme vultus vitiū.
Heu quis secretos nescit ignarus
   dolos?
Et mille patrui machinas? quis sibi
   prius
Promissa fratris regna fraude non
   videt?
Dolis petitū publicè regnū negat.
Inventa damnat sceptra ficta sanctitas,
Qualis negat bis consecrari pontifex.
qui sacra tamen ambit colenda forsi-
   tan.
Talis sua rex sponte compulsus gerit
erepta pueris sceptra. Sed decit
   magis
Spectare tantas plæbeos tragædias,
Quicquid libet, regi licet, nec legibus
Semp piis nec vota metitur sua
Crebro juvat nescire, quod scias
   tamen

ACTUS QUARTUS.

Dr. Shawe, Civis Amicus.

Civis.

Cur sic pigro miser gradu moues
   stupens,
Dubiusq sese pes incerto tenet?
corpus cupis referre progressu licet?
Hæret animus, ponisq nolentem pe-
   dem
Quid triste consiliū diu torques?
   modū
Nec invenis? quid civiū vultus fugis
Insane? vince quicquid obstitit,
   expedi
Mentem tuā, teq restituas tibi.

Doct. Shaw.

Heu mihi animus semet scelere plenus
   fugit.
vetat quæ scire pectus oneratū malis,
mentisq consciæ pavor, dolor æstuat,
animus non potest venenū expellere.
Scelerisq mordet sæva conscientia
Quis, quis coëgit dæmon adversus
   mihi,
fœdare stupro regis Eduardi thoros?
heu mihi tuos Eduarde natos prodidi,
et ore nuntio nefando adulteros :
tuā coronā possidet jussu meo
Richardus ; hei mihi, voce fœdavi
   mea
natos tuos : mendatiis sacra miscui
et ore scripturas imani pollui.

Civis.

Cur triste pœnis gravib[9] infestus
   graves?
nutritus alias colligit dolor faces,
renovatq durū molle sanari malū,
Frœnos capit prudens dolor, et ex-
   tinguitur,
vincit dolorem, quisquis eximere
   cupit,
et pfidū sanare conatur malū.

Doct. Sha.

Psæceps monentem mens fugit, redit
   statim
concepta frustra concilia repetens,
   sequi
cogit scelus priora, virtutem timet,
Accendit ipse semet infestus dolor,
lapsasq vires inregrat, nunquā meas
cessabit in pœnas scelus, nunquā quies
nocturna curis solvit, alit altus sopor.
Noctu diem voco, repeto noctem die,
semp memet fugio, non possū scelus.

Civis.

Malū nequis sanare.

D. Sha.

Si possim mori.

Civis.

At dedecus demi licet magnū potest.

Dr. Sha.

Nisi turpis hæret usq vestigiū labis.

Civis.

Mors sola maculā demere infanda potest.

Dr. Sha.

Fœdata nescit vita crimen ponere.

Civis.

At pœnitenti sera parcunt Numina.

Dr. Sha.

Sceleris novi mater prius natu scelus.

Civis.

Sanare cessas, qui nimis vulnus times?

Dr. Sha.

Sanare non potes facilè vulnus grave.

Civis.

Nulli parcet quisquis haud parcit sibi.

Dr. Sha.

Priùs ipse crimen solus accusa tuū.

Civis.

Absolve te quem judicas ultus satis.

Dr. Sha.

Nemo satis ulcisci scelus dirū potest.

Civis.

Crimen nimis judex acerbus vendicas.

Dr. Sha.

Nisi mordet acre, fœda sordent vulnera.

Civis.

Dum cogitas severa, nil curas reū.

Dr. Sha.

Dolor doloris est medela : nescit pcere
cœlū crimen videt nefandū conscia
tanti fuit dedecoris et tellus vaga.
Ruina mentis fœda tam me disparem
fecit mihi, ut memet nil fugiam magis,
et factus infœlix mei sum pfuga,
animusq serū corporis divortiū :
precatur anxius, necat quisquis jubet
vivere : quisquis mori jubet vitam
dedit.
tantùm potest placere quicquid displicet.
de me viri quid loquuntur futiles ?

Cives.

Te sceleris arguunt nefandi consciū.

Dr Sha.

Sed quid tumultus civiū istuc convolat ?

Civis.

Ubi civium regnare jussu cœperat
princeps Glocestrius : loco primū studet
rex prius ab illo subditis fari suis,
Ubi voce lex Anglis loqui viva solet.
Nunc ergo ab aulā comigrat Westminsteri.
Rex ut prius legū peritis imperet :
Ne prava mens legū minas adulteret,
discescit infœlix, pati nec civiū
vultus potest : huic verba pandā
principis.

Dux Glocest.

Juvabat Astreæ locatū sedibus,
et hoc tribunali tremendo Minois,
auro caput sepire primū fulgido,
Justaq cives lege regere patriæ
Rex providere debet id potissimū

ut urbiū columna lex firmissima
in curio dominetur æquali potens.
vestrū domare pectus haud metū decet,
quorū superbū claruit titulis genus :
Non cæca regnat ira vinci nescia
Nunc ense fessum miles exonerat
  latus :
Omnes amoris vincula jungere juvat,
contempta nec patrū jacebūt stemata ;
Vos laudo patres jure doctos patrio,
qui continetis legibus rempublica,
ne jurgiis lacerata mutuis Anglia
languescat : amplo vos honore psequar,
et mente cives gaudeāt lassa licet,
e sordidis qui nutriuntur artib⁹,
nec causa vos agitata judici premet,
nec fera clangor bella pstrepat tubæ :
Nam concidunt res prosperæ discordiis :
Hinc falsa mens vultu minatur inte-
  gro:
Hinc omne fluxit civitatib⁹ malū.
Sedabit hos fluctus amor, pietas,
  fides :
his vinculis fœlix cohoret Angliā,
quæ nec furor contundet domesticus,
Nec robur hostiū potest infringere
Odii recentis pereat omnis memoria.
Statim mihi Foggū satelles liberet,
supplex asylo qui metu nostro latet.
Sit finis iræ, nec minas jactet furor,
Sumo laboret impetu mens impia
à subditis vultu benigno conspici.
Heu quàm velim fides vigeret aurea,
tantùm vetustis nota quondā sæeulis,
aut quæ fucos experta virtus non
  fuit.
Mox sit decorū numen adversū mihi,
si lingua mentis fallat interpres suæ.
Noli timere (Fogge) concedas propè
sociemus animos : pignus hoc fidei
  cape,
conjunge dextram, et me vicissim de-
  lige.

ACTUS QUINTUS.

HOSPES, CIVES.

Hospes.

Domesticum narras malū, terū, grave
Imensa regni moles invidiæ capax
quantis cietur fluctib⁹ ? victū licet,
potuisse vinci non sibi credit tamen.
Graves procellas concitat regni fames,
Dum cæca quassavit libido principis
Quot urbiū projecta sunt cadavera ?
Qualem maris salsi secantem gurgitem
puppim benignam turbo concussit
  gravis
et volvit horrens concitū flatu fretū,
dum latera scindit, et geminat minas :
Talis premit vehemens statim mutatio.
Affare (quæso) cur freqens huc convolat
populus, notatq proximos occulis
  locos?
Theatra stupidus specta usq splendida
et singulis sternuntur omnia fulgidis,
regale spendat atq soliū principis.

Civis.

Hospes fidelis mihi, coronâ cingitur
Rex Angliæ Richardus : assensu pari
cujusvis hæres approbatur ordinis.

Hospes.

Hoc sparsit olim rumor ambigu⁹.

Cives.

                                    Locus
Hic maximis datur comitiis, iminet
  horā.

Hosp.

Bona diū pius creatur rex : mala,

Si nequior : rex si bonus sit, civiū
. salus :
rex si malus sit, civitatis pestis est.

Civis.

Qui regio natus supbo stemate,
duos nepotes principes tutor suā
suscepit in fidem patruus : en Angliæ
rex ipse conventu creatur maximo.

Hosp.

Ubi reguli duo ? nefas regere patruū
hi dum supsint.

Civis.

　　　Hoc facit regni sitis :
in arce regni carceris cæci luem
patiuntur.

Hosp.

　　O scelus !

Civis.

　　　Sed principis tamen

Hosp.

Magis hoc nefandū.

Civis.

　　　Propter imperiū simul.

Hosp.

Pietas decet regem, nec impio licet
parare regnum pretio.

Civis.

　　　Semp tamen
imperia constant pretio bene quolibet.

Hosp.

Nunquam diu male pta succedunt.

Civis.

　　　　　Satis
semel est regere.

Hosp.

　　Statim labi duplex malū
fœlicitas brevis labor regni gravis.

Civis.

Prout lubet, regendo minuitur labor.

Hosp.

Crescit magis odiū.

Civis.

　　Hoc metu restinguitur.

Hosp.

Potius fide.

Civis.

　　Quin deme tantos spiritus
Lacerare dictis principem diris grave
　　　est,
statimq suspectos sibi mori jubent.
Jam parce dictis : tempori decet ob-
　　　sequi
nuper nimis blande salutat obvios :
abjicere se cogit mens mali conscia,
regemq vultus pene servilis docet.
Hinc liberavit Cardinalem vinculis,
Et Stanleium emisit solutū carcere.
Hujus timebat filiū Lancastriæ,
Ne sæva patris vindicaret vincula.
At Eliensem præsulem clausū domi
retinere Buckinghamiū jussit Ducem.
Sed regis adventū sonat clangor tubæ
Comites, Ducesq, Marchiones, Præ-
　　　sides,
præire torquibus mirantes cernimus.

Hosp.

Effare (civis) nitida quid calcaria
aurata signant, quæ comes manu gerit

Civis.

Sunt Bellicæ virtutis hæc insignia.

Hosp.

Baculū quid.

Civis.

Eduardi fuit regis pii
id illius nunc memoria pferąnt.

Hosp.

Sed absq cuspide gladius, quem fert
caput
nudus, quid indicat?

Civis.

Clementiā.

Hosp.

Aure⁹

Clavus, quid?

Civis.

Officiū Comestabilis Angliæ
Equitum magister publico hunc cœtu
gerit.

Hosp.

Enses quid à dextris feruntur principis
et à sinistris fulgidi duo simul?

Civis.

Sunt arma justitiæ: scelus cleri
simul
Laiciq puniunt salubri vulnere.

Hosp.

Nudi duo feruntur enses cuspide
nullo.

Civis.

[*Hiant Codices.*]

Hosp.

Quidnā loquuntur sceptra?

Civis.

Pacē.

Hosp.

Quid Globus,
Cujus sup crux elevatur verticem?

Civis.

Monarchiam.

Hosp.

Ecce alius vagina conditū
et arte sūma fulgidū gladiū gerit
itemq magnū.

Civis.

Sūma dignitatis est
honore sūmo spatha.

Hosp.

Quis locū
splendore mediū maximo, radiis quasi
nitidis micans, rubroq tinctus murice
tenet.

Civis.

Iste fecialis est sui ordinis
primus atq regis ipse nomine.

Hosp.

Virgula quid alba præ se fert ducis?

Civis.

Hanc sūmus Angliæ Archichamerinus
gerit.

Hosp.

Quid alba Reginæ columba denotat?

Hosp.

Notat avis iñocentiā nihil nocens.

The Shewe of the Coronation.

Trumpetts
Choristers
Singing-men
Præbendaries
Bishopps
Cardinall
Heralds
Aldermen of London
Esquires, Knights, Noblemen
Gilt spurrs borne by the Earle of Huntingdon
St Edward's stafe.   Earle of Bedford
The point of ye sword naked.   E. of Northumberland
The great mace.   Lord Stanly
Two naked swordes, E. of Kent. L. Lovell
The grete scepter.   Duke of Suffolke
The ball wth the crosse.   E. of Lincolne
The sword of estate.   E. of Surrey
Three togather.   The Kinge of heralds
The Maior of London with a mace
On the right hand the gentleman usher
on the left hand,
The King's crowne.   Duke of Norfolke
The Kinge under a canopy betwixt two Bishops
The Duke of Buckinghā wth a white staffe caringe up the
      King's traine
Noblemen
The Queen's scepter
The white dove wth a white rod
The Queene's crowne
The Queene wth a circlet on her head under a Canopie
The Lady Margaret bearinge up the Queene's traine
A Troupe of Ladies
Knights and Esquires
Northren Souldiers well armed.

During the solemnity of the Coronation
lett this songe followinge be songe wth
instruments.

Festū diem colamus assensu pari
quo principis caput corona cingitur.

Decora Regni possidet
Regis propago nobilis
Illustre principis caput
fulva corona cingitur.
Nunc voce læti consona
cantū canamus principem.
    Regnū premebat dedicus
    Libido Regis polluit.

TERTIA ACTIO.

DRAMATIS PERSONÆ.

Mr. PALMER, Richardus Rex
Mr. STRINGER, Dux Buckinghamius
D. SHEPARD, Elizabetha Regina
D. TITLEY, Filia Eduardi regis major
D. PILKINGTON, Ancilla
Mr. STANTON, Epis. Eliensis
Mr. FOXCROFT, Brakenburius præfectus arcis
Mr. SNELL, Tyrellus generosus
Mr. ROBSON, Ludovicus medicus
Mr. GARGRAVE, Anna Regina uxor Richardi
Mr. SEDWICK, Nuntius primus
D. HILL, Nuntius secundus
HOULT, Nuntius tertius
Mr. BAYLY, Lovellus heros
Mr. ROBINSON, Catesbeius
Ds. MORRELL, Nuntius quartus
              Nuntius quintus
Mr. HICKMAN, Henricus comes Richmondiæ
Mr. DIGBY, Comes Oxonii
Mr. HILL se : Dux Norfolciensis
Mr. LINSELL, Rhesus Thomæ Wallicus
Ds. HARRIS, Nuntius
              Mulier
              Alia Mulier
              Anus
D. HARRISON, Hungerford ⎫
Mr. ROBINSON, Burchier   ⎬ equestris ordinis
           Miles   ⎭

Mr. HODSON, Stanleius heros
Mr. CONSTABLE, Gent. Filius Stanlei Dominus
         Strange.
         Centurio
         Braa servus comitissæ Richmond
REDFERNE, Dighton carnifex, a big sloven
Mr. DUCKET, Comes Northumbriæ

MUTES.

The yonge kinge and his brother lyinge dead on a bed.
Foure daughters of King Edward.
Souldiers unarmed and armed.

———

ARGUMENTUM.

FUROR.

Quorsum furor secreta volvis pectora
minasq spiras intimas, nec expedis
faces tuas? scelus expleas Glocestriũ:
Glocestrios invise rex olim tuos:
et sceptra jactes, prætiu sane necis,
dubiosq regni volve fraterni metus.
Decora spectant ora Eboracũ stupens
miretur excelsũ decus vulgus leve.
Quorsũ moras trahis lenes? totus miser
fias, magisq sæviat nefas breve.
Aude scelus mens quicquid atrox cogitat,
Regnũq verset ultimũ Regis scelus.
Nondũ madebant cæde cognata manu:
nondũ nepotes suffocantur Regii
et frustra poscas neptis incestos thoros:
imple scelere domũ patris tui: illico
discat furor sævire Buckinghamius:
macta tyrannũ, deme sceptra si potes:
sed non potes: pænasq dignas pferes
tanti tumultus.   En venit Richmondius,
exul venit, promissa regna vendicat,
regniq juratos priùs thoros: age,
stringantur enses, odia misce, funera
dirãq stragem: impone finem litibus
En regnet exul, rex nec auxiliũ impetret,
tuaq cadat (Henrice) Richardus manu.
Actum est satis: parcam furor Britanniæ
posthac, novasq jam mihi quæram sedes.

ACTUS PRIMUS.

BRAKENB. ORDINIS EQUESTRIS,
TIRELLUS.

Brak.

O rector alme cœlitum et terræ decus,
quisquis gubernas, parce Brakenburio
Clemens furorem siste dūri principis,
pœnaq certam libera gravi fidem
Horrere nunquā cessat imperii sitis,
'curis nec usquā solvitur ægra ambitio.
Regni metu Richardus æstuat ferox,
injusta sceptra possidet trepida manu,
novasq suspicatur insidias sibi.
Stipante dum magna caterva rex suā
inviseret Glocestriā, famam occupans
incerta sortis cogitans ludibria,
quàmq facili injusta ruit impetu po-
     tentia,
rcgniq ludibriū nimis statū tremens,
dum spiritu vescatur ælherio nepos :
mox ut suo reddat dolori spiritū
geminus nepos, et sanguine extin-
     guant suo
Regni metū pueri, ferox patruus studet
Nuper Johannes Greeñus intento
     sacris
Mihi, traditas à regc literas dedit
Parare tristem Regulis jubet necem,
Et principib⁹ adferre crudeles manus
quos vinculis præfectus arcis com-
     primo.
Solus potest mactare Brakenburius
natos tuos Eduarde? solus pdere
stirpem tua? mandala regis excquar.
Lubens tibi Richarde promptus servio.
Necare stirpem fratris, ah, pietas
     vetat.
Intus jacent squalente miseri carcere,
Solusq captivis ministrat carnifex.

O principis dirū nefas, tetrū, ferox.
Inter metū animus spemq dubius vol·
     vitur,
mentemq distractā tumultus verberat.
Nunc regis horreo minas : notus mihi
animus satis vetat timere : conscius
nihil mihi, quò fata vellicant, sequor.
Quid in tuū Richarde subditū paras?
crudele quid spiras? quid atrox
     cogitas?
Pius fui : cruore regem pollui
nunquā manus meas : quid incusas?
     fidem
tuebar : ulcisi bonū iñensū paras.
Testor deorū numen iñocens eram
insons eram. Solumne regnū uón
     timct
maculā? quid aula ptinax fugis pudor
humilemq casā quæris? aulā deserat
quisquis piè vivet : micans splendor
     nimis
Sortis beatæ lumen impedit piū,
Et turpiter collisa mens impingitur
sin fata me morentur, adveniā lubens
tibi de tuorū cæde tristis nuntius
Eduarde, pculsus miser ferro simul
A rege sed Tirellus huc quid advolat?
an non perimus? heu metu cor pal-
     pitat
Quā, quā parant pænā gravē fido
     mihi?
Ferrē libenter quicquid est, ruā licet.

Tyrell.

Ignava mens, quid jussa regis exequi
dubitas? inanes et metus fingis tibi?
Haud leve timebit, tristis quisquis
     cogitat.
Quid principi Tirelle gratari times?
rex imperat : crit inocens necessitas :

magna anxiū cura Richardū liberas,
et longa te regis beabunt præmia.
Principe suo Eborū domus contenta
    erit,
prolesq regiæ spiritū inimicū expuant
pro mortuis pugnare quis stultè cupit?
aut principum demens tueri cogitat
exangue corpus? quicquid est auden-
    dū erit.
malus minister regis anxius pudor
Equestris ordinis decus Brakenbūri,
regis parentis adulterū vivit genus?

Brak.

Tantū moratur ultimū vitæ diem.

Tirell.

Nihil horrescis tremendā principis?

Brak.

Sequar lubens, quocunq fata me vo-
    cant.

Tirell.

An non decet mandata Regis exequi?

Brak.

Nunquam decet jubere regem pessima.

Tirell.

Fas est eos vivere, quos princeps
    oderit?

Brak.

Nefas eos odisse quos omnes amant.

Tirell.

Regni metu angi Principem nū æquū
    putas?

Brak.

Scelere mederi vulneri scelus reor.

Tirell.

Constare regnū illis nequit viventibus.

Brak.

Illis mortuis invisum erit.

Tirell.

Ars prima sceptri posse te invidiā
pati.

Brak.

Quem sepè casus transit, aliquando
    opprimit.

Tirell.

Regnare non vult esse qui invisus
    timet.

Brak.

Invisa nunquam imperia retinentur
    diu.

Tirell.

Tua interest vivat puer vel occidat.

Brak.

Parū nisi ut occisore me non occidat.

Tirell.

Tua ecquid imbelles timet pueros
    mānus?

Brak.

Qui castra non timeo, scelus tamen
    horreo.

Tirell.

Hanc immemor regi reponis gratiā.

Brak.

Quod in scelere nullā repono gratiā.

Tirell.

Nil sævientis principis iram times?

Brak.

Generosa mens terrore nunquā con-
    cidit.

Tirell.

At multa rex tibi miniatur horridus
En serus alto jungitur Phœbus salo,

Nudumq lustrandū sorori deserit
cœlu? ergo sume regis ad te literas,
claves ut arcis illico mandes mihi,
hac nocte regis exequi jussa ut queā.

BRAKENB. TYRELL, JOHAN :
DIGHTON.

Brak.

O cæca regnandi libido, ô scelus
Regis furentis triste nimis, ô patrui
Nefanda sceptra, quæ suorū sanguine
madent. Propinquæ vos manus heu
    destruunt,
υ nobĩles pueri, pupillos opprimunt
Hostemq dare genus vestrum potest.
Amissa postquā regna cognovit puer,
et possidere rapta sceptra patruū :
Sic fatur infœlix lachrymis genas
    rĩgans
ab imo pectore trahens suspiria,
Regnū nihil moror : precor vitā mihi
hanc patruus ne demat.   Heu quis
    Caucasus
lachrymis potest, aut decus Indus
    pcere ?
Nunquā deinde ornare se miserū
    juvat :
Nullo solutæ vestes diffluunt nodo.
Imago semp errat ante occulos mihi
tristis gementis principis, nec desinit
pulsare mœstum animū quærela
    Reguli.
Sed huc refert Tirellus infaustū gradū.

Tirell.

Cædis fidele munus intus occupant
Vastusq Dighton, et Forestus carnifex,
Mortem morabor principū dū pferant.

Brak.

Uterq fato cessit inimico puer ?

Tirell.

Vivunt adhuc, illis tamen necem pa-
    rant.

Brak.

Aliter placari regis irą non potest ?

Tirell.

Regem metus non ira crudelem facit.

Brak.

Effare quo rex ore responsū tulit
quod ense nunquā cæderent meo.

Tirell.

Ut ista primū novit, ingenti statim
stupore torpet, sanguis ora deserit,
totusq cineri similis expallet simul
suspiria imis efflat è pcordiis,
lævaq cordi proximū feriens latus,
regale subitò deserit soliū, furens
graditur citatis · passibus, quassans
    caput,
tacitoq secum dirus imungit sinu,
ubi sanguis è fornace veluti denuo
proruit adustus, fervidis torret genas
rubetq totus, puncio velut mari
immersus, aut minio fuisset plitus.
Oculi scintillant flamei obtuitu truci
velutiq setis horret erectis coma.
His tanquā Orestes accensus facib⁹
    fuit
Nam de suorū cæde convellunt pares
utrumq furiæ : discrepapt uno tamen.
Agitatur umbra matris ille mortuæ :
gravi nepotū ast ille vivorū metu.
Et graviter in te exarsit ira turbida,
responsa rex qua nocte pcepit tua :
Coram tacendæ functionis assecla
ingemuit et in hos mœstus erupit
    sonos.
Proh, cui quis ullā sanus adjunget
    fidem ?
Ubi gratus animus, quovè pietas ex-
    ulat ?

Terras relinquens scelere pollutas
  latet
Viris nec ullis jam licet confidere.
Quos ego velut gnatos parens enutrio
si quando tristis urgeat necessitas :
Hi me pentem deserunt, violant
  fidem,
meoq jussu prorsus audebunt nihil.
Respondet illico principi astans assecla,
At proximo stratus cubili vir jacet
(audacter istud audio nunc dicere)
id esset arduū nimis, quod is neget
unquā subire, placeat modò tibi.
Quū rex ab illo tū quis esset quæreret,
me dixit : ad cubile rapitur illico,
ibi me fratremq offendit in lectū datos.
Rex tū jocosè, Tam citò (inquit) vos
  thoro
componere juvat? tū seorsim me vocat
panditq mentis triste consiliū suæ
de Regulorū celeri et occulta nece.
Ego quis moneret intuens, qualis simul
ipse fuerim, lamentata nec regis ferens.
meā ultro regi tū lubens opem tuli :
Quocerca primo mane mihi literas
  dedit
ad te notatas, quas mea ferrē manu :
Jussitq claves turris excelsæ mihi
ut traderes, quò Regis exequar
Fidele mandatū nocte comissū mihi.

Dighton.

Uterq suffocatur exanguis puer.

Brak.

Hei mihi, p̄ ārtus horror excurrit vagus.

Tirell.

Quo sunt perempti genere læthi parvuli ? •

Dighton.

Cū triste cœlū stella lustraret vaga,
serasq gallus cecinit umbras pvigil :
en, dum nepos uterq lecto sternitur,

dulcesq somnos caperet geminus puer:
cubile nos intramus occulto pede,
fratresq subito stragulis convolvimus
sumis volutos virib⁹ depressimus,
Ubi plumeā clauduntur ora culcitra,
vocemq prohibent pressa pulvinaria :
mox suffocantur adempto uterq spiritu,
quia perviū spirantibus non est iter,
En, ambo cæsi lectulo strati jacent.

Brak.

Videone corpora Regulorū livida ?
funestus heu jā cæde puerili thorus
Quis lachrymas durus malis vultus
  negat ?
Hei mihi, perempti fraude patrui
  jacent.
Quis Colchus hæc? quæ Caspiū tan-
  gens mare
gens audet ? Atq sedis incertæ Scytha.
Nunquā tuas Busiris aspersit ferox
puerilis aras sanguis, aut gregibus suis
epulanda parva membra Diomedes
  dedit.

Tirell.

Bene est : fratris Richarde nunc soliū
  tene
securus, et decora regni posside,
Sepelite tetri carceris gradu infimo :
satis prófunda fossa fratres contegat,
et saxeo mox obruuntur aggere,
de morte passim sparge rumores
  vagos,
quod fato sponte trina condulsit soror,
Periisse subita morte finge regulos.
Sunt Regis hæc mandata, cura sedulò,
Jam sume claves [ptinax Brakenburi.]

Brak.

O sæva nostri temporis credulitas
ô regis animus dirus ! ô mens barbara,
secura turbans jura naturæ ferox !
Tune iñocentes principes, pueros pios

monstrū Procustes, tune mactasti
 tuos?
ô terra, cœlū, mœstūq regnū Tartari,
scelus videtis triste ? Sustines nefas
tantū, trisulco horrens Saturnie fulmine
Acheronte toto merge Syderiū caput
radiate Tytan, pereat et mundo dies,
Quis quo suo generi hostis infestus
 fuit,
adeo ut cruentet cæde puerili manus.
Jam Nero pius es ? scelere materno
 madens
nefande Pelops cæde, majus hic nefas
Sola teneros Medea mactat liberos.
Jugulare civem semp indignū fuit
privare luce fœminā tetrū nimis :
at inōcentes, parvulos, infantulos,
(qui vita quid sit, non p ætatem
 sciunt)
spoliare vita, facinus horrendū nimis.
Quid parcet aliis qui suos ferox necat ?
qui nocte pueros mulctat atra iñoxios,
quos sumā charos cura comendat sibi.
Heu, heu, quib⁹ jactaris Angla fluctibus ?
Discede pietas, et locū quærat fides,
en longa sanguinis sitis regno iminet.

REGINA, ANCILLA.

Regina.

Eheu recenti corda palpitant metu
gelidus per artus vadit exangues tremor,
Nocturna sic me visa miserā territant,
Et dira turbant inquietā somnia
At tu pater qui clara volvis sydera,
et igne flamiferū vago regis jubar,
omen nefandū averte, funestū, tetrū.
Jam cuncta passim blanda straverat
 quies,
somnusq fessis facilis obrepsit genis
vidi minantem concito cursu heu aprū
natosq frendens dente laniavit truci

utrosq sævus mactat. Ætheriæ potens
dominator aulæ, fata si quid filiis
dirū minantur, in hoc caput crescat
 furor,
matremq priùs jam fulmen irati petat.

Ancilla.

Quando vacabit tempus ullū cladibus ?
modūq ponit matris attonitæ dolor ?
Nam triste matri nunciū demens
 taces ?
totas an animus gaudet ærumnas suas
tractare, longos et dolores claudere ?
O regio quondā tumens fastu, potens
Regina.

Regina.

Misera voce quid media stupes ?
exire jussus non reperit viā sonus ?
fusisq turpes lachrymis genæ madent.

Ancilla.

Sævit cruento dente frendens aper.

Reg.
 Adhuc
quicquāne sceleri restat.

Ancil.
 Ah, gnati tui.

Regina.

Audire cupio miserias statim meas.

Ancil.

Heu ambo scelere suffocantur principes,
Labefacta mens succumbit : assurge :
 hei mihi,
rursus cadentem misera spiritū leva.
spirat, revixit, tarda mors miseros
 fugit.

Regina.

Regnare nunc sceleste patrue potes,
 nihil
timebit imbelles ferox pueros furor.

scelesta vibres sceptra : adhuc unū
  deest
sceleri tuo, jam sanguinē nostrum
  pete,
tui furoris misera testis haud ero.
Quem defleā infœlix ? propinquos ?
  liberos ?
anne malis superesse fata quem si-
  nunt
tantis ? Ego meos mater occidi, latus
Eduarde quando comite nudavi tuo,
et tunc asylū deseris dulcis puer.
Te, te, precor supplex mater genib⁹
  minor,
qui vindicās flamās vibras tonans pater,
et hunc vibrentur tela pjurū tua,
Spolies Olimpū irate fulminibus tuis,
et impiū cœli ruina vindicet.

Ancilla.

Quin placida cogites, animūq mitiga,
mentemq sana turbidā curis leva.

Regina.

O patrui monstrū nefandū, quale nec
Dirus Procustes novit, aut Colchos
  ferox.
O Cardinalis impii fallax fides,
cui filiū vesana mandavi meū.
O filii charissimi, ô liberi,
quos patrui crudelis ensis eripit,
suo nec unū sufficit sceleri nefas
vestrumq matri funus invident mihi.

ACTUS SECUNDUS.

Dux Buckingha: Episc. Eliensis.

Buck.

Venerande præsul Eliensis insulæ,
depone mœstitiā : prius liber licet
nunc ædibus captivus hæreas meis :
nam te meæ cum crederet fidei ferox

Princeps, parū promitto sæverū fore
Parem tibi potius amicū possides
Jam pristinæ vitæ status reminscere
et non quis es quis fuisti cogita,

Eliens.

O me beatū (pace quod dicā tua)
carcere quòd isto liberū me sentiā
Sed fata quid non graviter incusem
  mea ?
Quod mentis initiū benevolæ desinit
virtus sed animi rebus afflictis tui
solamen est quæ non potentis respi-
  cit
tam copiā, quàm quæ voluntas indigi.

Buck.

Gratū est voluntatis tuæ indiciū mihi,
Adversa quamvis singula videntur
  tibi :
Cum sic amicè me colis indignū
  tamen,
conabor, ut quæ voce jactentur mea,
hæc vera tandū expertus affirmes
  fore,
Nec fata damnes dura, quin potiùs
  probes,
tantū nec æstimes malum, te liberū
Non esse quantū est gaudiū vita frui
duras tyrannus regni habenas dū
  tenet
Quin capite quod non plecteris lucrū
  puta :
vitā dedit, dum non admit audax
  furor.
Quot cædibus cruentat insanas manus?
Quot destinavit ad necem mentis
  furor ?
dicere nequeo, nec verba sufficiunt
  mihi :
dolor tacere jussit. O nullo scelus
credibile in ævo, quodq posteritas negat.
Patruus nepotes patris heu regno ex-
  pulit.

Tantū exuit regno? necem miseris
    dedit.
Frænos dolor vix patitur, ulcisci cupit.

Eliens.

Præclara suades, inclytū durū genus.
Hoc patribus percrebuit olim pris-
    tinis,
IMPERIA SCELERE PARTA SOLVUN-
    TUR STATIM.
Tanto medelā vulneri nisi feceris,
quæret lues secreta regni vulnera.
Perdere tyrannū laus vel hostem æqua-
    lis est.

Buck.

At sceptra tutus ut regat potiùs ve-
    lim
(cujus furor paucis nocebat forsitan)
quam sede dimoveri pulsū regia
Nec talis est, ut in suos sic sæviat :
Stimulo coëgit ira, quæ nescit modū
Cujus tamen regno scio prudens ca-
    put
consulere, pax florebit æqua civibus.
Laudandus ergo, cura quem regni
    tenet,
et cui suorū civiū chara est salus.

Eliens.

Superbus eructat animus, nec con-
    tinet
sese, secretā miscet irā laudibus.
Sic principes illi cautus odiū concita,
ut te tamen sequi puteris nunc magis
stultū est diu occultare, quod prodas
    statim
Nullā mihi fidem dabis certò scio,
diversa modò si vellem juvare tibi.
Testor deū, si non fuissent irrita
Vota mea et Eduardo quod obtigit
    duci
Stetisset Henrico, stabile regni decus
Henrice, partes non reliquissem tuas.
Sed cùm secus tulere fatorū vices,
sceptraq regi deferant Eduardo, magis

quæ voluerā Henrico remansisse inte-
    gsa :
non sic furore pcitus miser fui,
ut mortui patronus illudar pius.
Calcare victorem quis audet invidus ?
Post ego sequens victoris arbitriū
    sagax,
in gratiā receptus illico fui,
vivoq nunquā fefelli tibi : tu fidem
Eduarde liberis precabor, et tuis
decora regni sceptra : longas Angliæ
tractent habenas regis orti stemate.
At quæ deus contexuit, retexere
non est meū : sed qui fuit regni
    modò
protector, is nunc regio fulget throno.
Cohibebo me : quin sacra præsulem
    vocant
senem magis, non studia regni : jam
    meis
doctus malis satis : at preces decent
    modò.

Buck.

De rege fatus obmutescit : audio
lubens, sagax de rege quidnā cogitat.
Quin perge pater, egressa verba ne
    premas,
animiq tutus vota psequere tui.
Hinc non modo periculi nihil, sed
    gratius
votis tuis mox comodu eveniet tibi.
Consultor eris in rebus incertis mihi :
Quod cogitabā, a rege cùm precib[9]
    meis
impetro tuā domi meæ custodiā.
Alterius esset fortè carcer tibi magis
molestus, hic te liberū potiùs puta.

Eliens.

Factis parem habeo gratiā (dux in-
    clyte)
at non placet tractare gesta principiū
Hic sæpe blanda tecta fronte fraus
    latet

Quæ dicta sunt bene, sæpe torquent non bene,
curamq fabula suadet Æsopi Phrigis.
Legem tulit princeps talem feris leo
passim necis pænā minatur horridus,
Cornuta silvas bellua nisi deserat
tantū tumens vesana fronte bestia
Jussus tremens regis, parat miserā fugā.
Fortè properanti vulpes occurrit sibi,
causāq mirabundus exquirit fugæ.
Sylvam fugio : Leonis (inquit) horreo
mandata : Ridet vulpes, affatur ferā,
Falsò times demens, nihil de te Leo
tantùm tumet frons tibi, gerit cornū nihil
Satis (inquit) hoc inermis et novi fera,
Sin esse cornu dixerit frendens Leo,
quid tum perempta pulchrā sane disputo :
Subridet, omnia sorte felici cadent.

Buck.

Nihil time, leo nil nocebit rugiens,
aper ne dente vulnus infliget tibi.
Nil audiet princeps eorum, quæ tu mihi
Narras secretus,

Eliens.

Hercle aures si suas
hic sermo pulset, ipse nec sumat male :
Nil tū timerem, forsitan grates daret.
Sin mala (quod auguror) potiùs affectio
interpres esset, veritatis nec penditur :
utriq verba grande conflarent malū.

Buck.

Hoc quicquid est audire mens avida cupit.

culpam lubens præstabo quamlibet, haud time
tantū meis morem geras votis pater.

Eliens.

Nihii herclè dico, sceptra quando possidet
Protector, hæc quo jure princeps vendicat,
Præcarer at suplex tamen, quod patriæ
salus requirit, cujus ille frena jam
moderatur, et pars ego fidelis extiti,
dotes ad illas addat ut clemens deus
(his licet abundat, laude nec nostra indiget
Quod in tuo numen benignū fusius
spasserit honore, dotibus abundat magis
regniq tractet meliùs habenas sui.
Cohibebo me : hæc tacere me decet magis.

Buck.

Miror quid hæret, voce quid media stupet ?
Quin seriò cum patre tremulo colloquor ?
Venerande pater, animū quid incertū tenes ?
seseq vox egressa continet statim
dum fundis interupta, concludis nihil
et crebrò spiras. Qua fide regem colas
neq scio, nec tuus amor in nos quis fuit
nostras quòd ornas præco virtutes (licet
in me reperio laudibus dignū nihil)
id me magis nunc mentis incertū tenet
sed tuā odio ardere mentem suspicor
vel amore ductus ista cæco concipis,
vel obstat ut audias vanus timor,
vel impedit pudor senem parū decens,

Effare : honorem pignoro dubio tibi tuti recessus, surdus audiā.

Eliens.

Quid est Promissa cernis, dux nimis fastu tumet, avidus honores haurit, odit principem secretus huic aperire mentem quid times ? aut regis exitiū paras, vel dū faces accendas irarū duci, tuā fugā. Captivus ex quo Regis arbitrio tuus fueram (liceat hac voce pace uti tua) Quanquā molesti carceris sentio nihil, libris levabam pectus attonitū malis, sententiā dedici revolvens optimā, quod nemo liber nascitur solū sibi Victurus, at partem parentes vendicant, partem propinqui, maxime sed patria debet parens comūnis allicere piū. dem mente volvo, debitū patriæ juvat præstare, cujus (heu) statū dum cogito; quantū micabat sumā regū gloria, tantū tyrannus nunc jugo premit gravi : Regni ruinā sceptra promittunt sua. Sed magna miseris non deest spes civibus dum corpus aspicio tuū, pulchrū decus, ignis acumen, vimq dicendi parem, sumas opes raramq virtutem ducis, præ ceteris cui chara patriæ salus patriæ labanti gratulor, cui contigit heros mederi quis malis tantis potest qui regni habenas tractet æquali manu, quas nunc tirannis opprimet Glocestria. Retineat ille nomen antiquū, novū parum placet, quod jure sceptra non tenet.

Nec invideo regnum, pios si non honor Mores simul mutasset effrænis ducis, novamq mentem nomen acciperet novū, O gravia passū nobile imperiū Angliæ graviora passurū, tyrannus si imperet Imanis usq scelera quid psequar ? Agnosco qualem stravit ad regnū viā En optimatū cæde fœdavit manus, obstare votis quos putabat improbis. O sacra regnandi sitis, quò animos trahis mortaliū ? scelestus at pgit furor. quantuq libuit audet, sceleris haud modū ponit, patravit majus et fide scelus. Ætasne credat ulla, matrem filius quòd damnet insanus probri solus suā ? Impius inurit criminis falsi notā, fratresq geminos spurios falso vocat, nec non nepotes impia notat labe, stirpemq fratris damnat ambiguā sui. Hoc est familiæ nobile tueri decus. Sed cur queror? nū sceleris hic finis fuit ? gradus mali fuit, hactenus non stat nefas. Jam regna fratris possidens non timet audire majora : miser heu implet manus funere suorū patruus, insontes necans; Erumpat ergo vis corrusca fulminis : an parcet aliis qui suos mactat ferox ? sperare quis meliora nunc demens potest ? Majora monstra triste præsagit nefas. Nunc ergo moveat temporū tandem status. Per numen æternū, p Anglorū decus; titulis superbū si genus charū tibi, succurre miseris, rumpe fatorū moras, capesse regnū, sede pulsū deprime tyrannū, ademptū vindica regni decus. Nec justa dubiū causa terreat nimis,

defende cives, chara sit patriæ salus
Comes laboris haud deesse jam potest :
plebs tota defectū rebellis murmurat:
magis subibunt barbari Turcæ regnū,
quam rex suo impius cruore luderet.
Quanto magis nunc te crearet principem,
in quo genus refulget excelsū ? meis
quiesce votis, Angliæ oblatū thronum
Nec respuas, prodesse multis dū potes,
nec te labor deterreat, si quem putas
inesse; sed sit arduū : minime tamen
pro pace patriæ deserendū publica,
Quod si recusas ptinax, nec te sinas
vinci precibus : adjuro p verū deū,
p maximi ducis fidem, sancto simul
quondam p astrictā fidem Georgio
insignis ascitus eques ordinis Garterii
quando fuisti primùm, ut in nostrū
   caput
sermonis hujus culpa grassetur nihil.
Hoc publicis imploro precib⁹ civiū
Sin alterius optanda sceptra dexteræ
quæris : throno Lancastriæ pulsū genus
addas paterno, aut filiū Eduardi patris
throno superbo nobilis jungas viri.
Sic impiū tyrannus exitiū feret,
et cladibus defessa gens ponet modū,
habes meā de rebus his sententiā.
Cur sic tacet ? miror : metuo multū
   mihi :
suspiriū ducit : fidemne decipit ?

Buck.

Video timore distrahi pectus pater.
doloris ansā (doleo) quod tacens dedi.
tu macte sis virtute : non fallā fidem.
O magne cœli rector, et mundi arbiter,
quantū tibi devincta gens est Anglica ?
qui fluctuantem sæpiùs regni statu
Clemens deus manu benigna protegis ?
Jam statue tandem gravibus ærumnis
   modū,

clementer animi spiritū inspira pater,
ut principem quæramus auspiciis tuis,
qui justa tractet sceptra regali manu,
statimq rebus collocet lassis opem
Reverende sedis præsul Eliensiū,
specimen dedisti mentis erga me tuæ
clarā satis amoremq testor patriæ
par culpa nostri, quare nil time dolos
de rege mentis sensa prorsus eloquar,
vires cur illi adjutor adjunxi meas.
retinere postquā non potest fati colos
Eduardus ejus nominis quartus, mori
sed fata cogunt : liberis parū suis
fui benevolus, ille quod meritis parūm
dignū referret præmiū, generis mei
titulos nec altos æstimavit invidus
Ergo minùs orbos tū colebā liberos
patris inimici. Vulgo jactatur vetus
dictū facilè regnū labi, cujus tenet
rex puer habenas : Cœpta tū comes
   tua
Richarde faveo, judicavi tū virū
fuisse clementem, atq nunc video ferū
hac fraude plurimùm allicit mentes
   pias,
ut publico Protector assensu Angliæ
renunciatus esset, et regis simul.
accensa sic honore mens fuit novo,
ut cùm secundū possidet regni locū,
tantùm placere sceptra cœperunt
   statim.
Regni decora poscit ad tempus sibi
teneros nepos dum complet annos debilis.
Dubitare postquā nos videt, regni
   fidem
nec fallimus, spurios nepotes tū probat
patruus scelestus : credimus tandem
   sibi,
statimq nostri fræna regni tradimus.
damnavit hæredem ducis Clarentiæ.
crimen paternū, jura avita pdidit
Regni thronū, Richarde sic paras tibi
ruisq tandem, quò furor traxit tuus
regnare liceat (ut lubet) jam neminē

æquū est metuere, nullus est hostis
ferox,
obstare sceptris nemo jam potest tuis.
At quis minister funeris tanti fuit ?
Tu, tu tyrannus natus ad patriæ luem,
tu prole matrem sævus orbaris sua,
nec abstines à cæde cognita miser,
teneros nepotes patruus injustus necas.
Quorū necis cū fama penetrasset meas.
aures, trementes horror occupat vagus
artus, venas deserit hiantes intimus
cruor, soluta membra diffluunt.
Nobis salubre pollicemur inscii,
incerta dū sit propriæ domus salus
Mihi damnat injustū frequens injuria.
Avita si ad justus hæres prædia
sumiq vendico munus comestabulis.
graviter repulsā læsus ingratā tuli.
Nunquid dabit nova, qui suū nunquā
dedit.
At si dedisseꝉ non tamen gratis daret.
Ope namꝗ nostra possidet imperii
decus.
Agnosco culpā, quū mea carens ope
Nunquā feroci sceptra gestasset manu.
Fratris redundat in meū crimen caput,
manuq patriæ vulnus inflixi meæ.
Hoc expiabo si medelā fecero ;
medebor ergo, sicq decrevi priùs,
justā querelā durus ubi tū respuit
Non amplius me contineo : dicā ordine
quodcunq mente absconditū tacita
latet,
Cum regis animū scelere plenū cernerē
in odium amor imutatur, ulcisci paro,
Quem sū passus ejus aspectū statim
tuli molestè, ferre nec vultū queo.
Aulā relinquo regiā, domū peto,
dum cœpi iter, mea facile tunc dextera
erepta posse sceptra transferri puto,
regnare postquā populus iratus jubet.
Quo mihi placebā ludicro titulo diu,
et justus hæres domus Lancastriæ
mihi falsò videor, ambiens regni
thronū.

Hæc cogitanti subitò me rogat obvia
Richmondiæ comitissa, redditū filio
precarer exuli : si rex benignus an-
nuat,
tum regis Eduardi relictæ filiæ
natū suū despondet ad castos thoros :
dotem nihil moratur, una dos erit
Regis favor, nec amplius mater petit.
Hic nostra pereunt regna : tū mihi
exciderat animo filio primū suo
matriq jus patêre regni : somniū
thronus fuit, regnūq frustra vendico.
Contemno primū vota Comitissæ pia.
Mens altius dum cogitat matris preces,
tum spiritu impulsā sacro matrem,
bonū
sensisse regni nesciā imensū puto,
Infensa si domus thronos jungit pios,
quæ sceptra jure dubia vendicat suo
æterna fieret civib[9] tranquillitas,
solidamq pacis alliget rectæ fidem,
hæresq dubiæ certus esset Angliæ.

Eliens.

O recta patriæ spes, salus, solatiū
respicere cœpit mitis afflictos deus.
O sancta lecti jura legitimi, Anglia,
tibi gratulor, lætare, solamen venit.

Buck.

Nunc tata quib[9] arcana tuti pandim[9]
Matris priùs mentem decet cognos-
cere.

Eliens.

Jam nostra votis cœpta succedent
satis
Servus fidelis ecce Comitissæ venit,
ut nos licèt lentus juvas miseros deus !
Brai potentis servū Comitissæ, tuæ
domine salutis gratus esto nuntius.
Jactata pacis appulit portū ratis :
mox natus horæ sceptra gestabat
manu,
si jure jurando suā astringet fidem
face velit sibi jugali jungere
quæ nata major regis Eduardi fuit.

Nati ergo faustos mater ambiet
  thronos,
ut sede pellatur sua rex impius.

Bra.

Tam læta domine, nuncius ferā
  lubens.
quamcunq vobis atq prestabo fidem.

Buck.

De rege tandem memet ulciscar
  probè :
de sede malè parta triumphabit parū.
Nunc sævus infensū inveniet aper sibi
fortem leonem, qui unguib⁹ tantū valet
quantū ille dente : jā scelere cumula
  scelus :
Crudelis imple cæde funestas manus :
adhuc iniquè jura detineas mihi :
dominare tumidus, spiritus altos gere :
sequitur superbos ultor à tergo deus,
Reddes coactus, sponte quæ negas
  mihi :
Nuper superbus Eboraci fastu tumens,
Cinctus corona, vestibus claris nitens
spectanda præbet ora stupidis civibus,
diadema pariter cinxit uxoris caput,
celebratq plebs honore divino levis :
portendit excelsus ruinā spiritus.

Eliens.

Tu tu tyrannū morte mulctabis ferox
si liber essem, vinculis nudus tuis,
meaq septus insula tota satis,
nihil furentis horreā regis minas :
nunc ergo liceat pace discedā tua.

Buck.

Dispersa perdit turba vires debilis,
unita fortiùs minatur hostibus manus;
morare paulùm, milites dū colligo :
defendet armatus tuā miles viā.

LODOVICUS MEDICUS.

Comitissa mater læta Braii nuntia
postquā sui nati de nuptiis acceperat,
ut regis Eduardi priori filiæ
si sacra lecti iura sponderet comes
Richmondius, speraret amissū thronū,
adire reginā jubet celeri gradu,
tentare mentem sponte quasi pulsā
  mea :
ut qui peritus arte medicorū fui,
fœdera medelis sacra miscerem meis,
Lectumq promissū comitis Richmondii.
Nunc ergo Lodovice, jussus exequi
decet fideles, vince matrem, ne thoros
comiti negaret conjugales filiæ.

EPŪS ELIENSIS FUGIENS.

Deserere nolens cogor hospitiū ducis
turbata magnū consilia suadent metū.
Nunc ergo consulā mihi celeri fuga.
Quàm nunc manus miser hostiū sævas
  tremo ?
sed cautus incedā, insulā petā meā,
sulcabo salsa nave mox et æquora,
hopesq tutus bella spectabo procul.
Te, te potens mundi arbiter supplex
  precor,
ab hoste servū protegas sævo tuū.

LODOVICUS, REGINA.

Lod.

Regina servans conjugis casta fide
lectū jugalem, siste misera lachrimas,
adesse spera jam malis finem tuis.
Parumper aure verba facilis percipe
vacato nostris precib⁹: inveni modū
quo trux tyrannus debitas pœnas luat,
tractentq rursus sceptra felici manu
tui nepotes, rege dejecto truci :
procerū sibi, plebisq concitat odiū

Richardus, invisū eximere regno student.
Jam vulgus insano crebescit murmure,
quàm ferre possunt gravius imponi
jugū,
an sceptra speremus benigna principis?
neci nepotes patruus infantes dedit.
Querela civiū frequens pulsat Jovem
amare nequiunt, quem execrantur
publicè
servile collo populus excuteret jugū
si notus hæres esse imperii sibi.
Richmondiæ (nunc exul) Henricus
comes
hæres familiæ certus est Lancastriæ:
huic filiæ sociare si thalamos jubes,
nullus de regni jure hæses disputat.

Regina.

Quod pepulit aures nuntiū lætū meas?
quid audio? nū misera mens est credula?
hæc facilè credunt quod minis miseri
volunt.
Sed quod volunt, fortuna contumax
vetat.
Prona est timori semper in pejus
fides.
Regnat tyrannus, exul Henricus
comes,
est vulgus anceps, dubius et populi
favor
Quæ filiæ facilis patet meæ via
ad sceptra?

Lodov.

Voto tremulus obstabit timor.
Confide causæ, civiū pugnat salus:
prudens familiæ consulas mater tuæ:
cædis recentis immemor sobolis jaces
cur sic inultā te sinis? stimulet dolor
cædis tuorū, et conjugis chari probrū.

Regina.

Spem pollicetur animus invitam trahens.
Dotāre thalamo filiā Elizabeth velim:
sed spernet illā forsan Henrici parens
illam petas; scrutare nū maneat vetus
domus simultas, exulis gnati potest
Flecti malis, ut fieret ex misero potens.

Lodov.

Regina, peragam jussa.

Reg.

Respiret deus
consilia læta, perge non dubio gradu.

DUX BUCK. AD MILITAS.

Ultrice dextrā, milites, sævus cadat
comunis hostis ille, tum quisquis
comes
fuerit tyranni, jaceat et pene comes.
Quid ira posset, durus expromat dolor
Utinā cruorē capitis invisi deo
libare possim! multa mactatur Jovi
opima magis arasve tinxit victima
quam rex iniquus [aut tirannus im-
pius].
Violenta nemo imperia continet diu,
sperare tanti sceleris quis demens potest
regnū salubre, vel fidem tutā dui?
vobis scelestæ mentis exponā dolū.
Bellū parari dū videt, mox literas
mittit benignas, spondet agros, nil
negat
sensi dolū, morā traho, veniā peto.
Ægre repulsā passus imperat statim
venire? adhuc recuso; sed veniā tamen,
Veniam, Richarde, sed malo tandem
tuo

Et ultor adero inimicus infensus tibi
miseris Britannis pacis autor publicæ.
Fugiéns asylū Marchio Dorcestrius
vim militū magnā Eboraci colligit.
Ducem sequuntur Devoniensis Curt-
　　næū.
viresque fratris adjuvat sacrū caput
Episcopi Exetrensis : infesto agmine
Gilfordus impiū tyrannū eques petit,
frequensq Cantii caterva militū.
Mactetur hostis, bella poscunt, im-
　　pias
dirus suorū carnifex pœnas luat.
Ergo tyrannū patriæ pestem suæ
trucidate, cū sit grata civibus hostia,
præsidia cum sint tanta, quæ partes
　　student
nostras tueri, et patriæ vitā dare,
omnesq dux ferā lubens angustias,
ut hostis pereat vester ferox Nero.
Quid desidemus? arma cur cessant
　　pia?
cedendo vinci ut perfidos hostes putes
stultè nimis votisq pulsando Jovem
vibrentur enses, copias jungi decet ;
ad arma ruite, vos ferox hostis manet :
pugnate validi, vir viro inferat manus
tollantur altè signa, bellū tuba canat,
et excitetur classico miles truci.

ACTUS TERTIUS.

RICHARDUS REX SOLUS.

O sæva fata semper, ô sortem as-
　　perā
cum sævit et cum parcit ex æquo
　　malā
Fortuna fallax rebus humanis nimis
insultat, agili cuncta pvertens rota.
Quos modò locavit parte suprema,
　　modò
ad ima eosdem trudit et calcat pede.
Subitio labantis ecce fortunæ impetu

quis non potentem cernit eversa
　　domū?
Heu gnatus. heu primò unicus periit
　　meus
(ô dura fata, et lugubrem sortem
　　nimis)
qui clara patris regna sperat mortui.
Ut ille magni parvus armenti comes,
primisq vixdum cornibus frontem
　　gerens
cervice subito celsus, et capite arduus
gregem paternū ducit, et pecori im-
　　perat.
O suave pignus, ô decus domus
Regalis, ô Britanniæ fumus tuæ,
O patris heu spes vana, cui demens
　　ego
laudes Achillis bellicas, et Nestoris
annos precabar, luce privavit deus.
Nunquā potenti sceptra gestabis manu
felix, Britanno jura nec populo dabis,
victasq gentes sub tuū mittes jugum:
Non Franca subiges terga, non Scotos
　　trahes
in tua rebelles imperia, sine gloria
jacebis alto clausus in tumulo miser.
Porro exul hærens finib[9] Britanniæ
dirū parat bellū Comes Richmondius.
viresq cogit sceptra rapturus mea.
Domi cruorem populus en nostrū
　　petit,
incendit animos ptinax nimiū furor,
sceleris ministros armat in nostrā
　　necem
Quidā minantem virib[9] Richmondiū
juvare ; quida firma præsidia arcibus
locare? quidā clanculū armatos domi
servare, quidā subditos ; fidem ut suā
fallant, rogare precibus infensi student
Nescire velim, cuncta simulavi lubens
dum cæca potui cœpta, concilia dolos
sentire, militūq vires jungere.
Hujus furoris cū ducem Bucking-
　　hamiū
caput esse scirem, et totius fontem
　　mali

Vel marte aperto trahere, vel precibus piè
allicere cepi, ne fidem muttat suā,
Dedi benignas ad ducem magis literas,
Felix ad aulā convolet celeri gradu :
Sentit dolos dux, texuit causas moræ
stomachiq se dolore rudit premi,
Omnem statim morā jubebā rumpere.
Venturū ad hostem patriæ sese negat.
Et milites cogens suos dux pessimus,
in me nefanda bella demens comovit.
Quid facio ? amicus qui mihi sumus
fuit
auferre regna quærit : odit maximè
qui maximè colebat : ô scelus impiū !
et dux profundo devovende Tartaro.
At plebs velut procella ventis turbida,
agmine scelesto principem neci petit :
Solus Richardus causa cantatur mali
Quid nunc agendū restat ? aut quem
consulā ?
Infecta facta reddere haud quivis potest.
Si populus odit, pereo ? sed populi
favor
servetur, isto macula tolletur modo,
qua nomen indui scelestus heu meū ;
ut in Britannos si quid erumpat malū
damnent nihil, jam mitis, humanus,
pius,
et iiberalis civibus meis ero,
et scelere vindicabo nomen impio.
Centū sacrifitiis alta surgent mœnia,
curis soluti ut precibus incumbant
piis :
Legesq patriæ utiles ferā meæ
fortasse nostras populus in ptes ruet,
pietate falsa ductus : auri montibus,
blandisq verbis ducitur vulgus leve.

NUNTIUS, REX RICHARDUS.

Nuntius.

Aurero ducem fugisse Buckinghamiū,
magnæq quid nunc dissipantur copiæ.

Rich. Rex.

Quæ causa subitò terga vertendi fuit ?

Nuntius.

Ubi Wallicorū numerat ingentē manu,
qua sylva sese porrigit Danica, viā
pandit superbus, et Sabrinā nobile
superare flumen properat, agmini suo
ut Courtneorū jungat agmen ; at
minas
dum spirat horrens impio dux agmine,
at non genus mortale curant Numina ?
dum milites vicina spectant flumina
altasq ripas non datur adhuc tangere,
subitò gravis terrā ruina cœli verberat
divesq pluviis laxat imbres humidūs
Auster, et agros altùm tegit frequens
aqua.
En piscis ignotas in auras tollitur,
Lectis jacentes arboribus hærent, agris
eversa, tecta : vagit in cunis puer
passim per agros, montibus natant
feræ,
terrā diebus obruunt aquæ decem
Stupet miles, cū Courtneiorū copiis
jungere pfusus agmen haud fluvius
sinit.
At Wallicorū turba nulla præmio
invita serviens duci, carens simul
misera cibariis, statim illū deserunt :
Nullis minis gens Cambria adduci
potest
aut precibus, ut maneat simul belli
comes,
aut pergat ultra. Præda nudus hostibus
suis relictus, cepit infœlix fugam.

Rex Rich.

Fœlix ad aures nuntius nostras venit
prius labantem fausta tollunt numina.
Portus ad omnes miles undiq sepiat,
dux exteras ne erumpat ad gentes.
Comes

Richmondius quidnā parat, quærat
   simul :
nun cœpta linquat, an minetur amplius.
Princeps honorem testor, illū qui mihi
captū reducet, præmiū dignū feret.
Si servus ille fuerit emittā manu :
sin liber, illū mille ditabo libris.
Classis Britannū armatạ sulcabit mare,
ne perfidus premat Angliā Richmondius.
Aude scelera, ne crescat malū :
exprimere jus est ense, quod nequeant
   preces.
Quicunq sceleris socius in nostras
   manus
veniet, piabit sanguine inceptū nefas.

NUNTIUS, REX RICHARDUS.

Nuntius.

Captus tenetur vinculis Buckinghamius.

Rex Rich.

Sacris colamus prosperā votis diem.
O mihi propitios, sed tamen lentos
   dies [*al.* deos] !
hostis quib⁹ captus dolis sit, explica !

Nuntius.

Ubi Cambrio dux milite orbatū vidit,
obstupuit illicò, atq sorte tā gravi
pculsus, animū pene despondit suū
consilii egenus, sed sibi fidit tamen,
Banisteri tremens ad ædes clā fugit,
cui dux amore eximio priùs favebat,
et semp auxit dignitate plurimùm :
hujus latêre clā studebat ædibus,
donec cohortem reparet, et belli
   ruinas
nudusve mare fugeret secans Britannū,

Comitiq sese jungeret Richmondio.
At malè deorū si quis invisus duci
fuerit, paratū non potest fugere malū.
Servus Banister, seu vitæ timens suæ,
tuisve ductus præmiis, Salopiæ
Proconsul, tum Mitton proditum
   ducem
Is militū stipante pgit agmine,
servi præhendit ab ædib⁹ sui haud
   procul,
dum fata sylvis dira solus cogitat,
tibiq vinctū fidus adducit virū.

Richardus.

Si non fides me sacra regno contin-
   ent,
tentabo mea stabilire sceptra sanguine,
et regna duro sævus imperio regā
Nunc ergo dux pœnas gravissimas
   luat.
Obrumpat ensis noxiū tristis caput,
nullamq pene carnifex reddat morā.
Regnare nescit, odia qui timet nimis.
Non tua mihi Stanleie dubia fides
   fuit.
Comes sitit Richmondius honores
   meos.
Gener tuus sibi sceptra despondet
   mea.
uxor suo comitissa quærit filio
Victrice dextra rapta sceptra tradere.
rapidis volabis gressibus Lancastriā :
illā intimis reclude mox penetralibus,
pateat nec nullū fœminæ servoru iter,
ad filiū nullas mater det literas,
ne patriæ demens luem tristem paret,
et sceptra mihi mulier rebellis auferat,
At Strangeū præstantem honore filiū
fidei tuæ mecū relinques præsidem :
testabitur puer patris constantiā
Natura mentem fœminæ pronā malo
dedit, dolisq pectuš instruxit, negat
vires, malū ut tantū queat vindicare.

Dux Buckinghamius.

O blandientis lubricū sortis decus !
ô tristis horrendi nimis belli casus !
heu, heu fatis mortale luditur genus.
Quisquāne sibi spondere tā firmū
   potest
quod non statim metuenda convellat
   dies !
Cujus refulsit nomen Anglis inclytū
modò, pallidos nunc ad lacus trudor
   miser.
Quid (heu) juvat jactare magnos
   spiritus ?
Fallacis aulæ fulgor (heu) quos perdidit ?
Heu blanda nimiū dona fortunæ !
   mare
non sic aquis refluentibus turget, aut
   undis
turbatus ab imis pontus Euxinus
   tumet,
ut cæca casus heu fortuna magnatū
   vocat.
Funestus heu dirusq Richardi favor
quid illa deplorem miser tempora,
   quibus
fretus meo consilio aper frendens, sibi
regnū cruento dente raptū comparat ?
En, hujus ictu nunc atroci corruo.
Natale solū, illustre decus ô Angliæ,
horrenda quæ te fata nunc manent ?
   ferox
postquā jugo tyrannus oppressū tenet
heu, heu, miser Stygeas ad undas de-
   primor,
Crudelis et collo securis iminet.

ACTUS QUARTUS.

RICARD. REX, NUNTIUS, LOVELL :
   HEROS, CATESBEIUS.

Richardus.

Quid me potens fortuna fallaci nimis
blandita vultu graviūs ut ruerem, edita

de rupe tollis ! finis alterius mali
gradus est futuri : dira conspirat
   manus
in me rebellis, torqueor metu miser.
disrumpor æstuante curarū salo.
Richmondiensis ille pfidus comes
in transmarinis ambit (heu) regnū
   locis :
In cujus arma jurat turba civiū
inimica : mox hujus mali tanti metu
famulos cruenta morte mulctavi meos.
at fama vexat turgidū pectus magis :
thalamos jugales filiæ Richmondio
Comiti studet regina mater jungere.
O triste facinus, hostis in nostra
   potens
regnabit aula, meq fatis destinat.

Nunt.

Richmondiensis incubat ponto comes.

Rex.

O flenda fata ! Gesta quæ sunt, explica.

Nunt.

Ubi ter, quatuor, implesset October
   dies,
Oculis profundū mane spectantes
   fretū,
Vagas carinas vidimus appellere.
Portū petunt Dorcestriū, quem Polū
vocant. Dubia nos turba spectontes
   diu
manemus illic. Nave tum prætoria
comitem ferocem novimus Richmondiæ
Auxilia forsan alia sperantes manent
aliquot diebus : ut nos celsas vident
ripas tenentes, littus appellant simul
Num simus hostes, miles an charus
   duci
quærunt : vafros nos fingimus vultu
   dolos
ibi milites locasse Buckinghamium,
ut comitis adventū maneret exulis,

dubiūq mox ad castra deducant ducis
Junctæ facilè possent phalanges vincere.
Rex maximo sepultus obruitur metu.
Hi blanda verba suspicantes, carbasa
complente vento laxa comittunt mari,
velisq pansis advolant Britanniā.

Rex.

Cur ludis inconstans nimis miserū
dea?
nup locatū me levas sumā rota,
auraq molli prosperos affers dies :
illico supinū lubrico affligis solo.
Quàm varia? quàm maligna? quam
levis dea?

Lovell.

Cur vexat animū cura vesanū gravius?
ubi prisca virtus? pellat ignavos
metus
excelsus animus : [fortis haud novit
metum.]
Mullo periculo nobilis virtus labat.
Quorsū ducis manes tremiscis mortui?
quorsū rebelles cæteros? an non jacent
terra sepulti? pulverem demens times?
Promissus hymen, et fides Scotis data
illos fideles pacis officio tenent.
Mandata legati duci Britanno
tua deferunt, agros sibi rebelliū
promittis, armis sceptra si juvet tua.
Quem non movebunt ampla promittā
præmi
desine timere : quod satis tutū est
times.

Cates.

Si præmiis dux pertinax ductus tuis
non exeitetur aliud incœptū manet.
Richmondio disjunge promissos thoros
neptis tuæ : Lancastriis si non opem
ferat domus Eborū (fremat licet ferox)
frustra minatur : differa connubiū

Richmondii, nec filiæ Eduardi faces
celebrent jugales, si frui voto vellis.

Rex.

Rapietur illico, finietq nuptias
districtus ensis, Tartaro nubet priùs.

Lovell.

At est asyli grande violati nefas :
meliora cogita : ista non prodest tuo
medicina morbo : culpa non sanat
reos,
nec est aperto scelere pugnandū
scelus.
Et nuper allectus tibi populus fuit
quem plurimis dudū modis colere
studes.
statim scelere pculsus inani, oderit.

Cates.

Quod impetrari mollibus precibus
potest,
non est minis duris parandū, voce vel
sæva tyranni neq frigido metu.

Rex.

Tædasne demens patiar invisas mihi
meoq sceptro contrahi? nunquā ac-
cidet.
Scelesta nostrū firmat impietas thronū
audebo quodvis : scelere vincendū
scelus :
violare jura facilè regnanti licet.
In rebus aliis usq pietatem colas.
Stringatur ensis: Regna tutatur cruor.

Lovell.

Regina tenera mollibus verbis potest
utrinq torqueri facilè, mox deferant
jussus tuos legati ad illā, ut filias
suas in aulā adduci mater sinat.

Cates.

Si socia thalami fortè moriatur tui,
neptem statim vince ducendā tibi,
illoq pacto fracta spes comitis erit.

Rex.

Placet, quod inquis ! potius quā
   regnū ruat,
tentanda cuncta : triste consiliū tamen
dum vivit uxor : hanc decet lætho
   dari.

Lovell.

Frequentet illā rumor esse mortuā.

Rex.

Cum salva fuerit illa, quid rumor potest.

Lovell.

Fortasse longa oppressa curarū tabe
morietur : utq mors sit illi certior,
illico suborna qui susurret clanculū
fecunda quid non sit, fore infestā tibi.
Arcenda thalamis sterilis uxor tuis est.
Aulā beare sobole fœlici decet
Regem : doloris sæva ppetua lues
matura timidæ fata fœminæ dabit.

Rex.

Mactabo potiùs, ense læthali, priùs
tollam veneno, quā mea pestis throni
cladesq fuerit : vosq quos semp colo
faciles animi, fida Magnatū manus,
adite templū, tum meis verbis piè
matrem salutantes, colere me dicite,
vitæq sordes esse mutatas meæ
contendo, quævis opprimat silentiū.
Populi favorem nequeo nancisci priùs
quam fratris ut complectar olim filias,
quorū duós miser fratres neci dedi,
natumq Marchionem honore prosc-
   quar.
amplos agros promitte, magnas et
   opes,
si gratus Anglia exul illico venerit.

RICHARDUS REX SOLUS.

Animū tumultus volvit attonitus, rupit
regni metus, quiescere nec usquā
   potest,

sanare nunc malū queo solū, face
neptem jugali si maritus jungerem
Uxor sed obstat : scelera novimus
   prius
quid conjugem cessas veneno tollere ?
aude anime, nū peccata formidas tuā ?
serò pudet : peracta pars sceleris mei
olim fuit maxima : piū esse quid
   juvat ?
post tanta miserū facinora, nihil facis.
Parat animus nefanda, parva nec placent.
Regnū tuemur : omnis in ferro salus.

LOVELL : REGINA ELIZAB. REX RICHARDUS.

Lovell.

O socia thalami regis olim, fœmina
illustris, ad te nos legatos principis
fecere jussus, ut soluta sacro carcere
aulā sequaris splendidam mater potens.
Nec moveat antè Regis imensū scelus,
quem tantopere vitæ scelestæ pœnitet :
matura sanctè suadet ætas vivere
Vitā cupit mens lapsa spurcā ponere,
serumq cepit vitii fastidiū.
Dum vincere cupis, arma delectant
   magis
nescit modū sibi strictus ensis ponere :
at placida victori magis pax expedit,
quem civiū quivis tumultus territat
Partā priùs ne perderet iterū gloriā,
a plebe rex quæsivit ardenter coli.
Hoc efficere priùs nequit princeps
   pius,
nisi tê tuasq filias sancte colat,
et splendidis illas locaret nuptiis,
cujus necavit filios heu turpiter,
En concidit dolore confectus gravi,
fletu rigantur ora sceleris vindice :
vitæ tantùm corrigendæ defuit.
honos tuarū, filiusq marchio

Dorcettus heros, qui p̄ oras nunc
      vagus
incognitas perrat exul. Si domū
reversus, arma deserat Richmondii,
florebit alto clarus imperio statim
illustris heros, sibi patebunt omnia
fulgentis aulæ dona : nil frustra petet.
Nunc ergo quæras lumen aulæ splen-
      didū,
In gratiā, Regina cum principe redi
nec regis animū sperne tam charū tibi :
sed dulce pignus filias animi tui
mittas ad aulā, adhuc nec obscuro
      horreant
loco, pius quas diligit rex unice.
Quid mœsta terram conticescis in-
      tuens ?
errore quid pectuṣ vago versas tuū ?

Regina.

Ergo filiorū sanguine madentes
      manus ?
non liberos crudelis occidit fratris ?
nostrosq conspersit thoros falsa labe ?
an non potest matri scelestus parcere,
infame generi vulnus inflixit suo
Sævire ferrū cessat, ubi regnat furor ?
Quisquamne putet ullū deesse nequitæ
      moḍū ?
Sævire cum ratione num quisquā po-
      test ?
Strictus tuetur ensis, invitis tuis
quicquid tenere te scias, quicquid
      scelus
peperit, tuetur majus admissū scelus.
Haud dulcis aula, cruore quæ meo
      fluit.
Quas nuptias meorū meorū sanguine ?
An filiarū nuptias celebret ? priùs,
reddat sepulcrū filiorū, plangere
funera meorū mater efflagito priùs,
suis debetur atq mortuis honor.

Lovell.

Sepulta quid renovas odia ? pectus
      premet

æterna vesanū ira ? patratū liceat
scelus expiare : quid juvat gemitu
      adeo
opplere cœlū ? vel lamentis æthera
pulsare ? toties vulneri quid heu
      manus
adfers ? medelā nec pati potes mali ?
Si quisq quoties peccat, illico Jupiter
iratus ignes vindices jaculabitur :
orbis jacebit squalido turpis situ
et tanta damna sobole turpis situ
et tanta damna sobole repararet sua
nunquā Venus cunctis petita viris ?
      adhuc
ferrūne terret.

Reg.

Cujus ictu concidi.

Lovell.

At melius infligens mededetur vulneri.

Reg.

Ad arma nova perrumpit ira sæpius.

Lovell.

Despecta magis irascitur clementia.

Reg.

Veteratus at nescit furor clementiā.

Lovell.

Quid arma metuis, ira quando extin-
      guitur ?

Reg.

Haud sanguinis saties sitim, nisi ex-
      pleas.

Lovell.

At in cruore quod est necesse sufficit.

Reg.

At triste furioso necesse quod libet ?

Lovell.

At ira vana luditur sine viribus,
cœptiq mox timerarii nimis pudet.
Quod si furore pectus attonitus times,
Et regis horres impias adhuc minas :
hæc sola spes relicta : pugnandū
prece :
Luctantibus nihil valebis viribur,
Sed fortius cōmota mens ebulliet,
nullamq vim patitur sibi resistere.

Reg.

Heu mihi mulier, heu, heu, quid infœlix agā ?
animus vacillans fluctuat, timet omnia,
sperare rursus jussit omissus thronus,
Tradamne regi filias ? egone meas
honore privabo ? aula filias decet.
At quid facis ? cui credis ? insontes
tuos
mactavit, an parcit sorori ? Jus idem
utriq regni. Cujus heu thoro meas
Rex filias cōmendat, has qui turpiter
matre editas mentitus est adultera ?

Lovell.

Errore quorsū pectus uris anxiū ?
Sin vita regis sancta ñil psuadeat,
Sed hujus animū adhuc ferocem som-
nias
quantū tibi iratus minetur, cogita,
Hujus benigna vota si contempseris.

Reg.

An morte quicquā minatur amplius ?

Lovell.

Exosa vitā filias num destrues ?

Reg.

O filiæ charissimæ, heu, heu, filiæ.
dotare vos thalamis beatis rex parat,
abite, vos fortuna quò miseras jubet,
et supplices ad genua patrui sternite

dedisce regnū infausta proles principis,
privata vos decent magis : regnū
nocet :
facre juvet, quicquid necessitas jubet.
Omnia timore plena : metuendū tamen
palam nihil : nunquā preces spernit
leo
timidæ feræ, nec supplices temnit
sonos.
Si sors beabit fausta, jussit en parens
vos ire : sin crudele fatū pderet,
Ulciscar ipse morte eadem me simul,
meiq pœnas mater incœpti ferā.
Adsis fidelis particeps mentis meæ :
celeri gradu oras Galliæ mox advola,
gnatoq Marchioni reditū suadeas,
dubium nil rerū exitū pavesceret,
nec horreat minas cruenti principis.
Sceleris sui regem nefandi pœnitet,
deflet cruenta miser nepotū funera,
sibiq larga pollicetur præmia,
magnosq honores, atq liberā malis
vitam : ergo præceps vela pandat
prospera,
charamq rursus patriā reddat sibi.

Rex. Rich.

Geminas video sorores : ô faustū
diem.
Compone vultum, amplectar illas
arctius.
Neptes amandæ, quàm libens vos os-
culor.
vestræ miserandam doleo fortunæ
vicem,
itaq sacro ægrè carcere inclusas tuli.
Quapropter hunc mutabo luctū flebi-
lem
in gaudiū, atq veste præclara induā,
vobisq magnatū parabo nuptias.
Jam gaudet animus ; pace sperata
fruor.
Has nuptias uxoris invisū caput

perturbat.   Anna huc confert tristem
   gradū :
Concepta ménte scelera vultu contegā,
ægrāq verbis molliā mentem piis.

REGINA ANNA, RICHARD. REX,
   NUNTIUS.

Reg. Anna.

Heu quantis curarū fluctibus æstuo?
Quid mihi horrendi præsagit animus
   mali?
In lugubres rumpamne suspiria voces?
et quærulis ferā corusca sydera planc-
   tīs?
Quid misera faciam? fata deplorā
   mea?
En, rumor perebuit vitā oblatā mihi,
et garrula volavit fama funeris mei :
ergo vivæ mihi sepulcrū quæritur,
Et nostra lachrymis viva decoro
   funera,
cogorq jussa mihi nunc psolvere.
Cur mihi meus minatur ingratus necem?
nihilq nostros amores crudelis æsti-
   mat?
Cardinalis antistes mihi gravis pater
fletu genis madentib⁹ nunciat.
Rex (inquit) jamdudū saturavit amorē,
nec dabit amplexus, aut oscula figet
   ducia :
Te sterilem esse, Regali nec aptā
   thoro.
Talem regiæ conjugem poscunt faces,
Qualis liberorū possit procreare magnū
   decus,
qui tenera patris sceptra gestabit
   manu.
Variis animus curarū fluctib⁹ æstuat,
rumorq vexat scelestus augur fati
   mei.
Quid faciam misera? en quærunt neci
Nostræq vitæ ultimos claudere dies,
vitæq rupta fila eripere sororibus.

Illustre Britanniæ decus, rector potens,
quid misera merui? quid ad mortē
   trahor :
En mortem pstrepunt garrulæ voces,
et ad sepulcrū funesta turba vocat.
Si non placet thalamis fides tuis
   data,
aut si tuū demens honorem læsi, invida
aut manibus pudica moriar tuis,
et scelesta tuus fodiat ensis viscera,
nec populi millies suis vulnerent vocibus,
et sordidis regina civibus occidam.

Rex. Rich.

Nunquā miser charæ pararem conjugi
mortem, castasq tuo cruore manus
   spargerem.
Nec te minæ pturbent, cū futilis
erroris esse populus magister solet :
nec principi plebs novit garrula parcere.
Jam siste lachrymas, teq cura molliùs.
En nos graves premunt curæ Britanniæ,
motusq turbidos cives rebelles con-
   citāt ;
Hos maximū decet ducem compes-
   cere :
post, mutuis simul fruemur amplexibus.

Nuntius.

Fugit manus Comes Richmondius
   tuas.

Rich.

Effare, carcerem cur evasit tetrū?

Nunt.

Postquā sinus complente laxos vince-
   rent
Impulsa vento vela fluctus turbidos,

littusq puppis tangeret Britannicū,
mandata monstramus duci statim tua.
Hujus dolor premebat artus languidos
nec rebus ullis æger animus sufficit,
Hinc jussa rerū cura Thesaurario
soli fuit, Petrū vocant Landosiū :
Huic mox agros promittimus rebelliū,
fortuna vel benigna quicquid addidit,
·si patriæ restituat exulem suæ
Richmondiū, comitesq cæteros fugæ.
Promissa vincunt ampla thesaurariū,
Anglisq tanti gaudet autor muneris,
quò se tueri possit Anglorū potens
viribus, et hostis frangat iras invidi.
Mox concito quærit gradū comitē
velox
at sensit astus callidos comes priùs,
furtoq se subduxit ille Parisiis.
Tum dura quos fortuna jungit trans-
fugas
comites sequuntur : at dolet Lando-
sius
prædam sibi ereptam esse, sed serò
dolet
Cæleri cupit vi prævertere elapsū
licèt,
terramq calcantes pede ruunt concito
hastas vibrantes extra equites, si
queaut
tardare fugientem : tamen redeunt
statim
illisq tantus cessit incassū labor.
Nam Rege fretus Gallico tutus satis,
implorat adversā tuis sceptris opem.
Nec finis hic mali : solutus carcere
Oxonii fugit comes Callisiis.
Comitiq jungit supplici supplex comes.

Rex.

'O nuntium infestium ! ô nitida pal-
latia,
passura graviorem exitū Oedipodæ
domo !

O luce splendens principis falsa decus !
O sors acerba ! ô fata Regnis invida !
Sed parce diis demens scelere quos
irritas.
Opaca regna Ditis, et cæcū Chaos.
exangue vulgus, numen abstruxi Jovis,
et quicquid arcet, huc novos spargite
dolos.
Vestras manus Richmondiū vocat
nefas,
ut spiritus illico scelestos expuat,
nisi graviores expetat pœnas dolor.

NUNTIUS, REX.

Nuntius.

Regina florens Anna dudū mortua
est.

Rex.

O dira fata ! sæva nimis ô numina !
res possident mortaliū certi nihil ;
Consors unica vitæ, et chara conjux,
vale.
Crudele tristis indica exitii genus.

Nunt.

Postquā lugubris sedisset mœsta diu,
suspiria gravibus mista cū singulti-
bus
heu sæpe fundit : sæpe falsis lachrymis
diris querelis conjugem ingratū premit.
Tandem inquietam capit attonitus
furor,
nuncq huc èt illuc currit erranti gradu,
tanquā tumultū patiens in se turbidū :
Statimq quærit (voces infractæ sono)
Quæ cor revellit dextera crudelis
meū ?
An non est maritus, inquit ? heu
fidele cor

O

valde est ineptū munus ingrato viro.

Postea pupillæ prorsus occultæ latent,
et solū aperta pallidè albugo micat :
vomitiones inde crebras extulit,
animæq in altū sæpe deliquiū cadit :
Artus p omnes frigidus sudor meat
orisq subitò nitidus evanuit color :
frons flava marcet, livida ardent tem-
    pora
et palpebrarū omnes defluunt pili
Cærulia turpi labia liquescunt situ,
et lingua (visu horribile) specie lurida
prominet hiante ex ore solito gran-
    dior,
unguesq nunc haud amplius clari
    nitent,
sed quasi veneno perliti pereunt :
    cadit
tandem misera luctata fatis fœmina.

Rex.

Nunc fausta neptis ambio connubia,
neptisq fallam frustra promissos
    thoros.
Sed neptis huc dubio venit gradu
    mea,
tentare procus hujus instituā thoros.

REX, FILIA EDUARDI MAJOR.

Rex.

O regia de stirpe derivans genus,
et digna sceptris virgo : postquā
    (proh dolor)
rapuere fata conjugem.tam tristia :
quæ sit magis mihi juncta Regali
    face,
quàm genere quæ regis superbo nas-
    citur ?
Sociemus animos, et thori sponde
    fidem,
accipe maritū. Quid truci vultu siles ?

Filia.

Egone, ô nefandum scelus, expiandū
    rogis
nullis ! egone manus misera conjux,
    meas
rubente mortuorū sanguine imbuā ?
Olimpus uxori deerit antè suæ,
Luanq gubernabit diem, noctemq sol :
Prius Ætna gelidas emittet ardens
    aquas,
Nilusq vagus ignitas laminas vomet.
Egone silebo parvulos misera invidos
tibi nepotes, at mihi charos fratres
crudelitèr tua pemptos dextera ?
Sceleste patrue ? prius ab extremo
    sinu
Hespera Tethys lucidū attollet diem :
Lepus fugabit invidū priùs canem.
Punit nefandū quamvis abditū scelus
Jupiter, et astutos sinit nunquā dolos.
Humeros premebant saxa Sisiphi
    lubrica,
sævus Procustes asperā pœna luit,
quoniam suos vim necarunt hospites.
Non hospites tu, sed nepotes (heu)
    tuos
nuper relictis fasciis miser necas.

Rich.

Agedum effrenatas virgo voces amove,
ne ob unū scelus corpora pereant duo.
Cruore soliū fateor acquiri meū
et inocentiū morte : sic fatis placet.
Cecidere fratres ? doleo; facti pœnitet
Sunt mortui ? factū prius nequit infici
Num flebo mortuos ? lachrymæ nil
    valent.
Quid vis facerem ? an fratrū geminā
    necem
hac dextera effuso rependā sanguine ?
faciā ? paratis ensibus pectus dabo :
et si placet magis, moriar ulnis tuis
ignes, aquas, terram, aut minacem
    Caucasū

petā, petam Tartara, vel umbrosū nemus
atræ Stygis ; nullū laborem desero
si gratus essem tibi. [virago regia]

Filia.

Sit amor, sit odiū, sit ira, vel sit fides;
non curo : placet odisse, quicquid cogitas.
Tuus priùs penetrabit ensis pectora,
libido quàm cognata corpus polluat.
O Jupiter sævo peritus fulmine.
Cur non trisulca mundus ignescit
face ?
Cur non hiulca terra devorat illico ?
Immane portentū ferocis principis,
terrore superans Gorgóneū genus.

Rich.

Pessima, tace : solū silet in armis
fides.
nihilne valet amor? nihil thorus movet
regius? acerbæ neq lacyrymæ valent ?
est imperandi principi duplex via,
Amor et metus : utrumq regibus utile.
Cogere.

Filia.

Si cogas mori sequor lubens.

Rich.

Moriere.

Filia.

Grata mors erit magis mihi
et præstat ærumnis mori oppressā
statim,
quam luce curis obsitā frui diu.

Rich.

Moriere demens.

Filia.

Nil minaris ampliùs ?
mallem mori virgo, tyranno quā viro
incesta vivere, diis, hominibusq invida.

Rich.

Hem quid agis infœlix? thoros spernet tuos.
Regina vivas, sis mea, miseros sile
fratres.

Filia.

Miser non est quisquis mori sciet

Rich.

Anne lubens ? en nullus est ferro metus,
strictusq nescit ensis unquā parcere.

Filia.

Neronis umbræ, atq furiæ Cleopatræ
truces resurgite, similem finem date
his nuptiis, qualem tulit Oedipodæ
domus.
Nec sufficit fratres necasses tuos principes?
Et nobili fœdare cæde dexterā ?
quin et integrā stuprare quæras vir-
ginē
maritus? ô mores, nefanda ô tempora !
at sæva priùs evadat ales viscera :
in me feras priùs tuas atrox nemus
emitte, vel quod triste monstrum nu-
trias,
quàm casta thalamos virgo sequor
adulteros.

Rich.

Discessit, et nostros fugit demens
thoros
negligit amores stulta virgo regios.
Nunc ista differam ; minæ forsan cadent
rabidæ puellæ, patriæ dū consula.

NUNTIUS, REX.

Nunt.

Gerebat altos nup animos insolens

Richmondius, celso superbus vertice
tumebat : at cecidit miser tandem :
sui
serò pudet cœpti, atq fraguntur minæ.

Rex.

O grata lux, quæ sceptra confirmat
mea !
Jam solida certe pacis emergit fides.
at cuncta narras : nam spes miseros
alit.

Nunt.

Adhuc juventæ flore vix primo viget
rex Galliæ, nec prima depinxit genas
barba, nec sceptra puerilis manus
satis tuetur ; quin tenera tutoribus
curanda datur ætas, virilis pòst vigor
dum regna discat : hos frequens pulsat
comes
votis iniquis, rebus et fessis opem
implorat ardens, nec preces frustra
sinit
perire. Dum multos fatigat anxius
multo labore, nec pati potest moras
mens lassa, planctus atq frustravi suos
ægrè tulit tam sæpe ; dū longā pati
cogit repulsā multiplex procerū favor :
desperat animus, optat exul vivere
potiùs, inanis et laboris pœnitet.

Rex.

Festū diem celebrare jam lætos decet,
ô mihi dies albo lapillo nobilis !
Jam sors beatis mitior rebus fluit.
Quot modò procellas concitat frustra
Comes.
et quàm graves nuper minatur exitus ?
Quin in suū redibit authorem scelus.
Jam frustra placido classis incumbit
mari,
Richmondios jam falsò reditus excu-
bat,
ergo rates hærere nunc ponto veta,
milesq portū quisquis adversā cavet,
deponat arma, finis hic malorū erìt.

Tutò licet regnare : jam cessit timor,
nisi quid timendū non sit, id timeas
tamen.

ACTUS QUINTUS.

NUNTIUS, MULIER, MULIER, ANUS.

Nunt.

Quis me p auras turbo raptat conci
tus ?
fuge, fuge, civis, hæret à tergo Comes :
minatur horrendū furor Richmondius :
portū pedite Milfordiū im̄ani premit.
totamq calcat proditā sibi Walliā :
furens comes toti minatur Angliæ.

Mulier.

Quo, quo fugis charā marite conjugem ?
frustraq tot perire patieris preces
uxoris ; en fletu genæ multo fluunt
miserere ; sin fugere lares dulces juvat;
det simul conjux itineris pvū onus.

Alia Mul.

Heare let divers Te p deorū numen et
mutes run over   datam fidem
yᵉ stage from
divers places thori, p annos   filii
for feare.   teneros precor,
              ne deseras im̄itis ah
tristem domū.

Anus.

Matris tuæ solamen ô fili mane.
Sin hostibus domū relinques pfuga,
scrutetur ensis nota quondam filio
ubera ; tuo mater peribo vulnere.

HENRICUS COMES, RHESUS THOMÆ
WALLICUS.

Hen. Com.

Optata tandem tecta cerno patriæ,
miserisq nosco maximū exulibus bonū.

ô chara salve terra, sed salve diu,
frendentis apri dente lacerata impio.
Da (patria) veniam, bella si geram
  pia,
da quæso veniā : causa comovit tua ;
dirumq principis nefas bellū vocat.
Rex est peremptus : occupat regnū
  Nero :
cum rege fratre parvulus periit puer
Solū tuentur templa reginā sacra.
Regū cruoris ultor adveni pius :
pœnas dabit Richardus Henrico :
  dedit,
si nostra clemens vota concedat Deus.
Rhesū Thomæ de stirpe video Wal-
  lica.

Rhes. Thom.

O clare princeps regia stirpe edite,
honore præcellens Comes Richmondiæ,
heros Britanniæ gentis auxiliū unicū :
Optatus Anglis civibus venis tuis.

Henricus.

Post multa vota, et temporis longas
  moras.
natale semper mente complector solū :
servile collo strenuus excutiam jugo.

Rhes.

Tu patriæ nunc columen, et verū caput :
tu solus affers rebus afflictis opem :
Et rege tanto læta gaudet Anglia.

Hen.

Non quem fatentur ore principem suo,
hunc corde semp intimo cives colunt.

Rhes.

Deus trisulca qui quatit flama polos,
et in profunda pfidos Proserpinæ
detrudit antra, me premat vivū nigra
tellure, si datā fidem fallā tibi.

Si signa campis Cambriæ ponere
  jubes,
in Wallicū agrū messor impius, ruam.
Quoscunq velles disjici muros, citò
hac aries actus saxa disperget manu :
Nec miles ullus in meis castris erit
quin te sequetur.

Hen

Rhese, grata est mihi fides
Si cœpta Numen prosperet mea,
  spondeo
te præsidem toti futurū Walliæ.

BURCHER : HUNGERFORD : MILES.

Hungerf.

Splendens equestri clare Burcher ordine,
lætus scelestas hostis effugi manus :
agmenq lubens Duci Brakenburio
p noctis umbras abstuli densas miser.

Burch.

Quot per recessus labimur Hungerford vagi
huc usque nostro terga vertentes duci ?
At ô quieta noctis almæ tempora,
tuq miseris præbens opem Phœbi soror,
adhuc tuere : differas Titan diem,
donec tyranni tuti ab armis, inclyti
tentoria Henrici comitis attingimus.

Miles.

Let heare allso   Fœlix tuas fugio p um
divers mutes,   bras cæca nox
armed soul-
diore, run over mactetur ense quisquis
the stage one   obstabit mihi.
after another
to ye Earle of
Richmond.   *Hen. Rex. [Comes.]*

Quis hic locus, quæ regio quæ regni
  plaga ?
ubi sū ? ruit nox : heu ubi satellites

Inimica cuncta : fraude quis vacat locus
quem quod rogabo? tuta sit fides, vide,
nativus artus liquit internos calor,
rigore frigent membra : vix loquor metu :
tremesco solus, cura mentem concoquit.
Hos vitricus luctus dedit meus mihi
Stanleus : illū tantæ quæ tent moræ?
Dum varia sortis cogito ludibria,
dumbiamq solus civiū volvo fidem,
exercitum præire jussi : tum moras
damnare tantas vitrici cœpi mei.
Postquā metus cor, spesq dubiū verberat,
et quicquid obstat mente dum volvo satis :
densas per umbras lapsus aspectū fugit
exercitus, suo errat orbatus duce :
sum nudus hostib⁹ relict⁹ perfuga.

Com. Oxon.

Ingens premebat cura sollicitos (comes
illustris) animos horror excussit gravis,
dux milites quòd absens deseris,
dum nocte cæca sumā montiū juga
vincunt, nec ullus jussa privatus facit.
Mox triste pectus mœror invasit gravis :
nunc voce miles frustra compellat ducem :
nunc civiū timemus incertā fidem,
lætiq sero fruimur aspectu, licèt
animus adhuc turbatur excusso metu.

Henri.

Quorsū times, pellatur ignavus metus :
solū juvat secreta sæpe volvere.

Hunger.

Sævi tyranni ereptus insidiis miser

supplex tuo vivere sub imperio, comes
illustris, atq signa cupio sequi.

Henri.

Propago clara, equitūq generosū genus ;
jam vos sequetur digna factis gloria.
me grata delectat voluntas civiū,
vestramq tantā lætus amplector fidem.
At quas tyrannus cogias ducit, doče.

Hungerf.

Pauci sequuntur sponte signa militis,
et cogit arma jungere Richardi metus :
sese magis dubius metuit exercitus,
suis nil armis miles audet credere.

Henri.

Tu transferas ad castra milites sua.

HENRICUS COMES, STANLEUS HEROS.

Henri.

Nisi vota fallunt, vitricus venit meus,
domus suæ Stanleius eximiū decus.
verumne video corpus? an fallor tua
deceptus umbra? Spiritus vires capit :
exultat anlmus, et vacat pectus metu.

Stan.

Et nostra dulce membra recreat gaudiū :
generū juvat videre : complexus mihi
redde expetitos. Sospitem qui te dedit,
det tua vicissim cœpta pficiat deus ;

Henri.

Dabit, tuo si liceat auxilio frui.

Stanl.

Utinā liceret quæ velim.

Henr.

Quidni potes ?
quid non licebit.

Stanl.

Sæpe quod cupis tamen
non absq magno pfici potest damno.

Henr.

Quidnam times, dū patriā juvis tuā ?

Stanl.

Quod vita chara filii fuit mei.

Henr.

Serat Richardus obsidem fidei tuæ.

Stanl.

Ne te juvarem, pignori datū tenet.

Henr.

O subdolū scelus, ô tyrannū bar-
barū !
amore quos fidos parū credit sibi,
horū fidem crudelis exprimit metus.

Stanl.

Irā coërce, pectus et nobile doma
palā juvare si nequeo, furtim tamen
subsidia nunquā nostra deerunt tibi.

Henr.

Discescit : heu, me lenta vitrici fides
pturbat : hujus quanta spes fulsit
mihi ?
Frustra at quærelis pectus uritur
anxium,
vanisq juvat implere cœlū quæstibus :
quin triste præcipitare consillū decet.

DUX NORFOLCIENS : RICH : REX.

Dux Norf.

Armatus expectet suū miles ducem
bellū ciebunt æra, nec moras sinent.

Richardus huc dubio venit princeps
gradu :
secreta solus volvit, et curæ premunt.
Quæ subita vultus causa turbavit
tuos ?
quid ora pallent ? mente quid dubia
stupes.

Richard.

Norfolciæ charū caput, dux nobilis,
cujus fuit mihi semp illustris fides ;
falso celabo nihil fronte pfidus.
Horrenda noctis visa terrent prox-
imæ.
Postquā sepulta nox quietem suaserat,
altusq teneris somnus obrepsit genis :
subitò premebant dira furiarū cohors,
sævòq laceravit impetu corpus tremens,
et fœda rabidis præda sū dæmonibus :
somnosq tandem magnus excussit
tremor,
et pulsat artus horridus nostros metus.
Heu ! quid truces minantur umbræ
Tartari ?

Dux Norf.

Quid somnia tremis ? noctes et vanas
minas ?
quid falsa terrent mentis et ludibria ?
Jam strictus ensis optimū augurīū
canit :
aude satis, nec vota formides tua.
Tibi rebelles spolia tot cives dabunt,
vinctæ fatebuntur manus victoriā.

Richard.

Nil pectus ullus verberat tremulū metus,
ignava nec quassat tumultus corpora
audere didicimus priùs : telis locos
hostes vicinos jam premunt, bellū vocant :
acies in armis nostra ex adversis sta-
bit.

Dux Norf.

Quid agimus? hem quid cæca fata cogitant?
quidnā parat suspecta civiū fides?
Inventa nup scripta me talia monent:

> NORFOLCIENSIS INCLYTE
> NIL CŒPERIS AUDACIUS:
> NAM VENDITUS REX PRETIO
> RICHARDUS HEROS PERDITUR.

At nulla nostram macula damnabit
fidem:
Richardi nunquam signa vivus de-
seram.

ORATIO RICHARDI AD MILITES.

Comites fideles, milites et subditi
Crudele quamvis facinus, et dirū
scelus
olim patravi: lachrymis culpā piis
satis piavi, sceleris et pœnas dedi:
satis dolore crimen ultus sum suo.
vos tanta moveat ergo pœnitentia.
Partū tueri melius est quā quærere.
Pugnate fortes, regna parta viribus
vestris studete fortiter defendere.
Non est opus cruore multo: Wallicus
oppugant hostis, regna vendicat impudens.
Illum sequuntur pfidæ Anglorū manus
sicarii nequā, genusq prodigū,
vestræq flamma patriæ gens Gallica.
at civiū me credidit manibus deus,
quorū fides spectata mihi semp fuit:
quorū paravi viribus regni decus
orisq nisi decipiar interpres, truces
victoriā vultus ferunt, [dandum mihi]
oculi diris necem minantur hostibus.
Vicistis, inquā, vicit Anglorū manus:
suo video cruore manantes agros:
simulq Gallos, Cambrios simul leves
mox fœda victos strages absumet
mea?

Sed fata quid moror? cur his vocibus
vos irruentes teneo? mihi veniā date:
Nunc quanta clemens ultro concedit
deus?
Si vincat ille, vos manent diræ cruces.
ferrū, cathenæ, et duro collo serv-
itus:
et nostra membra quærit ensis hostiū
me nil morabor: curā sit vestri salus:
consulite vobis, liberis, uxoribus:
prospicite patriæ: hæc opem vestrā
petit:
estote fortes; victus hostes occidat,
dubiūq martis exitum nemo horreat.
Nobis triumphi signa dantur maxima:
Non vos latet, sūma ducis prudentia
niti sālutem militū: nullos habet
En vultus: Henrici minas frustra
times
et robur invictū ducis Richmondii.
Infesta quare signa campis fulgeant:
cursu citato miles infestus ruat,
et hostis hostem vulneret ferus ferū
vos, vos triumphus (nobiles socii) manent:
Hac namq dextra spiritū ejus haureā,
qui causa bellorū fuit civiliū.
Aut moriar hodie, aut parabo gloriā.

NUNTIUS, REX RICHARD: DUX NORFOL.

Nunt.

Magnanime princeps, jussa pfeci tua.
Respondet ore Stanleius duro nimis,
si filiū mactes suū plures habet.

Rex Rich.

Detractat ergo pfidus jussus meos
ingratus hostis, et scelestus proditor?
Mactabo gnatū, vota psolvā statim
te digna patre. Tam diu cur filius
vivit scelesti patris? ô patiens nimis,
ô segnis ira post nefas tantū mea!

Tu jussa page : mitte qui velox mihi
ejus pempti referat abscissū caput.

Dux Norf.

Animū doma nec impius vexat pater:
jam bella poscunt, tempus aliud petit:
Signis vicina signa fulgent hostiū.

Rex Rich.

Parcamne gnato inultus impii patris ?

Dux Norf.

Post bella gnatus patris expiet scelus.

Rex Rich.

Ergo nefandi patris invisam prolem
in castra ducite.   Marte confecto
    statim
capite paterni criminis pœnas dabit.

ORATIO HENRICI COMITIS AD MILITES.

O sceleris ultrix, signa quæ sequeris
    mea
Britanna gens, vanos metus nil som-
    nies,
Sin ulla justūs bella curet Jupiter,
nobis favebit regis excusso jugo,
quos liberam videre patriā juvat.
En rapta fraude sceptra jure posci-
    mus.
Quæ causa belli melior afferri potest
quam patriæ ?   Hostis regiæ stirpis
    lues
ergo tyrannus morte crudeli cadat.
Scelere Richardus impios vicit Scy-
    thas :
Te (Nero) vicit cæde matris nobilem.
Suos nepotes ense mactat impio :
matris probro nihil pepercit filius :
stuprare neptem audet libido patrui.
Sic fratris exhibes honores manibus ?
Cesset timor, et infestus hostem vul-
    neres :

nil arma metuas tanta : media ducem
linquent arena.   Quos sequi cogit
    metus,
parùm ducem tuentur inimici suū.
At sint fideles, nec suū spernāt ducem:
pugnent acritèr, et millibus multis
    ruant :
non copiarū numerus, at virtus ducis
victoriā potitur, et laudem feret.
Hujus timebis arma, qui scelus timet
nullū ? nepotes morte confecit suos.
Asyla rupta, frater occisus, stupro
tentata neptis, falsa cui deniq fides.
Quid non patravit patriæ pestis suæ
adversus hostem corpus ense cingite.
In bella ruite, agmenq strenuè rum-
    pite,
tollantur altè signa. [quisquis occidat]
Bello fidelis pfidos, pius impios,
placidus tyrannū, mitis imitem petis
Quòd si liceret (salvo honore prin-
    cipis)
ad genua vestra volverer supplex,
    petens
ut verus hæres Anglici Henricus
    throni
vincat Ricardū, sceptra qui furto
    tenet,
Sin vincat ille, vester Henricus vagus
patria exulabit, aut luet pœnas graves:
et vos pudebit colla victori dare.
Petatur ultro dñ parat vires modò.
Heare ye hattell Aut perdat, aut peribit,
  is joyned.   hoc certū est mihi.

Uppon his retourne, lett gunns goe
    of, and trumpetts sound, wth all
    stir of Souldiers wth out ye hall,
    untill such time as ye lord Stanly
    be one ye stage ready to speake.

STANLEUS AD MILITES.

Properate, solvite patriā tyrannide
infesta ferte signa, pugna dū calet,
ut verus hæres regna teneat Angliæ.

Pugnabit adversus scelus virtus pia
Pugnate tantùm, vestra   ye battell.
   cum victoria.
Si vincitis, patria tyranno libera
medios in hostes ruite passu concito.

Let heare bee the like noyse made as
before, as soone as ye Lord Stanley
hath spoken, who followéth the
rest to the feild.   After a little
space, let the L. Northumberland
come with his band from ye feild,
att whose speach let the noyse
cease.

Oratio Comitis Northumbriæ ad milites.

Northumbriorū illustre nil damnes
   genus,
nostramve lunā (miles) ignavā putes,
quod tella fugiens hostiū terga dedi
Immane regis execror tan-
   dem scelus :   ye Battell.
horreo suorū sanguine mandentes manus.
Suasit vetustas fatidica regi fore
victoriā, manus prius si conferat
Mutata quàm sit luna.   Luna nos
   sumus :
Mox ergo lunā (milites) mutavimus,
tyrannus ut dignas scelere pœnas
   luat.

Let hear be the like noyse as before,
and after a while let a captaine run
after a souldier or two, wth a sword
drawne driveinge them againe to
the feild, and say as followeth.

Centurio.

Ignave miles, quo fugis? nisi redis
   meo peribis ense.

After the like noise againe, let 'souldiers run from ye feild, over the

stage one after the another, fling-
inge of their harnesse, and att
length let some come haltinge and
wounded.   After this let Henerye,
Earle of Richmoud come tryumph-
ing, haveing ye body of K. Richard
dead on a horse : Catesby and Rat-
liffe and others bound.

Nuntius.

Sedata lis est.   Juditiū Mavors tulit,
Iacet Ricardus, at Duci similis jacet.
Postquā feroces mutuò sese acies vident,
et signū ad arma classicū cecinit tuba :
sævus paratū miles in bellū ruit.
fugiente tandem milite, comitem videns,
equo Richardus admisso in illū ruit,
Catulis Nemæus ut furens raptis leo
per arva passim rugiens sævus volat.
Vexilla Comitis fortè Brandonus
   tulit,
Cruore cujus hastam tepefacit suā.
Hinc se Richardo Chæneiius armis
   valens
offert : Richardus hic viribus unà
   cadit.
ventū est ad hostem : quem validè
   solū petit,
In Comite solo comorabatur ferox
Contrà, potenti dextra sese Comes
defendit : æquo Marte pugnatur diu,
donec tot hostes convolent illò simul,
ut ille multis vulneribus fossus cadat.
O laude bellica inclytū verè ducem,
Si sæva Gallus arma sensisset tua,
vel pfidus fallens datam Scotus fidem.
Sed sceleris ultor cœlitū potens pater
est serò vitā, sed satis ultus tuā.

Oratio Henrici Comitis.

Rector potens Olympi, et astrorū
   decus,
terrestriū qui pastor es fideliū,

et principū cujus est potestas cordiū :
tu læta Regibus trophæa collocas :
Nitida caput cingis corona regiū,
Solus deorū falsa vincis numina,
hostesq generi affligis invidos sùo :
Ingens honor debetur et gratia tibi,
qui splendidū triumphū indulseras.
Cedit tuis armata jussibus cohors,
Si straga quis sæviret Astyages ferox
Phrygiove Pelops rege natus Tan-
talo.
expectet ille Cyrū, et ultorem tre-
mat.
Henricus audebat Richardū pellere.
At tu nitentis ô gubernator poli
Quem terra colit et vasta mundi fab-
rica,
dum corpus aura vescitur, nec ultimū
diem claudunt fati sorores invidæ,
teneros levis dum nutrit artus spiritus,
te laude perpetua canemus, debitas
tibi afferemus gratias, potens deus :
Tu belluā meis domandā viribus
mitis dabis, heu civibus pestem suis.
At vos graves passi dolores milites,
curate mox inflicta membris vulnera,
crudele ne quò serpat ulcus longiùs.
Reliqui sepulcra mortuis mites date.
Et inferis debetur excellens honor.

STRAUNGE HEROS PUER, HEN.
COMES, STANLEIUS.

Straunge.

Non semp æquor fluctibus rabidis
tumet.

Non semp imbre Jupiter pulsat mare.
Non semp acres Æolus ventos ciet.
Nec semp humiles cæca calcat sors
viros.
Aliquando fluctus sternitur rabidi
maris.
Illico caput radiatus et Titan micat,
Pressosq tollet æqua sors tandem
viros,
rex olim exul Gallicis et Britonū
latens in otis, victor en potens suo
regno potitur. Regis ô charū caput
salve, tuoq lætus in solio sede,
multos in annos Angliæ verū decus.
felix deinceps subditis vivas tuis,
fideiq captivos tuæ hos clemens cape.

Henricus Comes.

O Stanleiorū chara progenies mihi.
O Straunge nobilis, en libens te con-
spicor :
quos mihi dedisti, reddo captivos tibi.

Stanl.

Rediisse charū patri salvū filiū
crudelis elapsū tyranni dexterā,
exultat animus lætus, ô fili, mihi
pericula post tam dira quod sospes
venis.

Hen. Rex.

Regno mihiq gratulor : regno, gravi
quòd sit tyranno liberū : porro mihi,
quod sceptra regni tracto regalia mei.
Quare supremo regna qui dedit deo
laudes canamus ore supplices pio.

Let a noble man putt on yᵉ Crowne upon kinge Henries head att the end of his oration, and yᵉ Song sunge wᶜʰ is in yᵉ end of the booke. After an Epilogue is to bee made, wherein lett bee declared the happy unite-inge of both houses, of whome the Queenes majestie came, and is undoubted heyre, wishinge her a prosperous raigne.

EPILOGUS.

Extincta vidistis Regulorū corpora,
horrenda magnatū furentem funera :
funesta vidistis potentū prælia
et digna quæ cepit tyrannus præmia.
Henricus illustris Comes Richmondius
turbata pacavit Richardi sanguine,
Antistitis comotus Eliensiū
sermone fœlici, sagaci pectore
et gloriosi marte Buckinghamii,
tum Margaretæ matris impulsu suæ,
illustre quæ nostrū hoc Collegiū
Christoq fundavit dicatū sumptibus :
Quæ multa regalis reliquit dexteræ
nunquam laudatæ satis mentis suæ
præclara cunctis signa quondā sæculis.
Hic stirpe regali satus Lancastriæ
accepit uxorem creatam sanguine
Eboracensi : sic duarū fœdere
finiunt æterna domorū jurgia.
Hinc portus, hic Anglis quietis perditis
finisq funestæ fuit discordiæ.
Hinc illa manavit propago nobilis
hæresq certus, qui Britanni Cardinem
regni gubernas jure vexit jam suo,
Henricus Henrici parentis filius.
Qui verus afflictæ patronus patriæ,
tum singulis unū reliquit comodis
præstantius multò, licèt quàm plurimis,
Cum tam potentem procreraet principem.
Elizabethā, patre dignā filiā,
canosq vencentem seniles virginem.
Quæ regna tot Phœbi phractis cursibus
comissa rexit pace fœlix Anglia.
quam dextra supremi tonantis protegat
illus et vitam tegendo protrahet.

FINIS.

KING JOHN.

EDITIONS.

———o———

The Troublesome Raigne of Iohn King of England, with the discouerie of King Richard Gordelions Base Sonne (vulgaly named, The Bastard Fawconbridge) : also the death of King Iohn at Swinstead Abbey. As it was (sundry times) publikely acted by the Queenes Maiesties Players, in the honourable Citie of London. Imprinted at London for Sampson Clarke, and are to be solde at his shop, on the backe-side of the Royall Exchange. 1591. 4°.

THIS play was reprinted in 1611, from which edition it has been republished by Nichols in his "Six Old Plays," 1779. The copy of the original 4° of 1591 in the Capel collection is the only one with which I am acquainted.

On the title of the reprint of 1611 the bookseller placed the initials W. Sh., ostensibly for the purpose of creating a belief that the play was Shakespeare's.

TO THE GENTLEMEN READERS.

—o——

You that with friendly grace of smoothed brow
Haue entertaind the Scythian Tamburlaine,
And giuen applause vnto an Infidel:
Vouchsafe to welcome (with like curtesie)
A warlike Christian and your Countreyman.
For Christs true faith indur'd he many a storme,
And set himselfe against the Man of Rome,
Vntill base treason (by a damned wight)
Did all his former triumphs put to flight,
Accept of it (sweete Gentles) in good sort
And thinke it was preparde for your disport.

The Troublesome Raigne of King Iohn.

——o——

Enter *K. Iohn*, Queene *Elinor*, his Mother, *William
Marshall*, Earle of *Pembrooke*, the Earles of *Essex*
and of *Salisbury*.

Q. El. BARONS of England, and my noble
Lords;
Though God and Fortune haue bereft from vs
Victorious Richard scourge of Infidels,
And clad this Land in stole of dismall hieu :
Yet giue me leaue to ioy, and ioy you all,
That from this wombe hath sprung a second hope,
A King that may in rule and vertue both
Succeede his brother in his Emperie.

K. Iohn. My gracious mother Queene, and Barons
all ;
Though farre vnworthie of so high a place,
As is the Throne of mightie England's King ;
Yet Iohn your Lord, contented vncontent,
Will (as he may) sustaine the heauie yoke
Of pressing cares, that hang vpon a Crowne.
My Lord of Pembrooke and Lord Salsbury,
Admit the Lord Shattilion to our presence ;

That we may know what Philip King of Fraunce
(By his Ambassadors) requires of vs.
  Q. El. Dare lay my hand that Elinor can gesse
Whereto this weightie Embassade doth tend:
If of my Nephew Arthur and his claime,
Then say, my Sonne, I haue not mist my aime.

Enter *Chattilion* and the two Earles.

  Iohn. My Lord Chattilion, welcome into England!
How fares our Brother Philip King of Fraunce?
  Chat. His Highnesse at my comming was in
      health,
And wild me to salute your Maiestie,
And say the message he hath giuen in charge.
  Iohn. And spare not man, wee are preparde to heare.
  Chat. Philip, by the grace of God most Christian
K. of France, hauing taken into his guardain and
protection Arthur Duke of Brittaine sonne & heire to
Jeffrey thine elder brother, requireth in the behalfe of
the said Arthur, the Kingdom of England, with the
Lordship of Ireland, Poiters, Aniow, Torain, Main:
and I attend thine aunswere.
  Iohn. A small request: belike he makes account,
That England, Ireland, Poiters, Aniow, Torain, Main,
Are nothing for a King to giue at once:
I wonder what be meanes to leaue for me.
Tell Philip, he may keepe his Lords at home,
With greater honour than to send them thus
On Embassades that not concerne himselfe,
Or if they did, would yeeld but small returne.
  Chat. Is this thine answere?
  Iohn. It is, and too good an answer for so proud a
      message.
  Chat. Then King of England, in my Masters
      name,

And in Prince Arthur Duke of Britaines name,
I doo defie thee as an Enemie,
And wish thee to prepare for bloodie warres.

   Q. El. My Lord (that stands vpon defiance thus)
Commend me to my Nephew, tell the boy,
That I Queene Elianor (his Grandmother)
Vpon my blessing charge him leaue his Armes
Whereto his head-strong Mother pricks him so :
Her pride we know, and know her for a Dame
That will not sticke to bring him to his ende,
So she may bring her selfe to rule a realme.
Next, wish him to forsake the King of Fraunce,
And come to me and to his Uncle here,
And he shall want for nothing at our hands.

   Chat. This shall I doo, and thus I take my leaue.

   Iohn. Pembrooke, conuey him safely to the sea,
But not in hast : for as we are aduisde,
We meane to be in Fraunce as soone as he,
To fortefie such townes as we possesse
In Aniou, Torain, and in Normandy.   [Exit Chatt.

   Enter the Shriue and whispers the Earle of *Salisbury*
               in the eare.

   Sals. Please it your maiestie, heere is the Shriue of
Northamptonshire, with certaine persons that of late
committed a riot, and haue appeald to your maiestie,
beseeching your Highnes for speciall cause to heare
them.

   Iohn. Will them come neere, and while wee heare
      the cause,
Goe Salisbury and make prouision,
We meane with speede to pass the Sea to Fraunce.
                         [Exit Sals.
Say Shriue, what are these men, what haue they done ?
Or whereto tends the course of this appeale ?

   Shrieue. Please it your maiesty, these two brethren

vnnaturally falling at odds about their father's liuing,
haue broken your Highnes peace, in seeking to right
their own wrongs without cause of Law, or order of
Iustice, vnlawfully assembled themselues in mutinous
manner, hauing committed a riot, appealing from triall
in their Countrey to your Highnes : and here I Thomas
Nidigate shrieue of Northamptonshire do deliuer them
ouer to their triall.

John. My Lord of Essex, will the offenders to stand
foorth, and tell the cause of their quarrell.

Essex. Gentlemen, it is the Kings pleasure that you
discouer your griefes, & doubt not but you shall haue
iustice.

Phil. Please it your Majestie the wrong is mine :
yet wil I abide all wrongs, before I once open my
mouth to vnrippe the shamefull slaunder of my parents, the dishonour of my selfe, & the wicked dealing
of my brother in this princely assembly.

Rob. Then, by my Prince his leaue, shall Robert
    speake,
And tell your maiestie what right I haue
To offer wrong, as he accounteth wrong.
My father (not vnknowen vnto your Grace)
Receiud his spurres of Knighthood in the Field,
At Kingly Richards hands in Palestine,
When as the walls of Acon gaue him way :
His name Sir Robert Fauconbridge of Mountbery.
What by succession from his Ancestors,
And warlike seruice vnder Englands Armes,
His liuing did amount too at his death
Two thousand markes rcuenew euery yeare :
And this (my Lord) I challenge for my right,
As lawfull hcire to Robert Fauconbridge.

Phil. If first-borne sonne be heire indubitate
By certaine right of Englands auncient Lawe,
How should myselfe make any other doubt,
But I am heire to Robert Fauconbridge.

Iohn. Fond Youth, to trouble these our Princely
  eares,
Or make a question in so plaine a case :
Speake, is this man thine elder Brother borne ?

  Rob. Please it your Grace with patience for to
  heare,
I not denie but he mine Elder is,
Mine elder Brother too : yet in such sort,
As he can make no title to the land.

  Iohn. A doubtfull tale as euer I did heare,
Thy Brother, and thine elder, and no heire :
Explaine this darke *Ænigma.*

  Rob. I graunt (my Lord) he is my mothers sonne,
Base borne, and base begot, no Fauconbridge.
Indeede the world reputes him lawfull heire,
My father in his life did count him so :
And here my Mother stands to prooue him so :
But I (my Lord) can prooue, and doo auerre
Both to my Mothers shame, and his reproach,
He is no heire, nor yet legitimate.
Then (gracious Lord) let Fauconbridge enioy
The liuing that belongs to Fauconbridge.
And let him not possesse anothers right.

  Iohn. Prooue this, the land is thine by Englands
  law.

  Q. El. Ungracious youth, to rip thy mothers
  shame,
The wombe from whence thou didst thy being take,
All honest eares abhorre thy wickednes,
But gold I see doth beate downe natures law.

  Mother. My gracious Lord, & you thrice reuerend
  Dame,
That see the teares distilling from mine eyes,
And scalding sighes blowne from a rented heart :
For honour and regard of womanhood,
Let me entreate to be commaunded hence.
Let not these eares heere receiue the hissing sound

Of such a viper, who with poysoned words
Doth masserate the bowells of my soule.

    Iohn. Ladie, stand vp, be patient for a while :
And fellow, say, whose bastard is thy brother?

    Phil. Not for my selfe, nor for my mother now,
But for the honour of so braue a Man,
Whom he accuseth with adulterie :
Here I beseech your Grace vpon my knees,
To count him mad, and so dismisse vs hence.

    Rob. Nor mad, nor mazde, but well aduised, I
Charge thee before this royall presence here
To be a Bastard to King Richards selfe,
Sonne to your Grace, and Brother to your Maiestie.
Thus bluntly, and—

    Elianor. Yong man, thou needst not be ashamed
      of thy kin,
Nor of thy Sire.   But forward with thy proofe.

    Rob. The proofe so plaine, the argument so
      strong,
As that your Highnesse and these noble Lords,
And all (saue those that haue no eyes to see)
Shall sweare him to be Bastard to the King.
First, when my Father was Embassadour
In Germanie vnto the Emperour,
The king lay often at my father's house :
And all the Realme suspected what befell :
And at my fathers back-returne agen
My Mother was deliuered, as tis sed,
Sixe weekes before the account my father made.
But more than this : looke but on Philips face,
His features, actions, and his lineaments,
And all this Princely presence shall confesse,
He is no other but King Richards Sonne,
Then gracious Lord, rest he King Richards Sonne,
And let me rest safe in my Fathers right,
That am his rightfull sonne and onely heire.

    Iohn. Is this thy proofe and all thou hast to say?

Rob. I haue no more, nor neede I greater proofe.

Iohn. First, where thou saidst in absence of thy Sire
My Brother ofteñ lodged in his house :
And what of that ? base groome to slaunder him,
That honoured his Embassador so much,
In absence of the man to cheere the wife ?
This will not hold, proceede vnto the next.

Q. El. Thou saist she teemde sixe weeks before
    her time,
Why good Sir Squire, are you so cunning growen,
To make account of womens reckonings ?
Spit in your hand and to your other proofes :
Many mischaunces hap in such affaires,
To make a woman come before her time.

Iohn. And where thou saist, he looketh like the King,
In action, feature and proportion :
Therein I hold with thee, for in my life
I neuer saw so liuely counterfeit
Of Richard Cordelion, as in him.

Robert. Then good my Lord, be you indiffrent Iudge,
And let me haue my liuing and my right.

Q. El. Nay, heare you Sir, you runne away too
    fast :
Know you not, *Omne simile non est idem* ?
Or haue read in.   Harke ye good sir,
Twas thus I warrant, and no otherwise.
She lay with Sir Robert your father, and thought vppon
King Richard my Sonne, and so your Brother was
formed in this fashion.

Rob. Madame, you wrong me thus to iest it out,
I craue my right : King Iohn, as thou art King,
So be thou iust, and let me haue my right.

Iohn. Why (foolish boy) thy proofes are friuolous,
Nor canst thou chalenge any thing thereby.
But thou shalt see how I will helpe thy claime :
This is my doome, and this my doome shall stand
Irreuocable, as I am King of England.

For thou knowst not, weele aske of them that know,
His mother and himselfe shall ende this strife :
And as they say, so shall thy liuing passe.
Rob. My Lord, herein I challenge you of wrong,
To giue away my right, and put the doome
Unto themselues.   Can there be likelihood
That she will loose ?
Or he will giue the liuing from himselfe ?
It may not be my Lord.   Why should it be ?
Iohn. Lords, keepe him back, & let him heare the
   doome.
Essex, first aske the Mother thrice who was his Sire ?
Essex. Ladie Margaret, Widow of Fauconbridge,
Who was Father to thy Sonne Philip ?
Mother. Please it your Maiestie, Sir Robert Faucon-
   bridge.
Rob. This is right, aske my felow there if I bc a
   thiefe.
Iohn. Aske Philip whose Sonne he is.
Essex. Philip, who was thy father ?
Phil. Mas my Lord, and thats a question : and
you had not taken some paines with her before,
I should haue desired you to aske my Mother.
Iohn. Say, who was thy father ?
Phil. Faith (my Lord) to answere you, sure he is
my father that was neerest my mother when I was
gotten, & him I thinke to be Sir Robert Faucon-
bridge.
Iohn. Essex, for fashions sake demaund agen,
And so an ende to this contention.
Rob. Was euer man thus wrongd as Robert is ?
Essex. Philip speake I say, who was thy Father ?
Iohn. Young man how now, what art thou in a
   traunce ?
Elianor. Philip awake, the man is in a dreame.
Phil. Philippus atauis ædite Regibus.
What saist thou Philip, sprung of auncient Kings ?

Quo me rapit tempestas ?
What winde of honour blowes this furie forth?
Or whence proeede these fumes of Maiestie?
Me thinkes I heare a hollow Eccho sound,
That Philip is the Sonne vnto a King :
The whistling leaues vpon the trembling trees,
Whistle in consort I am Richards Sonne :
The bubling murmur of the waters fall,
Records *Philippus Regius filius :*
Birds in their flight make musicke with their wings,
Filling the ayre with glorie of my birth :
Birds, bubbles, leaues, and mountaines, Eccho, all
Ring in mine eares, that I am Richards Sonne.
Fond man, ah whither art thou carried?
How are thy thoughts ywrapt in honors heauen?
Forgetfull what thou art, and whence thou camst.
Thy Fathers land cannot maintaine these thoughts,
These thoughts are farre vnfitting Fauconbridge :
And well they may ; for why this mounting minde
Doth soare too high to stoupe to Fauconbridge.
Why how now? knowest thou where thou art?
And knowest thou who expects thine answere here?
Wilt thou vpon a frantick madding vaine
Goe loose thy land, and say thy selfe base borne?
No, keepe thy land, though Richard were thy Sire,
What ere thou thinkst, say thou art Fauconbridge.
        Iohn. Speake man, be sodaine, who thy Father
    was.
        Phil. Please it your maiestie, Sir Robert
Philip, that Fauconbridge cleaues to thy iawes :
It will not out, I cannot for my life
Say I am Sonne vnto a Fauconbridge.
Let land and liuing goe, tis Honors fire
That makes me sweare King Richard was my Sire.
Base to a King addes title of more State,
Than knights begotten, though legittimate.
Please it your Grace, I am King Richards Sonne.

Rob. Robert reuiue thy heart, let sorrow die,
His faltring tongue not suffers him to lie.
   Mother. What head-strong furie doth enchaunt my
     sonne ?
   Phil. Philip cannot repent, for he hath done.
   Iohn. Then Philip blame not me, thy selfe hath lost
By wilfulnesse, thy liuing and thy land.
Robert, thou art the heire of Fauconbridge,
God giue thee ioy, greater than thy desert.
   Q. El. Why how now Philip, giue away thine
     owne ?
   Phil. Madame, I am bold to make my selfe your
     nephew,
The poorest kinsman that your Highnes hath :
And with this prouerb gin the world anew,
Help hands, I haue no lands, Honor is my desire ;
Let Philip liue to shew himselfe worthie so great a
     Sire.
   Elinor. Philip, I think thou knewst thy Grandams
     minde :
But cheere the boy, I will not see thee wante
As long as Elinor hath foote of land ;
Henceforth thou shalt be taken for my sonne,
And waite on me and on thine Uncle heere,
Who shall giue honour to thy noble minde.
   Iohn. Philip kneele down, that thou maist throughly
     know
How much thy resolution pleaseth vs,
Rise vp Sir Richard Plantaginet King Richards Sonne.
   Phil. Graunt heauens that Philiponce may shew
     himself
Worthie the honour of Plantaginet,
Or basest glorie of a Bastards name.
   Iohn. Now Gentlemen, we will away to France,
To checke the pride of Arthur and his mates :
Essex, thou shalt be Ruler of my Realme,
And toward the maine charges of my warres,

Ile ceaze the lasie Abbey lubbers lands
Into my hands to pay.my men of warre.
The Pope and Popelings shall not grease themselues
With golde and groates, that are the souldiers due.
Thus forward Lords, let our commaund be done,
And march we forward mightiely to Fraunce.

       [Exeunt.   Manet Philip and his Mother.

    Phil. Madame, I beseech you deigne me so much
leasure as the hearing of a matter I long to impart
to you.
    Mother. Whats the matter Philip? I thinke your
sute in secret, tends to some money matter, which
you suppose burns in the bottom of my chest.
    Phil. No Madam, it is no such sute as to beg or
      borrow,
But such a sute, as might some other grant,
I would not now haue troubled you withall.
    Mother. A Gods name let vs heare it.
    Phil. Then Madame thus, your Ladiship sees well,
How that my scandall growes by meanes of you,
In that report hath rumord vp and downe,
I am a bastard, and no Fauconbridge.
This grose attaint so tilteth in my thoughts,
Maintaining combat to abridge mine ease,
That field and towne, and company alone,
What so I doo, or wheresoere I am,
I cannot chase the slaunder from my thoughts.
If it be true, resolue me of my Sire,
For pardon Madam, if I thinke amisse.
Be Philip Philip, and no Fauconbridge,
His Father doubtles was as braue a man.
To you on knees, as sometimes Phaeton,
Mistrusting silly Merop for his Sire,
Strayning a little bashfull modestie,
I beg some instance whence I am extraught.
    Mother. Yet more adoo to haste me to my graue,

And wilt thou too become a Mothers crosse?
Must I accuse myself to close with you?
Slaunder myself, to quiet your affects?
Thou mooust me Philip with this idle talke,
Which I remit, in hope this mood will die.
   Phil. Nay Ladie mother, heare me further yet,
For strong conceipt driues dutie hence awhile :
Your husband Fauconbridge was Father to that sonne
That carries marks of Nature like the Sire,
The sonne that blotteth you with wedlocks breach,
And holds my right, as lineall in descent
From him whose forme was figured in his face,
Can Nature so dissemble in her frame,
To make the one so like as like may be,
And in the other print no character
To challenge any marke of true descent?
My brothers minde is base, and too too dull.
To mount where Philip lodgeth his affects,
And his external graces that you view,
(Though I report it) counterpoise not mine :
His constitution plaine debilitie,
Requires the chayre, and mine the seate of steele.
Nay, what is he, or what am I to him?
When any one that knoweth how to carpe,
Will scarcely iudge vs both one Countrey borne.
This Madame, this, hath droue me from my selfe ·
And here by heauens eternall lampes I sweare,
As cursed Nero with his mother did,
So I with you, if you resolue me not.
   Mother. Let mothers teares quench out thy angers
     fire,
And vrge no further what thou dost require.
   Phil. Let sonnes entreatie sway the mother now,
Or else she dies : Ile not infringe my vow,
   Mother. Vnhappy taske : must I recount my shame,
Blab my misdeedes, or by concealing die?
Some power strike me speechlesse for a time,

Or take from him a while his hearings vse.
Why wish I so, vnhappy as I am?
The fault is mine, and he the faultie frute,
I blush, I faint, oh would I might be mute.
    Phil. Mother be briefe, I long to know my
      name.
    Mother. And longing dye, to shrowd thy Mothers
      shame.
    Phil. Come Madame come, you neede not be so
      loth.
The shame is shared equall twixt vs both.
Ist not a slacknes in me, worthie blame,
To be so olde, and cannot write my name.
Good Mother resolue me.
    Mother. Then Philip heare thy fortune, and my
      griefe,
My honours losse by purchase of thy selfe,
My shame, thy name, and husbands secret wrong,
All maimd and staind by youths vnruly sway.
And when thou knowest from whence thou art ex-
      traught,
Or if thou knewest what sutes, what threates, what
      feares,
To mooue by loue, or massacre by death.
To yeeld with loue, or end by loues contempt.
The mightines of him that courted me,
Who tempred terror with his wanton talke,
That something may extenuate the guilt.
But let it not aduantage me so much :
Vpbraid me rather with the Romane Dame.
That shed her blood to wash away her shame.
Why stand I to expostulate the crime
With *pro & contra*, now the deede is don?
When to conclude two words may tell the tale,
That Philips Father was a Princes Son,
Rich Englands rule, worlds onely terror hee,
For honours losse left me with childe of thee :

Whose Sonne thou art, then pardon me the rather,
For faire King Richard was thy noble Father.
    Phil. Then Robin Fauconbridge I wish thee ioy,
My Sire a King, and I a landles Boy.
Gods Ladie Mother, the world is in my debt,
There's something owing to Plantaginet.
I marrie Sir, let me alone for game,
Ile act some wonders now I know my name.
By blessed Marie Ile not sell that pride
For Englands wealth, and all the world beside.
Sit fast the proudest of my Fathers foes,
Away good Mother, there the comfort goes. [Exeunt.

Enter *Philip* the French King, and *Lewis, Limoges,
Constance,* and her sonne *Arthur.*

    King. Now gin we broach the title of thy claime,
Young Arthur in the Albion Territories,
Scaring proud Angiers with a puissant siedge :
Braue Austria, cause of Cordelions death,
Is also come to aide thee in thy warres;
And all our Forces ioyne for Arthurs right.
And, but for causes of great consequence,
Pleading delay till newes from England come,
Twice should not Titan hide him in the West,
To coole the set-locks of his wearie teame,
Till I had with an vnresisted shock
Controld the mannage of proud Angiers walls,
Or made a forfet of my fame to Chaunce.
    Cons. May that be Iohn in conscience or in feare
To offer wrong where you impugne the ill,
Will send such calme conditions backe to Fraunce,
As shall rebate the edge of fearefull warres :
If so, forbearance is a deed well done.
    Arth. Ah Mother, possession of a Crowne is
      much,
And Iohn as I haue heard reported of.

For present vantage would aduenture farre.
The world can witnes, in his Brothers time,
He tooke vpon him rule, and almost raigne :
Then must it follow as a doubtfull poynt,
That hee'le resigne the rule vnto his Nephew.
I rather thinke the menace of the world
Sounds in his eares, as threats of no esteeme,
And sooner would he scorne Europaes power,
Than loose the smallest title he enioys ;
For questionles he is an Englishman.
    Lewis. Why are the English peereles in compare ?
Braue caualiers as ere that Island bred,
Haue liude and dide, and darde, and done inough,
Yet neuer gracde their countrey for the cause :
England is England, yeelding good and bad,
And Iohn of England is as other Iohns.
Trust me yong Arthur, if thou need my reede,
Praise thou the French that helpe thee in this neede.
    Lym. The Englishman hath little cause I trow,
To spend good speaches on so proud a foe.
Why Arthur heres his spoyle that now is gon,
Who when he liud outrou'de his brother Iohn :
But hastie curres that lie so long to catch,
Come halting home, and meete their ouermatch.
But newes comes now, heers the Embassadour.

Enter *Chattilion.*

    K. Phil. And in good time, welcome my Lord
        Chattilion :
What newes? will Iohn accord to our commaund ?
    Chat. Be I not briefe to tell your Highnes all,
He will approach to interrupt my tale :
For one selfe bottome brought vs both to Fraunce.
He on his part will trie the chaunce of warre,
And if his words inferre assured truth,
Will loose himselfe, and all his followers,

Ere yeeld vnto the least of your demaunds,
The Mother Queene she taketh on amaine
Gainst Ladie Constance, counting her the cause
That doth effect this claime to Albion,
Coniuring Arthur with a Grandames care,
To leaue his mother : willing him submit
His state to Iohn, and her protection,
Who (as shee saith) are studious for his good.
More circumstance the season intercepts :
This is the summe, which briefly I haue showne.

   K. Phil. This bitter wind' must nip somebodies
      spring !
Sodaine and briefe, who so, 'tis haruest weather.
But say Chattilion, what persons of accompt are with
      him ?

   Chat. Of England, Earle Pembrooke and Salsbury,
The onely noted men of any name.
Next to them, a Bastard of the Kings deceast,
A hardy wildehead, tough and venturous,
With many other men of high resolue.
Then is there with them Elinor mother queene,
And Blanch her Neece, daughter to the King of
      Spaine :
These are the prime Birds of this hot aduenture.

     Enter *John* & his followers, Queene, Bastard,
         Earles, &c.

   K. Phil. Me seemeth Iohn, an ouer-daring spirit
Effects some frenzie in thy rash approach,
Treading my Confines with thy armed Troupes.
I rather lookt for some submisse reply
Touching the claime thy Nephew Arthur makes
To that which thou vniustly dost vsurpe.

   K. Iohn. For that Chattilion can discharge you all,
I list not pleade my Title with my tongue.
Nor came I hether with intent of wrong

To Fraunce or thee, or ony right of thine,
But in defence and purchase of my right,
The Towne of Angiers: which thou doost begirt
In the behalfe of ladie Constance Sonne,
Wheretoo nor he nor she can lay iust claime.
    Cons. Yes (false intruder) if that iust be iust,
And headstrong vsurpation put apart,
Arthur my Sonne, heire to thy elder Brother,
Without ambiguous shadow of discent,
Is soveraigne to the substance thou withholdst.
    Q. El. Misgouernd gossip, staine to this resort,
Occasion of these vndecided iarres,
I say (that know) to check thy vaine suppose,
Thy sonne hath naught to doo with that he claymes.
For proof whereof, I can inferre a Will,
That barres the way he vrgeth by discent.
    Cons. A Will indeede, a crabbed Womans will,
Wherein the Diuell is an ouerseer,
And proud dame Elinor sole Exocutresse:
More wills than so, on perill of my soule,
Were neuer made to hinder Arthurs right.
    Arth. But say there was, as sure there can be
        none,
The Law intends such testaments as voyd,
Where right discent can no way be impeacht.
    Q. El. Peace Arthur peace, thy mother makes
        thee wings
To soar with perill after Icarus,
And trust me yongling for the Fathers sake,
I pitie much the hazard of thy youth.
    Cons. Beshrew you els how pittiful you are,
Readie to weepe to heare him aske his owne;
Sorrow betide such Grandames and such griefe.
That minister a poyson for pure loue.
But who so blinde, as cannot see this beame,
That you forsooth would keepe your cousin downe,
For feare his Mother should be vsde too well?

I theres the griefe, confusion catch the braine,
That hammers shiftes to stop a Princes raigne.

Q. El. Impatient, frantike, common slanderer,
Immodest Dame, vnnurtvred quarreller,
I tell thee I, not enuie to thy Son,
But iustice makes me speake as I haue don.

> *K. Phil.* But heres no proof that showes your son
> a King.
>
> *K. Iohn.* What wants, my sword shal more at large
> set down.
>
> *Lewis.* But that may breake before the truth be
> knowne.
>
> *Bast.* Then this may hold till all his right be
> showne.
>
> *Lym.* Good words sir sauce, your betters are in
> place.
>
> *Bast.* Not you sir doughtie, with your Lions case.
>
> *Blanch.* Ah ioy betide his soule, to whom that spoile
> belong'd :

Ah Richard, how thy glorie here is wrong'd.

> *Lym.* Me thinkes that Richards pride & Richards
> fall,

Should be a president t'affright you all.

> *Bast.* What words are these? how doo my sinews
> shake ?

My Fathers foe clad in my Fathers spoyle,
A thousand furies kindle with reuenge,
This hart that choller keepes a consistorie,
Searing my inwards with a brand of hate :
How doth Alecto whisper in mine eares?
Delay not Philip, kill the villaine straight,
Disrobe him of the matchles moniment
Thy Fathers triumph ore the Sauages,
Base heardgroome, coward, peasant, worse than a
threshing slave,
What makst thou with the Trophie of a King?
Shamst thou not coystrell, loathsome dunghill swad,

To grace thy carkasse with an ornament
Too precious for a monarchs couerture?
Scarce can I temper due obedience
Unto the presence of my Soueraigne,
From acting outrage on this trunke of haté:
But arme thee traytor, wronger of renowne,
For by his soule I sweare, my Fathers soule,
Twice will I not reuiew the Mornings rise,
Till I have torne that Trophie from thy back,
And split thy heart for wearing it so long.
Philip hath sworne, and if it be not done,
Let not the world repute me Richards Sonne.
   Lym. Nay soft sir Bastard, harts are not split so
     soone,
Let them reioyce that at the ende doo win:
And take this lesson at thy foeman's hand,
Pawne not thy life to get thy Fathers skin.
   Blanch. Well may the world speake of his knightly
     valor,
That winnes this hide to weare a Ladies fauour.
   Bast. 'Ill may I thriue, and nothing brooke with
     mee,
If shortly I present it not to thee.
   K. Phil. Lordings forbeare, for time is comming
     fast,
That deedes may trie what words cannot determine,
And to the purpose for the cause you come.
Me seemes you set right in chaunce of warre,
Yeelding no other reasons for your claime,
But so and so, because it shall be so.
So wrong shall be subornd by trust of strength
A Tyrants practize to inuest himselfe,
Where weake resistance giueth wrong the way.
To check the which, in holy lawfull Armes,
I, in the right of Arthur, Geoffreys Sonne,
Am come before this Citie of Angiers,
To barre all other false supported clayme,

From whence, or howsoere the error springs.
And in his quarrell on my Princely word,
Ile fight it out vnto the latest man.

    Iohn. Know King of Fraunce, I will not be com-
maunded,
By any power or Prince in Christendome,
To yeeld an instance how I hold mine owne,
More than to answere, that mine owne is mine,
But wilt thou see me parley with the Towne,
And heare them offer me allegeance,
Fealtie and homage, as true liege men ought.

    K. Phil. Summon them, I will not beleeue it till
I see it,
and when I see it, Ile soone change it.

    [They summon the Towne, the Citizens appeare
vpon the walls.

    K. Iohn. You men of Angiers, and as I take it my
loyall Subiects, I haue summoned you to the walls :
to dispute on my right, were to thinke you doubtfull
therein, which I am perswaded you are not. In few
words, our Brothers Sonne, backt with the King of
Fraunce, haue beleagred your Towne vpon a false
pretented title to the same : in defence whereof I
your liege Lord haue brought our power to fence you
from the Usurper, to free your intended seruitude,
and vtterly to supplant the foemen, to my right &
your rest. Say then, who keepe you the town for?

    Citizen. For our lawfull King.

    Iohn. I was no lesse perswaded : then in Gods
name open your gates, and let me enter.

    Citizen. And it please your Highness we comptroll
not your title, neither will we rashly admit your
entrance : if you bee lawfull King, with all obedience
we keepe it to your vse, if not King, our rashness to
be impeached for yeelding, without more considerate
triall : wee answere not as men lawles, but to the
behoofe of him that prooues lawfull.

Iohn. I shall not come in then ?

Citizen. No my Lord, till we know more.

K. Phil. Then heare me speake in the behalfe of
Arthur, Sonne of Geffrey, elder Brother to Iohn, his
title manifest, without contradiction, to the Crown
and Kingdome of England, with Angiers, and diuers
Townes on this side the sea ; will you acknowledge
him your liege Lord, who speaketh in my word, to
intertaine you with all fauors, as beseemeth a King to
his subiects, or a friend to his wel willers : or stand
to the perill of your contempt, when his title is prooued
by the sword.

Citizen. We answere as before, till you haue prooued
one right, we acknowledge none right, he that tries
himselfe our Soueraigne, to him will we remain firme
subiects, and for him, and in his right we hold our
Towne, as desirous to know the truth, as loath to
subscribe before we knowe : More than this we
cannot say, & more than this we dare not doo.

K. Phil. Then Iohn I defie thee, in the name and
behalfe of Arthur Plantaginet, thy King and cousin,
whose right and patrimonie thou detainest, as I
doubt not, ere the day ende, in a set battel make
thee confesse ; whereunto, with a zeale to right, I
challenge thee.

K. Iohn. I accept the challenge, and turne the
defiance to thy throate.

Excursions.   The Bastard chaseth *Lymoges* the
      Austrich Duke, and maketh him leaue the Lyons
      skinne.

Bast. And art thou gone, misfortune haunt thy
      steps,
And chill colde feare assaile thy times of rest.
Morpheus leaue here thy silent Eban caue,
Besiedge his thoughts with dismal fantasies.

And ghastly obiects of pale threatning *mors.*
Affright him every minute with stearne lookes,
Let shadowe temper terror in his thoughts,
And let the terror make the coward mad,
And in his madnes let his feare pursute,
And so in frenzie let the peasant die.
Here is the ransome that allayes his rage,
The first freehold that Richard left his sonne :
With which I shall surprize his liuing foes,
As Hectors statue did .the fainting Greekes.   [Exit.

Enter the Kings Herolds with trumpets to the wals
      of Angiers : they summon the Towne.

Eng. Herolds. Iohn by the grace of God King of
England, Lord of Ireland, Aniou, Toraine, &c. demaundeth once againe of you his subiects of Angiers,
if you will quietly surrender vp the Towne into his
hands ?
Fr. Herold. Philip by the grace of God King of
Fraunce, demaundeth in the behalfe of Arthur Duke
of Britaine, if you will surrender vp the Towne into
his hands, to the vse of the said Arthur.
Citizens. Herrolds goe tell the two victorious
Princes, that we the poore inhabitants of Angiers,
require a parle of their Maiesties.
Herolds. We goe.

Enter the Kings, Queen *Elianor, Blanch, Bastard,*
      Lymoges, Lewis, Castilean, Pembrooke, Salis-
      bury, Constance, and *Arthur* Duke of Brittaine.

Iohn. Herold, what answer doo the Townsmen
      send ?
Philip. Will Angiers yield to Philip King of
      Fraunce ?
Eng. Her. The Townsmen on the wals accept your
      Grace.

Fr. Her. And craue a parley of your Maiesty.

Iohn. You Citizens of Angiers, haue your eyes
Beheld the slaughter that our English bowes
Haue made vpon the coward frawdfull French?
And haue you wisely pondred therewithall
Your gaine in yeelding to the English King?

Phil. Their losse in yeelding to the English King.
But Iohn, they saw from out their highest Towers
The Cheualiers of *France* and crossebow-shot
Make lanes of slaughterd bodies through thine hoast,
And are resolu'd to yeeld to Arthurs right.

Iohn. Why Philip, though thou brauest it fore the
        wals,
Thy conscience knowes that Iohn hath wonne the field.

Phil. What ere my conscience knows, thy armie
        feeles
That Philip had the better of the day.

Bast. Philip indeede hath got the Lyons case,
Which here he holds to Lymoges disgrace.
Base Duke to flye and leaue such spoyles behind:
But this thou knewst of force to make mee stay.
It farde with thee as with the marriner,
Spying the hugie Whale, whose monstrous bulke
Doth beare the waues like mountaines fore the winde,
That throwes out empty vessels, so to stay
His furie, while the ship doth saile away,
Philip, t'is thine: and fore this Princely presence,
Madame, I humbly lay it at your feete,
Being the first aduenture I atchieu'd,
And first exployt your Grace did me enioyne:
Yet many more I long to be enjoynd.

Blanch. Philip I take it, and I thee command
To weare the same as earst thy Father did:
Therewith receiue this fauour at my hands,
T'incourage thee to follow Richards fame.

Arth. Ye Citizens of Angiers are ye mute?
Arthur or Iohn, say which shall be your King?

Citizen. We care not which, if once we knew the
   right,
But till we know, we will not yeeld our right.
   Bast. Might Philip counsell two so mightie kings,
As are the Kings of England and of Fraunce,
He would aduise your Graces to vnite
And knit your forces gainst these Citizens,
Pulling their battered wals about their ears.
The Towne once wonne, then striue about the claime,
For they are minded to delude you both.
   Citizen. Kings, Princes, Lords, & Knights assembled
      here,
The Cittizens of Angiers all by me
Entreate your Maiestie to heare them speake :
And as you like the motion they shall make,
So to account and follow their aduice.
   Iohn. *Phil.* Speake on, we giue thee leaue.
   Citizen. Then thus : whereas the yong and lusty
      knight
Incites you on to knit your kingly strengths :
The motion cannot chuse but please the good,
And such as loue the quiet of the State.
But how my Lords, how should your strengths be knit ?
Not to oppresse your subiects and your friends,
And fill the world with brawles and mutinies :
But vnto peace your forces should be knit
To liue in Princely league and amitie :
Doo this, the gates of Angiers shall giue way,
And stand quite open to your harts content.
To make this peace a lasting bond of loue,
Remains one onely honorable meanes,
Which by your pardon I shall here display.
Lewis the Dolphin and the heire of Fraunce,
A man of noted valor through the world,
Is yet vnmarried : let him take to wife
The beauteous daughter of the King of Spaine,
Neece to K. Iohn, the louely Ladie Blanch,

Begotten on his Sister Elianor.
With her in marriage will her vnkle giue
Castles and Towers, as fitteth such a match.
The Kings thus ioynd in league of perfect loue,
They may so deale with Arthur Duke of Britaine,
Who is but yong, and yet vnmeete to raigne,
As he shall stand contented euerie way.
Thus haue I boldly (for the common good)
Deliuered what the Citie gaue in charge.
And as vpon conditions you agree,
So shall we stand content to yeeld the Towne.

   Arth. A proper peace, if such a motion hold ;
These Kings beare armes for me, and for my right,
And they shall share my lands to make them friends.

   Q. El. Sonne Iohn, follow this motion, as thou
     louest thy mother.
Make league with Philip, yeeld to any thing :
Lewis shall haue my Neece, and then be sure
Arthur shall haue small succour out of Fraunce.

   Iohn. Brother of Fraunce, you heare the Citizens :
Then tell me, how you meane to deale herein.

   Cons. Why Iohn, what canst thou giue vnto thy
     Neece,
Thou hast no foote of land but Arthurs right.

   Lewis. Byr lady Citizens, I like your choyce,
A louely damsele is the Ladie Blanche,
Worthie the heire of Europe for her pheere.

   Cons. What Kings, why stand you gazing in a
     trance ?
Why how now Lords ? accursed Cittizens`
To fill and tickle their ambicious ears,
With hope of gaine, that springs from Arthurs losse.
Some dismall Planet at thy birth-day raign'd,
For now I see the fall of all thy hopes.

   K. Phil. Ladie, and Duke of Brittaine, know you both,
The King of Fraunce respects his honor more,
Than to betray his friends and fauourers,

Princesse of Spaine, could you affect my Sonne,
If we vpon conditions could agree?
    Bast. Swounds Madam, take an English Gentleman;
Slaue as I was, I thought to haue mooude the match.
Grandame you made me halfe a promise once,
That Lady Blanch should bring me wealth inough,
And make me heire of store of English land.
    Q. El. Peace Philip, I will looke thee out a
        wife,
We must with policie compound this strife.
    Bast. If Lewis get her, well, I say no more :
But let the froelicke Frenchman take no scorne,
If Philip front him with an English horne.
    Iohn. Ladie, what answere make you to the King
        of Fraunce?
Can you affect the Dolphin for your Lord?
    Blanch. I thanke the King that likes of me so
        well,
To make me Bride vnto so great a Prince :
But giue me leaue my Lord to pause on this,
Least beeing too too forward in the cause,
It may be blemish to my modestie.
    Q. El. Sonne Iohn, and worthie Philip K. of
        Fraunce,
Doo you confer a wnile about the Dower,
And I will schoole my modest Neece so well,
That she shall yeeld as soone as you haue done.
    Cons. I, theres the wretch that broacheth all this ill,
Why flye I not vpon the Beldames face,
And with my nayles pull foorth her hatefull eyes.
    Arth. Sweet Mother cease these hastie madding
        fits ;
For my sake, let my Grandame haue her will.
O would she with her hands pull forth my heart,
I could affoord it to appease these broyles.
But (mother) let vs wisely winke at all,
Least farther harmes ensue our hastie speech.

Phil. Brother of England, what dowrie wilt thou
   giue
Vnto my Sonne in marriage with thy Neece?
   Iohn. First Philip knowes her dowrie out of Spaine,
To be so great as to content a King :
But more to mend and amplifie the same,
I giue in money thirty thousand markes,
For land I leaue it to thine owne demaund.
   Phil. Then I demand Volquesson, Torain, Main,
Poiters and Aniou, these fiue Provinces,
Which thou as King of England holdst in Fraunce :
Then shall our peace be soone concluded on.
   Bast. No less than fiue such Provinces at once?
   Iohn. Mother what shall I doo? my brother got
   these lands
With much effusion of our English bloud :
And shall I giue it all away at once?
   Q. Elin. Iohn giue it him, so shalt thou liue in
   peace,
And keepe the residue sans ieopardie.
   Iohn. Philip, bring forth thy Sonne, here is my Neece,
And here in mariage I doo giue with her
From me and my Successors English Kings,
Volquesson, Poiters, Anjou, Torain, Main,
And thirtie thousand markes of stipend coyne.
Now Citizens, how like you of this match?
   Citiz. We ioye to see so sweete a peace begun.
   Lewis. Lewis with Blanch shall euer liue content,
But now King Iohn, what say you to the Duke?
Father, speake as you may in his behalfe.
   Phil. K. Iohn, be good vnto thy Nephew here,
And giue him somewhat that shall please thee best.
   Iohn. Arthur, although thou troublest Englands
   peace   .
Yet here I giue thee Brittaine for thine owne,
Together with the Earledome of Richmont,
And this rich Citie of Angiers withall.

Q. El. And if thou seeke to please thine Uncle
  Iohn,
Shalt see my Sonne how I will make of thee.
  Iohn. Now euery thing is sorted to this end,
Lets in, and there prepare the mariage rytes,
Which in S. Maries Chappell presently
Shal be performed ere this presence part.
      [Exeunt. Manent Constance & Arthur.
  Arth. Madam good cheere, these drouping languish-
    ments,
Addc no redresse to salue our awkward haps,
If heauens haue concluded these euents,
To small auaile is bitter pensiuenes :
Seasons will change, and so our present griefe
May change with them, and all to our reliefe.
  Cons. Ah boy, thy yeares I see are farre too greene
To looke into the bottome of these cares.
But I, who see the poyse that weigheth downe
Thy weale, my wish, and all the willing meanes
Wherewith thy fortune and thy fame should mount,
What ioye, what ease, what rest can lodge in me,
With whom all hope and hap doe disagree ?
  Art. Yet Ladies teares. and cares, and solemne
    shows,
Rather then helpes, heape vp more worke for woes.
  Cons. If any Power will heare a widdowes plaint,
That from a wounded soule implores reuenge :
Send fell contagion to infect this Clyme,
This cursed Countrey, where the traytors breath,
Whose periurie (as prowd Briareus,)
Beleaguers all the Skie with mis-beliefe.
He promist Arthur, and he sware it too,
To fence thy right, and check thy foemans pride :
But now black-spotted Periure as he is,
He takes a truce with Elnors damned brat,
And marries Lewis to her iouely Neece,
Sharing thy fortune, and thy birth-dayes gift

Betweene these louers : ill betide the match.
And as they shoulder thee from out thy owne,
And triumph in a widowes tearefull cares :
So heavens crosse them with a thriftles course,
Is all the bloud yspilt on either part,
Closing the cranies of the thirstie earth,
Growne to a loue-game and a Bridall feast ?
And must thy birthright bid the wedding banes ?
Poore helples boy, hopeles and helpeles too,
To whom misfortune seemes no yoke at all.
Thy stay, thy state, thy imminent mishaps
Woundeth thy mothers thoughts with feeling care,
Why lookst thou pale ? the colour flyes thy face :
I trouble now the fountaine of thy youth,
And make it moodie with my doles discourse,
Goe in with me, reply not louely boy,
We must obscure this mone with melodie,
Least worser wrack ensue our malecontent. [Exeunt.

Enter the King of *England,* the King of *France,*
    Arthur, Bastard, Lewis, Lymoges, Constance,
    Blanche, Chattileion. Pembrooke, Salisburie, and
    Elianor.

Iohn. This is the day, the long desired day,
Wherein the Realmes of England and of Fraunce
Stand highly blessed in a lasting peace.
Thrice happie is the bridegroome and the bride,
From whose sweete bridal such a concord springs,
To make of mortall foes immortall friends.
    Cons. Vngodly peace made by anothers warre.
    Phil. Vnhappie peace, that ties thee from reuenge,
Rouze thee Plantaginet, liue not to see
The butcher of the great Plantaginet.
Kings, Princes, and ye Peeres of either Realmes,
Pardon my rashnes, and forgiue the zeale
That carries me in furie to a deede

Of high desert, of honour, and of armes.
A boone (O Kings) a boone doth Philip beg
Prostrate vpon his knee : which knee shall cleaue
Unto the superficies of the earth,
Till Fraunce and England grant this glorious boone.
    Iohn. Speake Philip. England grants thee thy re-
    quest.
    Phil. And Fraunce confirmes what ere is in his
    power.
    Bast. Then Duke sit fast, I leuell at thy head,
Too base a ransome for my fathers life.
Princes, I craue the Combat with the Duke
That braues it in dishonor of my Sire.
Your words are past, nor can you now reuerse
The Princely promise that reuiues my soule,
Whereat me thinks I see his sinnews shake :
This is the boon (dread Lords) which granted once
Or life or death are pleasant to my soule;
Since I shall liue and die in Richards right.
    Lym. Base Bastard, misbegotten of a King,
To interrupt these holy nuptiall rytes
With brawles and tumults to a Dukes disgrace ;
Let it suffice, I scorne to ioyne in fight,
With one so farre vnequall to myselfe.
    Bast. A fine excuse, Kings if you wil be Kings,
Then keepe your words, and let vs combat it.
    Iohn. Philip, we cannot force the Duke to fight,
Beeing a subiect vnto neither Realme :
But tell me Austria, if an English Duke
Should dare thee thus, wouldst thou accept the chal-
    lendge ?
    Lym. Els let the world account the Austrich Duke
The greatest coward liuing on the Earth.
    Iohn. Then cheere thee Philip, Iohn will keepe his
    word,
Kneele downe, in sight of Philip King of Fraunce,
And all these Princely Lords assembled here,

I gird thee with the sword of Normandie,
And of that Land I doo inuest thee Duke :
So shalt thou be in liuing and in land
Nothing inferiour vnto Austria.
    Lym. K. Iohn, I tell thee flatly to thy face,
Thou wrongst mine honour : and that thou maist see
How much I scorne thy new made Duke and thee,
I flatly say, I will not be compeld :
And so farewell Sir Duke of low degree,
Ile finde a time to match you for this geere.   [Exit.
    Iohn. Stay Philip, let him goe, the honors thine.
    Bast. I cannot liue unles his life be mine.
    Q. El. Thy forwardnes this day hath ioyd my
        soule,
And made me thinke my Richard liues in thee.
    K. Phil. Lordlings lets in, and spend the wedding
        day
In maskes and triumphs, letting quarreles cease.

Enter a Cardynall from *Rome.*

    Car. Stay King of France, I charge thee ioin not
        hands
With him that stands accurst of God and men.
    Know Iohn, that I Pandulph, Cardinall of Millaine,
and Legate from the Sea of Rome, demaund of thee
in the name of our holy Father the Pope Innocent,
why dost (contrarie to the lawes of our holy mother
the Church, and our holye Father the Pope) disturbe
the quiet of the Church, and disannul the election of
Stephen Langhton, whom his holines hath elected
Archbishop of Canterburie : this in his Holines name
I demaund of thee?
    Iohn. And what hast thou or the Pope thy maister
to doo to demaund of me, how I employ mine own?
Know Sir Priest, as I honour the Church and holy
Churchmen, so I scorne to be subiect to the greatest

Prelate in the world. Tell thy Maister so from me, and say, Iohn of England said it, that neuer an Italian Priest of them all, shal either haue tythe, tole, or polling penie out of England; but as I am King, so will I raigne next vnder God, supreame head both ouer spiritual and temrall: and hee that contradicts me in this, Ile make him hoppe headlesse.

K. Phil. What King Iohn, know you what you say, thus to blaspheme against our holy father the Pope?

Iohn. Philip, though thou and all the Princes of Christendome suffer themselues to be abusde by a Prelates slauery, my minde is not of such base temper. If the Pope will bee King in England, let him winne it with the sword, I know no other title he can alleage to mine inheritance.

Car. Iohn, this is thine answer?

Iohn. What then?

Car. Then I Pandulph of Padoa, Legate from the Apostolike Sea, do in the name of Saint Peter and his successor our holy Father Pope Innocent, pronounce thee accursed, discharging euery one of thy subiectes of all dutie and fealtie that they doo owe to thee, and pardon and forgiuenes of sinne to those or them whateuer, which shall carrie armes against thee, or murder thee: This I pronounce, and charge all good men to abhorre thee as an excommunicate person.

Iohn. So sir, the more the Fox is curst the better a fares: if God blesse me and my Land, let the Pope and his shauelings curse and sparc not.

Car. Furthermore, I charge thee Philip King of France, and al the Kings and Princes of Christendome, to make war vpon this miscreant: and whereas thou hast made a league with him, and confirmed it by oath, I doo in the name of our foresaid father the Pope, acquit thee of that oath, as vnlawfull, beeing made with an heretike; how saist thou Philip, doost thou obey?

Iohn. Brother of Fraunce, what say you to the
Cardinall?

Phil. I say, I ant sorrie for your Majestie, request-
ing you to submit your selfe to the Church of Rome.

    Iohn. And what say you to our league, if I doo not
      submit?

    Phil. What should I say? I must obey the Pope.

    Iohn. Obey the Pope, and breake your oath to
      God?

Phil. The Legate hath absolu'de me of mine oath :
Then yeeld to Rome, or I defie thee heere.

    Iohn. Why Philip, I defie the Pope and thee,
False as thou art, and periured King of Fraunce,
Unworthie man to be accompted King.
Giu'st thou thy sword into a Prelates hands?
Pandulph, where I of Abbots, Monkes, and Friers
Haue taken somewhat to maintaine my warres,
Now will I take no more but all they haue.
Ile rowze the lazie lubbers from their Cells,
And in despight Ile send them to the Pope.
Mother come you with me, and for the rest
That will not follow Iohn in this attempt,
Confusion light vpon their damned soules.
Come Lords, fight for your King, that fighteth for
    your good.

    Phil. And are they gone? Pandulph thy selfe shalt
      see
How Fraunce will fight for Rome and Romish rytes.
Nobles to armes, let him not passe the seas,
Lets take him captiue, and in triumph lead
The K. of England to the gates of Rome.
Arthur bestirre thee man, and thou shalt see
What Philip K. of Fraunce will doo for thee.

    Blanche. And will your Grace vpon your wedding
      day
Forsake your Bride, and follow dreadfull drums?
Nay, good my Lord, stay you at home with mee.

Lewis. Sweete hearte content thee, and we shall
　agree.
Phil. Follow me Lords, Lord Cardynall lead the
　way,
Drums shal be musicque to this wedding day.
　　　　　　　　　　　　　　　　[Exeunt.

Excursions.　The *Bastard* pursues *Austria,* and
　　　　　kils him.

Bast. Thus hath K. Richards sonne performde his
　vowes.
And offred Austria's bloud for sacrifice
Unto his fathers euerliuing soule.
Braue Cordelion, now my heart doth say,
I haue deserude, though not to be thy heire,
Yet as I am, thy base begotten sonne,
A name as pleasing to thy Philips heart,
As to be cald the Duke of Normandie.
Lie there a pray to euery rauening fowle :
And as my father triumpht in thy spoyles,
And trode thine Ensignes vnderneath his feete,
So doo I tread vpon thy cursed selfe,
And leaue thy bodie to the fowles for food.　　[Exit.

Excursions.　*Arthur, Constance, Lewis,* having taken
　　　　Q. *Elianor* prisoner.

Cons. Thus hath the God of Kings with conquering
　arme
Dispearst the foes to true succession,
Proud, and disturder of thy Countreyes peace,
Constance doth liue to tame thine insolence,
And on thy head will now auenged be
For all the mischiefes hatched in thy braine.
　Q. El. Contemptuous Dame, vnreuerent Dutches
　　thou,
To braue so great a Queene as Elianor,

Base scolde, hast thou forgot, that I was wife
And mother to three mightie English Kings?
I charge thee then, and you forsooth sir Boy,
To set your Grandmother at libertie,
And yeeld to Iohn your Uncle and your King.

    Cons. 'Tis not thy words proud Queene shal carry it.
    Elianor. Nor yet thy threates proud dame shal
      daunt my mind.
    Arth. Sweete Grandame, and good Mother, leaue
      these braules.
    Elianor. Ile finde a time to triumph in thy fall.
    Cons. My time is now to triumph in thy fall.
And thou shalt know that Constance will triumph.
    Arth. Good mother, weigh it is Queene Elianor.
Though she be captiue, vse her like herselfe.
Sweete Grandame, beare with what my Mother says,
Your highnes shal be vsed honourably.

Enter a Messenger.

    Mess. Lewis my Lord, Duke Arthur, and the rest,
To armes in hast, K. Iohn relyes his men,
And ginnes the sight afresh : and sweares withall
To lose his life, or set his Mother free.
    Lewis. Arthur away, tis time to looke about.
    Elianor. Why how now dame, what is your courage
      coold?
    Cons. No Elianor my courage gathers strength,
And hopes to lead both Iohn and thee as slaues :
And in that hope, I hale thee to the field.   [Exeunt.
[Excursions. *Elianor* is rescued by *Iohn*, and *Arthur*
    is taken prisoner. *Exeunt.* Sound Victorie.

Enter *Iohn, Elianor,* and *Arthur* prisoner, *Bastard,*
    Pembrooke, Salisbury, and *Hubert de Burgh.*

    Iohn. Thus right triumphs, and Iohn triumphs in
      right :

Arthur thou seest, Fraunce cannot bolster thee :
Thy Mothers pride hath brought thee to this fall.
But if at last Nephew thou yeeld thy selfe
Into the gardance of thine Unckle Iohn,
Thou shalt be vsèd as becomes a Prince.

    Arth. Unckle, my Grandame taught her Nephew this,
To beare captivitie with patience.
Might hath preuayld, not right, for I am King
Of England, though thou weare the Diadem.

    Q. El. Sonne Iohn, soone shall wee teach him to
      forget
These proud presumptions, and to know himselfe.

    Iohn. Mother, he neuer will forget his claime,
J would he liude not to remember it.
But leauing this, we will to England now,
And take some order with our Popelings there,
That swell with pride and fat of lay mens lands.
Philip, I make thee chiefe in this affaire,
Ransack the Abbeys, Cloysters, Priories,
Conuert their coyne vnto my souldiers vse :
And whatsoere he be within my Land,
That goes to Rome for iustice and for law,
While he may haue his right within the Realme,
Let him be iudgde a traitor to the state,
And suffer as an enemie to England.
Mother, we leaue you here beyond the seas,
As Regent of our Prouinces in Fraunce,
While we to England take a speedie course,
And thanke our God that gaue vs victorie.
Hubert de Burgh take Arthur here to thee,
Be he thy prisoner : Hubert keepe him safe,
For on his life doth hang thy Soueraignes Crowne.
But in his death consists thy Soueraignes blisse :
Then Hubert, as thou shortly hearst from me,
So vse the prisoner I haue giuen in charge.

    Hub. Frolick yong Prince, though I your keeper be,
Yet shall your keeper liue at your commaund.

Arth. As please my God, so shall become of me.
Q. El. My Sonne, to England, I will see thee shipt,
And pray to God to send thee safe ashore.
Bast. Now warres are done, I long to be at home,
To diue into the Monkes and Abbots bags,
To make some sport among the smooth skin Nunnes,
And keepe some reuell with the fanzen Friers.
Iohn. To England Lords, each looke vnto your
charge,
And arme yourselues against the Romane pride.
[Exeunt.

Enter the King of France, *Lewes* his sonne, Cardinall
Pandolph, Legate, and *Constance.*

Phil. What, euery man attacht with this mishap?
Why frowne you so, why droop ye Lords of Fraunce?
Me thinkes it differs from a warlike minde,
To lowre it for a checke or two of Chaunce.
Had Lymoges escapt the bastards spight,
A little sorrow might haue serude our losse.
Braue Austria, heauen ioyes to haue thee there.
Card. His sowle is safe and free from Purgatorie,
Our holy Father hath dispenst his sinnes,
The blessed Saints haue heard our Orisons,
And all are Mediators for his soule,
And in the right of these most holy warres,
His Holinese free pardon doth pronounce
To all that follow you gainst English heretiques,
Who stand accursed in our mother Church.

Enter *Constance* alone.

Phil. To aggrauate the measure of our griefe,
All malecontent comes Constance for her Sonne.
Be breefe good madame, for your face imports
A tragick tale behinde thats yet vntolde,
Her passions stop the organ of her voyce,

Deepe sorrow throbbeth misbefalne euents,
Out with it Ladie, that our Act may end
A full Catastrophe of sad laments.
 Cons. My tongue is tunde to storie forth mishap :
When did I breath to tell a pleasing tale?
Must Constance speake? let teares preuent her talke:
Must I discourse? let Dido sigh and say,
She weepes againe to heare the wracke of Troy :
Two words will serue, and then my tale is done :
Elnors proud brat hath robd me of my Sonne.
 Lewis. Haue patience Madame, this is chaunce of
  warre :
He may be ransomde, we reuenge his wrong.
 Cons. Be it ner so soone, I shall not liue so long.
 Phil. Despaire not yet, come Constance, goe with
  me,
These clouds will fleet, the day will cleare againe.
            [Exeunt.
 Card. Now Lewes, thy fortune buds with happie
  spring,
Our holy Fathers prayers effecteth this.
Arthur is safe, let Iohn alone with him,
Thy title next is fairst to Englands crowne :
Now stirre thy Father to begin with Iohn,
The Pope sayes I, and so is Albion thine.
 Lewes. Thankes my Lord Legat for your good
  conceipt,
'Tis best we follow now the game is faire,
My Father wants to worke him your good words.
 Card. A few will serue to forward him in this,
Those shal not want; but lets about it then. [Exeunt.

Enter *Philip* leading a Frier, charging him show
  where the Abbots golde lay.

 Phil. Come on you fat Franciscan, dallie no longer,
but shew me where the Abbots treasure lyes, or die.

Frier. *Benedicamus Domini,* was euer such an
iniurie?
Sweete S. Withold of thy lenitie, defend vs from
extremitie,
And heare vs for S. Charitie, oppressed with austeritie.
In nomine Domini, make I my homilie,
Gentle gentilitie grieue not the cleargie.
　Phil. Grey-gownd good face, coniure ye,
　　nere trust me for a groate
If this waste girdle hang thee not
　　that girdeth in thy coate.
Now balde and barefoote Bungie birds,
　　when vp the gallowes climing,
Say Philip he had words inough,
　　to put you downe with ryming,
　Frier. O pardon, *O parce,* S. Frauncis for mercie,
Shall shield thee from nightspels, and dreaming of
diuells,
If thou wilt forgiue me, and neuer more grieue me,
With fasting and praying, and *Haile Marie* saying,
From black Purgatorie, a penance right sorie :
Frier Thomas will warme you,
It shall neuer harme you.
　Phil. Come leaue off your rabble,
Sirs, hang vp this lozell.
　2 *Frier.* For charitie I beg his life,
　　Saint Francis chiefest Frier,
The best in all our couent Sir,
　　to keepe a Winters fier.
O strangle not the good olde man,
　　My hostesse oldest guest,
And I will bring you by and by
　　Vnto the Priors chest.
　Phil. I, saist thou so, & if thou wilt the Frier is at
libertie,
If not, as I am honest man, I hang you both for com-
panie.

Frier. Come hether, this is the chest, though simple
    to behold,
That wanteth not a thousand pound in siluer and in
    gold.
My selfe will warrant full so much, I know the Abbots
    store,
Ile pawne my life there is no lesse, to haue what ere
    is more.
    Phil. I take thy word, the ouerplus vnto thy share
    shall come,
But if there want of full so much, thy neck shall pay
    the sum.
Breake vp the Coffer, Frier.
    Frier. Oh I am vndun, faire Alice the Nun
Hath tooke vp her rest in the Abbots chest.
Sancte benedicite, pardon my simplicitie.
Fie Alice, confession will not salue this transgression.
    Phil. What haue wee here, a holy Nun? so keepe
    mee God in health,
A smooth facte Nunne (for ought I knowe) is all the
    Abbots wealth.
Is this the Nonries chastitie?
Beshrewe me but I thinke
They go as oft to Venery as niggards to their
    drinke,
Why paltry Frier and Pandar too, ye shamelesse shauen
    crowne,
Is this the chest that held a hoord,
    at least a thousand pound?
And is the hoord a holy whore?
    Well, be the hangman nimble,
Hee'le take the paine to paye you home,
    and teach you to dissemble.
    Nunne. O spare the Frier Anthony,
    a beggar neuer was
To sing a Dirige solemnly,
    or read a morning masse.

If money be the meanes of this,
   I know an ancient Nunne,
That hath a hoord these seuen yeares,
   did neuer see the sunne ;
And that is yours, and what is ours,
   so fauour now be shown,
You shall commaund as commonly,
   as if it were your owne.
   Frier. Your honour excepted.
   Nunne. I Thomas, I meane so.
   Phil. From all saue from Friers.
   Nunne. Good sir, doo not think so.
   Phil. I thinke and see so :
why how camst thou here ?
   Frier. To hide here from lay men.
   Nunne. Tis true sir, for feare.
   Phil. For fear of the laytie : a pitifull dred
When a Nunne flies for succour to a fat Friers
   bed.
But now for your ransome my Cloyster-bred Conney,
To the chest that you speake of where lyes so much
   money.
   Nunne. Faire sir, within this presse, of plate &
   money is
The valew of a thousand markes, and other things
   by gis.
Let vs alone, and take it all, tis yours sir, now you
   know it.
   Phil. Come on sir Frier, pick the locke, this geere
   dooth cotton hansome,
That couetousnes so cunningly must pay ye letchers
   ransom.
What is in the hoord ?
   Frier. Frier Laurence my Lord, now holy water
   help vs,
Some witch or some diuell is sent to delude vs :
Haud credo Laurentius, that thou shouldst be pend thus

In the presse of a Nun we are all vndone,
And brought to discredence if thou be Frier Laurence.
    Frier. Amor vincit omnia, so Cato affirmeth,
And therefore a Frier whose fancie soone burneth,
Because he is mortall and made of mould,
He omits what he ought, and doth more than he
    should.
    Phil. How goes this geere? the Friers chest filde
    with a sausen Nunne.
The Nunne again lockes Friar vp,
    to keep him from the Sun.
Belike the press is Purgatorie,
    or penance passing grieuous :
The Friers chest a hel for Nunnes !
    how doo these dolts deceive us ?
Is this the labour of their liues, to feede and liue at
    ease ?
To reuell so lasciuiously as often as they please ?
Ile mend the fault or fault my ayme,
    if I do misse amending,
Tis better burn the Cloisters down,
    than leaue them for offending.
But holy you, to you I speake,
    to you religious diuell,
Is this the presse that holds the summe,
    to quite you for your euill?
    Nunne. I crie *Peccavi, parce me,*
    good Sir I was beguild.
    Frier. Absolue Sir for charitie,
    she would bee reconcilde.
    Phil. And so I shall, sirs binde them fast,
    this is their absolution,
go hang them vp for hurting them,
    haste them to execution.
    Fr. Lawrence. O tempus edax rerum,
Giue children bookes they teare them.
O *vanitas vanitatis,* in this waning *ætatis.*

At threescore wel-neere, to goe to this geere,
To my conscience a clog, to dye like a dog.
Exaudi me Domine, si uis me parce
Dabo pecuniam, si habeo veniam.
To goe and fetch it, I will dispatch it,
A hundred pounds sterling, for my liues sparing.

Enter *Peter* a Prophet, with people.

Peter. Hoe, who is here? S. Frauncis be your speed,
Come in my flock, and follow me,
    your fortunes I will reed.
Come hether boy, goe get thee home,
    and clime not ouer hie,
For from aloft thy fortune stands, in hazard thou shalt
    die.

Boy. God be with you Peter, I pray you come to
our house a Sunday.

Peter. My boy show me thy hand, blesse thee my
    boy,
For in thy palme I see a many troubles are ybent to
    dwell,
But thou shalt scape them all, and doo full well.

Boy. I thanke you Peter, theres a cheese for your
labor : my sister prayes ye to come home, & tell her
how many husbands she shall haue, and shee'l giue
you a rib of bacon.

Peter. My masters, stay at the towns end for me.
Ile come to you all anon : I must dispatch some
busines with a Frier, and then Ile read your fortunes.

Phil. How now, a Prophet ! Sir prophet whence
are ye ?

Peter. I am of the world and in the world, but liue
not as others, by the world : what I am I know, and
what thou wilt be I know. If thou knowest me now,
be answered : if not, enquire no more what I am.

Phil. Sir, I know you will be a dissembling knaue,

that deludes the people with blinde prophecies : you
are him I looke for, you shall away with me : bring
away all the rabble, and you Frier Laurence, remember
your raunsome a hundred pound, and a pardon for
your selfe, and the rest come on. Sir Prophet, you
shall with me, to receiue a Prophets rewarde. [Exeunt.

Enter *Hubert de Burgh* with three men.

Hub. My masters, I haue shewed you what warrant I haue for this attempt; I perceiue by your
heauie countenances, you had rather be otherwise
imployed, and for my owne part, I would the King
had made choyce of some other executioner : onely
this is my comfort, that a King commaunds, whose
precepts neglected or omitted, threatneth torture for
the default. Therefore in briefe, leaue me, and be
readie to attend the aduenture : stay within that entry,
and when you hear me crie, God save the King, issue
sodainly foorth, lay handes on Arthur, set him in his
chayre, wherein (once fast bound) leaue him with me
to finish the rest.

Attendants. We goe, though loath.   [Exeunt.

Hub. My Lord, will it please your Honour to take
the benefite of the faire euening ?

Enter *Arthur* to *Hubert de Burgh.*

Arth. Gramercie Hubert for thy care of me,
In or to whom restraint is newly knowen,
The ioy of walking is small benefit,
Yet will I take thy offer with small thankes,
I would not loose the pleasure of the eye.
But tell me curteous Keeper if you can,
How long the King will haue me tarrie here.

Hub. I know not Prince, but as I gesse, not long.
God send you freedome, and God saue the King.
                              [They issue forth.

Arth. Why now sirs, what may this outrage meane?
O help me Hubert, gentle Keeper helpe ;
God send this sodaine mutinous approach
Tend not to reaue a wretched guiltless life.
Hub. So sirs, depart, and leaue the rest for me.
Arth. Then Arthur yeeld, death frowneth in thy face,
What meaneth this ?   Good Hubert plead the case.
Hub. Patience yong Lord, and listen words of woe,
Harmfull and harsh, hells horror to be heard :
A dismall tale fit for a furies tongue.
I faint to tell, deepe sorrow is the sound.
Arth. What, must I die ?
Hub. No newes of death, but tidings of more hate,
A wrathfull doome, and must vnluckie fate :
Deaths dish were daintie at so fell a feast,
Be deafe, heare not, its hell to tell the rest.
Arth. Alas, thou wrongst my youth with words of
    feare,
Tis hell, tis horror, not for one to heare :
What is it man if needes be don,
Act it, and end it, that the paine were gon.
Hub. I will not chaunt such dolour with my tongue,
Yet must I act the outrage with my hand.
My heart, my head, and all my powers beside,
To aide the office haue at once denide.
Peruse this Letter, lines of treble woe,
Reade ore my charge, and pardon when you know.

Hubert, these are to commaund thee, as thou tendrest
    our quiet in minde, and the estate of our person,
    that presently vpon the receipt of our commaund,
    thou put out the eies of Arthur Plantaginet.

Arth. Ah monstrous damned man ! his very breath
    infects the elements.
Contagious venyme dwelleth in his heart,
Effecting meanes to poyson all the world.

Unreuerent may I be to blame the heauens
Of great iniustice, that the miscreant
Liues to oppresse the innocents with wrong.
Ah Hubert ! makes he thee his instrument,
To sound the tromp that causeth hell triumph ?
Heaven weepes, the Saints do shed celestiall teares,
They feare thy fall, and cyte thee with remorse,
They knock thy conscience, moouing pitie there,
Willing to fence thee from the rage of hell
Hell, Hubert, trust me all the plagues of hell
Hangs on performance of this damncd deede.
This seale, the warrant of the bodies blisse,
Ensureth Satan chieftaine of thy soule :
Subscribe not Hubert, giue not Gods part away,
I speake not only for eyes priuiledge,
The chiefe exterior that I would enioy :
But for thy perill, farre beyond my paine,
Thy sweete soules losse, more than my eyes vaine lack :
A cause internall, and eternall too.
Aduise thee Hubert, for the case is hard,
To loose saluation for a Kings reward.

   Hub. My Lord, a subiect dwelling in the land
Is tyed to execute the Kings commaund.

   Arth. Yet God commands whose power reacheth
      further,
That no commaund should stand in force to murther.

   Hub. But that same Essence hath ordained a law,
A death for guilt, to keepe the world in awe.

   Arth. I pleade, not guiltie, treasonlesse and free.

   Hub. But that appeale, my Lord, concernes not
    me.

   Arth. Why thou art he that maist omit the perill.

   Hub. I, if my Soueraigne would remit his quarrell.

   Arth. His quarrell is vnhallowed false and wrong.

   Hub. Then be the blame to whom it doth belong.

   Arth. Why thats to thee if thou as they proceede,
Conclude their iudgement with so vile a deede.

Hub. Why then no execution can be lawfull,
If Iudges doomes must be reputed doubtfull.
    Arth. Yes where in forme of Lawe in place and
        time,
The offender is conuicted of the crime.
    Hub. My Lord, my Lord, this long expostula-
        tion,
Heapes vp more griefe, than promise of redresse ;
For this I know, and so resolude I end,
That subiects liues on Kings commaunds depend.
I must not reason why he is your foe,
But doo his charge since he commaunds it so.
    Arth. Then doo thy charge, and charged be thy
        soule
With wrongfull persecution done this day.
You rowling eyes, whose superficies yet
I doo behold with eyes that Nature lent :
Send foorth the terror of your Moouers frowne,
To wreake my wrong vpon the murtherers
That rob me of your faire reflecting view :
Let hell to them (as earth they wish to mee)
Be darke and direfull guerdon for their guylt,
And let the black tormenters of deepe Tartary
Upbraide them with this damned enterprise,
Inflicting change of tortures on their soules.
Delay not Hubert, my orisons are ended,
Begin I pray thee, reaue me of my sight :
But to performe a tragedie indeede,
Conclude the period with a mortal stab.
Constance farewell, tormenter come away,
Make my dispatch the Tyrants feasting day.
    Hub. I faint, I feare, my conscience bids desist :
Faint did I say ? fear was it that I named :
My King commaunds, that warrant sets me free :
But God forbids, and he commaundeth Kings,
That great Commaunder counterchecks my charge,
He stayes my hand, he maketh soft my heart.

Goe cursed tooles, your office is exempt,
Cheere thee young Lord, thou shalt not loose an
    eye,
Though I should purchase it with losse of life.
Ile to the King, and say his will is done,
And of the langor tell him thou art dead,
Goe in with me, for Hubert was not borne
To blinde those lampes that nature pollisht so.
    Arth. Hubert, if euer Arthur be in state,
Looke for amends of this receiued gift,
I tooke my eyesight by thy curtesie,
Thou lentst them me, I will not be ingrate.
But now procrastination may offend
The issue that thy kindness vndertakes:
Depart we, Hubert, to preuent the worst.   [Exeunt.

    Enter *K. Iohn, Essex, Salisbury, Penbrooke.*

    Iohn. Now warlike followers, resteth ought vn-
    done
That may impeach vs of fond ouersight?
The French haue felt the temper of our swords,
Cold terror keepes possession in their sowles,
Checking their ouerdaring arrogance
For buckling with so great an ouermatch,
The Arche prowd titled Priest of Italy,
That calls himselfe grand Vicar vnder God,
Is busied now with trentall obsequies,
Masse and months minde, dirge and I know not
    what,
To ease their sowles in painefull purgatory,
That haue miscarried in these bloudy warres.
Heard you not, Lords, when first his Holines
Had tidings of our small account of him,
How with a taunt vaunting vpon his toes,
He urgde a reason why the English asse
Disdaignd the blessed ordinance of Rome?

The title (reuerently might I inferre)
Became the Kings that earst haue borne the load,
The slauish weieht of that controlling Priest :
Who at his pleasure temperd them like waxe
To carrie armes on danger of his curse,
Banding their sowles with warrants of his hand.
I grieue to thinke how Kings in ages past
(Simply deuoted to the Sea of Rome)
Haue run into a thousand acts of shame.
But now for confirmation of our State,
Sith we haue proynd the more than needfull braunch
That did oppresse the true wel-growing stock,
It resteth we throughout our Territories
Be reproclaimed and inuested King.
   Pemb. My Liege, that were to busie men with
    doubts,
Once were you crownd, proclaimd, and with ap-
    plause
Your Citie streetes haue ecchoed to the eare,
God saue the King, God saue our Soueraigne Iohn,
Pardon my feare, my censure doth infer
Your Highnes not deposde from Regall State,
Would breed a mutinie in peoples mindes,
What it should meane to haue you crownd againe.
   Iohn. Pembrooke, performe what I haue bid thee
    doo,
Thou knowst not what induceth me to this.
Essex goe in, and Lordings all begon
About this taske, I will be crownd anon.

Enter the Bastard.

Philip what newes, how doo the Abbots chests ?
Are Friers fatter than the Nunnes are faire?
What cheere with Churchmen, had they golde or
   no?
Tell me, how hath thy office tooke effect ?

Phil. My Lord, I haue performd your Highnes
    charge :
The ease bred Abbots, and the bare-foote Friers,
The Monkes, the Priors, and holy cloystred Nunnes,
Are all in health, and were my Lord in wealth
Till I had tythde and tolde their holy hoords.
I doubt not when your Highnes sees my prize,
You may proportion all their former pride.
    Iohn. Why so, now sorts it Philip as it should :
This small intrusion into Abbey trunkes,
Will make the Popelings cxcommunicate,
Curse, ban, and breath out damned orisons,
As thick as hailestones fore the Springs approach :
But yet as harmeles and without effect,
As is the eccho of a Cannons crack
Dischargd against the battlements of heauen.
But what newes else befell there Philip ?
    Bast. Strange newes my Lord: within your territories
Nere Pomfret is a Prophet new sprong vp,
Whose diuination volleys wonders foorth :
To him the Commons throng with Countrey gifts,
He sets a date vnto the Beldames death,
Prescribes how long the Virgins state shall last,
Distinguisheth the moouing of the heauens,
Giues limits vnto holy nuptiall rytes,
Foretelleth famine, aboundeth plentie forth :
Of fatc, of fortune, life and death he chats,
With such assurance, scruples put apart,
As if he knew the certaine doomes of heauen,
Or kept a Register of all the Destinies.
    Iohn. Thou telst me mcruailes, would thou hadst
    brought the man,
We might haue questiond him of things to come.
    Bast. My Lord, I tooke a care of had I wist,
And brought the Prophet with me to the Court,
He stayes my Lord but at the Presence doore :
Pleaseth your Highnes, I will call him in.

Iohn. Nay stay awhile, wee'l haue him here anon,
A thing of weight is first to be performd.

Enter the Nobles and crowne King *John*, and then
cry God save the king.

Iohn. Lordings and friends supporters of our State,
Admire not at this vnaccustomd course,
Nor in your thoughts blame not this deede of yours.
Once ere this time was I inuested King,
Your fealtie sworne as Liegmen to our state :
Once since that time ambicious weeds haue sprung
To staine the beauty of our garden plot :
But heauens in our conduct rooting thence
The false intruders, breakers of worlds peace,
Haue to our ioy, made sunshine chase the storme.
After the which, to try your constancie,
That now I see is worthie of your names,
We craude once more your helps for to inuest us
Into the right that envie sought to wrack.
Once was I not deposde, your former choyce ;
Now twice been crowned and applauded King?
Your cheered action to install me so,
Infers assured witnes of your loues,
And binds me ouer in a Kingly care
To render loue with loue, rewards of worth
To ballance downe requitall to the full.
But thankes the while, thankes Lordings to you all :
Aske me and vse me, try me and finde me yours.
   Essex. A boon my Lord, at vauntage of your
     words
We ask to guerdon all our loyalties.
   Pemb. We take the time your Highnes bids vs
     aske :
Please it you graunt, you make your promise good,
With lesser losse than one superfluous haire
That not remembred falleth from your head.

Iohn. My word is past, receiue your boone my Lords,
What may it be? Aske it, and it is yours.
    Essex. We craue my Lord to please the Commons with
The liberty of Lady Constance Sonne:
Whose durance darkeneth your Highnes right,
As if you kept him prisoner, to the end
Your selfe were doubtfull of the thing you haue.
Dismisse him hence, your Highnes needes not feare,
Twice by consent you are proclaimed our King.
    Pemb. This if you graunt, were all vnto your good:
For simple people muse you keepe him close.
    Iohn. Your words haue searcht the center of my thoughts,
Confirming warrant of your loyalties,
Dismisse your counsell, sway my state,
Let Iohn doo nothing, but by your consents.
Why how now Philip, what extasie is this?
Why casts thou vp thy eyes to heauen so?
               [There the five Moones appeare.
    Bast. See, my Lord, strange apparitions,
Glauncing mine eye to see the Diadem
Placte by the Bishops on your Highnes head,
From foorth a gloomie cloude, which courtainelike
Displaide it selfe, I sodainly espied
Fiue Moones reflecting, as you see them now:
Euen in the moment that the Crowne was placte
Gan they appeare, holding the course you see.
    Iohn. What might portend these apparitions,
Vnvsuall signes, forerunners of euent,
Presagers of strange terror to the world:
Beleeue me Lords, the obiect feares me much.
Philip thou toldst me of me of wizzard late,
Fetch in the man to descant of this show.
    Pemb. The heauens frowne vpon the sinfull earth,

When with prodigious vnaccustomd signes
They spot their superficies with such wonder.
    Essex. Before the ruines of Ierusalem,
Such Meteors were the Ensignes of his wrath,
That hastned to destroy the faultfull Towne.

Enter the Bastard with the prophet.

    Iohn. Is this the man ?
    Bast. It is my Lord.
    Iohn. Prophet of Pomfret, for so I heare thou art,
That calculatst of many things to come :
Who by a power repleate with heauenly gifte,
Canst blab the counsell of thy Makers will.
If fame be true, or truth be wrongd by thee,
Decide in cyphering, what these fiue Moones
Portend this Clyme, if they presage at all.
Breath out thy gift, and if I liue to see
Thy diuination take a true effect,
Ile honour thee aboue all earthly men.
    Peter. The Skies wherein these Moones have
        residence,
Presenteth Rome the great Metropolis,
Where sits the Pope in all his holy pompe.
Fowre of the Moones present fowre Provinces,
To wit, Spaine, Denmarke, Germanie, and France,
That beare the yoke of proud commaunding Rome,
And stand in feare to tempt the Prelates curse.
The smallest Moone that whirles about the rest,
Impatient of the place he holds with them,
Doth figure foorth this Island Albion,
Who gins to scorne the See and State of Rome,
And seekes to shun the Edicts of the Pope :
This showes the heauen, and this I doo auerre
Is figured in the apparitions.
    Iohn. Why then it seemes the heauens smile on us,
Giving applause for leauing of the Pope.

But for they chaunce in our Meridian,
Doo they effect no priuate growing ill
To be inflicted on vs in this clyme?
    Peter. The Moones effect no more than what I
      said :
But on some other knowledge that I haue
By my prescience, ere Ascension day
Haue brought the Sunne vnto his vsuall height,
Of Crowne, Estate, and Royall dignitie,
Thou shalt be cleane dispoyld and dispossest.
    Iohn. False Dreamer, perish with thy witched
      newes,
Villaine thou woundst me with thy fallacies :
If it be true, die for thy tidings price ;
If false, for fearing me with vaine suppose :
Hence with the witch, hells damned secretarie.
Lock him vp sure ; for by my faith I sweare,
True or not true, the Wizzard shall not liue.
Before Ascension day : who shall be cause hereof?
Cut off the cause, and then the effect will dye.
Tut, tut, my mercie serues to maime my selfe,
The roote doth liue, from whence these thornes
      spring vp,
I and my promise past for his deliuery :
Frowne friends, faile faith, the diuell goe withall,
The brat shall dye, that terrifies me thus.
Pembrooke and Essex, I recall my graunt,
I will not buy your fauours with my feare :
Nay murmur not, my will is law enough,
1 loue you well, but if I lou'de you better,
I would not buy it with my discontent.

Enter *Hubert.*

How now, what newes with thee?
    Hub. According to your Highnes strict commaund,
Young Arthurs eyes are blinded and extinct.

Iohn. Why so, then he may feele the crowne, but
  never see it.
Hub. Nor see nor feele, for of the extreame paine,
Within one hower gaue he vp the ghost.
Iohn. What is he dead?
Hub. He is my Lord.
Iohn. Then with him dyes my cares.
Essex. Now ioy betide thy soule.
Pemb. And heauens reuenge thy death.
Essex. What haue you done my Lord? was euer
  heard
A deede of more inhumane consequence?
Your foes will curse, your friends will crie reuenge.
Unkindly rage, more rough than Northern winde,
To chip the beautie of so sweete a flower.
What hope in vs for mercie on a fault,
When kinsman dyes without impeach of cause,
As you haue done, so come to cheere you with,
The guilt shall neuer be cast in my teeth.   [Exeunt.
Iohn. And are you gone? the diuell be your guide :
Proud Rebels as ye are, to braue me so :
Saucie, vnciuill, checkers of my will.
Your tongues giue edge vnto the fatall knife,
That shall haue passage through your traitrous throats.
But husht, breathe not buggs words too soone abroad,
Least time preuent the issue of thy reach.
Arthur is dead, I there the corzie growes :
But while he liude, the danger was the more ;
His death hath freed me from a thousand feares,
But it hath purchast me ten times ten thousand foes.
Why all is one, such luck shall haunt his game,
To whome the diuell owes an open shame :
His life a foe that leueld at my Crowne,
His death a frame to pull my building downe.
My thoughts harpt still on quiet by his end,
Who liuing aymed shrowdly at my roome :
But to preuent that plea, twice was I crownd,

Twice did my subiects sweare me fealtie,
And in my conscience lou'de me as their liege,
In whose defence they would haue pawnd their liues.
But now they shun me as a Serpents sting,
A tragick Tyrant, sterne and pitiles,
And not a title followes after Iohn,
But Butcher, blood-sucker, and murtherer.
What Planet gouernde my natiuitie,
To bode me soueraigne types of high estate,
So interlacte with hellish discontent,
Wherein fell furie hath no interest?
Curst be the Crowne, chiefe author of my care,
Nay curst my will, that made the Crowne my care :
Curst be.my birthday, curst ten times the wombe
That yeelded me aliue into the world.
Art thou there villaine, Furies haunt thee still,
For killing him whom all the world laments.

    Hub. Why heres my Lord your Highnes hand & seale,
Charging on liues regard to doo the deede.

    Iohn. Ah dull conceipted peazant, knowst thou not
It was a damned execrable deede?
Showst me a seale? Oh villaine, both our soules
Haue sold their freedome to the thrall of hell
Under the warrant of that cursed Seale.
Hence villaine, hang thy selfe, and say in hell
That I am comming for a kingdome there.

    Hub. My Lord, attend the happie tale I tell,
For heauens health send Sathan packing hence
That instigates your Highnes to despaire.
If Arthurs death be dismall to be heard,
Bandie the newes for rumors of vntruth :
He liues my Lord, the sweetest youth aliue,
In health, with eysight, not a hair amisse.
This hart tooke vigor from this froward hand,
Making it weake to execute your charge.

      Iohn. What, liues he! Then sweete hope come
      home agen,

Chase hence despaire, the purueyor for hell.
Hye Hubert, tell these tidings to my Lords
That throb in passions for yong Arthurs death :
Hence Hubert, stay not till thou hast reueald
The wished newes of Arthurs happy health.
I go my selfe, the ioyfulst man aliue
To storie out this new supposed crime.   [Exeunt.

THE ENDE OF THE FIRST PART.

The

Second part of the

troublesome Raigne of King

John, conteining the death

of Arthur Plantaginet,

the landing of Lewes, and

the poysoning of King

John at Swinstead

Abbey

As it was (sundry times) publikely acted by the

Queenes Maiesties Players, in the ho-

nourable Citie of

LONDON.

TO THE GENTLEMEN READERS.

—o—

The changeles purpose of determinde Fate
Giues period to our care, or harts content
When heauens fixt time for this or that hath end
Nor can earths pomp or policie preuent
The doome ordained in their secret will.
  Gentles we left King John *repleate with blisse*
That Arthur *liude, whom he supposed slaine;*
And Hubert *posting to returne those Lords,*
Who deemd him dead, and parted discontent:
Arthur *himselfe begins our latter Act.*
Our Act of outrage, desperate furie, death;
Wherein fond rashness murdereth first a Prince,
And Monkes falsnes poysoneth last a King.
First Scene shews Arthurs *death in infancie,*
And last concludes Johns *fatall tragedie.*

The Troublesome Raigne of King Iohn.

THE SECOND PART.

——o——

Enter yong Arthur on the walls.

NOW helpe good hap to further mine entent,
   Crosse not my youth with any more extreames :
I venter life to gaine my libertie,
And if I die, worlds troubles haue an end.
Feare gins disswade the strength of my resolue,
My holde will faile, and then alas I fall,
And if I fall, no question death is next :
Better desist, and liue in prison still.
Prison said I? nay, rather death than so :
Comfort and courage come againe to me,
Ile venter sure : tis but a leape for life.

*He leapes, ana brusing his bones, after he was from
his traunce, speakes thus :*

Hoe, who is nigh? some bodie take me vp.
Where is my mother? let me speake with her.
Who hurts me thus? speake hoe, where are you gone?
Ay me poore Arthur, I am here alone.
Why cald I mother, how did I forget?

My fall, my fall, hath kilde my Mothers sonne.
How will she weepe at tidings of my death ?
My death indeed, O God, my bones are burst.
Sweet Jesu saue my soule, forgiue my rash attempt,
Comfort my Mother, shield her from despaire,
When she shall heare my tragick ouerthrowe.
My heart controules the office of my toonge,
My vitall powers forsake my brused trunck,
I dye I dye, heauen take my fleeting soule,
And Lady Mother all good hap to thee.   [He dies.

Enter *Penbrooke, Salsburie, Essex.*

Essex. My Lords of Pembroke and of Salsbury,
We must be carefull in our policie,
To vndermine the kepers of this place,
Else shall we neuer find the princes graue.
    Penb. My Lord of Essex, take no care for that,
I warrant you it was not closely done.
But who is this ? lo Lords the withered flowre,
Who in his life shin'de like the Mornings blush,
Cast out a doore, denide his buriall right,
A pray for birds and beasts to gorge vpon.
    Sals. O ruthfull spectacle ! O damned deede !
My sinewes shake, my very heart doth bleede.
    Essex. Leaue childish teares braue Lords of England,
If waterfloods could fetch his life againe,
My eyes should conduit foorth a sea of teares.
If sobbs would helpe, or sorrowes serue the turne,
My heart should vollie out deepe piercing plaints.
But bootlesse were't to breath as many sighes
As might ecclipse the brightest Sommers sunne,
Heere rests the helpe, a seruice to his ghost.
Let not the tyrant causer of this dole,
Liue to triumph in ruthfull massacres,
Giue hand and hart, and Englishmen to armes,
Tis Gods decree to wreake vs of these harmes.

Pemb. The best aduice : But who commes posting
heere ?

Enter *Hughbert.*

Right noble Lords, I speake vnto you all,
The King entreates your soonest speed
To visit him, who on your present want,
Did ban and cursse his birth, himselfe and me,
For executing of his strict commaund.
I saw his passion, and at fittest time,
Assurde him of his cousins being safe,
Whome pitie would not let me doo to death :
He craues your company my Lords in haste,
To whome I will conduct young Arthur streight,
Who is in health vnder my custodie.
  Essex. In health base villaine, wert not I leaue the
    crime
To Gods reuenge, to whome reuenge belongs,
Heere shouldst thou perish on my Rapires point.
Cal'st thou this health ? such health betide thy friends,
And all that are of thy condition.
  Hugh. My Lords, but heare me speake, & kil me
    then,
If heere I left not this yong Prince aliue,
Maugre the hastie Edict of the King,
Who gaue me charge to put out both his eyes.
That God that gaue me liuing to this howre,
Thunder reuenge vpon me in this place :
And as I tendred him with earnest loue,
So God loue me, and then I shall be well.
  Sals. Hence traytor hence, thy counesel is herecin.
                                    [Exit Hughbert.
Some in this place appoynted by the King,
Haue throwne him from this lodging here aboue,
And sure the murther hath bin newly done,
For yet the body is not fully colde.

Essex. How say you Lords, shal we with speed
    dispatch
Vnder our hands a packet into Fraunce,
To bid the Dolphin enter with his force,
To claime the Kingdome for his proper right,
His title maketh lawfull strength thereto.
Besides, the Pope, on perill of his cursse,
Hath bard vs of obedience vnto Iohn,
This hatefull murder, Lewis his true descent,
The holy charge that we receiu'd from Rome,
Are weightie reasons, if you like my reede,
To make vs all perseuer in this deede.
    Pemb. My lord of Essex, well haue you aduis'de,
I will accord to further you in this.
    Sals. And Salsbury will not gainsay the same :
But aid that course as far foorth as he can.
    Essex. Then each of vs send straight to his allyes.
To winne them to this famous enterprise :
And let vs all yclad in Palmers weede,
The tenth of April at Saint Edmonds Bury
Meete to confer, and on the Altar there
Sweare secrecie and aid to this aduise.
Meane while, let vs conueigh this body hence,
And giue him buriall, as befits his state,
Keeping his months minde, and his obsequies
With solemne intercession for his soule.
How say you Lordings, are you all agreed ?
    Pemb. The tenth of Aprill at Saint Edmunds Bury,
God letting not, I will not faile the time.
    Essex. Then let vs all conuey the body hence.
                                            [*Exeunt.*

Enter *King Iohn*, with two or three, and the Prophet.

    Iohn. Disturbed thoughts, foredoomers of mine ill,
Distracted passions, signes of growing harmes,
Strange Prophecies of imminent mishaps,

Confound my wits, and dull my senses so,
That euery obiect these mine eyes behold,
Seeme instruments to bring me to my end.
Ascension day is come, Iohn feare not then
The prodigies this pratling Prophet threates.
Tis come indeede : ah were it fully past,
Then were I careles of a thousand feares.
The Diall tells me, it is twelue at noone.
Were twelue at midnight past, then might I vaunt,
False seers prophecies of no import.
Could I as well with this right hand of mine
Remove the Sunne from our Meridian,
Unto the moonsted circle of th' antipodes,
As turne this steele from twelue to twelue agen,
Then Iohn, the date of fatall prophecies,
Should with the Prophets life together end.
But *Multa cadunt inter calicem supremaque labra.*
Peter, vnsay thy foolish doting dreame,
And by the Crowne of *England* heere I sweare,
To make thee great, and greatest of thy kin.
 Peter. King Iohn, although the time I haue pre-
  scribed
Be but twelue houres remayning yet behinde,
Yet do I know by inspiration,
Ere that fixt time be fully come about,
King Iohn shall not be King as heeretofore.
 Iohn. Uain buzzard, what mischaunce can chaunce
  so soone,
To set a King beside his regall Seate ?
My heart is good, my body passing strong,
My Land in peace, my enemies subdew'd,
Only my Barons storme at Arthurs death,
But Arthur liues, I there the challenge growes,
Were he dispatcht vnto his longest home,
Then were the King secure of thousand foes.
Hubert, what news with thee, where are my Lords ?
 Hub. Hard newes my Lord, Arthur the louely Prince,

Seeking to escape ouer the Castle walles,
Fell headlong downe, and in the cursed fall
He brake his bones, and there before the gate
Your Barons found him dead, and breathlesse quite.
Iohn. Is Arthur dead? then Hubert without more
    words hang the Prophet.
Away with Peter, villen out of my sight,
I am deafe, be gone, let him not speake a word.
Now Iohn, thy feares are vanisht into smoake,
Arthur is dead, thou guiltlesse of his death.
Sweet Youth, but that I striued for a Crowne,
I could haue well affoorded to thine age,
Long life, and happines to thy content.

Enter the Bastard.

Iohn. Philip what newes with thee?
Bas. The newes I heard was Peters prayers,
Who wisht like fortune to befall vs all :
And with that word, the rope his latest friend,
Kept him from falling headlong to the ground.
Iohn. There let him hang, and be the Rauens food,
While Iohn triumphs in spight of Prophecies.
But whats the tidings from the Popelings now?
What say the Monkes and Priests to our proceedings?
Or where's the Barons that so sodainly
Did leaue the King vpon a false surmise?
Bas. The Prelates storme & thirst for sharpe
    reuenge :
But please your Majestie, were that the worst,
Is little skild : a greater danger growes,
Which must be weeded out by carefull speede,
Or all is lost, for all is leueld at.
Iohn. More frights and feares ! what ere thy tid-
    ings be,
I am preparde : then Philip, quickly say,
Meane they to murder, or imprison me,

To giue my Crowne away to Rome or Fraunce;
Or will they each of them become a King?
Worse than I thinke it is, it cannot be.

Bast. Not worse my Lord, but euerie whit as bad.
The nobles have elected Lewis King,
In right of Ladie Blanch, your Neece, his Wife:
His landing is expected euery hower.
The Nobles, Commons, Clergie, all Estates,
Incited chiefly by the *Cardinall,*
Pandulph that lies here Legate for the Pope,
Thinks long to see their new elected King.
And for vndoubted proofe, see here my Liege,
Letters to me from your Nobilitie,
To be a partie in this action:
Who vnder shew of fained holines,
Appoynt their meeting at S. Edmonds Bury.
There to consult, conspire, and conclude
The ouerthrow and downfall of your State.

Iohn. Why so it must be: one hower of content,
Matcht with a month of passionate effects.
Why shines the Sunne to favour this consort?
Why doo the windes not breake their brazen gates,
And scatter all these periured complices,
With all their counsells, and their damned drifts?
But see the welkin rolleth gently on,
Theres not a lowring clowde to frowne on them;
The heauen, the earth, the sunne, the moone and all,
Conspire with those confederates my decay.
Then hell for me, if any power be there,
Forsake that place, and guide me step by step,
To poyson, strangle, murder in their steps
These traitors: oh that name is too good for them,
And death is easie: is there nothing worse,
To wreake me on this proud peace-breaking crew?
What saist thou Philip? why assists thou not?

Bast. These curses (good my Lord) fit not the season:
Help must descend from heauen against this treason?

Iohn. Nay thou wilt proove a traitor with the rest,
Goe get thee to them, shame come to you all.
　Bast. I would be loath to leaue your Highnes
　　thus,
Yet you command, and I, though grieu'd, will goe.
　Iohn. Ah Philip, whither goest thou? come againe.
　Bast. My Lord, these motions are as passions of a
　　mad man.
　Iohn. A mad man Philip, I am mad indeed,
My hart is mazd, my senses all foredone.
And Iohn of *England* now is quite vndone.
Was euer King as I opprest with cares?
Dame Elianor my noble Mother Queene,
My onely hope and comfort in distresse,
Is dead, and *England* excommunicate,
And I am interdicted by the Pope,
All churches curst, their doores are sealed vp,
And for the pleasure of the Romish Priest,
The seruice of the Highest is neglected,
The multitude (a beast of many heads)
Doo with confusion to their Soueraigne :
The Nobles blinded with ambitions fumes,
Assemble powers to beat mine Empire downe,
And more than this, elect a forren King.
O *England,* wert thou euer miserable,
King Iohn of *England* sees thee miserable :
Iohn, tis thy sinnes that makes it miserable,
Quic quid delirunt Reges, plectuntur Achiui.
Philip, as thou hast euer loude thy King,
So show it now : post to S. Edmonds Bury,
Dissemble with the Nobles, know their drifts,
Confound their diuellish plots, and damned deuises.
Though Iohn be faultie, yet let subiects beare,
He will amend, and right the peoples wrongs.
A Mother though she were vnnaturall,
Is better than the kindest Stepdame is :
Let neuer Englishman trust forraine rule.

Then Philip shew thy fealtie to thy King,
And mongst the Nobles plead thou for the King.
    Bast. I goe my lord : see how he is distraught,
This is the cursed Priest of Italy
Hath heapt these mischiefes on this haplesse Land.
Now, Philip, hadst thou Tullyes eloquence,
Then mightst thou hope to plead with good successe.
                                         [Exit.
    Iohn. And art thou gone? successe may follow
      thee :
Thus hast thou shewd thy kindnes to thy King.
Sirra, in hast goe greete the Cardinall,
Pandulph I meane, the Legate from the Pope.
Say that the King desires to speake with him.
Now Iohn bethinke thee how thou maist resolue :
And if thou wilt continue Englands King,
Then cast about to keep thy Diadem ;
For life and land, and all is leueld at.
The Pope of Rome, tis he that is the cause,
He curseth thee, he sets thy subiects free
From due obedience to their Soueraigne :
He animates the Nobles in their warres,
He giues away the Crowne to Philips Sonne,
And pardons all that seeke to murther thee :
And thus blind zeale is still predominant.
Then Iohn there is no way to keepe thy Crowne,
But finely to dissemble with the Pope :
That hand that gaue the wound must giue the salue
To cure the hurt, els quite incurable.
Thy sinnes are farre too great to be the man
T'abolish Pope, and Poperie from thy Realme :
But in thy seate, if I may gesse at all,
A King shall raigne that shall suppresse them all.
Peace Iohn, here comes the Legate of the Pope,
Dissemble thou, and whatsoere thou saist,
Yet with thy heart wish their confusion.

Enter *Pandulph.*

Pand. Now Iohn, vnworthie man to breath on
earth,
That dost oppugne against thy Mother Church :
Why am I sent for to thy cursed selfe?
Iohn. Thou man of God, Vicegerent for the Pope,
The holy Vicar of S. Peters Church,
Upon my knees, I pardon craue of thee,
And doo submit me to the Sea of Rome,
And vow for penaunce of my high offence,
To take on me the holy Crosse of Christ,
And carry Armes in holy Christian warres.
Pand. No Iohn, thy crowching and dissembling
thus
Cannot deceiue the Legate of the Pope,
Say what thou wilt, I will not credit thee :
Thy Crowne and Kingdome both are tane away,
And thou art curst without redemption.
Iohn. Accurst indeed to kneele to such a drudge,
And get no help with thy submission,
Unsheath thy sword, and sley the misprowd Priest,
That thus triumphs ore thee a mighty King :
No Iohn, submit againe, dissemble yet,
For Priests and Women must be flattered.
Yet holy Father thou thy selfe dost know,
No time to late for sinners to repent,
Absolue me then, and Iohn doth sweare to doo
The vttermost what euer thou demaundst.
Pand. Iohn, now I see thy harty penitence,
I rew and pitty thy distrest estate,
One way is left to reconcile thy selfe,
And only one which I shall shew to thee.
Thou must surrender to the sea of Rome
Thy Crowne and Diademe, then shall the Pope
Defend thee from th' inuasion of thy foes.
And where his Holinesse hath kindled Fraunce,

And set thy subiects hearts at warre with thee,
Then shall he curse thy foes, and beate them downe,
That seeke the discontentment of the King.
   Iohn. From bad to woorse, or I must loose my
     realme,
Or giue my Crowne for penance vnto Rome :
A miserie more piercing than the darts
That breake from burning exhalations power.
What ? shall I giue my Crowne with this right hand ?
No : with this hand defend thy Crowne and thee.
What newes with thee ?

Enter Messenger.

   Please it your maiestie, there is discried on the
Coast of Kent an hundred Sayle of Ships, which of
all men is thought to be the French fleete, vnder the
conduct of the Dolphin, so that it puts the Countrie
in a mutinie, so they send to your Grace for succour.
   K. Iohn. How now Lord Cardinall, whats your
     best aduise ?
These mutinies must be allayd in time,
By pollicy or headstrong rage at least.
O Iohn, these troubles tyre thy wearyed soule,
And like to Luna in a sad Eclipse,
So are thy thoughts and passions for this newes.
Well may it be, when Kings are grieued so,
The vulgar sort worke Princes ouerthrow.
   Card. K. John, for not effecting of thy plighted
     vow,
This strange annoyance happens to thy land :
But yet be reconcild vnto the Church,
And nothing shall be grieuous to thy state.
   Iohn. Oh Pandulph, be it as thou hast decreed,
Iohn will not spurne against thy sound aduise,
Come lets away, and with thy helpe I trow,
My Realme shall florish, and my Crowne in peace.

Enter the Nobles, *Pembrooke, Essex, Chester, Bew-
        champe, Clare,* with others.

Pemb. Now sweet S. Edmond holy Saint in heauen,
Whose Shrine is sacred, high esteemd on earth,
Infuse a constant zeale in all our hearts,
To prosecute this act of mickle waight,
Lord Bewchampe say, what friends have you procurde.
   Bewch. The L. Fitz Water, L. Percy, and L. Rosse,
Uowd meeting heere this day the leuenth houre.
   Essex. Under the cloke of holie Pilgrimage,
By that same houre on warrant of their faith,
Philip Plantagenet, a bird of swiftest wing,
Lord   Eustace,   Vescy,   Lord   Cressy,   and   Lord
        Mowbrey,
Appointed meeting at S. Edmonds Shrine.
   Pemb. Untill their presence, ile conceale my tale,
Sweete complices in holie Christian acts,
That venture for the purchase of renowne,
Thrice welcome to the league of high resolue,
That pawne their bodies for their soules regard.
   Essex. Now wanteth but the rest to end this worke,
In Pilgrims habit comes our holie troupe
A furlong hence, with swift vnwonted pace,
May be they are the persons you expect.
   Pemb. With swift vnwonted gate, see what a thing
        is zeale,
That spurrs them on with feruence to this Shrine,
Now ioy come to them for their true intent :
And in good time, heere come the warmen all,
That sweate in body by the minds disease :
Hap and heartsease braue Lordings be your lot.

        Enter the Bastard *Philip, &c.*

Amen my Lords, the like betide your lucke,
And all that trauell in a Christian cause.

Essex. Cheerely replied braue braunch of kingly
    stock,
A right Plantaginet should reason so.
But silence Lords, attend our commings cause :
The seruile yoke that payned vs with toyle,
On strong instinct hath framed this conuentickle,
To ease our necks of seruitudes contempt.
Should I not name the foeman of our rest,
Which of you all so barraine in conceipt.
As cannot leuell at the man I meane ?
But least Enigma's shadow shining truth,
Plainely to paint, as truth requires no arte.
Th' effect of this resort importeth this,
To roote and cleane extirpate tirant Iohn,
Tirant, I say, appealing to the man,
If any heere that loues him, and I aske,
What kindship, lenitie, or christian raigne,
Rules in the man, to barre this foule impeach ?
First I inferre the Chesters bannishment :
For reprehending him in most vnchristian crimes,
Was speciall notice of a tyrants will.
But were this all, the diuill should be saud,
But this the least of many thousand faults,
That circumstance with leisure might display.
Our priuate wrongs, no parcell of my tale
Which now in presence, but for some great cause
Might wish to him as to a mortall foe.
But shall I close the period with an acte
Abhorring in the eares of Christian men,
His Cosens death, that sweet vnguilty childe,
Untimely butcherd by the tyrants meanes,
Heere is my proofes, as cleere as grauell brooke,
And on the same I further must inferre,
That who vpholds a tyrant in his course,
Is culpable of all his damned guilt.
To show the which, is yet to be describd.
My Lord of Penbrooke, shew what is behinde,

Only I say, that were there nothing else
To mooue us, but the Popes most dreadfull curse,
Whereof we are assured, if we fayle,
It were inough to instigate vs all,
With earnestnesse of spirit, to seeke a meane
To dispossess Iohn of his regiment.

    Penb. Well hath my Lord of Essex tolde his tale,
Which I auer for most substanciall truth,
And more to make the matter to our minde,
I say that Lewis in chalenge of his wife,
Hath title of an vncontrouled plea,
To all that longeth to an English crowne.
Short tale to make, the Sea Apostolick,
Hath offerd dispensation for the fault.
If any be, as trust me none I know,
By planting Lewis in the vsurpers roome:
This is the cause of all our presence heere,
That on the holy Altar we protest,
To ayde the right of Lewis with goods and life,
Who on our knowledge is in Armes for England.
What say you Lords?

    Sals. As Pembrooke sayth, affirmeth Salsburie :
Faire Lewis of Fraunce that spoused Lady Blanch,
Hath title of an vncontrouled strength
To England, and what longeth to the Crowne ;
In right whereof, as we are true informd,
The Prince is marching hitherward in Armes.
Our purpose, to conclude that with a word,
Is to inuest him as we may deuise,
King of our Countrey, in the tyrants stead :
And so the warrant on the Altar sworne,
And so the intent for which we hither came.

    Bast. My Lord of Salsbury, I cannot couch
My speeches with the needfull words of arte,
As doth beseeme in such a waightie work,
But what my conscience and my dutie will,
I purpose to impart.

For Chesters exile, blame his busie wit,
That medled where his dutie quite forbade :
For any priuate causes that you haue,
Me thinke they should not mount to such a height,
As to depose a King in their reuenge.
For Arthurs death, King Iohn was innocent,
He desperat was the deathsman to himselfe,
With you, to make a colour to your crime, iniustly do
    impute to his default,
But where fell traytorisme hath residence,
There wants no words to set despight on worke.
I say tis shame, and worthy all reproofe,
To wrest such pettie wrongs in tearmes of right,
Against a King annoynted by the Lord.
Why Salsburie, admit the wrongs are true,
Yet subiects may not take in hand reuenge,
And rob the heauens of their proper power,
Where sitteth he to whom reuenge belongs.
And doth a Pope, a Priest, a man of pride,
Giue charters for the liues of lawfull Kings ?
What can he blesse, or who regards his cursse,
But such as giue to man, and takes from God ?
I speake it in the sight of God aboue,
Theres not a man that dyes in your beliefe,
But sels his soule perpetually to payne.
Ayd Lewis, leave God, kill Iohn, please hell,
Make havock of the welfare of your soules,
For heere I leaue you in the sight of heauen,
A troupe of traytors, foode for hellish feends ;
If you desist, then follow me as friends,
If not, then doo your worst as hatefull traytors.
For Lewis his right, alas tis too too lame,
A senslesse clayme, if truth be titles friend.
In briefe, if this be cause of our resort,
Our Pilgrimage is to the Diuils Shrine.
I came not Lords to troupe as traytors doo,
Nor will I counsaile in so bad a cause :

Please you returne, wee goe againe as friends,
If not, I too my King, and you where traytors please
           [Exit.
 Per. A hote yong man, and so my Lords proceed,
I let him go, and better lost than found.
 Penb. What say you Lords, will all the rest pro-
  ceed,
Will you all with me sweare vpon the Altar,
That you wil to the death, be ayd to Lewis & enemy
  to Iohn ?
Euery man lay his hand by mine, in witnes of his
  harts accord,
Well then, euery man to armes to meete the King,
Who is alreadie before London.

Enter Messenger.

 Penb. What newes Harrold ?
 The right Christian Prince my Master, Lewis of
Fraunce, is at hand, comming to visit your honors,
directed hether by the right honorable Richard Earle
of Bigot, to conferre with your Honors.
 Penb. How neere is his Highnesse ?
 Mess. Ready to enter your presence.

Enter *Lewis*, Earle *Bigot*, with his troupe.

 Lewes. Faire Lords of England, Lewis salutes you
  all
As friends, and firme welwillers of his weale
At whose request, from plenty flowing Fraunce,
Crossing the Ocean with a Southern gale,
He is in Person come at your commaunds,
To vndertake and gratifie withall,
The fulnesse of your fauours proffred him.
But worlds braue men, omitting promises,
Till time be minister of more amends,

I must acquaint you with our fortunes course.
The heauens dewing fauours on my head,
Haue in their conduct safe with victorie,
Brought me along your well manured bounds,
With small repulse, and little crosse of chaunce.
Your Citie Rochester, with great applause,
By some diuine instinct layd armes aside :
And from the hollow holes of Thamesis,
Eccho apace replide, *Viue la roy.*
From thence, along the wanton rowling glade
To Troynouant, your fayre Metropolis,
With luck came Lewes, to shew his troupes of Fraunce,
Wauing our Ensignes with the dallying windes,
The fearefull obiect of fell frowning warre ;
Where after some assault, and small defence,
Heauens may I say, and not my warlike troupe,
Temperd their hearts to take a friendly foe
Within the compasse of their high built walles,
Giuing me title, as it seemd they wish.
Thus fortune (Lords) acts to your forwardnes,
Meanes of content, in lieu of former griefe :
And may I liue but to requite you all,
Worlds' wish were mine, in dying noted yours.
 Salis. Welcome the balme that closeth vp our
  wounds,
The soueraigne medcine for our quick recure,
The anchor of our hope, the onely prop,
Whereon depends our liues, our lands, our weale,
Without the which, as sheep without their heard,
(Except a shepheard winking at the wolfe)
We stray, we pine, we run to thousand harmes.
No meruaile then, though with vnwonted ioy,
We welcome him that beateth woes away.
 Lewes. Thanks to you all of this religious league,
A holy knot of Catholique consent.
I cannot name you Lordings, man by man,
But like a stranger vnacquainted yet,

In generall I promise faithfull loue :
Lord Bigot brought me to S. Edmonds shrine,
Giuing me warrant of a Christian oath,
That this assembly came deuoted heere,
To sweare according as your packets showd,
Homage and loyall seruice to our selfe,
I neede not doubt the suretie of your wills,
Since well I know, for many of your sakes,
The townes haue yeelded on their owne accords :
Yet for a fashion, not for misbeliefe,
My eyes must witnes, and these eares must heare
Your oath vpon the holy Altar sworne,
And after march, to end our commings cause.

   Sals. That we intend no other than good truth,
All that are present of this holy League,
For confirmation of our better trust,
In presence of his Highnes, sweare with me,
The sequel that my selfe shall vtter heere.

   I Thomas Plantaginet, Earle of Salisbury, sweare
vpon the Altar, and by the holy Armie of Saints,
homage and allegeance to the right Christian Prince
Lewes of France, as true and rightfull King to England, Cornwall, & Wales, and to their Territories : in
the defence whereof, I vpon the holy Altars sweare
all forwardnes.   [All the Eng. Lords sweare.

   As the noble Earle hath sworne, so sweare we
    all.

   Lewes. I rest assured on your holy oath.
And on this Altar in like sort I sweare
Loue to you all, and Princely recompence
To guerdon your good wills vnto the full.
And since I am at this religious Shrine,
My good welwillers giue us leaue awhile,
To vse some orisons our selues apart,
To all the holy companie of heauen,
That they will smile vpon our purposes,
And bring them to a fortunate event.

Sals. We leaue your Highnes to your good intent.
　　　　　　　[Exeunt Lords of England.
Lewes. Now Uicount Meloun, what remaines be-
　　hinde ?
Trust me these traitors to their Soueraigne State,
Are not to be beleeude in any sort.
　　Meloun. Indeed my Lord, they that infringe their
　　oths,
And play the Rebels gainst their natiue King,
Will for as little cause reuolt from you,
If euer opportunitie incite them so :
For once forsworne, and neuer after found,
Theres no affiance after periury.
　　Lewes. Well Meloun, well, lets smooth with them
　　awhile,
Untill we haue as much as they can doo :
And when their vertue is exhaled drie,
Il hang them for the guerdon of their help :
Meane while wee'l vse them as a precious poyson,
To vndertake the issue of our hope.
　　Fr. Lord. Tis policie (my Lord) to bait our hookes
With merry smiles, and promise of much waight :
But when your Highnes needeth them no more,
Tis good make sure worke with them, lest indeede
They prooue to you as to their naturall King.
　　Meloun. Trust me my Lord, right well haue you
　　aduisde,
Venyme for vse, but neuer for a sport
Is to be dallyed with, least it infect.
Were you instald, as soone I hope you shall :
Be free from traitors, and dispatch them all.
　　Lewes. That so I meane, I sweare before you all
On this same altar, and by heauens power,
Theres not an English traytor of them all,
Iohn once dispatcht, and I faire Englands King,
Shall on his shoulders beare his head one day,
But I will crop it for their guilts desert :

Nor shall their heires inioy their Signories,
But perish by their parents fowle amisse.
This haue I sworne, and this will I performe,
If ere I come vnto the height I hope.
Lay downe your hands, and sweare the same with me.
                    [The French Lords swear.
Why so, now call them in, and speake them faire,
A smile of France will feed an English foole.
Beare them in hand as friends, for so they be :
But in the hart like traitors as they are.

Enter the *English* Lords.

Now famous followers, chieftaines of the world,
Haue we solicited with heartie prayer
The heauen in fauour of our high attempt.
Leaue we this place, and march we with our power
To rowse the Tyrant from his chiefest hold :
And when our labours haue a prosperous end,
Each man shall reape the fruite of his desert.
And so resolude, braue followers let vs hence.

Enter K. *Iohn, Bastard, Pandulph,* and a many
              Priests with them.

Thus Iohn, thou art absolude from all thy sinnes,
And freed by order from our Fathers curse.
Receiue thy Crowne againe, with this prouiso,
That thou remaine true liegeman to the Pope,
And carry armes in right of holy Rome.
    Iohn. I holde the same as tenaunt to the Pope,
And thanke your Holines for your kindnes showne.
    Phil. A proper iest, when Kings must stoop to
        Friers,
Neede hath no law, when Frier must be Kings.

Enter a Messenger.

Mess. Please it your Maiestie, the Prince of Fraunce,
With all the Nobles of your Graces Land
Are marching hetherward in good aray.
Where ere they set their foote, all places yeeld :
Thy Land is theirs, and not a foote holds out
But Dover Castle, which is hard besiegd.
  Pand. Feare not king Iohn, thy kingdome is y*e*
    Popes,
And they shall know his Holines hath power,
To beate them soone from whence he hath to doo.

Drums and Trumpets. Enter *Lewes, Melun, Salisbury, Essex, Pembrooke,* and all the˘ Nobles from
Fraunce and *England.*

  Lewes. Pandulph, as gaue his Holines in charge,
So hath the Dolphin mustred vp his troupes,
And wonne the greatest part of all this Land.
But ill becomes your Grace Lord Cardinall,
Thus to conuerse with Iohn that is accurst.
  Pand. Lewes of France, victorious Conqueror,
Whose sword hath made this Iland quake for fear ;
Thy forwardnes to fight for holy Rome,
Shall be remunerated to the full :
But know my Lord, K. Iohn is now absolude,
The Pope is pleasde, the Land is blest agen,
And thou hast brought each thing to good effect.
It resteth then that thou withdraw thy powers,
And quietly returne to Fraunce againe :
For all is done the Pope would wish thee doo.
  Lewes. But al's not done that Lewes came to do.
Why Pandulph, hath K. Philip sent his sonne
And been at such excessiue charge in warres,
To be dismist with words ? king Iohn shall know,
England is mine, and he vsurps my right.

Pand. Lewes, I charge thee and thy complices
Upon the paine of Pandulphs holy curse,
That thou withdraw thy powers to Fraunce againe,
And yeeld vp London and the neighbour Townes
That thou hast tane in England by the sword.

Melun. Lord Cardinall by Lewes princely leaue,
It can be nought but vsurpation
In thee, the Pope, and all the Church of Rome,
Thus to insult on Kings of Christendome,
Now with a word to make them carie armes,
Then with a word to make them leaue their armes.
This must not be : Prince Lewes keepe thine owne,
Let Pope and Popelings curse their bellyes full.

Bast. My Lord of Melun, what title had the Prince
To England and the Crowne of Albion,
But such a title as the Pope confirmde :
The Prelate now lets fall his fained claime :
Lewes is but the agent for the Pope,
Then must the Dolphin cease, sith he hath ceast :
But cease or no, it greatly matters not,
If you my Lords and Barons of the Land
Will leave the French, and cleaue vnto our King.
For shame yee Peeres of England suffer not
Your selues, your honours, and your land to fall :
But with resolued thoughts beate backe the French,
And free the Land from yoke of seruitude.

Salis. Philip, not so, Lord Lewes is our King,
And we will follow him vnto the death.

Pand. Then in the name of Innocent the Pope,
I curse the Prince and all that take his part,
And excommunicate the rebell Peeres
As traytors to the King and to the Pope.

Lewes. Pandolph, our swords shall blesse our selues
    agen :
Prepare thee Iohn, Lords follow me your King.
                                        [Exeunt.

Iohn. Accursed Iohn, the Diuell owes thee shame,

Resisting Rome, or yeelding to the Pope, alls one.
The diuell take the Pope, the Peeres, and Fraunce :
Shame be my share for yeelding to the Priest.
 Pand. Comfort thy selfe K. Iohn, the Cardnall
    goes
Upon his curse to make them leaue their armes.
                                              [Exit.
 Bast. Comfort my Lord, and curse the Cardinall,
Betake your self to armes, my troupes are prest
To answere Lewes with a lustie shocke :
The English archers haue their quiuers full,
Their bowes are bent, the pykes are prest to push :
God cheere my Lord, K. Richards fortune hangs
Upon the plume of warlike Philips helme.
Then let them know his brother and his sonne
Are leaders of the Englishmen at armes.
 Iohn. Philip, I know not how to answer thee :
But let vs hence, to answere Lewes pride.

 Excursions.   Enter *Meloun* with English Lords.

 Mel. O I am slaine, Nobles, Salsbury, Pembrooke,
My soule is charged, heare me : for what I say
Concernes the Peeres of England, and their State.
Listen, braue Lords, a fearfull mourning tale
To be deliuered by a man of death.
Behold these scarres, the dole of bloudie Mars
Are harbingers from natures common foe,
Cyting this trunke to Tellus prison house ?
Lifes charter (Lordings) lasteth not an hower :
And fearfull thoughts, forerunners of my end,
Bids me giue Phisicke to a sickly soule.
O Peeres of England, know you what you doo ?
There's but a haire that sunders you from harme,
The hooke is bayted, and the traine is made,
And simply you runne doating to your deaths.
But least I dye, and leaue my tale vntolde,
With silence slaughtering so braue a crew,

This I auerre, if Lewes win the day,
There's not an Englishman that lifts his hand
Against King Iohn to plant the heire of Fraunce,
But is already damnd to cruell death.
I heard it vowd ; my selfe amongst the rest
Swore on the Altar aid to this Edict.
Two causes Lords, makes me display this drift,
The greatest for the freedome of my soule,
That longs to leaue this mansion free from guilt :
The other on a naturall instinct,
For that my Grandsire was an Englishman.
Misdoubt not Lords the truth of my discourse,
No frenzie, nor no brainsick idle fit,
But well aduisde, and wotting what I say,
Pronounce I here before the face of heauen,
That nothing is discouered but a truth.
Tis time to flie, submit your selues to Iohn,
The smiles of Fraunce shade in the frownes of death,
Lift vp your swords, turne face against the French,
Expell the yoke thats framed for your necks.
Back warmen, back, imbowell not the clyme,
Your seate, your nurse, your birth days breathing
        place,
That bred you, beares you, brought you vp in armes.
Ah! be not so ingrate to digge your Mothers graue,
Preserue your lambes and beate away the Wolfe.
My soule hath said, contritions penitence
Layes hold on mans redemption for my sinne.
Farewell my Lords ; witnes my faith when we are met
        in heauen,
And for my kindnes giue me graue roome heere.
My soule doth fleete, worlds vanities farewell.
    Sals. Now ioy betide thy soule wel-meaning man,
How now my Lords, what cooling card is this?
A greater griefe growes now than earst hath been.
What counsell giue you, shall we stay and dye?
Or shall we home, and kneele vnto the King.

Pemb. My hart misgaue this sad accursed newes:
What haue we done? fie Lords, what frenzie moued
Our hearts to yeeld vnto the pride of Fraunce?
If we perseuer, we are sure to dye:
If we desist, small hope againe of life.

Sals. Beare hence the bodie of this wretched man,
That made vs wretched with his dying tale,
And stand not wayling on our present harmes,
As women wont: but seeke our harmes redresse.
As for my selfe, I will in haste be gon:
And kneele for pardon to our Souereign Iohn.

Pemb. I, theres the way, lets rather kneele to him,
Than to the French that would confound vs all.

[Exeunt.

Enter king *John* carried betweene 2 Lords.

Iohn. Set downe, set downe the load not woorth
  your pain,
For done I am with deadly wounding griefe:
Sickly and succourles, hopeles of any good,
The world hath wearied me, and I haue wearied it:
It loaths I liue, I liue and loath my selfe.
Who pities me? to whom haue I been kinde?
But to a few; a few will pitie me.
Why dye I not? Death scornes so vilde a pray.
Why liue I not, life hates so sad a prize.
I sue to both to be retaynd of either,
But both are deafe, I can be heard of neither.
Nor death nor life, yet life and neare the neere,
Ymixt with death, biding I wot not where.

Phil. How fares my Lord, that he is caryed thus?
Not all the aukward fortunes yet befalne,
Made such impression of lament in me.
Nor euer did my eye attaynt my heart
With any obiect mouing more remorse,
Than now beholding of a mighty King,
Borne by his Lords in such distressed state.

Iohn. What news with thee ?   If bad, report it
    straite :
If good, be mute, it doth but flatter me.
    Phil. Such as it is, and heauy though it be,
To glut the world with tragick elegies,
Once will I breath to agrauate the rest,
Another moane to make the measure full.
The brauest bowman had not yet sent forth
Two arrowes from the quiuer at his side,
But that a rumor went throughout our Campe,
That Iohn had fled, the King had left the field.
At last the rumor scald these eares of mine,
Who rather chose as sacrifice for Mars,
Than ignominious scandall by retyre.
I cheerd the troupes, as did the prince of Troy
His weery followers gainst the Mermidons,
Crying alowde, S. George, the day is ours.
But feare had captiuated courage quite,
And like the Lamb before the greedie Wolfe,
So hartlesse fled our warmen from the feeld.
Short tale to make, my selfe amongst the rest,
Was faine to flie before the eager foe.
By this time night had shadowed all the earth.
With sable curteines of the blackest hue,
And fenct vs from the fury of the French,
As Io from the iealous Iunoes eye,
When in the morning our troupes did gather head,
Passing the washes with our carriages,
The impartiall tyde deadly and inexorable,
Came raging in with billowes threatning death,
And swallowed up the most of all our men,
My selfe vpon a Galloway right free, well paced,
Out stript the flouds that followed waue by waue,
I so escapt to tell this tragick tale.
    Iohn. Griefe vpon griefe, yet none so great a griefe
To end this life, and thereby rid my griefe.
Was euer any so infortunate,

The right Idea of a curssed man,
As I, poore I, a triumph for despight,
My feuer growes, what ague shakes me so?
How farre to Sminsteed, tell me, do you know?
Present vnto the Abbot word of my repaire.
My sicknesse rages, to tirannize vpon me,
I cannot liue vnlesse this feuer leaue me.

Phil. Good cheare my Lord, the Abbey is at hand,
Behold my Lord, the Churchmen come to meete you.

Enter the Abbot and certayne Monkes.

Abb. All health & happines to our soueraigne Lord
the King.

Iohn. Nor health nor happines hath Iohn at all.
Say Abbot, am I welcome to thy house?

Abb. Such welcome as our Abbey can afford,
Your maiestie shal be assured of.

Phil. The King thou seest is weake and very faint,
What victuals hast thou to refresh his Grace?

Abb. Good store my Lord, of that you neede not
feare,
For Lincolneshire, and these our Abbey grounds
Were neuer fatter, nor in better plight.

Iohn. Philip, thou neuer needst to doubt of cates,
Nor King nor Lord is seated halfe so well,
As are the Abbeis throughout all the land,
If any plot of ground do passe another,
The Friers fasten on it streight :
But let vs in to taste of their repast,
It goes against my heart to feed with them,
Or be beholden to such Abbey groomes. [Exeunt.

Manet the Monk.

Monk. Is this the King that neuer lou'd a Frier?
Is this the man that doth contemne the Pope?
Is this the man that robd the holy Church?
And yet will flye vnto a Friory?

Is this the King that aymes at Abbeys lands?
Is this the man whom all the world abhorres,
And yet will flie vnto a Friorie?
Accurst be Swinsted Abbey, Abbot, Friers,
Monks, Nuns, and Clarks, and all that dwells therein,
If wicked Iohn escape aliue away.
Now if that thou wilt looke to merit heauen,
And be canònized for a holy Saint:
To please the world with a deseruing worke,
Be thou the man to set thy cuntrey free,
And murder him that seeks to murder thee.

Enter the Abbot.

Abb. Why are not you within to cheere the King?
He now begins to mend, and will to meate.
Monk. What if I say to strangle him in his sleepe?
Abb. What, at thy Mumpsimus? away,
And seeke some meanes for to pastime the King.
Monk. Ile set a dudgeon dagger at his heart,
And with a mallet knock him on the head.
Abb. Alas, what meanes this Monke to murder me?
Dare lay my life heel kill me for my place.
Monk. Ile poyson him, and it shall neere be knowne,
And then shall I be chiefest of my house.
Abb. If I were dead indeed he is the next.
But Ile away, for why the Monke is mad,
And in his madnesse he will murder me.
Monk. My L. I cry your Lordship mercy, I saw you
not.
Abb. Alas good Thomas, do not murther me, and
thou shalt haue my place with thousand thanks.
Monk. I murther you! God sheeld from such a
thought.
Abb. If thou wilt needs, yet let me say my prayers.
Monk. I will not hurt your Lordship good my Lord:
but if you please,
I will impart a thing that shall be beneficiall to vs all.

Abb. Wilt thou not hurt me holy Monke? say on.

Monk. You know, my Lord, the King is in our house.

Abb. True.

Monk. You know likewise the King abhors a Frier.

Abb. True.

Monk. And he that loues not a Frier is our enemy.

Abb. Thou saist true.

Monk. Then the King is our enemy.

Abb. True.

Monk. Why then should we not kil our enemy, & the King being our enemy, why then should we not kil the King.

Abb. O blessed Monke! I see God moues thy minde to free this land from tyrants slauery.
But who dare venter for to do this deede?

Monk. Who dare? why I my Lord dare do the
    deede,
Ile free my Country and the Church from foes,
And merit heauen by killing of a King.

Abb. Thomas kneel downe, and if thou art re-
    solu'd,
I will absolue thee heere from all thy sinnes,
For why the deede is meritorious.
Forward, and feare not man for euery month,
Our Friers shall sing a Masse for Thomas soule.

Monk. God and S. Francis prosper my attempt,
For now my Lord I goe about my worke.   [Exeunt.

Enter Lewes and his armie.

Lewes. Thus victory in bloudy Lawrell clad,
Followes the fortune of young Lodowike,
The Englishmen as daunted at our sight,
Fall as the fowle before the Eagles eyes,
Only two crosses of contrary change
Do nip my heart, and vexe me with vnrest.

Lord Melons death, the one part of my soule,
A brauer man did neuer liue in Fraunce.
The other griefe, I thats a gall indeede
To thinke that Douer Castile should hold out
Gainst all assaults, and rest impregnable.
Yee warlike race of Francus Hectors sonne,
Triumph in conquest of that tyrant Iohn,
The better halfe of England is our owne :
And towards the conquest of the other part,
We haue the face of all the English lords,
What then remaines but ouerrunne the land ?
Be resolute my warlike followers,
And if good fortune serue as she begins,
The poorest pesant of the realme of Fraunce
Shall be a maister ore an English Lord.

Enter a Messenger.

Lewes. Fellow, what newes?

Mess. Pleaseth your Grace, the Earle of Salsbury,
Penbroke, Essex, Clare, and Arundell, with all the
Barons that did fight for thee, are on a sodeine fled
with all their powers, to ioyne with Iohn to drive thee
back againe.

Enter another Messenger.

Mess. Lewes my Lord, why standst thou in a maze ?
Gather thy troups, hope not of help from Fraunce,
For all thy forces being fiftie sayle,
Conteyning twenty thousand souldiers,
With victuall and munition for the warre,
Putting them from Callis in vnluckie time,
Did crosse the seas, and on the Goodwin sands,
The men, munition, and the ships are lost.

Enter another Messenger.

Lewes. More newes? say on.
Mess. Iohn (my Lord) with all his scattered troupes,

Flying the fury of your conquering sword,
As Pharaoh earst within the bloody sea,
So he and his enuironed with the tyde,
On Lincolne washes all were ouerwhelmed,
The Barons fled, our forces cast away.

Lewes. Was euer heard such vnexpected newes?

Mess. Yet Lodowike reuiue thy dying heart,
King Iohn and all his forces are consumde.
The lesse thou needst the ayd of English Earles,
The lesse thou needst to grieue thy Nauies wracke,
And follow tymes aduantage with successe.

Lewes. Braue Frenchmen armde with magnani-
mitie,
March after Lewes, who will leade you on
To chase the Barons power that wants a head,
For Iohn is drownd, and I am Englands King.
Though our munition and our men be lost,
Philip of Fraunce will send vs fresh supplyes.

[Exeunt.

Enter two Friers laying a Cloth.

Frier. Dispatch, dispatch, the King desires to eate,
Would a might eate his last for the loue hee bears to
Churchmen.

Frier. I am of thy minde too, and so it should be
and we might be our owne caruers.
I meruaile why they dine here in the Orchard.

Frier. I know not, nor I care not. The King coms.

Iohn. Come on Lord Abbot, shall we sit together?

Abb. Pleaseth your Grace sit downe.

Iohn. Take your places sirs, no pomp in penury,
all beggers and friends may come, where Necessitie
keepes the house, curtesie is bard the table, sit downe,
Philip.

Bast. My Lord, I am loth to allude so much to
ye prouerb, honors change manners: a King is a
King, though Fortune do her worst, & we as dutifull

in despite of her frowne, as if your highnesse were now in the highest type of dignitie.

Iohn. Come, no more ado, and you will tell me much of dignitie, youle mar my appetite in a surfet of sorrow.

What cheere Lord Abbot, me thinks ye frowne like an host that knowes his guest hath no money to pay the reckning?

Abb. No my Liege, if I frowne at all, it is for I feare this cheere too homely to entertaine so mighty a guest as your Maiestie.

Bast. I thinke, rather, my Lord Abbot, you remember my last being heere, when I went in progresse for powtches, and the rancor of his heart breakes out in his countenance, to shew he hath not forgot me.

Abb. Not so my Lord, you, and the meanest follower of his maiesty, are hartily welcome to me.

Monk. Wassell my Liege, and as a poore Monke may say, welcome to Swinsted.

Iohn. Begin Monke, and report hereafter thou wast taster to a King.

Monk. As much helth to your Highnes as to my own hart.

Iohn. I pledge thee kinde Monke.

Monk. The meriest draught yᵗ euer was dronk in England.

Am I not too bold with your Highnesse?

Iohn. Not a whit, all friendes and fellowes for a time.

Monk. If the inwards of a Toad be a compound of any proofe : why so it workes.

Iohn. Stay Philip, wheres the Monke?

Bast. He is dead my Lord.

Iohn. Then drinke not Philip for a world of wealth.

Bast. What cheere my liege? your cullor begins to change.

Iohn. So doth my life : O Philip, I am poysond.
The Monke, the Diuill, the poyson gins to rage,
It will depose my selfe a King from raigne.
  Bast. This Abbot hath an interest in this act.
At all aduentures take thou that from me.
There lye the Abbot, Abbey, Lubber, Diuill.
March with the Monke vnto the gates of hell.
How fares my Lord ?
  Iohn. Philip, some drinke, oh for the frozen Alpes,
To tumble on and coole this inward heate,
That rageth as the fornace seuenfold hote.
To burne the holy tree in Babylon,
Power after power forsake their proper power,
Only the hart impugnes with faint resist
The fierce inuade of him that conquers Kings,
Help God, O payne ! dye Iohn, O plague
Inflicted on thee for thy grieuous sinnes.
Philip, a chayre, and by and by a graue,
My leggs disdaine the carriage of a King.
  Bast. A good my Liege, with patience conquer
    griefe,
And beare this paine with kingly fortitude.
  Iohn. Me thinkes I see a cattalogue of sinne,
Wrote by a fiend in Marble characters,
The least enough to loose my part in heauen.
Me thinkes the Diuill whispers in mine eares,
And tels me, tis in vayne to hope for grace,
I must be damned for Arthurs sodaine death,
I see I see a thousand thousand men
Come to accuse me for my wrong on earth,
And there is none so mercifull a God
That will forgiue the number of my sinnes.
How haue I liu'd, but by anothers losse ?
What haue I loud, but wracke of others weale ?
Where haue I vowd, and not infring'd mine oath ?
Where haue I done a deede deseruing well ?
How what, when, and where, haue I bestow'd a day,

That tended not to some notorious ill?
My life repleat with rage and tyranie,
Craues little pittie for so strange a death,
Or, who will say that Iohn deceasd too sonne?
Who will not say, he rather liud too long?
Dishonor did attaynt me in my life,
And shame attendeth Iohn vnto his death.
Why did I scape the fury of the French,
And dyde not by the temper of their swords?
Shamelesse my life, and shamefully it ends,
Scornd by my foes, disdainèd of my friends.
    Bast. Forgiue the world and all your earthly foes,
And call on Christ, who is your latest friend.
    Iohn. My tongue doth falter: Philip, I tell thee
        man:
Since Iohn did yeeld vnto the Priest of Rome,
Nor he nor his haue prospred on the earth:
Curst are his blessings, and his curse is blisse.
Bnt in the spirit I cry vnto my God,
As did the Kingly Prophet Dauid cry,
(Whose hands, as mine, with murder were attaint)
I am not he shall build the Lord a house,
Or roote these Locusts from the face of earth:
But if my dying heart deceiue me not,
From out these loynes shall spring a Kingly braunch
Whose armes shall reach vnto the gates of Rome,
And· with his feete treads downe the Strumpets
        pride,
That sits vpon the chaire of Babylon.
Philip, my heart strings breake, the poysons flame
Hath ouercome in me weake Natures power,
And in the faith of Iesu Iohn doth dye.
    Bast. See how he striues for life, vnhappy Lord,
Whose bowels are diuided in themselues.
This is the fruite of Poperie, when true Kings
Are slaine and shouldred out by Monkes and
        Friers.

Enter a Messenger.

Mess. Please it your Grace, the Barons of the Land,
Which all this while bare armes against the King,
Conducted by the Legate of the Pope,
Together with the Prince his highnes Sonne,
Do craue to be admitted to the presence of the King.

Bast. Your Sonne, my Lord, yong Henry craves to
  see
Your Maiestie, and brings with him beside
The Barons that reuolted from your Grace.
O piercing sight, he fumbleth in the mouth,
His speech doth faile : lift vp your selfe my Lord,
And see the Prince to comfort you in death.

Enter *Pandulph*, yong *Henry*, the Barons with daggers
  in their hands.

Prince. O let me see my Father ere he dye :
O Uncle, were you here, and sufferd him
To be thus poysned by a damned Monke ?
Ah, he is dead, Father, sweet Father speake.

Bast. His speech doth faile, he hasteth to his end.

Pan. Lords, giue me leaue to joy the dying King,
With sight of these his Nobles kneeling here
With daggers in their hands, who offer vp
Their liues for ransome of their foule offence.
Then good my Lord, if you forgiue them all,
Lift vp your hand in token you forgiue.

Salis. We humbly thanke your royall Maiestie,
And vow to fight for England and her King :
And in the sight of Iohn our soueraigne Lord,
In spite of Lewes and the power of Fraunce,
Who hetherward are marching in all hast,
We crowne yong Henry in his fathers sted.

Hen. Help, help, he dyes; ah Father ! looke on
  mee.

Legat. K. Iohn, farewell : in token of thy faith,

And signe thou dyest the seruant of the Lord,
Lift vp thy hand, that we may witnes here,
Thou dyedst the seruant of our Sauiour Christ.
Now ioy betide thy soule : what noyse is this ?

Enter a Messenger.

Mess. Help Lords, the Dolphin maketh hetherward
With Ensignes of defiance in the winde,
And all our armie standeth at a gaze,
Expecting what their Leaders will commaund.

    Bast. Lets arme our selues in yong K. Henries
      right,
And beate the power of Fraunce to sea againe.

    Legat. Philip not so, but I will to the Prince,
And bring him face to face to parl with you.

    Bast. Lord Salsbury, your selfe shall march with
      me,
So shall we bring these troubles to an ende.

    King. Sweete Uncle, if thou loue thy Soueraigne,
Let not a stone of Swinsted Abbey stand,
But pull the house about the Friers eares :
For they haue killde my Father and my King.

                        [Exeunt.

A parle sounded, *Lewes, Pandulph, Salsbury, &c.*

    Pan. Lewes of Fraunce, yong Henry Englands
      King
Requires to know the reason of the claime
That thou canst make to any thing of his.
King Iohn that did offend, is dead and gone,
See where his breathles trunke in presence lyes,
And he as heire apparant to the crowne
Is now succeeded to his Fathers roome.

    Hen. Lewes, what law of Armes doth lead thee
      thus,
To keepe possession of my lawfull right ?

Answere; in fine, if thou wilt take a peace,
And make surrender of my right againe,
Or trie thy title with the dint of sword :
I tell thee Dolphin, Henry feares thee not,
For now the Barons cleaue vnto their King,
And what thou hast in England they did get.

    Lewes. Henry of England, now that Iohn is dead,
That was the chiefest enemie to Fraunce,
I may the rather be inducde to peace.
But Salsbury, and you Barons of the Realme,
This strange reuolt agrees not with the oath
That you on Bury Altare lately sware.

    Sals. Nor did the oath your Highnes there did take
Agree with honour of the Prince of Fraunce.

    Bast. My Lord, what answere make you to the
    King?

    Dol. Faith Philip this I say : it bootes not me,
Nor any Prince nor power of Christendome,
To seeke to win this Island Albion,
Vnlesse he haue a partie in the Realme
By treason for to help him in his warres.
The Peeres which were the partie on my side,
Are fled from me : then bootes not me to fight,
But on conditions, as mine honour wills,
I am contented to depart the realme.

    Hen. On what conditions will your Highnes yeeld?

    Lewes. That shall we thinke vpon by more aduice.

    Bast. Then Kings & Princes, let these broils haue
    end,
And at more leasure talke vpon the League.
Meanwhile to Worster let vs beare the King,
And there interre his bodie, as beseemes.
But first, in sight of Lewes, heire of Fraunce,
Lords take the crowne and set it on his head,
That by succession is our lawfull King.

They crown yong *Henry.*

Thus Englands peace begins in Henryes Raigne,
And bloody warres are closde with happie league
Let England liue but true within it selfe,
And all the world can neuer wrong her State.
Lewes, thou shalt be brauely shipt to France,
For neuer Frenchman got of English ground
The twentith part that thou hast conquered.
Dolphin, thy hand ; to Worster we will march :
Lords all, lay hands to beare your Soueraigne
With obsequies of honor to his graue :
If Englands Peeres and people ioyne in one,
Nor Pope, nor Fraunce, nor Spaine can doo them
    wrong.

FINIS.

KING HENRY V.

EDITION.

The Famovs Victories of Henry the fifth : Containing the Honourable Battell of Agincourt : As it was plaide by the Queenes maiesties Players. London Printed by Thomas Creede, 1598. 4°. Black letter.

THERE was a second edition in 1617 ; and the drama was licensed in 1594. The Malone copy of 1598 here reprinted is, however, the earliest impression known, as well as the only copy of that impression which has yet been found.

The second 4° was included in " Six Old Plays," 1779.

The Famous Victories of Henry the Fifth, Conteining the Honorable Battell of Agincourt.

———o———

Enter the yoong Prince, Ned, and Tom.

Henry V. COME away Ned and Tom.
   Both. Here my Lord.
Hen. V. Come away my Lads :
Tell me sirs, how much gold haue you got?
 Ned. Faith my Lord, I haue got fiue hundred
  pound.
 Hen. V. But tell me Tom, how much hast thou
  got?
 Tom. Faith my Lord, some foure hundred pound.
 Hen. V. Foure hundred pounds, brauely spoken
  Lads.
But tell me sirs, thinke you not that it was a villain-
ous part of me to rob my fathers Receuers?
 Ned. Why no my Lord, it was but a tricke of
  youth.
 Hen. V. Faith Ned, thou sayest true.
But tell me sirs, whereabouts are we?
 Tom. My Lord, we are now about a mile off
  London.
 Hen. V. But sirs, I maruell that sir Iohn Old-Castle
Comes not away : Sounds see where he comes.

Enters Iockey.

How now Iockey, what newes with thée?

Iockey. Faith my Lord, such newes as passeth,
For the Towne of Detfort is risen,
With hue and crie after your man,
Which parted from vs the last night,
And has set vpon, and hath robd a poore Carrier.

   Hen. V. Sownes, the vilaine that was wont to spie
Out our booties.

   Iock. I my Lord, euen the very same.

   Hen. V. Now baseminded rascal to rob a poore
    carrier,
Wel it skils not, ile saue the base vilaines life :
I, I may : but tel me Iockey, wherabout be the
    Receiuers ?

   Iock. Faith my Lord, they are hard by,
But the best is, we are a horse backe and they be a
    foote,
So we may escape them.

   Hen. V. Wel, I the vilaines come, let me alone
    with them.
But tel me Iockey, how much gots thou from the
    knaues ?
For I am sure I got something, for one of the
    vilaines
So belamd me about the shoulders,
As I shal féele it this moneth.

   Iock. Faith my Lord, I haue got a hundred
    pound.

   Hen. V. A hundred pound, now bravely spoken
    Iockey :
But come sirs, laie al your money before me,
Now by heauen here is a braue shewe :
But as I am true Gentleman, I wil haue the halfe
Of this spent to night, but sirs take vp your bags,
Here comes the Receiuers, let me alone.

Enters two Receiuers.

One. Alas good fellow, what shal we do?
I dare neuer go home to the Court, for I shall be
hangd.
But looke, here is the yong Prince, what shal we doo?
Hen. V. How now you vilaines, what are you?
One Recei. Speake you to him.
Other. No I pray, speake you to him.
Hen. V. Why how now you rascals, why speak you
not?
One. Forsooth we be. Pray speake you to him.
Hen. V. Sowns, vilains speak, or il cut off your
heads.
Other. Forsooth he can tel the tale better than I.
One. Forsooth we be your fathers Receiuers.
Hen. V. Are you my fathers Receiuers?
Then I hope ye haue brought me some money.
One. Money, Alas sir wee be robd.
Hen. V. Robd, how many were there of them?
One. Marry sir, there were foure of them :
And one of them had sir Iohn Old-Castles bay Hobbie,
And your blacke Nag.
Hen. V. Gogs wounds how like you this Iockey?
Blood you vilaines : my father robd of his money
abroad,
And we robd in our stables.
But tell me, how many were there[1] of them?
One Recei. If it please you, there were foure of them,
And there was one about the bignesse of you :
But I am sure I so belambd him about the shoulders,
That he wil féele it this month.
Hen. V. Gogs wounds you lamd them faierly,
So that they haue carried away your money.
But come sirs, what shall we do with the vilaines?

---

[1] [This word is omitted in first 4°.]

Both Recei. I beséech your grace, be good to vs.
Ned. I pray you my Lord forgiue them this once.
Well stand vp and get you gone,
And looke that you speake not a word of it,
For if there be, sownes ile hang you and all your kin.
　　　　　　　　　　　　　　　　　[Exit Purseuant.
Hen. V. Now sirs, how like you this?
Was not this brauely done?
For now the vilaines dare not speake a word of it,
I haue so feared them with words.
Now whither shall we goe?
　　All. Why my Lord, you know our old hostes at
　　Feuersham.
　　Hen. V. Our hostes at Feuersham, blood what shal
　　we do there?
We haue a thousand pound about vs,
And we shall go to a pettie Ale-house.
No, no: you know the olde Tauerne in Eastcheape,
There is good wine : besides, there is a prettie wench
That can talke well, for I delight as much in their
　　tongies,
As any part about them.
　　All. We are readie to waite vpon your grace.
　　Hen. V. Gogs wounds wait, we will go altogither,
We are all fellowes, I tell you sirs, and the King
My father were dead, we would be all Kings,
Therefore come away.
　　Ned. Gogs wounds, brauely spoken Harry

　　*Enter Iohn Cobler, Robin Pewterer, Lawrence
　　　　　　　　Costermonger.*

Iohn Cob. All is well here, all is well maisters.
　　Law. How say you neighbour Iohn Cobler?
I thinke it best that my neighbour
Robin Pewterer went to Pudding lane end,
And we will watch here at Billinsgate ward.
How say you neighbour Robin, how like you this?

Rob. Marry well neighbours :
I care not much if I goe to Pudding lanes end.
But neighbors, and you heare any adoe about me,
Make haste : and if I heare any adoe about you,
I will come to you. *Exit Robin.*
    Law. Neighbor, what newes heare you of yᵉ young
      Prince :
    Iohn. Marry neighbour, I heare say, he is a toward
      yoong Prince,
For if he met any by the hie way,
He will not let to talke with him,
I dare not call him théefe, but sure he is one of these
    taking fellowes.
    Law. Indéed neighbour, I heare say he is as liuely
A young Prince as euer was.
    Iohn. I, and I heare say, if he vse it long,
His father will cut him off from the Crowne :
But neighbour say nothing of that.
    Law. No, no, neighbour, I warrant you.
    Iohn. Neighbour, me thinkes you begin to sléepe,
If you will, we will sit down,
For I thinke it is about midnight.
    Law. Marry content neighbour, let vs sléepe.

Enter Dericke rouing.

    Der. Who, who there, who there ?   *Exit Dericke.*

Enter Robin.

    Rob. O neighbours, what meane you to sléepe,
And such ado in the stréetes ?
    Ambo. How now neighbor, whats the matter?

Enter Dericke againe.

    Der. Who there, who there, who there ?
    Cob. Why, what ailst thou ? here is no horses.
    Der. O alas man, I am robd, who there, who there ?
    Rob. Hold him neighbor Cobler.

Cob. Why I sée thou art a plaine Clowne.

Der. Am I a Clowne, sownes maisters,

Do Clownes goe in silke apparell?

I am sure all we gentlemen Clownes in Kent scant
goe so

Well: sownes you know clownes very well:

Heare you, are you Master Constable, and you be
speake?

For I will not take it at his hands.

Iohn. Faith I am maister Constable,

But I am one of his bad officers, for he is not here.

Der. Is not maister Constable here?

Well it is no matter, ile haue the law at his hands.

Iohn. Nay I pray you do not take the law of
vs.

Der. Well, you are one of his beastly officers.

Iohn. I am one of his bad officers.

Der. Why then I charge thée looke to him.

Cob. Nay but heare ye sir, you séeme to be an
honest

Fellow, and we are poore men, and now tis night:

And we would be loth to haue any thing adoo,

Therefore I pray thée put it vp.

Der. First, thou saiest true, I am an honest
fellow,

And a proper hansome fellow too,

And you séeme to be poore men, therfore I care not
greatly,

Nay, I am quickly pacified:

But and you chance to spie the théefe,

I pray you laie hold on him.

Rob. Yes that we wil, I warrant you.

Der. Tis a wonderfull thing to sée how glad the
knaue

Is, now I haue forgiuen him.

Iohn. Neighbors, do ye looke about you?

How now, who's there?

Enter the Theefe.

Theefe. Here is a good fellow, I pray you which
is the
Way to the old Tauerne in Eastcheape?
Der. Whoope hollo, now Gads Hill, knowest thou
me? I know thée for an Asse.
Theefe. I know thée for an Asse.
Der. And I know thée for a taking fellow,
Vpon Gads Hill in Kent:
A bots light vpon ye.
Theefe. The whorson vilaine would be knockt.
Der. Maisters, vilaine, and ye men stand to him,
And take his weapon from him, let him not passe you.
Iohn. My friend, what make you abroad now?
It is too late to walke now.
Theefe. It is not too late for true men to walke.
Law. We know thée not to be a true man.
Theefe. Why what do you meane to do with me?
Sownes I am one of the kings liege people.
Der. Heare you sir, are you one of the kings liege
people?
Theefe. I marry am I sir, what say you to it?
Der. Marry sir, I say you are one of the kings
filching people.
Cob. Come, come, lets haue him away.
Theefe. Why what haue I done?
Rob. Thou hast robd a poore fellow,
And taken away his goods from him,
Theefe. I neuer sawe him before.
Der. Maisters who comes here?

Enter the Vintners boy.

Boy. How now good man Cobler?
Cob. How now *Robin*, what makes thou abroad
At this time of night?
Boy. Marrie I haue béene at the Counter,

I can tell such newes as neuer you haue heard the
like.

Cob. What is that *Robin*, what is the matter ?

Boy. Why this night about two houres ago, there
came the young Prince, and thrée or foure more of
his companions, and called for wine good store, and
then they sent for a noyse of Musitians, and were
very merry for the space of an houre, then whether
their Musicke liked them not, or whether they had
drunke too much Wine or no, I cannot tell, but our
pots flue against the wals, and then they drew their
swordes, and went into the streete and fought, and
some tooke one part, & some tooke another, but for
the space of halfe an houre, there was such a bloodie
fray as passeth, and none coulde part them vntil such
time as the Maior and Sheriffe were sent for, and then
at last with much adoo, they tooke them, and so the
yong Prince was carried to the Counter, and then
about one houre after, there came a Messénger from
the Court in all haste, from the King, for my Lord
Maior and the Sheriffe, but for what cause I know
not.

Cob. Here is newes indéede *Robert.*

Law. Marry neighbour, this newes is strange indéede, I thinke it best neighbour, to rid our hands of
this fellowe first.

Theefe. What meane you to do with me ?

Cob. We mean to carry you to the prison, and there
to remaine till the Sessions day.

Theefe. Then I pray you let me go to the prison
where my maister is.

Cob. Nay thou must go to ye country prison, to
newgate, Therefore come away.

Theefe. I prethie be good to me honest fellow.

Der. I marry will I, ile be verie charitable to thée,
For I wil neuer leaue thée, til I sée thée on the
Gallowes.

*Enter Henry the fourth, with the Earle of Exeter
and the Lord of Oxford.*

Oxf. And please your Maiestie, héere is my Lord
Maior, and the Sheriffe of London, to speak with
your Maiestie.

K. Hen. IV. Admit them to our presence.

Enter the Maior and the Sheriffe.

Now my good Lord Maior of London,
The cause of my sending for you at this time, is to
tel you of a matter which I haué learned of my Councell : Herein I vnderstand, that you haue committed
my sonne to prison without our leaue and license.
What althogh he be a rude youth, and likely to giue
occasion, yet you might haue considered that he is a
Prince, and my sonne, and not to be halled to prison
by euery subiect.

Maior. May it please your Maiestie to giue vs leaue
to tell our tale ?

K. Hen. IV. Or else God forbid, otherwise you
might thinke me an vneqall Iudge, hauing more affection to my sonne, then to any rightfull iudgement.

Maior. Then I do not doubt but we shal rather
deserue commendations at your Maiesties hands, then
any anger.

K. Hen. IV. Go too, say on.

Maior. Then if it please your Maiestie, this night
betwixt two and three of the clocke in the morning,
my Lord the yong Prince with a very disordred companie, came to the old Tauerne in Eastcheape, and
whether it was that their musicke liked them not, or
whether they were ouercom with wine, I know not,
but they drew their swords, and into the stréete they
went, and some tooke my Lord the yong Princes part,
and some tooke the other, but betwixt them there
was such a bloodie fray for the space of halfe an

houre, that neyther watchmen, nor any other could stay them, till my brother the Sheriffe of London & I were sent for, and at the last with much adoo we staied them, but it was long first, which was a great disquieting to all your louing subiects thereabouts : and then my good Lord, we knew not whether your grace had sent them to trie vs, whether we would do iustice, or whether it were of their owne voluntarie will or not, we cannot tell : and therefore in such a case we knew not what to do, but for our own safegard we sent him to ward, where he wanteth nothing that is fit for his grace, and your Maiesties sonne. And thus most humbly beséeching your Maiestie to thinke of our answere.

Hen. IV. Stand aside vntill we haue further deliberated on your answere.   [*Exit Maior.*

Ah Harry, Harry, now thrice accursed Harry,
That hath gotten a sonne, which with gréefe
Will end his fathers dayes.
Oh my sonne, a Prince thou art, I a Prince in déed,
And to deserue imprisonment,
And well haue they done, and like faithfull subiects :
Discharge them and let them go.

L. Exe. I beséech your Grace, be good to my Lord the yong Prince.

Hen. IV. Nay, nay, tis no matter, let him alone.

L. Oxf. Perchance the Maior and the Sheriffe haue bene too precise in this matter.

Hen. IV. No : they haue done like faithfull subiects :
I will go my selfe to discharge them, and let them go.
                                        Exit omnes.

*Enter Lord chiefe Iustice, Clarke of the Office, Iayler,
   Iohn Cobler, Dericke, and the Theefe.*

Iudge. Iayler bring the prisoner to the barre.

Der. Heare you my Lord, I pray you bring the bar to the prisoner.

Iudge. Hold thy hand vp at the barre.

Theefe. Here it is my Lord.

Iudge. Clearke of the office, reade his inditement.

Clearke. What is thy name?

Theefe. My name was knowne before I came here.

And shall be when I am gone, I warrant you.

Iudge. I, I thinke so, but we will know it better before thou go.

Der. Sownes and you do but send to the next Iaile, We are sure to know his name,

For this is not the first prison he hath bene in, ile warrant you.

Clearke. What is thy name?

Theefe. What néed you to aske, and haue it in writing.

Clearke. Is not thy name Cutbert Cutter?

Theefe. What the Diuell néed you to ask, and know it so well.

Clearke. Why then Cutbert Cutter, I indite thée by the name of Cutbert Cutter, for robbing a poore carrier the 20 day of May last past, in the fourtéen yeare of the raigne of our soueraigne Lord King Henry the fourth, for setting vpon a poore Carrier vpon Gads hill in Kent, and hauing beaten and wounded the said Carrier, and taken his goods from him.

Der. Oh maisters stay there, nay lets neuer belie the man, for he hath not beaten and wounded me also, but hée hath beaten and wounded my packe, and hath taken the great rase of Ginger, that bouncing Bess with the iolly buttocks should haue had, that gréeues me most.

Iudge. Well, what sayest thou, art thou guiltie, or not guiltie?

Theefe. Not guiltie, my Lord.

Iudge. By whom wilt thou be tride?

Theefe. By my Lord the young Prince, or by my selfe whether you will.

Enter the young Prince, with Ned and Tom.

Hen. V. Come away my lads, Gogs wounds ye villain, what make you héere? I must goe about my businesse my selfe, and you must stand loytering here.

Theefe. Why my Lord, they haue bound me, and will not let me goe.

Hen. V. Haue they bound thée villain, why how now my Lord.

Iudge. I am glad to sée your Grace in good health.

Hen. V. Why, my Lord, this is my man,
Tis maruell you knew him not long before this,
I tell you he is a man of his hands.

Theefe. I Gogs wounds that I am, try me who dare.

Iudge. Your Grace shal finde small credit by acknowledging him to be your man.

Hen. V. Why my Lord, what hath he done?

Iudge. And it please your Maiestie, he hath robbed a poore Carrier.

Der. Heare you sir, marry it was one Dericke, Goodman Hoblings man of Kent.

Hen. V. What wast thou butten-breech?
Of my word my Lord, he did it but in jest.

Der. Heare you sir, is it your mans qualitie to rob folks in iest?
In faith, he shall be hangd in earnest.

Hen. V. Well my Lord, what do you meane to do with my man?

Iudge. And please your grace the law must passe on him,
According to iustice then he must be executed.

Der. Heare you sir, I pray you, is it your mans quality to rob folkes in iest? In faith he shall be hangd in iest.

Hen. V. Well my Lord, what meane you to do with my man?

Iudge. And please your grace the law must passe on him, According to iustice, then he must be executed.

Hen. V. Why then belike you meane to hang my man?

Iudge. I am sorie that it falles out so.

Hen. V. Why my Lord, I pray ye who am I?

Iudge. And please your Grace, you are my Lord the yong Prince, our King that shall be after the decease of our soueraigne Lord King Henry the fourth, whom God graunt long to raigne.

Hen. V. You say true my Lord :
And you will hang my man.

Iudge. And like your grace, I must néeds do iustice.

Hen. V. Tell me my Lord, shall I haue my man?

Iudge. I cannot my Lord.

Hen. V. But will you not let him go?

Iudge. I am sorie that his case is so ill.

Hen. V. Tush, case me no casings, shal I haue my man?

Iudge. I cannot, nor I may not my Lord.

Hen. V. Nay, and I shal not say, & then I am answered?

Iudge. No.

Hen. V. No : then I will haue him.

He giueth him a boxe on the eare.

Ned. Gogs wounds my Lord, shal I cut off his head?

Hen. V. No, I charge you draw not your swords,
But get you hence, prouide a noyse of Musitians,
Away, be gone.   [*Exeunt the Theefe.*

Iudge. Well my Lord, I am content to take it at your hands.

Hen. V. Nay and you be not, you shall haue more.

Iudge. Why I pray you my Lord, who am I?

Hen. V. You, who knowes not you?
Why man, you are Lord chiefe Iustice of England.

Iudge. Your Grace hath said truth, therefore in striking me in this place, you greatly abuse me, and not me onely but also your father : whose liuely person here in this place I doo represent. And therefore to teach you what prerogatiues meane, I commit you to the Fléete, vntill wee haue spoken with your father.

Hen. V. Why then belike you meane to send me to the Fléete?

Iudge. I indéed, and therefore carry him away.

Exeunt Henry V. with the Officers.

Iudge. Iayler, carry the prisoner to Newgate againe, vntil the next Sises.

Iayler. At your commandement my Lord, it shalbe done.

Enter Dericke and Iohn Cobler.

Der. Sownds maisters, heres adoo,
When Princes must go to prison :
Why Iohn, didst euer sée the like?

Iohn. O Dericke, trust me, I neuer saw the like.

Der. Why Iohn thou maist sée what princes be in choller,
A Iudge a boxe on the eare, Ile tel thée Iohn, O Iohn,
I would not haue done it for twentie shillings.

Iohn. No nor I, there had bene no way but one for vs,
We should haue been hangde.

Der. Faith Iohn, Ile tel thée what, thou shalt be my Lord chiefe Iustice, and thou shalt sit in the chaire,
And ile be the yong Prince, and hit thée a box on the eare,

And then thou shalt say, to teach you what prerogatiues meane, I commit you to the Fléete.

Iohn. Come on, Ile be your Iudge,
But thou shalt not hit me hard.

Der. No, no.

Iohn. What hath he done? ·

Der. Marry he hath robd Dericke.

Iohn. Why then I cannot let him goe.

Der. I must néeds haue my man.

Iohn. You shall not haue him.

Der. Shall I not haue my man, say no and you
dare :
How say you, shall I not haue my man ?

Iohn. No marry shall you not.

Der. Shall I not Iohn?

Iohn. No Dericke.

Der. Why then take you that till more come,
Sownes, shall I not haue him ?

Iohn. Well I am content to take this at your hand,
But I pray you who am I ?

Der. Who art thou, Sownds, doost not know thy
selfe ?

Iohn. No.

Der. Now away simple fellow,
Why man, thou art Iohn the Cobler.

Iohn. No, I am my Lord chiefe Iustice of England.

Der. Oh Iohn, Masse thou saist true, thou art indéed.

Iohn. Why then to teach you what prerogatiues
mean I commit you to the Flécte.

Der. Wel I wil go, but yfaith you gray beard knaue,
Ile course you.   *Exit.*   *And straight enters again.*
Oh Iohn, Come, come out of thy chaire, why what a
clown weart thou, to let me hit thée a box on the eare,
and now thou seest they will not take me to the
Fléete, I thinke that thou art one of these Worenday
Clownes.

Iohn. But I maruell what will become of thée?

Der. Faith, ile be no more a Carrier.

Iohn. What wilt thou doo then?

Der Ile dwell with thée and be a Cobler.

Iohn. With me, alasse, I am not able to kéepe thée,
Why thou wilt eate me out of doores.

Der. Oh Iohn, no Iohn, I am none of these great
slouching fellowes, that deuoure these great péeces of
béefe and brewes, alasse a trifle serues me, a Woodcocke, a Chicken, or a Capons legge, or any such
little thing serues me.

Iohn. A Capon, why man, I cannot get a Capon
once a yeare, except it be at Christmas, at some
other mans house, for we Coblers be glad of a dish of
rootes.

Der. Rootes, why are you so good at rooting?
Nay Cobler, wéele haue you ringde.

Iohn. But Dericke, though we be so poore,
Yet wil we haue in store a crab in the fire,
With nut-browne Ale, that is full stale,
Which wil a man quaile, and laie in the mire.

Der. A bots on you, and be but for your Ale,
Ile dwel with you, come lets away as fast as we can.

                                                    Exeunt.

Enter the yong Prince, with Ned and Tom.

Hen. V. Come away sirs, Gogs wounds Ned,
Didst thou not sée what a boxe on the eare
I tooke my Lord chiefe Iustice.

Tom. By gogs blood it did me good to sée it,
It made his téeth iarre in his head.

Enter sir Iohn Old-Castle.

Hen. V. How now sir Iohn Old-Castle?
What newes with you?

Ioh. Old. I am glad to sée your grace at libertie,
I was come I, to visit you in prison.

Hen. V. To visit me, didst thou not know that I

am a Princes son, why tis enough for me to looke
into a prison, though I come not in my selfe, but
heres such adoo now adayes, heres prisoning, heres
hanging, whipping, and the diuell and all : but I tel
you sirs, when I am King, we will haue no such things,
but my lads, if the old king my father were dead, we
would be all kings.

Ioh. Old. Hée is a good olde man, God take him
to his mercy the sooner.

Hen. V. But Ned, so soone as I am King, the first
thing I wil do, shal be to put my Lord chief Iustice
out of office. And thou shalt be my Lord chiefe
Iustice of England.

Ned. Shall I be Lord chiefe Iustice?
By gogs wounds Ile be the brauest Lord chiefe Iustice
That euer was in England.

Hen. V. Then Ned, Ile turne all these prisons into
Fence Schooles, and I will endue thée with them,
with landes to maintaine them withall : then I wil
haue a bout with my Lord chiefe Iustice, thou shalt
hang none but picke purses, and horse stealers, and
such base minded villaines, but that fellow that wil
stand by the highway side couragiously with his
sword and buckler and take a purse, that fellow
giue him commendations, beside that, send him to
me, and I will giue him an anuall pension out of my
Exchequer, to maintaine him all the dayes of his
life.

Ioh. Nobly spoken Harry, we shall neuer haue a
mery world til the old king be dead.

Ned. But whither are ye going now?

Hen. V. To the Court, for I heare say, my father
lies verie sicke.

Tom. But I doubt he wil not die.

Hen. V. Yet will I goe thither, for the breath shal
be no sooner out of his mouth, but I wil clap the
Crowne on my head.

Iock. Wil you goe to the Court with that cloake so ful of néedles?

Hen. V. Cloake, ilat-holes, néedles, and all was of mine owne devising, and therefore I wil weare it.

Tom. I pray you my Lord, what may be the meaning thereof?

Hen. V. Why man, tis a signe that I stand vpon thorns, til the Crowne be on my head.

Iock. Or that euery néedle might be a prick to their harts that repine at your doings.

Hen. V. Thou saist true Iockey but thers some wil say, the yoong Prince will bee a well toward yoong man and all this geare, that I had as leeue they would breake my head with a pot, as to say any such thing, but we stand prating here too long, I must néeds speake with my father, therfore come away.

Por. What a rapping kéep you at the Kings Courte gate?

Hen. V. Heres one that must speake with the King.

Por. The King is verie sicke, and none must speak with him.

Hen. V. No you rascall, do you not know me?

Por. You are my lord the yong Prince.

Hen. V. Then goe and tell my father, that I must and will speake with him.

Ned. Shall I cut off his head?

Hen. V. No, no, though I would helpe you in other places, yet I haue nothing to doo here, what you are in my father's Court.

Ned. I will write him in my Tables, for so soone as I am made Lord chiefe Iustice, I wil put him out of his Office.   *The Trumpet sounds.*

Hen. V. Gogs wounds sirs, the King comes,
Lets all stand aside.

Enter the King, with the Lord of Exeter.

Hen. IV. And is it true my Lord, that my sonne

is already sent to the Fléete? Now truly that man is more fitter to rule the Realme then I, for by no meanes could I rule my sonne, and he by one word hath caused him to be ruled. Oh my sonne, my sonne, no sooner out of one prison, but into an other, I had thought once whiles I had liued, to haue séene this noble Realme of England flourish by thée my soone, but now I sée it goes to ruine and decaie.

He wepeth.

Enters Lord of Oxford.

Oxf. And please your grace, here is my Lord your sonne,
That commeth to speake with you,
He saith, he must and wil speake with you,
　Hen. IV. Who my sonne Harry?
　Oxf. I and please your Maiestie.
　Hen. IV. I know wherefore he commeth,
But looke that none come with him.
　Oxf. A verie disordered companie, and such as make
Verie ill rule in your Maiesties house.
　Hen. IV. Well let him come,
But looke that none come with him.　　*He goeth.*
　Oxf. And please your grace,
My lord the King, sends for you.
　Hen. V. Come away sirs, lets go all togither.
　Oxf. And please your grace, none must go with you.
　Hen. V. Why, I must néeds have them with me,
Otherwise I can do my father no countenance,
Therefore come away.
　Oxf. The King your father commaunds.
There should none come.
　Hen. Well sirs then be gone,
And prouide me thrée Noyse of Musitians.

Exeunt knights.

Enters the Prince with a dagger in his hand.

Hen. IV. Come my sonne, come on a God's name,
I know wherefore thy comming is,
Oh my sonne, my sonne, what cause hath euer bene,
That thou shouldst forsake me, and follow this vilde
and
Reprobate company, which abuseth youth so mani-
festly :
Oh my sonne, thou knowest that these thy doings
Wil end thy fathers dayes.   *He weepes.*
I so, so, my sonne, thou fearest not to approach the
presence of thy sick father, in that disguised sort, I
tel thée my sonne, that there is neuer a néedle in thy
cloke, but it is a prick to my heart, & neuer an ilat-
hole, but it is a hole to my soule ; and wherefore
thou bringest that dagger in thy hande I know not,
but by coniecture.   *He weepes.*
Hen. V. My conscience accuseth me, most soueraign Lord, and welbeloued father, to answere first to
the last point, That is, whereas you coniecture that
this hand and this dagger shall be armde against your
life : no, know my beloued father, far be the thoughts
of your sonne, sonne said I, an vnworthie sonne for
so good a father : but farre be the thoughts of any
such pretended mischiefe : and I most humbly render
it to your Maiesties hand, and liue my Lord and
soueraigne for euer : and with your dagger arme show
like vengeance vpon the bodie of your sonne, I was
about say and dare not, ah woe is me therefore, that
your wilde slaue, tis not the Crowne that I come for,
sweet father, because I am vnworthie, and those wilde
& reprobate company I abandon, & vtterly abolish
their company for euer. Pardon sweete father,
pardon : the least thing and most desire : and this
ruffianly cloake, I here teare from my backe, and
sacrifice it to the diuel, which is maister of al mis-

chiefe : Pardon me, swéet father, pardō me : good
my Lord of Exeter, speak for me : pardon me,
pardō good father, not a word : ah he wil not speak
one word : A Harry, now thrice vnhappie Harry.
But what shal I do? I wil go take me into some
solitarie place, and there lament my sinfull life, and
when I haue done, I wil lay me downe and die.

Exit.

Hen. IV. Call him againe, call my sonne againe.

Hen. V. And doth my father call me againe ? now
Harry,

Happie be the time that thy father calleth thée againe.

Hen. IV. Stand vp my son, and do not think thy
father,

But at the request of thée my sonne, I wil pardon
thée,

And God blesse thée, and make thée his seruant.

Hen. V. Thanks good my Lord, & no doubt but
this day,

Euen this day, I am borne new againe.

Hen. IV. Come my son and Lords, take me by the
hands.   *Exeunt omnes.*

Enter Dericke.

Der. Thou art a stinking whore, & a whorson
stinking whore,

Doest thinke ile take it at thy hands ?

Enter Iohn Cobler running.

Iohn. Derick, D. D. Heuresta,

Do D. neuer while thou liuest vse that,

Why what wil my neighbors say, and thou go
away so ?

Der. Shées an arrant whore, and Ile haue the lawe
on you Iohn.

Der. Marry marke thou Iohn,
I wil proue it that I wil.
Iohn. What wilt thou proue?
Der. That she cald me in to dinner.
Iohn, marke the tale wel Iohn, and when I was set,
She brought me a dish of rootes, and a péece of barrel
    butter therin : and she is a verie knaue,
And thou a drab if thou take her part.
Iohn. Hearesta Dericke, is this the matter?
Nay, and it be no worse, we wil go home againe,
And all shall be amended.
Der. Oh Iohn, hearesta Iohn, is all well?
Iohn. I, all is wel.
Der. Then ile go home before, and breake all the
glass windowes.

Enter the King with his Lords.

Hen. IV. Come my Lords, I see it bootes me not
to take any phisick, for all the Phisitians in the world
cannot cure me, no not one. But good my Lords,
remember my last wil and Testament concerning my
sonne, for truly my Lordes, I doo not thinke but he
wil proue as valiant and victorious a King, as euer
raigned in England.
Both. Let heauen and earth be witnesse betwéene
us, if we accomplish not thy wil to the vttermost.
Hen. IV. I giue you most vnfained thanks, good
    my lords,
Draw the Curtaines and depart my chamber a while,
And cause some Musicke to rocke me a sléepe.
                He sleepeth.   Exeunt Lords.

Enter the Prince.

Hen. V. Ah Harry, thrice vnhappie that hath
neglèct so long from visiting of thy sicke father, I wil
goe, nay but why doo I not go to the Chamber of my
sick father, to comfort the melancholy soule of his

bodie, his soule said I, here is his bodie indéed, but
his soule is, whereas it néeds no bodie. Now thrice`
accursed Harry, that hath offended thy father so much,
and could not I craue pardon for all. Oh my dying
father, curst be the day wherin I was borne, and accursed
be the houre wherin I was begotten, but what shal I do?
if wéeping teares which come too late, may suffice the
negligence neglected to some, I wil wéepe day and night
vntil the fountaine be drie with wéeping. *Exit.*

Enter Lord of Exeter and Oxford.

Exe. Come easily my Lord, for waking of the King.
Hen. IV. Now my Lords.
Oxf. How doth your Grace féele your selfe.
Hen. IV. Somewhat better after my sléepe,
But good my Lords take off my Crowne,
Remoué my chaire a litle backe, and set me right.
    Ambo. And please your grace, the crown is také
    away.
Hen. IV. The Crowne taken away,
Good my Lord of Oxford, go sée who hath done this
    déed :
No doubt tis some vilde traitor that hath done it,
To depriue my sonne, they that would do it now,
Would séeke to scrape and scrawle for it after my
    death.

Enter Lord of Oxford with the Prince.

Oxf. Here and please your Grace,
Is my Lord the yong Prince with the Crowne.
Hen. IV. Why how now my sonne?
I had thought the last time I had you in schooling,
I had giuen you a lesson for all,
And do you now begin againe?
Why tel me my sonne,
Doest thou thinke the time so long,

That thou wouldest haue it before the
Breath be out of my mouth?

 Hen. V. Most soueraign Lord, and welbeloved
  father,
I came into your Chamber to comfort the melancholy
Soule of your bodie, and finding you at that time
Past all recouery, and dead to my thinking,
God is my witnesse: and what should I doo,
But with wéeping tears lament yᵉ death of you my
  father,
And after that, séeing the Crowne, I tooke it:
And tel me my father, who might better take it
  then I,
After your death? but séeing you liue,
I most humbly render it into your Maiesties hands,
And the happiest man aliue, that my father liue:
And liue my Lord and Father, for euer.

 Hen. IV. Stand vp my sonne,
Thine answere hath sounded wel in mine eares,
For I must néed confesse that I was in a very sound
  sléep,
And altogither vnmindful of thy comming:
But come neare my sonne,
And let me put thée in possession whilst I liue,
That none depriue thée of it after my death.

 Hen. V. Well may I take it at your maiesties hands,
But it shal neuer touch my head, so long as my father
  liues.

         He taketh the Crowne.
 Hen. IV. God giue thée ioy my sonne,
God blesse thée, and make thée his seruant,
And send thée a prosperous raigne.
For God knowes my sonne, how hardly I came by it,
And how hardly I haue maintained it.

 Hen. V. Howsoeuer you came by it, I know not,
And now I haue it from you, and from you I wil
  kéepe it:

And he that séekes to take the Crowne from my
    head,
Let him looke that his armour be thicker then mine,
Or I will pearce him to the heart,
Were it harder than brasse or bollion.
    Hen. IV. Nobly spoken, and like a King.
Now trust me my Lords, I feare not but my sonne
Will be as warlike and victorious a Prince,
As euer raigned in England.
    L. Ambo. His former life shewes no lesse.
    Hen. IV. Wel my lords I know not whether it be
    for sléep,
Or drawing neare of drowsie summer of death,
But I am verie much giuen to sléepe,
Therefore good my Lords and my sonne,
Draw the Curtaines, depart my chamber,
And cause some Musicke to rocke me a sléepe.
                Exeunt omnes.   *The King dieth.*

        Enter the Theefe.

    Theefe. Ah God, I am now much like to a Bird
Which hath escaped out of the Cage,
For so soone as my Lord chief iustice it heard
That the old King was dead, he was glad to let me go,
For feare of my Lord the yong Prince:
But here comes some of his companions,
I wil sée and I can get any thing of them,
For old acquaintance.

        Enter Knightes raunging.

    Tom. Gogs wounds the King is dead.
    Iock. Dead, then gogs blood, we shall be all kings.
    Ned. Gogs wounds, I shall be Lord chiefe Iustice
Of England.
    Tom. Why how, are you broken out of prison?
    Ned. Gogs wounds, how the villaine stinkes.

Iock. Why what wil become of thée now?
Fye vpon him, how the rascall stinkes.
   Theefe. Marry I wil go and serue my maister againe.
   Tom. Gogs blood, doost think that he wil haue any
     such
Scab'd knaue as thou art? what man he is a king now.
   Ned. Hold thée, heres a couple of Angels for thée,
And get thée gone, for the King wil not be long
Before he come this way:
And hereafter I wil tel the king of thée.   *Exit Theefe.*
   Iock. Oh how it did me good, to sée the king
When he was crowned:
Me thought his seate was like the figure of heauen,
And his person like vnto a God.
   Ned. But who would haue thought,
That the king would haue changde his countenance
     so?
   Iock. Did you not sée with what grace
He sent his embassage into France? to tel the French
     king
That Harry of England hath sent for the Crowne,
And Harry of England wil haue it.
   Tom. But twas but a litle to make the people be-
     léeue,
That he was sorie for his fathers death.
                  The Trumpet sounds
   Ned. Gogs wounds, the king comes,
Let all stand aside.

  Enter the King with the Archbishop, and the Lord of
              Oxford.

   Iock. How do you my Lord?
   Ned. How now Harry?
Tut my Lord, put away these dumpes,
You are a king, and all the realme is yours:
What man, do you not remember the old sayings,
You know I must be Lord chiefe Iustice of England,

Trust me my lord, me thinks you are very much
  changed,
And tis but with a litle sorrowing, to make folkes be-
  léeue
The death of your father gréeues you,
And tis nothing so.
  Hen. V. I prethée Ned, mend thy manners,
And be more modester in thy tearmes,
For my vnfeined gréefe is not to be ruled by thy flat-
  tering
And dissembling talke, thou saist I am changed,
So I am indeed, and so must thou be, and that
  quickly,
Or else I must cause thée to be chaunged.
  Iock. Gogs wounds how like you this?
Sownds tis not so swéete as Musicke.
  Tom. I trust we haue not offended your grace no
  way.
  Hen. V. Ah Tom, your former life gréeues me,
And makes me to abandō & abolish your company
  for euer
And therfore not vpō pain of death to approch my
  presence
By ten miles space, then if I heare wel of you,
It may be I wil do somewhat for you,
Otherwise looke for no more fauour at my hands,
Then at any other mans : And therefore be gone,
We haue no other matters to talke on.
                              Exeunt Knights:
Now my good Lord Archbishop of Canterbury,
What say you to our Embassage into France?
  Archb. Your right to the French Crowne of France,
Came by your great grandmother Izabel,
Wife to King Edward the third,
And sister to Charles the French King :
Now if the French king deny it, as likely inough he
  wil,

Then must you take your sword in hand,
And conquer the right.
Let the vsurped Frenchman know,
Although your predecessors haue let it passe, you wil
    not :
For your Countrymen are willing with purse and
    men,
To aide you.
Then my good Lord, as it hath bene alwaies knowne,
That Scotland hath bene in league with France,
By a sort of pensions which yearly come from thence,
I thinke it therefore best to conquere Scotland,
And thē I think that you may go more easily into
    France :
And this is all that I can say, My good Lord.
    Hen. V. I thanke you, my good lord Archbishop of
    Canterbury.
What say you my good Lord of Oxford?
    Oxf. And, And please your Maiestie,
I agree to my Lord Archbishop, sauing in this,
He that wil Scotland win, must first with France
    begin :
According to the old saying.
Therefore my good Lord, I think it best to inuade
    France,
For in conquering Scotland, you conquer but one,
And conquere France, and conquere both.

Enter Lord of Exeter.

    Exe. And please your Maiestie,
My Lord Embassador is come out of France.
    Hen. V. Now trust me my Lord,
He was the last man that we talked of,
I am glad that he is come to resolue vs of our an-
    swere,
Commit him to our presence.

Enter Duke of Yorke.

York. God saue the life of my soueraign Lord the king.

Hen. V. Now my good Lord the Duke of York,
What newes from our brother the French King?

York. And please your Maiestie,
I deliuered him my Embassage,
Whereof I tooke some deliberation,
But for the answere he hath sent,
My Lord Embassador of Burges, the Duke of Bur-
    gony,
Monsieur le Cole, with two hundred and fiftie horse-
    men,
To bring the Embassage.

Hen. V. Commit my Lord Archbishop of Burges
Into our presence.

Enter Archbishop of Burges.

Now my Lord Archbishop of Burges,
We do learne by our Lord Embassador,
That you haue our message to do
From our brother the French King:
Here my good Lord, according to our accustomed
    order,
We giue you frée libertie and license to speake,
With good audience.

Archb. God saue the mightie King of England,
My Lord and maister, the most Christian king,
Charles the seuenth, the great & mightie king of
    France,
As a most noble and Christian king,
Not minding to shed innocent blood, is rather con-
    tent
To yéeld somewhat to your vnreasonable demaunds,
That if fiftie thousand crownes a yeare with his
    daughter

The said Ladie Katheren, in marriage,
And some crownes which he may wel spare,
Not hurting of his kingdome,
He is content to yéeld so far to your vnreasonable
    desire.
    Hen. V. Why then belike your Lord and maister,
Thinks to puffe me vp with fifty thousand crowns a
    yere,
No tell thy Lord and maister,
That all the crownes in France shall not serue me,·
Except the Crowne and kingdome it selfe :
And perchance hereafter I wil haue his daughter.
    Archb. And may it please your maiestie,
My Lord Prince Dolphin greets you well,
With this present.
                    He deliuereth a Tunne of Tennis Balles.
    Hen. V. What a guilded Tunne ?
I pray you my Lord of Yorke, looke what is in it ?
    Yorke. And it please your Grace,
Here is a Carpet and a Tunne of Tennis balles.
    Hen. V. A Tunne of Tennis balles ?
I pray you good my Lord Archbishop,
What might the meaning thereof be ?
    Archb. And it please you my Lord,
A messenger you know, ought to kéepe close his
    message,
And specially an Embassador.
    Hen. V. But I know that you may declare your
    message
To a king, the law of Armes allowes no lesse.
    Archb. My Lord, hearing of your wildnesse before
    your
Fathers death, sent you this my good Lord,
Meaning that you are more fitter for a Tennis
    Court
Then a field, and more fitter for a Carpet then the
    Camp.

Hen. V. My lord Prince Dolphin is very pleasant[1]
  with me :
But tel him, that in stéed of balles of leather,
We wil tosse him balles of brasse and yron,
Yea such balles as neuer were tost in France,
The proudest Tennis Court shall rue it.
I and thou Prince of Burges shall rue it.
Therefore get thée hence, and tel him thy massage
  quickly,
Least I be there before thee : Away priest, be gone.
  Archb. I beséech your grace, to deliuer me your safe
Conduct vnder your broad seale Emanuel.
  Hen. V. Priest of Burges, know,
That the hand and seale of a King, and his word is
  all one,
And in stead of my hand and seale,
I will bring him my hand and sword :
And tel thy lord and maister, that I Harry of Eng-
  land said it,
And I Harry of England, wil performe it.
My Lord of Yorke, deliuer him our safe conduct,
Vnder our broad seale Emanuel.
            Exeunt Archbishop, and the Duke of Yorke.
Now my Lords, to Armes, to Armes,
For I vow by heauen and earth, that the proudest
French man in all France, shall rue the time that euer
These Tennis balles were sent into England.
My Lord, I wil y^t there be prouided a great Nauy of ships,
With all spéed, at South-Hampton.
For there I meane to ship my men,
For I would be there before him, if it [2] were possible,
Therefore come, but staie,
I had almost forget the chiefest thing of all, with chafing
With this French Embassador.
Call in my Lord chiefe Iustice of England.

---

[1] [Old copy, *pleansant.*]   [2] [Old copy, *it it.*]

Enters Lord chiefe Iustice of England.

Exe. Here is the King my Lord.

Iust. God preserue your Maiestie.

Hen. V. Why how now my lord, what is the matter?

Iust. I would it were vnknowne to your Maiestie.

Hen. V. Why what aile you?

Iust. Your Maiestie knoweth my griefe well.

Hen. V. Oh my Lord, your remember you sent me
to the Fléete, did you not?

Iust. I trust your grace haue forgotten that.

Hen. V. I truly my Lord, and for reuengement,
I haue chosen you to be my Protector ouer my
    Realme,
Vntil it shall please God to giue me spéedie returne
Out of France.

Iust. And if it please your Maiestie, I am far vn-
    worthie
Of so high a dignitie.

Hen. V. Tut my Lord, you are not vnworthie,
Because I thinke you worthie
For you that would not spare me,
I thinke wil not spare another,
It must néeds be so, and therefore come,
Let vs be gone, and get our men in a readinesse.
                    Exeunt omnes.

Enter a Captaine, Iohn Cobler and his wife.

Cap. Come, come, there's no remedie,
Thou must néeds serue the King.

Iohn. Good maister Captaine let me go,
I am not able to go so farre.

Wife. I pray you good maister Captaine,
Be good to my husband.

Cap. Why I am sure he is not too good to serue
    ye king?

Iohn. Alasse no : but a great deale too bad,
Therefore I pray you let me go.

    Cap. No, no, thou shalt go.

    Iohn. Oh sir, I haue a great many shooes at home
      to Cobble.

    Wife. I pray you let him go home againe.

    Cap. Tush I care not, thou shalt go.

    Iohn. Oh wife, and you had béen a louing wife to
      me,
This had not bene, for I haue said many times,
That I would go away, and now I must go
Against my will.   *He weepeth.*

Enters Dericke.

    Der. How now ho, Basillus Manus, for an old cod-
      péece,
Maister Captaine shall we away ?
Sowndes how now Iohn, what a crying ?
What make you and my dame there ?
I maruell whose head you will throw the stooles at,
Now we are gone.

    Wife. Ile tell you, come ye cloghead,
What doe you with my potlid ? heare you,
Will you haue it rapt about your pate ?
              She beateth him with her potlid.

    Der. Oh good dame, here he shakes her.
And I had my dagger here, I wold worie you all to
      péeces
That I would.

    Wife. Would you so, Ile trie that.   *She beateth him.*

    Der. Maister Captaine will ye suffer her?
Go too dame, I will go backe as far as I can,
But and you come againe,
Ile clap the law on your backe that flat :
Ile tell you maister Captaine what you shall dom ?
Presse her for a souldier, I warrant you,
She will do as much good as her husband and I too.

Enters the Theefe.

Sownes, who comes yonder?

Cap. How now good fellow, doest thou want a maister.

Theefe. I truly sir.

Cap. Hold thée then, I presse thée for a souldier,
To serue the King in France.

Der. How now Gads, what doest knowes thinkest?

Theefe. I, I knew thée long ago.

Der. Heare you maister Captaine?

Cap. What saist thou?

Der. I pray you let me go home againe.

Cap. Why what wouldst thou do at home?

Der. Marry I haue brought two shirts with me,
And I would carry one of them home againe,
For I am sure héele steale it from me,
He is such a filching fellow.

Cap. I warrant thée he wil not steale it from thée,
Come lets away.

Der. Come maister Captaine lets away,
Come follow me.

Iohn. Come wife, lets part lovingly.

Wife. Farewell good husband.

Der. Fie what a kissing and crying is here?
Sownes, do ye thinke he wil neuer come againe?
Why Iohn come away, doest thinke that we are so base
Minded to die among French men?
Sownes, we know not whether they will laie
Vs in their Church or no: Come M. Captain, lets away.

Cap. I cannot staie no longer, therefore come away.
Exeunt omnes.

*Enter the King, Prince Dolphin, and Lord
high Constable of France.*

King. Now my Lord high Constable,
What say you to our Embassage into England?

Con. And it please your Maiestie, I can say nothing,
Vntil my Lords Embassadors be come home,
But yet me thinkes your grace hath done well,
To get your men in so good a readinesse,
For feare of the worst.

King. I my Lord we haue some in a readinesse,
But if the King of England make against vs,
We must haue thrice so many moe.

Dol. Tut my Lord, although the King of England
Be yoong and wild headed, yet neuer think he will
   be so
Vnwise to make battell against the mightie King
   of France.

King. Oh my sonne, although the King of England be
Yoong and wilde headed, yet neuer thinke but he is
   rulde
By his wise Councellors.

Enter Archbyshop of Burges.

Archb. God saue the life of my soueraign lord the
   king.

King. Now my good Lord Archbishop of Burges,
What news from our brother the English King?

Archb. And please your Maiestie,
He is so far from your expectation,
That nothing wil serue him but the Crowne
And kingdome it selfe, besides, he bad me haste
   quickly,
Least he be there before me, and so far as I hearc,
He hath kept promise, for they say, he is alreadie
   landed
At Kidcocks in Normandie, vpon the Riuer of Sene,
And laid his siege to the Garrison Towne of Harflew.

King. You have made great haste in the meane
   time,
Haue you not?

Dol. I pray you my Lord, how did the King of
England take my presents ?

Archb. Truly my Lord, in very ill part,
For these your balles of leather,
He will tosse you balles of brass and yron.
Trust me my Lord, I was verie affraide of him,
He is such a hautie and high minded Prince,
He is as fierce as a Lyon.

Con. Tush, we wil make him as tame as a Lambe,
I warrant you.

Enters a Messenger.

Mess. God saue the mightie King of France.

King. Now Messenger, what newes ?

Mess. And it please your Maiestie,
I come from your poore distressed Towne of Harflew,
Which is so beset on euery side,
If your Maiestie do not send present aide,
The Towne will be yeelded to the English King.

King. Come my Lords, come, shall we stand still
Till our Country be spoyled vnder our noses ?
My Lords, let the Normanes, Brabants, Pickardies,
And Danes, be sent for with all spéede :
And you my Lord high Constable, I make Generall
Ouer all my whole Armie.
Monsieur le Colle, Maister of the Boas,
Signior Deuens, and all the rest, at your appoint-
ment.

Dol. I trust your Maiestie will bestow,
Some part of the Battell on me,
I hope not to present any otherwise then well.

King. I tell thée my sonne,
Although I should get the victory, and thou lose thy
life,
I should thinke my selfe quite conquered,
And the English men to haue the victorie.

Dol. Why my Lord and father,

I would haue the pettie king of England to know,
That I dare encounter him in any ground of the world.
  King. I know well my sonne,
But at this time I will haue it thus :
Therefore come away.
Exeunt omnes.

Enters Henry the fifth, with his Lords.

  Hen. V. Come my Lords of England,
No doubt this good lucke of winning this Towne,
Is a signe of an honourable victorie to come.
But good my Lord, go and speake to the Captaines
With all spéed, to number the hoast of the French
    men,
And by that meanes we may the better know
How to appoint the battell.
  Yorke. And it please your Maiestie,
There are many of your men sicke and diseased,
And many of them die for want of victuals.
  Hen. V. And why did you not tell me of it before ?
If we cannot haue it for money,
We will haue it by dint of sword,
The lawe of Armes allow no lesse.
  Oxf. I beséech your grace, to graunt me a boone.
  Hen. V. What is that my good Lord ?
  Oxf. That your grace would giue me the
Euantgard in the battell.
  Hen. V. Trust me my Lord of Oxford, I cannot :
For I haue alreadie giuen it to my vnc[l]e yᵉ Duke of
    York,
Yet I thanke you for your good will.
A Trumpet soundes.
How now, what is that ?
  Yorke. I thinke it be some Herald of Armes.

Enters a Herald.

  Her. King of England, my Lord high Constable,

And others of the Noble men of France,
Sends me to defie thée, as open enemy to God,
Our Countrey, and vs, and hereupon,
They presently bid thée battell.
    Hen. V. Herald tell them, that I defie them,
As open enemies to God, my Countrey, and me,
And as wron[g]full vsurpers of my right :
And whereas thou saist they presently bid me battell.
Tell them that I thinke they knowe how to please me :
But I pray thée what place hath my lord Prince Dol-
    phin
Here in battell.
    Her. And it please your grace,
My Lord and King his father,
Will not let him come into the field.
    Hen. V. Why then he doth me great iniurie,
I thought that he & I shuld haue plaid at tennis
    togither,
Therefore I haue brought tennis balles for him,
But other maner of ones then he sent me.
And Herald, tell my Lord Prince Dolphin,
That I haue inured my hāds with other kind of
    weapons
Then tennis balles, ere this time a day,
And that he shall finde it, ere it be long,
And so adue my friend :
And tell my Lord that I am readie when he will.
                                Exit Herald.
Come my Lords, I care not and I go to our Captaines,
And ile sée the number of the French army my selfe.
Strike up the Drumme.
                                Exeunt omnes.

               Enter French Souldiers.

    1. *Soul.* Come away Jack Drummer, come away
    all,
And me will tel you, what me wil doo,

Me wil tro one chance on the dice,
Who shall haue the king of England and his lords.

   2. Soul. Come away Iacke Drummer,
And tro your chance, and lay downe your Drumme.

Enter Drummer.

   Drum. Oh the braue apparrel that the English mans
Hay broth ouer, I will tel you what
Me ha donne, me ha prouided a hundreth trunkes,
And all to put the fine parel of the English mans in.

   1. Soul. What do thou meane by trunkea *(sic)*?

   2. Soul. A shest man, a hundred shests.

   1. Soul. Awee, awee, awee, Me wil tel you what,
Me ha put fiue children out of my house,
And all too litle to put the fine apparel of the
English mans in.

   Drum. Oh the braue, the braue apparel that we
Haue anon, but come, and you shall sée what we wil
    tro
At the kings Drummer and Fife,
Ha, me ha no good luckc, tro you.

   3. Soul. Faith me wil tro at ye Earle of Northum
    berland
And my Lord a Willowby, with his great horse,
Snorting, farting, oh braue horse.

   1. Soul. Ha, bur Ladie you ha reasonable good
    lucke,
Now I wil tro at the king himselfe,
Ha, me haue no good luckc.

Enters a Captaine.

   Cap. How now what make you here,
So farre from the Campe?

   2. Soul. Shal me tel our captain, what we haue done
    here?

   Drum. Awée, awée.

            Exeunt Drum and one Souldier.

2. *Soul.* I wil tel you what whe haue doune,
We haue bene troing on shance on the Dice,
But none can win the king.

Cap. I thinke so, why he is left behind for me,
And I haue set thrée or foure chaire-makers a worke,
To make a new disguised chaire to set that womanly
King of England in, that all the people may laugh
And scoffe at him.

2. *Soul.* Oh braue Captaine.

Cap. I am glad, and yet with a kindle of pitie,
To sée the poore king.
Why, who euer saw a more flourishing armie in France
In one day, then here is?   Are not here all the Péeres
of France?
Are not here the Normans with their firie hand-
Gunnes, and slaunching Curtleaxes?
Are not here the Barbarians with their bard horses,
And lanching speares?
Are not here Pickardes with their crosbowes & pierc-
ing Dartes.
The Henues with their cutting Glaues, and sharpe
Carbuckles.
Are not here the Lance knights of Burgondie?
And on the other side, a site of poore English scabs?
Why take an English man out of his warme bed
And his stale drinke, but one moneth,
And alas what wil become of him?
But giue the Frenchman a Reddish roote,
And he wil liue with it all the dayes of his life.
                                          Exit.

2. *Soul.* Oh the braue apparel that we shall haue of
the English mans.   *Exit.*

Enters the king of England, and his Lords.

Hen. V. Come my Lords and fellows of armes,
What company is there of the French men?

Oxf. And it please your Maiestie,

Our Captaines haue numbred them,
And so neare as they can iudge,
They are about thréescore thousand horsemen,
And fortie thousand footemen.
    Hen. V. They thréescore thousand,
And we but two thousand.
They thréescore thousand footemen,
And we twelue thousand.
They are a hundred thousand,
And we fortie thousand, ten to one.
My Lords and louing Countrey men,
Though we be fewer, and they many,
Feare not, your quarrel is good, and God wil defend
    you :
Plucke vp your hearts, for this day we shall either
    haue
A valiant victorie, or a honourable death.
Now my Lords, I wil that my vncle the Duke of
    Yorke,
Haue the auantgard in the battell.
The Earle of Darby, the Earle of Oxford,
The Earle of Kent, the Earle of Nottingham,
The Earle of Huntington, I wil haue beside the army,
That they may come fresh vpon them.
And I my selfe with the Duke of Bedford,
The Duke of Clarence and the Duke of Gloster,
Wil be in the midst of the battell.
Furthermore, I wil that my Lord of Willowby,
And the Earle of Northumberland,
With their troupes of horsemen, be côtinually running
    like Wings on both sides of the army :
My Lord of Northumberland, on the left wing.
Then I wil that euery archer prouide him a stake of
A trée, and sharpe it at both endes,
And at the first encounter of the horsemen,
To pitch their stakes downe into the ground before
    them,

That they may gore themselues vpon them,
And then to recoyle backe, and shoote wholly alto-
    gither,
And so discomfit them.

 Oxf. And it please your Maiestie,
I wil take that in charge, if your grace be therwith
    cōtent.

 Hen. V. With all my heart, my good Lord of
Oxford :
And go and prouide quickly.

 Oxf. I thanke your highnesse.   *Exit.*

 Hen. V. Well my Lords, our battels are ordeined,
And the French making of bonfires, and at their
    baukets,
But let them looke, for I meane to set vpon them.
          The Trumpet soundes.
Soft, here comes some other French message.

Enters Herauld.

 Her. King of England, my Lord high Constable,
And other of my Lords, considering the poore estate
    of thée
And thy poore Countrey men,
Sends me to know what thou wilt giue for thy ran-
    some ?
Perhaps thou maist agrée better cheape now,
Then when thou art conquered.

 Hen. V. Why then belike your high Constable,
Sends to know what I wil giue for my ransome ?
Now trust me Herald, not so much as a tun of ten-
    nis-bals
No not so much as one poore tènnis-ball,
Rather shall my bodie lie dead in the field to féed
    crowes,
Then euer England shall pay one penny ransome
For my bodie.

 Her. A kingly resolution.

Hen. V. No Herald, tis a kingly resolution,
And the resolution of a king :
Here take this for thy paines.   *Exit Herald.*
But stay my Lords, what time is it ?
    All. Prime my Lord.
    Hen. V. Then is it good time no doubt,
For all England praieth for vs :
What my Lords, me thinks you looke chéerfully
    vpon me ?
Why then with one voice and like true English hearts,
With me throw vp your caps, and for England,
Cry S. George, and God and S. George helpe vs.
        Strike Drummer, Exeunt omnes.

  The Frenchmen crie within, S. Dennis, S. Dennis,
    Mount Ioy, S. Dennis.

    The Battell.

  Enters King of England, and his Lords.

    Hen. V. Come my Lords come, by this time our
Swords are almost drunke with French blood,
But my Lords, which of you can tell me how many
    of our
Army be slaine in the battell ?
    Oxf. And it please your Maiestie,
There are of the French armie slaine
Aboue ten thousand, twentie sixe hundred
Whereof are Princes and Nobles bearing banners :
Besides, all the Nobilitie of France are taken prisoners.
Of your Maiesties Armie, are slaine none but the
    good
Duke of Yorke, and not aboue fiue or six and twentie
Common souldiers.
    Hen. V. For the good Duke of Yorke my vnckle,
I am heartily sorie, and greatly lament his misfortune,
Yet the honourable victorie which the Lord hath
    giuen vs,

Doth make me much reioyce.   But staie,
Here comes another French message.

> [*Sound Trumpet.*

Enters a Herald and kneeleth.

Her. God saue the life of the most mightie Con-
queror,
The honourable king of England.
Hen. V. Now Herald, me thinks the world is
changed
With you now, what I am sure it is a great disgrace
for a
Herald to kneele to the king of England,
What is thy message?
Her. My Lord & maister, the conquered king of
France,
Sends thée long health, with heartie gréeting.
Hen. V. Herald, his greetings are welcome,
But I thanke God for my health :
Well Herald, say on.
Her. He hath sent me to desire your Maiestie,
To giue him leaue to go into the field to view his
poore
Countrymen, that they may all be honourably buried.
Hen. V. Why Herald, doth thy Lord and maister
Send to me to burie the dead?
Let him bury them a Gods name.
But I pray thée Herald, where is my Lord hie Con-
stable,
And those that would haue had my ransome?
Her. And it please your maiestie,
He was slaine in the battell.
Hen. V. Why you may sée, you will make your
selues
Sure before the victorie be wonne, but Herald,
What Castle is this so néere adioyning to our Campe?

Her. And it please your Maiestie,
Tis cald the Castle of Agincourt.
Hen. V. Well then my lords of England,
For the more honour of our English men,
I will that this be for euer cald the battell of Agin-
court.
Her. And it please your Maiestie,
I haue a further message to deliuer to your Maiestie.
Hen. V. What is that Herald? say on.
Her. And it please your Maiestie, my Lord and
maister,
Craues to parley with your Maiestie.
Hen. V. With a good will, so some of my Nobles
View the place for feare of trecherie and treason.
Her. Your grace néeds not to doubt that.
Hen. V. Well, tell him then, I will come.

Exit Herald.

Now my lords, I will go into the field my selfe,
To view my country men, and to haue them honourably
Buried, for the French King shall neuer surpasse me in
Curtesie, while I am Harry King of England.
Come on my lords. *Exeunt omnes.*

Enters Iohn Cobler and Robbin Pewterer.

Robin. Now Iohn Cobler,
Didst thou sée how the King did behaue himselfe?
Iohn. But Robin, didst thou see what a pollicie
The King had, to sée how the French men were kild
With the stakes of the trées.
Robin. I Iohn, there was a braue pollicie.

Enters an English Souldier roming.

Soul. What are you my maisters?
Both. Why we be English men.
Soul. Are you English men, then change your lan-
guage

For all the Kings Tents are set a fire,
And all they that speake English will be kild.
    Iohn. What shall we do Robin? faith ile shift,
For I can speake broken French.
    Robin. Faith so can I, lets heare how thou canst
        speak.
    Iohn. Commodeuales Monsieur.
    Iohn. Thats well, come lets be gone.
                    Drum and Trumpet sounds.

*Enters Dericke roming. After him a Frenchman, and
            takes him prisoner.*
    Der. O good Mounser.
    French. Come, come, you villeaco.
    Der. O I will sir, I will.
    French. Come quickly you pesant.
    Der. I will sir, what shall I giue you?
    French. Marry, thou shalt giue me,
One, to, tre, foure, hundred Crownes.
    Der. Nay sir, I will giue you more,
I will giue you as many crowns as will lie on your
        sword.
    French. Wilt thou giue me as many crowns
As will lie on my sword?
    Der. I marrie will I, but you must lay downe your
Sword, or else they will not lie on your sworde.
        *Here the Frenchman layes downe his sword, and
            the clowne takes it vp, and hurles him downe.*
    Der. Thou villaine, darest thou looke vp?
    French. O good Mounsier comparteue
Monsieur pardon me.
    Der. O you villaine, now you lie at my mercie,
Doest thou remember since thou lambst me in thy
        short el?
O villaine, now I will strike off thy head.
            *Here whiles he turnes his back, the French-
                    man runnes his wayes.*

Der. What is he gone, masse I am glad of it,
For if he had staid, I was afraid he wold haue sturd
    again,
And then I should haue béene spilt,
But I will away, to kill more Frenchmen.

    Enters King of France, King of England, and
        attendants.

Hen. V. Now my good brother of France,
My comming into this land was not to shead blood,
But for the right of my Countrey, which if you can
    deny,
I am content peaceably to leaue my siege,
And to depart out of your land.
    Char. What is it you demand,
My louing brother of England.
    Hen. V. My Secretary hath it written, read it.
    Sec. Item, that immediately Henry of England
Be crowned King of France.
    Char. A very hard sentence,
My good brother of England.
    Hen. V. No more but right, my good brother of
    France.
    Fr. King. Well, read on.
    Sec. Item, that after the death of the said Henry,
The Crowne remaine to him and his heires for euer.
    Fr. King. Why then you do not onely meane to
Dispossesse me, but also my sonne.
    Hen. V. Why my good brother of France,
You haue had it long inough :
And as for Prince Dolphin,
It skils not though he sit beside the saddle :
Thus I haue set it downe, and thus it shall be.
    Fr. King. You are very peremptorie,
My good brother of England.
    Hen. V. And you as peruerse, my good brother of
    France.

Char. Why then belike, all that I haue here is
yours.
Hen. V. I euen as far as the kingdom of France
reaches.
Char. I for by this hote beginning,
We shall scarce bring it to a calme ending.
Hen. V. It is as you please, here is my resolution.
Char. Well my brother of England,
If you will, giue me a copie,
We will meet you againe to-morrow.
Exit King of France, and all their attendants.
Hen. V. With a good will my good brother of
France.
Secretary deliuer him a coppie.
My lords of England goe before,
And I will follow you.
Exeunt Lords. Speaks to himselfe.
Hen. V. Ah Harry, thrice vnhappie Harry.
Hast thou now conquered the French King,
And begins a fresh supply with his daughter,
But with what face canst thou seeke to gaine her loue,
Which hast sought to win her fathers Crowne?
Her fathers Crowne said I, no it is mine owne:
I but I loue her, and must craue her,
Nay I loue her and will haue her.

Enters Lady Katheren and her Ladies.

But here she comes:
How now faire Ladie Katheren of France,
What newes?
Kathren. And it please your Maiestie,
My father sent me to know if you will debate any of
these
Vnreasonable demands which you require.
Hen. V. Now trust me Kate,
I commend thy fathers wit greatly in this,

For none in the world could sooner haue made me
    debate it
If it were possible :
But tell me swéete Kate, canst thou tell how to loue ?
   Kate. I cannot hate my good Lord,
Therefore far vnfit were it for me to loue.
   Hen. V. Tush Kate, but tell me in plaine termes,
Canst thou loue the King of England ?
I cannot do as these Countries do,
That spend halfe their time in woing :
Tush wench, I am none such,
But wilt thou go ouer to England ?
   Kate. I would to God, that I had your Maiestie,
As fast in loue, as you haue my father in warres,
I would not vouchsafe so much as one looke,
Vntill you had related all these vnreasonable de-
    mands.
   Hen. V. Tush Kate, I know thou wouldst not vse
    me so hardly :
But tell me, canst thou loue the King of England ?
   Kate. How should I loue him, that hath dealt so
    hardly
With my father ?
   Hen. V. But ile deale as easily with thee,
As thy heart can imagine, or tongue can require,
How saist thou, what will it be ?
   Kate. If I were of my owne direction,
I could giue you answere :
But séeing I stand at my fathers direction,
I must first know his will.
   Hen. V. But shal I haue thy good wil in the mean
    season ?
   Kate. Whereas I can put your grace in no assur-
    ance,
    would be loth to put you in any dispaire.
   Hen. V. Now before God, it is a sweete wench.
       She goes aside, and speaks as followeth.

Kat. I may thinke my selfe the happiest in the
world,
That is beloued of the mighty King of England.
Hen. V. Well Kate, are you at hoast with me?
Swéete Kate, tel thy father from me,
That none in the world could sooner haue perswaded
me to
It then thou, and so tel thy father from me.
Kate. God kéepe your Maiestie in good health.
Exit Kat.
Hen. V. Farwel swéet Kate, in faith it is a swéet
wench,
But if I knew I could not haue her fathers good wil,
I would so rowse the Towers ouer his eares,
That I would make him be glad to bring her me,
Vpon his hands and knées. *Exit King.*

Enters Dericke with his girdle full of shooes.

Der. How now? Sownes it did me good to see how
I did triumph ouer the French men.

*Enters Iohn Cobler rouing, with a packe full
of apparell.*

Iohn. Whoope Dericke, how doest thou?
Der. What Iohn, Comedeuales, aliue yet.
Iohn. I promise thée Dericke, I scapte hardly,
For I was within halfe a mile when one was kild.
Der. Were you so?
Iohn. I trust me, I had like bene slaine.
Der. But once kild, why it is nothing,
I was foure or fiue times slaine.
Iohn. Foure or fiue times slaine.
Why how couldst thou haue béene aliue now?
Der. O Iohn, neuer say so,
For I was cald the bloodie souldier amongst them all.
Iohn. Why what didst thou?
Der. Why, I will tell thée Iohn,

Euery day when I went into the field,
I would take a straw, and thrust it into my nose,
And make my nose bléed, and then I wold go into
the field,
And when the Captaine saw me, he would say,
Peace a bloodie souldier, and bid me stand aside,
Whereof I was glad :
But marke the chance Iohn.
I went and stood behinde a tree, but marke then
Iohn,
I thought I had béne safe, but on a sodaine,
There steps to me a lustie tall Frenchman,
Now he drew, and I drew,
Now I lay here, and he lay there,
Now I set this leg before, and turned this backward,
And skipped quite ouer a hedge,
And he saw me no more there that day,
And was not this well done Iohn?
    Iohn. Masse Dericke, thou hast a wittie head.
    Der. I Iohn, thou maist sée, if thou hadst taken my
coūsel,
But what hast thou there ?
I thinke thou hast bene robbing the Frenchmen.
    Iohn. I faith Dericke, I haue gotten some reparrell,
To carry home to my wife.
    Der. And I haue got some shooes,
For ile tel thee what I did, when they were dead,
I would go take off all theyr shooes.
    Iohn. I, but Dericke, how shall we get home ?
    Der. Nay sownds and they take thée,
They wil hang thée,
O .Iohn, neuer do so, if it be thy fortune to be
hangd,
Be hangd in thy owne language whatsoeuer thou
doest.
    Iohn. Why Dericke the warres is done,
We may go home now.

Der. I but you may not go before you aske the
    king leaue,
But I know a way to go home, and aske the king no
    leaue.
Iohn. How is that Dericke?
Der. Why Iohn, thou knowest the Duke of Yorkes
Funerall must be carried into England, doest thou
    not?
Iohn. I that I do.
Der. Why then thou knowest wéele go with it.
Iohn. I but Dericke, how shall we do for to méet
    them?
Der. Sownds if I make not shift to méet them,
    hang me.
Sirra, thou knowst that in euery Towne there wil
Be ringing, and there wil be cakes and drinke,
Now I wil go to the Clarke and Sexton
And kéepe a talking, and say, O this fellow rings
    well,
And thou shalt go and take a péece of cake, then ile
    ring,
And thou shalt say, oh this fellow kéepe a good
    stint,
And then I will go drinke to thée all the way:
But I maruel what my dame wil say when we come
    home,
Because we haue not a French word to cast at a
    Dog
By the way?
Iohn. Why what shall we do Dericke?
Der. Why Iohn, ile go before and call my dame
    whore,
And thou shalt come after and set fire on the house,
We may do it Iohn, for ile proue it,
Because we be souldiers.   *The Trumpets sound.*
Iohn. Dericke helpe me to carry my shooes and
    bootes.

Enters King of England, Lord of Oxford and Exeter,
then the King of France, Prince Dolphin, and the
Duke of Burgondie, and attendants.

Hen. V. Now my good brother of France,
I hope by this time you haue deliberated of your
answere ?

Fr. King. I my welbeloued brother of England,
We haue viewed it ouer with our learned Councell,
But cannot finde that you should be crowned
King of France.

Hen. V. What not King of France, then nothing,
I must be King : but my louing brother of France,
I can hardly forget the late iniuries offered me,
When I came last to parley,
The French men had better a raked
The bowels out of their fathers carkasses,
Then to haue fiered my Tentes,
And if I knew thy sonne Prince Dolphin for one,
I would so rowse him, as he was neuer so rowsed.

Fr. King. I dare sweare for my sonnes innocencie
In this matter.
But if this please you, that immediately you be
Proclaimed and crowned heire and Regent of France,
Not King, because I my selfe was once crowned King.

Hen. V. Heire and Regent of France, that is well,
But that is not all that I must haue.

Fr. King. The rest my Secretary hath in writing.

Sec. Item, that Henry King of England,
Be Crowned heire and Regent of France,
During the life of King Charles, and after his death,
The Crowne with all rights to remaine to King Henry
Of England, and to his heires for euer.

Hen. V. Well my good brother of France,
There is one thing I must néeds desire.

Fr. King. What is that my good brother of England ?

Hen. V. That all your Nobles must be sworne to be
true to me.

Fr. King. Whereas they haue not stucke with
greater

Matters, I know they wil not sticke with such a trifle,
Begin you my Lord Duke of Burgondie.

Hen. V. Come my Lord of Burgondie,
Take your oath vpon my sword.

Burgon. I Philip Duke of Burgondie,
Sweare to Henry King of England,
To be true to him, and to become his league-man,
And that if I Philip, heare of any forraigne power
Comming to inuade the said Henry or his heires,
Then I the said Philip to send him word,
And aide him with all the power I can make,
And thereunto I take my oath.   *He kisseth the sword.*

Hen. V. Come Prince Dolphin, you must sweare too.
                               He kisseth the sword.

Hen. V. Well my brother of France,
There is one thing more I must néeds require of you,

Fr. King. Wherein is it that we may satisfie your
Maiestie?

Hen. V. A trifle my good brother of France.
I meane to make your daughter Quéene of England,
If she be willing, and you therewith content :
How saist thou Kate, canst thou loue the King of
England?

Kate. How should I loue thee, which is my fathers
enemy?

Hen. V. Tut stand not vpon these points,
Tis you must make vs friends :
I know Kate, thou art not a litle proud, that I loue
thée :
What wench, the King of England?

Fr. King. Daughter let nothing stand betwixt the
King of England and thée, agrée to it.

Kate. I had best while he is willing,

Least when I would, he will not :
I rest at your Maiesties commaund.

 Hen. V. Welcome swéet Kate, but my brother of
  France,
What say you to it?

 Fr. King. With all my heart I like it,
But when shall be our wedding day?

 Hen. V. The first Sunday of the next moneth,
God willing.   *Sound Trumpets.* *Exeunt omnes.*

THE SECOND PART OF KING HENRY VI.

EDITION.

The First Part of the Contention betwixt the Two Famous Houses of Yorke and Lancaster, with the Death of the good Duke Humphrey : And the banishment and death of the Duke of Suffolke, and the Tragicall end of the proud Cardinall of Winchester, with the notable Rebellion of Iacke Cade : And the Duke of Yorkes first claime vnto the Crowne. London Printed by Thomas Creed, for Thomas Millington, and are to be sold at his shop vnder Saint Peters Church in Cornwall. 1594. 4°.

MR HALLIWELL'S INTRODUCTION.[1]

———o———

ON the 2nd of April, 1798, Messrs Leigh and Sotheby,
the well-known booksellers and auctioneers, were
selling by auction the fourth day's division of the
" curious and valuable " library of Dr Samuel Pegge,
prebendary of Lichfield, and a distinguished anti-
quary. There was one particular lot in that day's
sale which has rendered the auction an era in Shake-
spearian bibliography—a very small octavo volume,
without covers, purchased by the author of " Cale-
donia " for £5, 15s. 6d., and described in the sale
catalogue, No. 938, as " Shakespeare's true Tragedie
of Richard Duke of Yorke, and the Death of good
King Henrie the Sixt, Lond. by P. S., 1595." This
little tract, so unpretendingly exhibited to competition, was no less than the *unique* copy of the play
upon which the Third Part of Henry VI. was founded,
which fetched the enormous sum of one hundred and
thirty pounds at Chalmers's sale in 1842, and concern-

---

1 [To the Shakespeare Society's edition, 8°, 1843. This introduction applies to the First Sketches of the Third, as well as
Second, Part of Henry VI.]

ing the nature of which so much was said in the public prints at the time of its producing the above sum, at the rate of more than three guineas for each leaf. This inestimable treasure was acquired by the Bodleian Library, and is one of the greatest rarities of the kind in that repository. It is the second tract presented to the reader in the following pages, who is indebted to the Shakespeare Society for this attempt to make it easily and generally accessible.

This celebrated "True Tragedie" was the Second Part of the play called "The Contention between the two famous Houses of York and Lancaster," on the First Part of which is founded the Second Part of Henry VI., which is now, for the first time, reprinted from an *unique* copy of the edition of 1594, also preserved in the Bodleian Library. Thus the possessor of the present volume will have the two plays upon which are founded the Second and Third Parts of Henry VI., both printed from *unique* copies —one a small octavo, the marketable value of which is one hundred and fifty pounds ; the other, a very thin, small quarto, which produced £64 several years ago, and would now probably realise more than twice that sum.

These early editions of 1594 and 1595 vary very considerably from the later impression of 1619, when they were published collectively. The amended play, in the form in which we have received it as Shakespeare's, appeared for the first time in the folio of 1623. All the various editions of the earlier drama have been collated for the notes, and will be found of some importance in a question to which I shall presently draw the reader's attention. This may be considered a part of the external evidence in the dispute concerning the exact portions of the Second and Third Parts of Henry VI., which may be attributed with safety to Shakespeare.

I. The First Part.

1. " The first part of the Contention betwixt the two famous Houses of Yorke and Lancaster, with the death of the good Duke Humphrey : And the banishment and death of the Duke of Suffolke, and the Tragicall end of the proud Cardinall of Winchester, with the notable Rebellion of Iacke Cade : And the Duke of Yorkes first claime vnto the Crowne. London Printed by Thomas Creed, for Thomas Millington, and are to be sold at his shop vnder Saint Peters Church in Cornwall. 1594."

A small quarto, containing 32 leaves, A to H in fours. The present copy, which is in the Bodleian Library, belonged to Heber, and is the only one known. See " Bibl. Heber.," vol. ii., No. 5479. Malone had a copy of it, and he has collated it with the second edition, marking the variations in his inlaid copy of the latter. Why Malone's copy was not inlaid with the rest of his early editions does not any where appear ; and Dr Bandinel, who is an excellent authority, says it was obtained improperly from Malone's possessions, and that the very one he used is that now in the Bodleian. At p. 33, l. 19, however, occurs the word " honouring," as in the Bodleian copy, which according to Malone's collation, was " thinking" in the exemplar that belonged to him. Unless, therefore, Malone made a mistaken alteration, these must have been different books, and an instance of the curious differences which sometimes occurs in various copies of the same edition. See p. 92. It was entered at Stationers' Hall on March 12th.

2. " The First Part of the Contention betwixt the two famous houses of Yorke and Lancaster, with the death of the good Duke Humphrey : And the banishment and death of the Duke of Suffolke, and the tra-

gicall end of the prowd Cardinall of Winchester, with the notable rebellion of Iacke Cade : And the Duke of Yorkes first clayme to the crowne. London : Printed by W. W. for Thomas Millington, and are to be sold at his shoppe vnder Saint Peters Church in Cornewall. 1600."

A small quarto, containing 32 leaves, A to H in fours. It was reprinted from the first edition, but carelessly, omitting about two dozen words necessary for the sense. It possesses, however, a few important corrections. This edition is very rare, and I have unwillingly used the Bodleian copy, which has a manuscript title.

3. "The First Part of the Contention betwixt the two famous houses of Yorke and Lancaster, with the death of the good Duke Humphrey : And the banishment and death of the Duke of Suffolke, and the Tragical end of the prowd Cardinall of Winchester, with the notable Rebellion of Iacke Cade : And the Duke of Yorkes first clayme to the Crowne. London Printed by Valentine Simmes for Thomas Millington, and are to be sold at his shop vnder S. Peters church in Cornewall. 1600."

This is the same impression as the preceding, excepting a very few trifling literal variations of no importance, with a different titlepage.   The only copy known is in the library of Trinity College, Cambridge, which is ατελ., having only the first 25 leaves, and concluding with the first leaf of Sig. G.. This edition is not mentioned by Lowndes, or any bibliographer.

II. THE TRUE TRAGEDIE.

1. "The True Tragedie of Richard *Duke of Yorke, and the death of* good King Henrie the Sixt, *with the whole contention betweene* the two houses Lancaster

and Yorke, as it was sundrie times acted by the Right
Honourable the Earle of Pembrooke his seruantes.
Printed at London by P. S. for Thomas Millington,
*and are to be sold at his shoppe vnder Saint Peters
Church in Cornwal.* 1595."

A small octavo, containing 40 leaves, A to E in
eights. Owing to its being printed with a narrow
page, the metre is often destroyed by the concluding
words of one line being inserted in the beginning of
the subsequent. This is corrected, in a great measure,
in the succeeding impressions. Very few early plays
are printed in this size; and so natural is it to consider nearly the whole of this class of literature as a
race of small quartos, that although Mr Knight in one
place very correctly describes the present volume as
"a small octavo," yet he afterwards refers to it as
"the *quarto* of 1595." On a fly-leaf, Chalmers has
written the following note :—" This very rare volume,
of which no other copy is known to exist, was purchased by Mr Chalmers at Dr Pegge's sale in 1796 [?].
It was then unbound, as it had been neglected by the
Doctor, who was unaware of its great value. By an
oversight of Mr Malone, and a singular mistake of
Mr Steevens, Mr Chalmers obtained it easily for
£5, 15s. 6d., without much competition; and Steevens
was enraged to find that it had gone for less than a
fifth of what he would have given for it." On the top
of the title-page some one has inscribed the name of
Shakespeare, which is not of much authority in the
question of authorship, if it was written, as Dr Bandinel says it was, by Dr Pegge.

2. "The True Tragedie of Richarde Duke of
Yorke, and the death of good King Henrie the sixt:
With the whole contention betweene the two Houses,
Lancaster and Yorke ; as it was sundry times acted
by the Right Honourable the Earle of Pembrooke his
seruantes. Printed at London by W. W. for Thomas

Millington, and are to be sold at his shoppe vnder Saint Peters Church in Cornewall.   1600."

A small quarto, containing 32 leaves, A to H in fours.   Malone mentions an edition of this date printed by Valentine Simmes.   See his "Shakespeare," by Boswell, xviii. 363, 543.   Malone says that Pavier's edition of 1619 was printed from this one, but I apprehend he has merely followed Capell's more general assertion that Pavier reprinted from the copies of 1600.   I have not succeeded in finding any evidence of the existence of an edition of " The True Tragedie" printed by Valentine Simmes ; for Malone confesses he has never seen a copy, although it is very possible that such a one may have been published.

3. " The Whole Contention betweene the two Famous Houses, Lancaster and Yorke.   With the Tragicall ends of the good Duke Humfrey, Richard Duke of Yorke, and King Henrie the sixt.   Diuided into two Parts : And newly corrected and enlarged. Written by William Shakespeare, Gent.   Printed at London, for T. P."

A small quarto, containing 64 leaves, A to Q in fours.   This contains the " First part of the Contention," as well as " The true Tragedie."   T. P. was Thomas Pavier, the publisher of other plays.   This edition has no date, but it is ascertained to have been printed in or about 1619 by the signatures.   The last signature of Pavier's edition is Q, and the first signature of the text of " Pericles," 4°. Lond. 1619, for the same bookseller, is R ; and on the recto of sig. I of this play, where the Second Part commences, is the same device as on the first page of that edition of Pericles.   The Second Part has no separate title-page, but is introduced as " The Second Part.   Containing the Tragedie of Richard Duke of Yorke, and the Good King Henrie the Sixt."

Pavier's edition was reprinted by Steevens in 1766,

and in general with accuracy,[1] although he has not considered it necessary to follow the rigid system I have pursued in the reprints now presented to the reader. Mistakes and peculiarities of all kinds I have retained as they stand in the original, capital letters, hyphens, punctuation, &c. : in all these particulars I have endeavoured to give as faithful a copy of the originals as I possibly could. The collations will be found in the notes, and with these a little judgment would form as good a text as could probably be made with the materials that have descended to our use.

In the books of the Stationers' Company, we have the following entries relative to these plays :

"12 March 1593-4.
"Tho. Millington.] A booke intituled the firste parte of the contention of the twoo famous Houses of York and Lancaster, with the Deathe of the good Duke Humphrey and the Banishment and Deathe of the Duke of *Suff.* and the tragicall Ende of the prowd Cardinall of Winchester, with the notable rebellion of Jack Cade and the Duke of Yorks first clayme unto the Crowne.

"19 April 1602.
"Tho. Pavier.] By assignment from Tho. Millington, *salvo jure cujuscunque,* the 1st and 2nd parts of Henry the VI : ij. books."

The last entry is a mistake for the First and Second Parts of the "Contention;" and we accordingly find that when Blount and Jaggard, in 1623, inserted a list of Shakespeare's plays "as are not formerly entered

---

[1] Steevens's reprints are excellently made, and the mistakes of importance do not average more than three or four in each play. I suspect that his successors have not improved. The Percy Society's reprint of "Kind-Harts Dreame" contains above one hundred and thirty errors, some of a portentous kind ; yet it is but a small tract, not so long as one of Shakespeare's plays. It is almost impossible to prevent occasional mistakes.

to other men," they omitted the first and second parts
of Henry VI., and only inserted "The Thirde Parte
of Henry the Sixt." In the same way, we find they
did not insert "King John" in the same list, although
there is no reason to suppose that any copy of that
play in its present form had previously been entered.
The probable inference is, that the list was hastily
compiled from the previous entries. Millington, it
appears, kept possession of the "Whole Contention,"
as Pavier afterwards called it, till 1602. There seems
something mysterious in the words, "salvo juris cujuscunque;" and it may be asked why Pavier kept them
so long without a republication, if the date of 1619
be correct. The entry is, however, important, for it
clearly shows that, as early as 1602, the present title
of "Henry VI." had superseded the older one.

I have called these plays "The First Sketches of
the Second and Third Parts of Henry VI.;" but it is
a question with the critics whether Shakespeare was
their author, or whether he merely borrowed from
some older dramatist.

The external evidence is in favour of Malone's
theory, that Shakespeare was *not* the author of the
two plays here reprinted. They appear to have been,
as I have said, in the hands of Millington till 1602,
and they were then transferred to Pavier, who retained them till 1626. Millington and Pavier managed
between them to monopolise nearly the whole of
Shakespeare's disputed plays. Thus Millington had
the "First Part of the Contention," the "Chronicle
History," and the "True Tragedie," which he transferred to Pavier in 1600 and 1602. In addition to
these, Pavier also had "Sir John Oldcastle," "Titus
Andronicus," "The Yorkshire Tragedy," "The
Puritan," and "Pericles," all of which seem to be
suspicious plays, to say the least of them. Again,

Millington, who published these plays in 1594, 1595, and 1600, did not put the name of Shakespeare to them, though it would have been for his advantage to have done so. After the year 1598, none of the undisputed plays of Shakespeare were published without having his name conspicuously inserted on the title,[1] and only three were ever published without his name, two in 1597, and one in 1598, although, between the years 1598 and 1655, forty-four quarto editions appeared with the authorship clearly announced. In 1600, when Millington published the Two Parts of the "Contention" without Shakespeare's name, six undisputed plays were published with his name, and seven disputed plays[2] without; but Pavier was afterwards bolder, and, out of the twenty-four editions of the disputed plays published between the years 1591 and 1635, we find eight with Shakespeare's name. This, however, was after 1609. The probability, therefore, is that the First Part of the "Contention," and the "True Tragedy," were published piratically, and altogether without Shakespeare's authority, if he had any share in them. In 1626, Pavier assigned to Edward Brewster and Robert Birde his right in the disputed plays, and we hear again of the two parts of the "Contention," for the last time, on November 8, 1630, as "Yorke and Lancaster," when they were assigned to Richard Cotes "by Mr Bird and consent of a full court."

The first edition of the "True Tragedy" does not

---

[1] I except the early editions of "Romeo and Juliet," and the first edition of "Hamlet," for these are not perfect copies, and, in all probability, were published piratically.

[2] Copies of "Sir John Oldcastle," 1600, as Mr Collier informs us, are also found with Shakespeare's name on the title-page, as well as without. This would seem to show that the name of our great dramatist could not always be used indiscriminately.

appear to have been entered at Stationers' Hall, and
it is probable that there is a secret history attached
to its publication that remains to be unravelled. The
first thing that strikes us is its title, and the reason
why it was not published as the "Second Part of the
Contention" till 1619. It will be remarked that the
title-page affirms it to contain "the *whole* contention." Could this have been done for the purpose
of deception? We may, however, infer that the
amended plays appeared after 1595, and before 1602,
or it is probable that the old titles would not have
been retained. Perhaps, however, the same argument holds with respect to the edition of 1600, and
this would place the date of the amended plays
within a very narrow compass. There are some
reasons for thinking that the Third Part of Henry
VI., in the form in which we now have it, was
written before 1598,[1] as, in one of the stage-directions
in the first folio, we have Gabriel, an actor, introduced, who, according to Mr Collier, was killed by
Ben Jonson in the September of that year. The
Third Part of Henry VI. also introduces Sinklo,
another actor, in a similar manner, who performed in
Tarlton's play of the "Seven Deadly Sins,"[2] and who

---

[1] It may one day be found that the allusion to enclosures at
Melford is valuable in the question of the chronology of the
earlier dramas. It is not unlikely that a dramatist may have
alluded to the popular dissatisfaction which enclosures generally
produce. The particular allusion may, perhaps, be discovered.
As early as 1549, there had been disturbances in that part of the
country in consequence of enclosures; but, as I am kindly informed by Mr Almack, of Melford, there is no local tradition
respecting it, nor do the parish books, although very ancient,
contain anything to the purpose. Perhaps the place is not included in the satire.

[2] Harvey, in his "Foure Letters," 1592, says that Nash's
"Pierce Penilesse" was not "dunsically botched-vp, but right-
formally conueied, according to the stile and tenour of Tarletons
president, his famous play of the seauen Deadly sinnes : which

probably, therefore, did not survive the year 1598. It is reasonable to suppose that the editors of the first folio used copies transcribed when those actors performed.

The constant offences against grammar which occur in these early copies may perhaps be another proof that they were not published by authority. For the reasons I have previously stated, very little doubt can be entertained of the fact that Pavier's copies of the older plays were piratically published ; and Shakespeare's name was *for the first time* appended to them in 1619, and not in 1600, probably because the poet was not alive to protect his interests, and in the latter case because he did not acknowledge them for his own. I will now place before the reader certain evidences, before unnoticed, which lead me to think that neither Malone, nor Knight, nor Collier, are exactly right in the results to which they have arrived concerning the authorship of the Second and Third Parts of Henry VI.

In a literary point of view, the first edition of the "First Part of the Contention" is far more valuable than the first edition of the "True Tragedy;" and considering that both are in the same library, it seems rather strange that Mr Knight should have collated the Second Part, and left the more valuable copy.

---

most-deadly, but most liuely playe, I might haue seene in London, and was verie gently inuited thereunto at Oxford, by Tarleton himselfe." Nash, in his "Apologie," 1593, angrily denies any similarity between his book and Tarlton's play. The original "platt of the secound Parte of the Seven Deadlie Sinns" is given in Malone's Shakespeare by Boswell, iii. 348. The exact date of Tarlton's death is not known ; but in the parish register of St Leonard, Shoreditch, for 1588, we have the following entry : " Richard Tarelton was buryed the third of September." It also appears from the same register that his residence was in " Haliwel Stret," so called from a famous well in the neighbourhood, but is now generally known as High Street, Shoreditch.

Perhaps, however, this remark is not necessary ; nor should I have alluded to the circumstance, had not Mr Knight written so extensively concerning these plays, that a reasonable doubt might be raised as to where new evidences, properly so called, could exist. To proceed.   In the two first editions of " The First Part of the Contention," 1594 and 1600, act i., sc. 2, we read—

> "This night when I was laid in bed, I dreampt that
> This, my staff, mine office-badge in court,
> Was broke in two, and on the ends were plac'd
> The heads of the Cardinal of Winchester,
> And William de la Poole, first duke of Suffolk."

This speech, in the edition of 1619, the only one used by Mr Knight, stands thus :

> " This night when I was laid in bed, I dreamt
> That this my staff, mine office-badge in court,
> Was broke in *twain ; by whom, I* cannot guess :
> *But, as I think, by the cardinal.   What it* bodes
> *God knows ;* and on the ends were plac'd
> The heads of *Edmund Duke of Somerset,*
> And William de la Poole, first duke of Suffolk."

Now let the reader carefully compare these different texts with the passage as corrected in the amended play :

> " Methought this staff, mine office-badge in court,
> Was broke in twain ; by whom, I have forgot,
> But as I think, it was by the cardinal ;
> And on the pieces of the broken wand
> Were plac'd the heads of Edmund duke of Somerset,
> And William de la Poole, first duke of Suffolk,
> This was my dream : what it doth bode God knows."

The words in italics in the second quotation are those which are common to the editions of 1619 and 1623, but are not found in the earlier impressions of 1594 and 1600.   We have thus *an intermediate composition* between the edition of 1594 and the amended play.   It will be at once seen that these differences

cannot be the result of emendation, in the way that
we account for the differences of the second folio.   I
will produce another and a stronger instance.   In
act i., sc. 2, the edition of 1594 has these two lines:

> "But ere it be long, I'll go before them all,
> Despite of all that seek to cross me thus."

Instead of these two lines, we have a different speech,
an elaboration of the other two—

> "I'll come after you, for I cannot go before,
> As long as *Gloster bears this base and humble mind :*
> *Were I a man*, and Protector, as he is,
> I'd reach to th' crown, or make some hop *headless :*
> *And being* but *a woman, I'll not* [be] behind
> For playing of *my part*, in spite of all
> That seek to cross me thus."

Again, compare these versions with the amended play:

> "Follow I must : I cannot go before,
> While Gloster bears this base and humble mind :
> Were I a man, a duke, and next of blood,
> I would remove these tedious stumbling blocks,
> And smooth my way upon their headless necks :
> And, being a woman, I will not be slack
> To play my part in fortune's pageant."

Here, perhaps, is a still stronger evidence of an
intermediate composition, and others of like importance may be seen from the notes.   But more than
this, the genealogy in act ii., sc. 2, in the edition of
1594, is entirely different from that given in the
edition of 1619, and this latter very nearly corresponds with the amended play.   It seems from these
instances, that it will be a difficult matter to ascertain
what really belongs to the first original play.   I am
inclined to think that there is a good deal of what
may be termed the amended play in the two parts of
the " Contention," and, although the evidence to my
mind is so strong that Shakespeare was not the author
of the whole of these plays, yet it appears little less

than absurd to form an arithmetical computation of what was written by Shakespeare, and what was the work of the author of the original dramas.

There are so many passages in the two plays now reprinted, that seem almost beyond the power of any of Shakespeare's predecessors or contemporaries, perhaps even not excepting Marlowe, that as one method of explaining away the difficulties which attend a belief in Malone's theory, my conjecture that when these plays were printed in 1594 and 1595, *they included the first additions which Shakespeare made to the originals,* does not seem improbable, borne out, as it is, by an examination of the early editions.   If I am so far correct, we have yet to discover the originals of the two parts of the " Contention," as well as that of 1 Henry VI.   The well-known passage in Greene's " Groatsworth of Wit " proves that Shakespeare was the author of the line :

> " O ! tiger's heart, wrapp'd in a woman's hide,"

before September 3, 1592, and the angry allusion to the "upstart crow, beautified with our feathers," may be best explained by supposing that Shakespeare had then superseded the older play, in which perhaps Greene may have had some very small share.   The attempt to generalise this passage fails, for Greene is speaking of Shakespeare as a writer, not as an actor, a point which Mr Knight does not sufficiently consider.   But that Greene " parodies a line of his own," as the other critics tell us, is assuming a power in Greene of penning the speech in which that line occurs; and it is only necessary to compare that speech with others in Greene's acknowledged plays, to be convinced that he was not equal to anything of the kind.

When Greene calls our great dramatist "in his own conceit the only Shake-scene in a country," it is

scarcely possible that he could allude to Shakespeare's power of dramatic arrangement; yet the
words imply something of the kind, and we may wish
to believe they really do. The notice just quoted is
the earliest introduction of Shakespeare in the printed
literature of this country, and so valuable an authority is it, that it is unfortunate any dispute or doubt
should arise relative to its meaning. That the
address in which it is inserted excited much attention
at the time, is told by more than one authority ;[1]
and it probably proved a source of considerable
vexation to Shakespeare himself, for shortly after its
publication we find Chettle, who edited Greene's tract,
apologising for the insertion of the offensive passage.
Nash also calls it, "a scald, trivial, lying, pamphlet,"
but there is no reason for supposing that the last epithet
was applied to the part now under consideration.
Chettle is enthusiastic. We may believe that he became acquainted with Shakespeare after the publication of Greene's work, and before the appearance of
"Kind-Hart's Dreame." He tells us that Shakespeare
was "excellent in the quality he professes," that is,
as an actor ; and had, moreover, a "facetious grace
in writing, that approves his art." [1] This was in No-

---

[1] And by none more clearly than a curious tract, entitled
"Greenes Newes both from *Heauen and Hell.* Prohibited the
first for writing of Bookes, and banished out of the last for dis-
playing of *Connycatchers. Commended to the Presse* By B. R.
At London, Printed, Anno. Domini. 1593," containing 31 leaves,
A to H 3, in fours. This is not by Greene, as Mr Dyce supposes, but perhaps by Barnaby Rich. As authors at that time
frequently transposed their initials, if this book were by the
same person who wrote "Greenes Funeralls," 1594, these two
were perhaps those alluded to in Barnefield's "Cynthia," 12mo.
Lond. 1595. "Howsoeuer vndeseruedly (I protest) I haue beene
thought (of some) to haue beene the authour of two Books here-
tofore. I neede not to name them, because they are too-well
knowne already : nor will I deny them, because they are dis-
lik't ; but because they are not mine."

vember or December 1592.   Shakespeare probably had
written part of the " True Tragedy" before that time.

There is another passage in " Kind-Harts Dreame,"
which seems rather at variance with the one just
quoted. Chettle, speaking of Greene, says, " of whom,
however some suppose themselves injured, I have learned
to speak, considering he is dead, *nil nisi necessarium.*
He was of singular plesance, *the very supporter,* and,
to no man's disgrace be this intended, the ONLY comedian of a vulgar writer in this country."   Chettle
here seems to recollect the offence that the " address "
had given ; he exclaims, " to *no* man's disgrace be
this intended," he was not wronging Shakespeare in
calling Greene " the *only* comedian of a vulgar writer
in this country."   Chettle professes to say nothing
more of Greene than is requisite ; this testimony to
his merits is given, notwithstanding his alleged friend-
liness to Shakespeare.   He probably alludes to
Shakespeare, when he says, " however some suppose
themselves injured."[2]   Mr Collier think Chettle im-

---

[1] A copy of " Kind-Harts Dreame," in the Bodleian, which
belonged to Burton, and cost him two-pence, reads, "*fatious*
grace in writing, *which* approoues his art." The passage was
corrected in passing through the press. A perfect copy of
this rare book is preserved in the King's Library in the
British Museum. The two copies in the Bodleian Library,
in the Burton and Malone collections, want the concluding
chapter. Burton's copy has several peculiar readings worthy
of notice. Thus at p. 16 of the reprint, we have :—" It
were to be wished, if they will not be warned, that, as well the
singers, as their supporters, were burned in the tongue, that they
might rather be ever utterly mute, than the *triumphers* of so
many mischiefs." The word " triumphers," which is clearly
wrong, is corrected in Burton's copy to " trumpets." If this
book be again reprinted, the editor would do well to notice this
and other variations.

[2] In case any one may chance to read the whole in the Percy
Society's reprint, it is necessary, for my own sake, to say that
this passage is there erroneously given, " howeuer some *may*
suppose themselves injured."

plies that Shakespeare had acquired no reputation as
an *original* dramatic poet in 1592; and it certainly
goes far to prove that his *comic* pieces had not then
appeared, or, if they had, had obtained little applause.
Our business is now with the histories; and the
"First Part of the Contention," and the "True
Tragedy," may have been *rifacimenti* by Shakespeare
as early as 1592.

When Greene parodied the line in "The True Tragedy," and alluded to the "crow beautified with *our*
feathers," it is probable he meant to insinuate that he
himself had some share in the composition of the
play, which in one state of its reconstruction or
amendment by Shakespeare fell under his satire.
This probability is considerably strengthened by the
following passage in "Greene's Funeralls, By R. B.
Gent.," 4°. Lond. 1594, a rare tract of twelve leaves,
preserved in the Bodleian Library:—

> " Greene is the pleasing Obiect of an eie ;
>   Greene pleasde the eies of all that lookt vppon him.
> Greene is the ground of eueric Painters die ;
>   Greene gaue the ground to all that wrote vpon him.
>   Nay more the men that so Eclipst his fame,
>   Purloynde his Plumes, can they deny the same."

This is "Sonnet ix." in this rare little volume,
which contains the terms "sugred sonnets," afterwards appropriated by Meres to Shakespeare. R. B.,
whoever he was, may write somewhat in partisanship,
but how Nash's indignant rejection of the authorship
of the other tract can be held a sufficient reply to
this plain statement seems mysterious. Yet so Mr
Knight would tell us, and adds that no "great author
appeared in the world who was not reputed, in the
outset of his career, to be a plagiarist." Was Har-
riot held a plagiarist, when he promulgated his original
theories? Was not his adoption of Vieta's notions
discovered afterwards? The cases are nearly parallel,

though there was no Vieta alive to claim the ground-work. We may not care to know who laid the foundation, but surely Greene's words are not to be altogether divested of any intelligible meaning.[1]

The " True Tragedy," as originally composed, was, as we learn from the title-page, played by the Earl of Pembroke's servants, for whom Greene was in the habit of writing. None of Shakespeare's undisputed plays were played by this company. " Titus Andronicus," an earlier drama, also has this external evidence against its authenticity. Mr Collier, indeed, tells that *before* 1592, "a popular play, written for one company, and perhaps acted by that company as it was written, might be surreptitiously obtained by another, having been at best taken down from the mouths of the original performers : from the second company it might be procured by a third, and, after a succession of changes, corruptions, and omissions, it might find its way at last to the press." This, as Mr Knight thinks, entirely overthrows Malone's argument on the point : but the " True Tragedy " was not printed till 1595, and according to Mr Collier, this system probably concluded two years previously. Besides, the title-page would probably exhibit the

---

[1] A writer of our own day, and, strange to say, since the publication of Mr Knight's " Essay," has given a gratuitous assertion quite as much the other way. The following announcement will be read with considerable astonishment by those who have paid any attention to this branch of literature. " Shakespeare was just then [1592] rising into notice ; and we know from various sources that he was employed in adapting and altering the productions of Nash, Greene, and other unprincipled companions—a circumstance which drew down upon him their hatred and abuse."—*Introduction to the Percy Society's reprint of Kind Heart's Dream*, 8º. Lond. 1841, p. xiv. Where are these various sources? Who were the *other* " unprincipled " companions? Shakespeare adapting and altering the productions of Nash!

name of the original company. If Malone is not right, it is very singular that the suspicious account should only appear on the titles of two suspicious dramas.

Passing over Malone's conclusions from inaccuracies and anachronisms, which can hardly be considered safe guides, when we reflect how numerous they are throughout Shakespeare's plays, there is yet one other circumstance worthy of notice, that indirectly associates the name of Greene with the older dramas. In "The First Part of the Contention," mention is made of "Abradas, *the great Macedonian pirate.*" Who Abradas was, does not any where appear, and the only other mention of him that has been discovered is in "Penelopes Web," 4°. Lond. 1588,[1] a tract written by Greene: "I remember, Ismena, that Epicurus measured euery mans dyet by his own principles, and Abradas, *the great Macedonian pirat,* thought euery one had a letter of mart that bare sayles in the ocean." These coincidences are perhaps more curious than important, but still they appear worth notice. It may likewise be mentioned, as a confirmatory circumstance, that Nash, in his "Apologie," 1593, mentions Greene "being chiefe agent for the companie, for hee writ more than foure other,[2] how well I will not say." If, therefore, Greene

---

[1] This book was entered, according to a MS. note by Malone, on the Stationers' Registers, by E. Aggas, Jan. 26th, 1587-8, and the book itself, "imprinted at London for T. C. and E. A.," was published that year without a date. Another edition appeared in 1601, which Mr Collier calls "the only known edition," but there is a copy of the *editio princeps* in the Bodleian. See Collier's "Shakespeare," v. 183.

[2] "He that was wont to solicite your mindes with many pleasant conciets, and to fit your fancies at the least euery quarter of the yere, with strange and quaint deuises, best beseeming the season, and most answerable to your pleasures."— *Greenes Newes both from Heauen and Hell,* 1593.

was so intimately connected with the Earl of Pembrook's servants, and Shakespeare not at all, the external evidence, as far as this goes, is strongly in favour of Greene's having had some share in the composition of the "True Tragedy," and, as a matter of course, "the First Part of the Contention."

I have followed Mr Hunter in saying that the allusion to Shakespeare in the "Groatsworth of Wit," entered at Stationers' Hall on September 20th, 1592, is the earliest introduction of our great dramatic poet in the printed literature of this country. If, however, the opinion of Chalmers may be relied on, Gabriel Harvey, in his "Four letters especially touching Robert Greene, and *other parties*, by him abused," 1592, alludes to Shakespeare in the third letter, dated September 9th, 1592, wherein he says : "I speak generally to every springing wit, but more especially to a few : and, at this instant, *singularly, to one*, whom I salute with a hundred blessings." These notices of Shakespeare are, however, digressions in this place, even if they prove that Shakespeare was not popularly known as a dramatic writer before 1592. Chettle's evidence in the same year is almost conclusive with respect to the histrionic powers of Shakespeare ; and it would be a curious addition to our poet's history to ascertain whether he performed in the plays now presented to the reader, after they had been altered and amended. There is a well-known epigram by Davies, in his "Scourge of Folly," 1611, p. 76, that has some theatrical anecdote connected with it, now perhaps for ever lost,[1] but which implies that Rowe was not .

---

[1] I do not know the authority for the following anecdote, which appears to illustrate Davies' epigram. "It is well known that Queen Elizabeth was a great admirer of the immortal Shakespeare, and used frequently, as was the custom with persons of great rank in those days, to appear upon the stage before the audience, or to sit delighted behind the scenes, when the

exactly right when he stated that "the top of his performance was the ghost of Hamlet." Another evidence may be adduced, from Davies' "Humours Heav'n on Earth," 8vo. Lond. 1609, p. 208, which has not been yet quoted :—

> " Some followed her [Fortune] by acting all men's parts,
>   These on a stage she rais'd, in scorn to fall,
> And made them mirrors by their acting arts,
>   Wherein men saw their faults, though ne'er so small :
> Yet some she guerdon'd not to their [1] deserts ;
>   But othersome were but ill-action all,
> Who, while they acted ill, ill stay'd behind,
>   By custom of their manners, in their mind. "

This alludes to Shakespeare and Burbage, as appears from the marginal note ; but the inference to be drawn from it is in favour of Shakespeare's capabilities as an actor. Davies is often rather unintelligible, and the allusion :

---

plays of our bard were performed. One evening, *when Shakespeare himself was personating the part of a king*, the audience knew of her majesty being in the house. She crossed the stage when he was performing, and, on receiving the accustomed greeting from the audience, moved politely to the poet, but he did not notice it. When behind the scenes, she caught his eye, and moved again, but still he could not throw off his character to notice her : this made her majesty think of some means by which she might know whether he would depart or not from the dignity of his character while on the stage. Accordingly, as he was about to make his exit, she stepped before him, dropped her glove, and recrossed the stage, which Shakespeare noticing, took up with these words, immediately after finishing his speech and so aptly were they delivered, that they seemed to belong to it :—

> ' And though now bent on this high embassy,
>   Yet stoop we to take up our cousin's glove.'

He then walked off the stage, and presented the glove to the queen, who was greatly pleased with his behaviour, and complimented him upon the propriety of it."—*Dramatic Table Talk*, 8°. Lond. 1825, ii., 156–7.

[1] " W. S., R. B."—*Marg. note in orig.*

" Some say, good Will, which I, in sport, do sing,
    Hadst thou not play'd some kingly parts in sport,
Thou hadst been a companion for a king,
    And been a king among the meaner sort. "

remains to be unravelled. It clearly alludes to some
circumstance which took place after the accession of
James I.

This digression is not without its use, because it
shows that we have good grounds for believing Chettle's testimony to Shakespeare's histrionic merits, and
we can the more readily give credence to his assertion
that our dramatist possessed a " facetious grace in
writing that approves his art." If the other passage
just quoted, which relates to Greene, proves that
Shakespeare was not known as a comic writer as early
as 1592, it by no means sufficiently outweighs Chettle's first testimony to make us doubt that Shakespeare had then largely contributed to the two parts
of the " Contention." Mr Knight tells us repeatedly
that if Malone's theory be adopted, Shakespeare was
the most unblushing plagiarist that ever put pen to
paper. Why so? Did Shakespeare adopt the labours
of others as his own? If he had done so, why was
his name effaced from the title-page of " Sir John
Oldcastle," and why was it not inserted on the early
editions of the present plays? He would have been
essentially a dishonest plagiarist, says Mr Knight.
But it was the common custom of the time for drama-
tists to be engaged to remodel and amplify the productions of others. A reference to Henslowe's Diary
will at once establish this fact. In 1601, Decker was
paid thirty shillings " for *altering* of Fayton ; " and,
in the following year, we find Ben Jonson paid £10
on account, " in earnest of a boocke called Richard
Croockback, and for *new adycions* for Jeronimo."
According to Mr Knight's theory, Decker, Jonson,
and every unfortunate playwright, who complied with

the custom of the time, were "unblushing plagiarists." The great probability is that the theatre for which Shakespeare wrote had become proprietor of the older plays, and that he made alterations, and added to them when necessary. There was no plagiarism in the case; and perhaps one day it will be discovered that little of the original dramas now remains in the Second and Third Parts of Henry VI.

From Henslowe's Diary it appears that a play called Henry VI. was acted thirteen times in the spring of 1592 by Lord Strange's players who, be it remembered, never performed any of Shakespeare's plays. This is conjectured with great probability to be the First Part of Henry VI. in some state or other of its composition, and the play whose power "embalmed" the bones of "brave Talbot" with the tears of ten thousand spectators. The death-scene of Talbot is, perhaps, the most powerfully-constructed part of the play; our national sympathies have been awakened in his favour, and we pity his woful end: but Nash gives like praise to the contemptible "Famous Victories." Mr Knight places great reliance on the unity of action in the First Part of the Contention and the first Part of Henry VI. to prove that they were both written by one and the same person; but surely these two plays have neither unity of characterisation, nor unity of style, and the want of these outweighs the unity of action. That there is considerable unity of action, I admit. In some cases, nearly the same expressions occur. Thus, in 1 Henry VI. act iv. sc. 1., King Henry says:

> "Cousin of York, we institute your grace
> To be our regent in these parts of France."

And in the First Part of the Contention, act i. sc. 1, he says—

> "Cousin of York, we here discharge your grace
> From being regent in the parts of France."

But I suspect these coincidences, and the evidences
of the unity of action, as well also as those scenes
which a cursory reader might suppose to have been
written for the purposes of continuation, may be attributed to the writer having adopted his incidents out
of the old chronicles, where such matters are placed
in not very strict chronological arrangement.   Thus,
in Richard III., the incident of the King sending
the Bishop of Ely for strawberries is isolated, adopted
in order with the other scenes from the chroniclers,
probably Holinshed, and useless for the purposes of
continuation.   With a discussion on the supposed
unity of style I will not occupy these pages.   Opinion
in this matter is sufficient, for the plays are accessible.
Mr Hallam thinks the First Part of Henry VI. might
have been written by Greene, and the very opening
of the play is in the bombastic style of the older dra-
matists.   Again, with respect to the characterisation,
is the Margaret of 1 Henry VI. the Margaret of the
First Part of the Contention ?   Perhaps her character
is not sufficiently developed in the first of these to
enable us to judge; but, in regard to the characters
that are common to both, we may safely decide that
not one characteristic of importance is to be found in
1 Henry VI. not immediately derived from the chroniclers.   Are we to suppose that Suffolk's instanta-
neous love was corresponded to by Margaret, or was
she only haughty and not passionate when she quietly
answers Suffolk in the speech in which she is introduced ?   I do not mean to assert that there is any
inconsistency in her being represented merely haughty
in one play, and passionate in the other, for different
circumstances would render this very possible ; but it
is not easy to infer the strict unity of characterisation
that is attempted to be established.

    If the First Part of Henry VI. were originally
written by Shakespeare, and with all these scenes for

the purposes of continuation, as Mr Knight would have us believe, how does Mr Knight account for the appearance of the Second Part of Henry VI. under the title of "The *First* Part of the Contention?" This is a point to which no attention has been given. Two editions of the "First Part of the Contention" were published in 1600 under the old title, but we find that in 1602 their later appellations as parts of Henry VI. had been given them. It seems reasonable to infer that, when Shakespeare remodelled the old plays, and formed the two parts of the "Contention," he had had nothing to do with the old play of Henry VI. mentioned by Henslowe, and had intended the play now called the Second Part of Henry VI. to be the first of his own Series. Afterwards, he might have been employed to make "new adycyons" to the old play of Henry VI. and then the three plays may have been amalgamated into a series, and the old play rendered uniform by scenes written for continuations previously made. Take the First Part of Henry VI. away, and the concluding chorus to Henry V. remains equally intelligible. The "True Tragedy" may also have been called "Edward IV., and so more naturally the series would have continued with Richard III.

In vain have I looked for any identity of manner in the scene between Suffolk and Margaret in the First Part of Henry VI. and the similar scene in the First Part of the Contention. But so much stress has been laid on this point, that I beg the reader will here carefully compare them together.

FIRST PART OF HENRY VI., Act v. sc. 3.

"*Suf.* Be what thou wilt, thou art my prisoner.
[*Gazes on her.*
O fairest beauty, do not fear, nor fly;
For I will touch thee but with reverent hands.
I kiss these fingers [*kissing her hand*] for eternal peace,

And lay them gently on thy tender side.
Who art thou? say, that I may honour thee.
  Mar. Margaret my name, and daughter to a king,
The king of Naples; whoso'er thou art.
  Suf. An earl I am, and Suffolk am I call'd.
Be not offended, nature's miracle,
Thou art allotted to be ta'en by me :
So doth the swan her downy cygnets save,
Keeping them prisoner underneath her wings.
Yet if this servile usage once offend,
Go, and be free again, as Suffolk's friend.
                              [*She turns away as going.*
O, stay!—I have no power to let her pass;
My hand would free her, but my heart says—no.
As plays the sun upon the glassy streams,
Twinkling another counterfeited beam,
So seems this gorgeous beauty to mine eyes."

FIRST PART OF THE CONTENTION, Act iii. sc. 2.
  "*Queen.* Sweet Suffolk, hie thee hence to France,
For if the king do come, thou sure must die.
  Suf. And if I go I cannot live : but here to die,
What were it else,
But like a pleasant slumber in thy lap?
Here could I breathe my soul into the air,
As mild and gentle as the new-born babe,
That dies with mother's dug between his lips.
Where from thy sight I should be raging mad,
And call for thee to close mine eyes,
Or with thy lips to stop my dying soul,
That I might breathe it so into thy body,
And then it liv'd in sweet Elysium.
By thee to die, were but to die in jest ;
From thee to die, were torment more than death :
Oh, let me stay, befal what may befal.
  Queen. Oh might'st thou stay with safety of thy life,
Then should'st thou stay ; but heavens deny it,
And therefore go, but hope ere long to be repeal'd.
  Suf. I go.
  Queen. And take my heart with thee.
                                    [*She kisses him.*
  Suf. A jewel lock'd into the wofull'st cask,
That ever yet contain'd a thing of worth.
Thus, like a splitted bark, so sunder we ;
This way fall I to death.   [*Exit Suffolk.*
  Quen. This way for me.   [*Exit Queen.*"

Mr Dyce could not have been far wrong, when he excluded the first of these plays from his chronology, as " exhibiting no traces of Shakespeare's peculiar style, and being altogether in the manner of an older school." This judicious writer thinks that it may be attributed either to Marlowe or Kyd, and we are occasionally reminded of the former author. Henslowe's " Diary " lets us a good deal into the prison-house secrets of the relative position between author and manager in those days ; we there find that sometimes four writers were occasionally employed on one play ; and there seems to be strong internal evidence that the First Part of Henry VI. was not wholly the work of one hand.

Capell, struck with the power of the death-scene of Henry VI., long since decided that it was unquestionably the work of Shakespeare. It is, indeed, a composition in Shakespeare's peculiar style ; and it occurs in the " True Tragedy," with only a few verbal alterations, and the omission of five unimportant lines at the commencement. In the same way, the speech beginning :—

" I will go clad my body in gay ornaments,"

is equal, if not superior, in smoothness and power, to a like speech in " Richard III." How can Mr Collier find it in his heart to deprive Shakespeare of these ? There is nothing equal to them in the First Part of Henry VI., and little superior to them in the other historical plays. It is, however, worthy of remark, that Meres in 1598 does not mention either Henry VI., or the Contention, which would seem to show that they were not highly estimated even in Shakespeare's own time.

Gildon tells us of a tradition, that Shakespeare, in a conversation with Ben Jonson, said that, " finding the nation generally very ignorant of history, he wrote plays in order to instruct the people in that particular." This is absurd. "Plays," says Heywood in 1612, "have made the ignorant more apprehensive, taught the unlearned the knowledge of many famous histories, instructed such as cannot read in the discovery of all our English chronicles; and what man have you now of that weak capacity, that cannot discourse of any ·notable thing recorded even from William the Conqueror, nay, from the landing of Brute, until this day?"[1] Henslowe mentions a play on the subject of William the Conqueror, and there can be little doubt that a complete series once existed, even up to Henry VIII., and perhaps even later. There was little authentic history in those days, and the researches of Cotton and Hayward were not popularly known. Most were content to take the "depraved lies" of the playwrights for truth, and, like the simpleton mentioned by Ben Jonson, prefer them to the sage chroniclers :—

> " No, I confess I have it from the play-books,
> And think they are more authentic."

It is ridiculous to talk of Shakespeare having invented an historical drama, that had been gradually growing towards the perfection it reached in his hands from the

---

[1] " Thirdly, he affirmes that playes have taught the ignorant knowledge of many famous histories. They have indeed made many to know of those histories they never did, by reason they would never take the paines to reade them. But these that know the histories before they see them acted, are ever ashamed, when they have heard what lyes the players insert amongst them, and how greatly they deprave them. If they be too long for a play, they make them curtals ; if too short, they enlarge them with many fables; and whither too long or too short, they corrupt them with a foole and his bables : whereby they make them like leaden rules, which men will fit to their worke, and not frame their worke to them. So that the ignorant instead of true history shall beare away nothing but fabulous lyes."—*A Refutation of the Apology for Actors*, 4°. Lond. 1615, p. 42.

middle of the sixteenth century. Let, therefore, Gildon's tradition be distributed with the other myths that the commencement of the seventeenth century interwove with the little that was then known of Shakespeare's authentic history.

There are other opinions that require notice in this place. It has been conjectured that the "First Part of the Contention" and the "True Tragedy" were not written by the same person, because the account of Clifford's death at the conclusion of the former play varies with that given of the same occurrence at the commencement of the other. The reader will find this mentioned in another place. On the same principle we might conclude that the Second Parts of Heny IV. and Henry VI. are not by the same hand, because the story of Althca is erroneously told in the first of these plays, and rightly in the second. It is difficult to account for these inconsistencies, but there they are, the ἁμαρτια κατα συμβεβηκος of Shakespeare. It seems paradoxical that Shakespeare should at one time remember a well-known classical story, and forget it at another; but these instances illustrate the correctness of Aristotle's definition, and can probably be explained in no other way.

Dr Johnson, who often speaks at random in these matters, asserts that the Second and Third Parts of Henry VI. were not written without a *dependence* on the first. Malone has answered him satisfactorily, by saying, "the old play of Henry VI. had been exhibited before these were written in any form; but it does not follow from this concession, either that the 'Contention' was written by the author of the former play, or that Shakespeare was the author of these two pieces, as *originally composed.*" This is exactly the point to which I would draw the reader's attention. I will leave the unity of action out of the question, because we are not dealing with works of imagination, and

this can be accounted for, as I have previously con-
tended, in the sources from which the incidents are
derived. Had there been two Parts to the "Tempest," and the same kind of unity of action, and similar instances of scenes written for the purposes of
continuation, the argument would hold in that case,
unless it could be shown that these were also to be
found in the original romance or drama upon which
it was founded. Here there is nothing of the kind.
I believe that, with the present evidence, it is impossible to ascertain the exact portions of the two Parts
of the "Contention," which were not written by
Shakespeare, and belong to the older drama. There
is nothing Shakesperian in this :—

> "These gifts ere long will make me mighty rich.
> The duchess she thinks now that all is well,
> But I have gold comes from another place,
> From one that hired me to set her on,
> To plot these treasons 'gainst the king and peers ;
> And that is the mighty duke of Suffolk.
> For he it is, but I must not say so,
> That by my means must work the duchess' fall,
> Who now by conjurations thinks to rise."

This is one of the most favourable specimens of
the rejections. Mr Knight would have us believe
that Shakespeare wrote the following speech, and put
it into the mouth of Richard, after he had slain
Somerset :—

> "So, lie thou there, and tumble in thy blood.
> What's here, the sign of the Castle?
> Then the prophecy is come to pass,
> For Somerset was forewarn'd of castles,
> The which he always did observe,
> And now behold, under a paltry alehouse sign,
> The Castle in St Alban's, Somerset
> Hath made the wizard famous by his death."

Is there in this one single characteristic of the language which *Shakespeare* gives to Richard? Is there

identity of manner ? Is not the style comparatively puerile? Let this and similar passages be given to the author or authors of the orginal play, but let us retain for Shakespeare the parts, that we may fairly judge from comparison to have been beyond the power of those of his contemporaries, whose works have descended to our times.

In these discussions, it ought to be recollected that the works of Shakespeare have met with a better fate than those of most of his contemporaries. There may have been "six Shakespeares in the field" at the time we have been speaking of, and the works of one only been preserved. Few had kind friends like Hemings and Condell to look to the interests of their posthumous reputation. It may be that few deserved such treatment, but we are by no means to decide conclusively, merely because the specimens of their talent which have come down to our time are so vastly inferior to the productions of the great bárd. The argument of authorship, as adopted by Mr Knight, is at best but a *reductio ad absurdum*, where *possibilities* exist, that even, if the predicates be proved, two conclusions may be drawn. Supposing we are satisfied that neither Peele, nor Kyd, nor Greene, nor even Marlowe, was equal to any given performance, it does not necessarily follow that there was no one of their contemporaries who was not capable of it, though the presumptive evidence may be in favour of the first position.

J. O. HALLIWELL.

Feb. 22nd, 1843.

The First Part of the Contention of the Two Famovs Houses of Yorke & Lancaster, with the death of the good Duke Humphrey.

——o——

Enter at one doore, King HENRY *the sixt, and* HUM-
PHREY *Duke of* GLOSTER, *the Duke of* SOMMER-
SET, *the Duke of* BUCKINGHAM, *Cardinall* BEW-
FORD, *and others.*
Enter at the other doore, the Duke of YORKE, *and the
Marquesse of* SUFFOLKE, *and Queene* MARGARET,
and the Earle of SALISBURY *and* WARWICK.

Suf. AS by your high imperiall Maiesties com-
mand,[1]
I had in charge at my depart for France,
As Procurator for your excellence,

---

[1] "This noble company came to the citie of Toures in
Tourayne, where they were honorably receiued, bothe of the
French kyng, and of the kyng of Scicilie. Wher the Marques
of Suffolke, as procurator to kyng Henry, espoused the said
Ladie in the churche of sainct Martyns. At whiche mariage
were present the father and mother of the bride, the Frenche
kyng himself, which was uncle to the husbande, and the Frenche
quene also, whiche was awnte to the wife. There were also the
Dukes of Orleance, of Calaber, of Alaunson, and of Britayn, vij
erles, xij barons, xx bishoppes, beside knightes and gentlemen."
—*Hall's Chronicle.* The historical information in these plays

To marry Princes Margaret for your grace,
So in the auncient famous Citie Towres,
In presence of the Kings of France & Cyssile,
The Dukes of Orleance, Calabar, Brittaine, and Alon-
son.[1]
Seuen Earles, twelue Barons, and then the[2] reuerend
Bishops,
I did performe my task and was espousde,
And now, most humbly on my bended knees,
In sight of England and her royall Peeres,
Deliuer vp my title in the Queene,
Vnto. your gratious excellence, that are the sub-
stance
Of that great shadow I did represent :
The happiest gift that euer Marquesse gaue,
The fairest Queene that euer King possest.
   King. Suffolke arise.
Welcome Queene Margaret to English Henries
Court,
The greatest show of kindnesse yet we can bestow,
Is this kinde kisse : Oh gracious God of heauen,
Lend me a heart repleat with thankfulnesse,
For in this beautious face thou hast bestowde
A world of pleasures to my perplexed soule.
   Queene. Th' excessiue loue I beare vnto your grace,
Forbids me to be lauish of my tongue,
Least I should speake more then beseemes a woman :
Let this suffice, my blisse is in your liking,

---

appears to be principally taken from this work, which was published under the title of "The Union of the two noble and
illustrate famelies of Lancastre and Yorke," fol. Lond. 1548.
Steevens quotes a similar passage from Holinshed, who appears
to have borrowed from Hall.
  [1] So all the editions ; but the second folio of the amended
play omits "and."
  [2] The edition of 1619 reads "twenty," as well as the amended
play ; which latter reading is the correct one, as readily appears
from the passage in Hall's "Chronicle" given above.

And nothing can make poore Margaret miserable,
Vnlesse the frowne of mightie Englands King.
   Kin. Her lookes did wound, but now her speech
      doth pierce,[1]
Louely Queene Margaret sit down by my side :
And vnckle Gloster, and you Lordly Peeres,
With one voice welcome my beloued Queene.
   All. Long liue Queene Margaret, Englands happi-
      nesse.
   Queene. We thank you all.[2]   [*Sound Trumpets.*
   Suf. My Lord Protector, so it please your grace,
Here are the Articles confirmde of peace,
Between our Soueraigne and the French King Charles,
Till terme of eighteene months be full expirde.
   Hum. Imprimis, It is agreed betweene the French
King Charles, and William de la Poule, Marquesse of
Suffolke, Embassador for Henry King of England,
that the said Henry shal wed and espouse the Ladie
Margaret, daughter to Raynard King of Naples,
Cyssels, and Ierusalem, and crown her Queene of
England, ere the 30. of the next month.[3]
   Item. It is further agreed betweene them, that the
Dutches of Anioy and of Maine,[4] shall be released
and deliuered ouer to the King her fa.
                        [*Duke* HUMPHREY *lets it fall.*

---

   [1] The word "her" is omitted in the two editions of 1600, but
restored again in that of 1619.   The amended play reads :

> "Her sight did ravish, but her grace in speech,
>   Her words y-clad with wisdom's majesty,
>   Makes me from wondering fall to weeping joys."

   [2] The first folio reads "all kneel," an addition omitted by
modern editors.
   [3] The edition of 1619 reads "ere the thirty day of the next
month."
   [4] The amended play in the first instance reads, "and the
county of Maine," in accordance with the chronicled accounts ;
but, when the cardinal repeats this part of the agreement, we
find the original form restored as in our text.

Kin. How now vnkle, whats the matter that you
stay so sodenly.

Hum. Pardon my Lord, a sodain qualme came.ouer
my hart,[1]
Which dimmes mine eyes that I can reade no more.[2]
Vncle of Winchester, I pray you reade on.[3]

Car. Item, It is further agreed betweene them,
that the Duches of Anioy and of Mayne, shall be
released and deliured ouer to the King her father, &
she sent ouer of the King of Englands owne proper
cost and charges without dowry.

King. They please vs well,[4] Lord Marquesse kneele
downe, We here create thee first Duke of Suffolke, &
girt thee with the sword. Cosin of Yorke, We here
discharge your grace from being Regent in the parts
of France, till terme of 18. months be full expirde.
Thankes vnckle Winchester, Gloster, Yorke, and
Buckingham, Somerset,[5] Salsbury and Warwicke.
We thanke you all for[6] this great fauour done,
In entertainment to my Princely Queene,

---

[1] The edition of 1619 reads "ore."
[2] The two quatto editions of 1600 read "that I can *see* no
more," while the edition of 1619 restores the old reading. The
amended play reads—

"Pardon me, gracious Lord,
Some sudden qualm hath struck me at the heart,
And dimm'd mine eyes, that I can read no further."

[3] In the amended play this line is more properly given to
King Henry. The edition of 1619 reads very differently :

" My lord of Yorke, I pray do you reade on ;"

and in Pavier's copy the next speech is accordingly given to
York. Perhaps the fact of Henry's thanking Winchester first
in order may sanction the older reading.
[4] The whole of this speech may be arranged in metre.
[5] The first folio of the amended play entirely omits the word
"and," while the second folio changes its position, and places it
before "Somerset." Malone follows our text, but Collier and
Knight adopt the reading of the first folio.
[6] The edition of 1619 reads, "We thanke you for all."

Come let vs in, and with all speed prouide
To see her Coronation be performde.
  [*Exet*[1] *King, Queene, and* SUFFOLKE, *and Duke*
  HUMPHREY *staies all the rest.*

  Hum. Braue Peeres of England, Pillars of the
    state,
To you Duke Humphrey must vnfold his griefe,
What did my brother Henry toyle himselfe,
And waste his subiects for to conquere France ?
And did my brother Bedford spend his time
To keep in awe that stout vnruly Realme ?
And haue not I and mine vncle Bewford[2] here,
Done all we could to keep that land in peace ?
And is all our labours then spent in vaine,[3]
For Suffolke he, the new made Duke that rules the
    roast,
Hath giuen away for our King Henries Queene,
The Dutches of Anioy and Mayne vnto her father.
Ah Lords, fatall is this marriage canselling our states,
Reuersing Monuments of conquered France,
Vndoing all, as none had nere bene done.
  Car. Why how now cosin Gloster, what needs this ?
As if our King were bound vnto your will,
And might not do his will without your leaue,
Proud Protector, enuy in thine eyes I see,
The big swoln venome of thy hatefull heart,
That dares presume [4] gainst that thy Soueraigne
    likes.

---

  [1] The Latinity is barbarous throughout this copy of the play.
  [2] Beaufort. The orthography in this old edition probably
occasioned Bedford and Beaufort being confused in some editions of the amended play.
  [3] "Is" may be a mistake for "are." The edition of 1619
reads, "spent quite in vain."
  [4] The two editions of 1600 have "dare," while that of 1619
restores the old reading. The latter part of this speech is
omitted in the amended play.

Hum. Nay my Lord[1] tis not my words that troubles[2] you,
But my presence, proud prelate as thou art:
But ile begone, and giue thee leaue to speake.
Farewell my Lords, and say when I am gone,
I prophesied France would be lost ere long.
                              [*Exet Duke* HUMPHREY.
  Car. There goes our Protector in a rage,
My Lords you know he is my great enemy,
And though he be Protector of the land,
And thereby couers his deceitfull thoughts,
For well you see,[3] if he but walke the streets,
The common people swarme about him straight,
Crying Iesus blesse your royall excellence,
With God preserue the good Duke Humphrey.
And many things besides that are not knowne,
Which time will bring to light in smooth Duke Hum-
      phrey.
But I will after him, and if I can
Ile laie a plot to heaue him from his seate.
                              [*Exet Cardinall.*
  Buc. But let vs watch this haughtie Cardinall,
Cosen of Somerset be rulde by me,
Weele watch Duke Humphrey and the Cardinall too,
And put them from the marke they faine would hit.
  Som. Thanks cosin Buckingham, ioyne thou with
      me,
And both of vs with the Duke of Suffolke,
Weele quickly heaue Duke Humphrey from his seate.
  Buc. Content, Come then let vs about it[4] straight,
For either thou or I will be Protector.
                              [*Exet* BUCKINGHAM *and* SOMERSET.

----

[1] The 4to. of 1619 reads, "Nay, my Lords," but erroneously.
[2] Probably "trouble."
[3] The edition of 1619 reads, "For you well see."
[4] The two editions of 1600 omit the word "then." The edition of 1619 agrees with our copy.

Sal. Pride went before, Ambition follows after.[1]
Whilst these do seeke their owne preferments thus,
My Lords let vs seeke for our Countries good,
Oft haue I seene this haughtie Cardinall
Sweare, and forsweare himself, and braue it out,
More like a Ruffin then a man of Church.[2]
Cosin Yorke,[3] the victories thou hast wonne,
In Ireland, Normandie, and in France,
Hath wonne thee immortall praise in England.
And thou braue Warwicke, my thrice valiant sonne,
Thy simple plainnesse and thy house-keeping,
Hath wonne thee credit amongst the common sort,
The reurence of mine age, and Neuels name,
Is of no little force if I command,
Then let vs ioyne all three in one for this,
That good Duke Humphrey may his state possesse,
But wherefore weeps Warwicke my noble sonne.
War. For griefe that all is lost that Warwick won.

---

[1] Perhaps in this line there is somewhat of proverbiality.
Steevens quotes the following from Wyntown's "Chronicle:"---

> "Awld men in thare prowerbe sayis,
> *Pryde gays before,* and schame alwayis
> Followys."

And this conjecture is proved by the following passage in Nash's
"Pierce Penilesse," 1592, ed. Collier, p. 8, which is more similar
to the line in our text : "It is a trim thing when Pride, the
sonne, goes before, and Shame, the father, followes after."

[2] The edition of 1619 reads—

> "More like a ruffian then a man of the church;"

which is worse metre than our edition, although it is adopted by
Mr Knight. The amended play reads—

> "More like a soldier than a man o' th' church;"

is given in the first two folios of 1623 and 1632. Modern editors write it somewhat differently.

[3] The amended play reads, "brother." York married Cicely,
the daughter of Ralph Nevil, Earl of Westmoreland, by Joan,
daughter to John of Gaunt, Duke of Lancaster, by his third
wife, dame Catharine Swinford. Richard Nevil, Earl of Salsbury, was son to the Earl of Westmoreland by a second wife.
Salsbury and York were, therefore, step brothers.

Sonñes.¹ Anioy and Maine, both giuen away at once
Why Warwick did win them, & must that then which
we wonne with our swords,² be giuen away with wordes.

Yorke. As I haue read, our Kinges of England
were woont to haue large dowries with their wiues,
but our King Henry giues away his owne.

Sal. Come sonnes away and looke vnto the maine.³

War. Vnto the Maine, Oh father Maine is lost,
Which Warwicke by main force did win from France,

---

¹ The edition of 1619 has this word in italics, as giving a separate speech to the remainder, and in this Pavier is followed by
Mr Knight. But if so, who were the *sonnes?* who were the
speakers? Salsbury cannot by any ingenuity be so called, and
why this singular mode? The expression, " Warwick did win
them," is not incompatible with the supposition that he himself
is speaking. I should rather be inclined to think that *sonnes* in
our text is merely a misprint for *sounes,* and then the speech
would very naturally run as follows : "Zounds, Anjoy and
Maine both given away at once! Why, Warwick did win
them! and must that then which we won with our swords be
given away with words?" The expression "*we won*" cannot
reasonably be considered an argument for one side or the other.
The corresponding passage in the amended play is nearly sufficient to establish my position:

> " *War.* For grief, that they are past recovery :
> For were there hope to conquer them again,
> My sword should shed hot blood, mine eyes no tears.
> Anjou and Maine ! Myself did win them both :
> Those provinces these arms of mine did conquer :
> And are the cities that I got with wounds,
> Deliver'd up again with peaceful words ?
> Mort Dieu !"

² In the amended play we have another jingle, as Johnson
styles it, substituted :

> "And are the cities, that I got with wounds,
> Deliver'd up again with peaceful words."

³ This and the next speech are thus altered in the amended
play, and will, perhaps, scarcely be thought improved :

> " *Sal.* Then let's make haste away, and look unto the main.
> *War.* Unto the main, O father ! Maine is lost ;
> That Maine, which by main force Warwick did win,
> And would have kept, so long as breath did last :
> Main chance, father, you meant ; but I meant Maine ;
> Which I will win from France, or else be slain."

Maine chance father you meant, but I meant Maine,
Which I will win from France, or else be slaine.
          [*Exet* SALSBURY *and* WARWICKE.
    Yorke. Anioy and Maine, both giuen vnto the
        French,
Cold newes for me, for I had hope of France,
Euen as I haue of fertill England.
A day will come when Yorke shall claime his owne,
And therefore I will take the Neuels parts,
And make a show of loue to proud Duke Humphrey :
And when I spie aduantage, claim the Crowne,
For thats the golden marke I seeke to hit :
Nor shall proud Lancaster vsurpe my right,
Nor hold the scepter in his childish fist,
Nor weare the Diademe vpon his head,
Whose church-like humours fits[1] not for a Crowne :
Then Yorke be still a while till time do serue,
Watch thou, and wake when others be a sleepe,
To prie into the secrets of the state,
Till Henry surfeiting in ioyes of loue,
With his new bride, and Englands dear bought queene,
And Humphrey with the Peeres be falne at iarres,
Then will I raise aloft the milk-white Rose,
With whose sweete smell[2] the aire shall be perfumde,
And in my Standard beare the Armes of Yorke,
To graffle[3] with the House of Lancaster :
And force perforce, ile make him yeeld the Crowne,
Whose bookish rule hath puld faire England downe.
                    [*Exet* YORKE.[4]

---

[1] So all the editions read. It ought to be "fit."

[2] Grey is rather hypercritical here in saying that "this thought
is not exactly just," though Spenser has given the preference to
the other colour :
> " She bath'd with roses red, and violets blue,
>   And all the sweetest flowers that in the forest grew."

[3] The older form of the word. The edition of 1619 reads
"grapple."

[4] This and some other stage directions have been omitted by
Mr Knight.

Enter Duke HUMPHREY, *and Dame* ELLANOR,
COBHAM *his wife.*

Eln. Why droopes my Lord like ouer ripened corne,
Hanging the head at Cearies plenteous loade,
What seeest thou Duke Humphrey King Henries
　　Crowne?
Reach at it, and if thine armes be too short,
Mine shall lengthen it.　Art not thou a Prince,[1]
Vnckle to the King, and his Protector?
Then what shouldst thou lacke that might content
　　thy minde.
Hum. My louely Nell, far be it from my heart,
To thinke of Treasons gainst my soueraigne Lord,
But I was troubled with a dreame to-night,
And God I pray, it do betide no ill.[2]
Eln. What drempt my Lord.　Good Humphrey
　　tell it me,
And ile interpret it, and when thats done,
Ile tell thee then, what I did dreame to night.
Hum. This night when I was laid in bed, I dreampt
　　that
This my staffe mine Office badge in Court,　　[Sig. B.]
Was broke in two,[3] and on the ends were plac'd,
The heads of the Cardinall of Winchester,
And William de la Poule first Duke of Suffolke.
Eln. Tush, my Lord, this signifies nought but this,
That he that breakes a sticke of Glosters groue,
Shall for th' offence, make forfeit of his head.
But now my Lord, Ile tell you what I dreampt,

---

[1] The edition of 1619 reads, " Art thou not a prince."
[2] The edition of 1619 reads, "It do betide none ill."
[3] The edition of 1619 contains two additional lines and variations :

> "Was broke in twaine, by whom I cannot gesse :
> But as I thinke by the Cardinall.　What it bodes
> God knowes ; and on tne ends were plac'd
> The heads of Edmund duke of Somerset,
> And William de la Pole, first duke of Suffolke."

Me thought I was in the Cathedrall Church
At Westminster, and seated in the chaire
Where Kings and Queenes[1] are crownde, and at my
    feete
Henry and Margaret with a Crowne of gold
Stood readie to set it on my Princely head.
    Hum. Fie Nell. Ambitious woman as thou art,
Art thou not second woman in this land,
And the Protectors wife belou'd of him,
And wilt thou still be hammering treason thus,
Away I say, and let me heare no more.
    Eln. How now my Lord. What angry with your
    Nell,
For telling but her dreame. The next I haue
Ile keepe to my selfe,[2] and not be rated thus.
    Hum. Nay Nell, Ile giue no credit to a dreame,
But I would haue thee to thinke on no such things.

Enters a Messenger.

    Mess. And it please your grace, the King and
Queene to morrow morning will ride a hawking to
Saint Albones, and craues[3] your company along with
them.
    Hum. With all my heart, I will attend his grace :
Come Nell, thou wilt go with vs vs[4] I am sure.
[*Exet* HUMPHREY.
    Eln. Ile come after you, for I cannot go before,
But ere it be long,[5] Ile go before them all,

---

[1] The two editions of 1600 read "where *the* kings and queenes," an interpolation omitted in the edition of 1619.

[2] The edition of 1619 reads " Ile keepe it to my selfe."

[3] Perhaps "crave."

[4] So in the original. This evident mistake is corrected in the later editions.

[5] Instead of this and the following line, we have in the edition of 1619—

    " As long as Gloster beares this base and humble minde :
    Were I a man, and protector as he is,

Despight of all that seeke to crosse me thus,
Who is within there?

Enter Sir IOHN HUM. [1]

What sir Iohn Hum, what newes with you?

Sir Iohn. Iesus preserue your Maiestie.

Eln. My Maiestie. Why man I am but grace.

Sir Iohn. I, but by the grace of God & Hums aduise,
Your graces state shall be aduanst ere long.

Eln. What hast thou conferd with Margery Iordaine,[2] the cunning Witch of Ely,[3] with Roger Bul-
ingbrooke and the rest, and will they vndertake to do
me good?

Sir Iohn. I haue Madame, and they haue promised
me to raise a Spirite from depth of vnder grounde,[4]
that shall tell your grace all questions you demaund.

Eln. Thanks good sir Iohn. Some two days hence
    I gesse

    I'de reache to' th' crowne, or make some hop headlesse.
    And being but a woman, Ile not behinde
    For playing of my part, in spite of all that seek to cross me thus."
We should perhaps read " be behinde," a mistake that might
very easily have occurred in the printing. In act iv. sc. 4, in
the first folio, p. 140, the word "be" is omitted before "betraid," and is supplied in the edition of 1632.

    [1] Priests in Shakespeare's time frequently had the title of
"Sir." So "Sir John Evans," in the "Merry Wives of
Windsor."

    [2] "Nono die Maii [1432], virtute brevis regii domino Waltero
Hungerford, constabulario castri regis de Wyndesore directi,
conduxit *Margeriam Jourdemayn,* Johannem Virley clericum, et
fratrem Johannem Ashewell, ordinis Sanctæ Crucis Londoniæ,
nuper custodiæ suæ pro *sorcerye* in dicto castro commissos, usque
Concilium regis apud Westmonasterium, et ibidem, de mandato
Dominorum de Concilio, deliberavit dictam Margeriam, Johannem, et fratrem Johannem domino cancellario, et exoneratus est
de cætero de eorum custodia."—Rymer's "Fædera," vol. x. p. 505.

    [3] The edition of 1619 reads "Rye," while Mr Knight follows
history in reading "Eye."

    [4] The two editions of 1600 read "from *the* depth of vnder-
grounde."

Will fit our time, then see that they be here :
For now the King is ryding to Saint Albones,
And all the Dukes and Earles along with him,
When they be gone, then safely they may come,[1]
And on the backside of my Orchard heere,
There cast their Spelles in silence of the night,
And so resolue vs[2] of the thing we wish,
Till when, drinke that for my sake, And so farwell.
                                        [*Exet* ELNOR.
    Sir Iohn. Now sir Iohn Hum,[3] No words but mum.[4]
Seale vp your lips, for you must silent be,

---

[1] The edition of 1619 reads, "then safely may they come."

[2] The word "vs" is omitted in the two editions of 1600, and restored in that of 1619.

[3] This seems to be intended to rhyme with the first part of the line, although in the amended play we have "Hume" instead of "Hum," an alteration which Mr Knight has inadvertently admitted in his "Library Shakespeare," vol. vi. p. 124.

[4] The following account by Hall of the detection of the Duchess of Gloucester is nearer the description given in the text than that related by any other chronicler: "Thys yere, dame Elyanour Cobham, wyfe to the sayd duke, was accused of treason, for that she, by sorcery and enchauntment, entended to destroy the kyng, to thentent to advaunce and promote her husbande to the croune : upon this she was examined in sainct Stephens chappell, before the Bishop of Canterbury, and there by examinacion convict and judged, to do open penaunce, in iii open places within the citie of London, and after that adiudged to perpetuall prisone in the Isle of Man, under the kepyng of sir Ihon Stanley, knight. At the same season wer arrested as ayders and counsaylers to the sayde Duchesse, Thomas Southwell, priest and chanon of saincte Stephens in Westmynster, Jhon Hum preest, Roger Bolyngbroke, a conyng nycromancier, and Margerie Jourdayne, surnamed the witche of Eye, to whose charge it was layed, that thei, at the request of the duchesse, had devised an image of waxe presenting the kyng, whiche by their sorcery, a litle and litle consumed, entendyng therby in conclusion to waist and destroy the kynges person, and so to bryng hym to death ; for the which treison, they wer adjudged to dye, and so Margery Jordayne was brent in Smithfelde, and Roger Bolinbroke was drawen and quartered at Tiborne, tayking upon his death, that there was never no suche thyng by them ymagened ; Ihon Hum

These gifts ere long will make me mightie rich,
The Duches she thinkes now that all is well,
But I haue gold comes from another place,
From one that hyred me to set her on,
To plot these Treasons gainst the King and Peeres,
And that is the mightie Duke of Suffolke.
For he it is, but I must not say so,
That by my meanes must worke the Duches fall,
Who now by Cuniurations thinkes to rise.[1]
But whist sir Iohn, no more of that I trow,
For feare you lose your head before you goe.   [*Exet.*

Enter two Petitioners, and PETER *the Armourers man.*

    1. *Pet.* Come sirs let vs[2] linger here abouts[3] a
while,
Vntill my Lord Protector come this way,
That we may show his grace our seuerall causes.
    2. *Pet.* I pray God saue the good Duke Humphries
life,[4]
For but for him a many were vndone,

---

had his pardon, and Southwell dyed in the toure before execu-
cion." Southwell is introduced by the author of the amended
play, so it is probable that he may have referred again to this
chronicle as well as to the original drama. Grafton (p. 587)
gives the same information as Hall. See also Higden's "Poly-
chronicon," translated by Trevisa, lib. ult. cap. 27. With respect
to the "image of waxe," it is observed by King James I., in his
"Dæmonology," that "the devil teacheth how to make pictures
of wax or clay, that, by roasting thereof, the persons that they
bear the name of may be continually melted, or dried away by
continual sickness."—See Dr Grey's "Notes upon Shakespeare,"
vol. ii. p. 18.

   [1] The two editions of 1600 read "raise." The edition of
1619 agrees with our text.

   [2] The edition of 1619 reads "lets."

   [3] The genuine old form of the word. Mr Knight alters it to
"hereabout."

   [4] The word "Duke" is accidentally omitted in the two editions of 1600.

That cannot get[1] no succour in the Court,
But see where he comes with the Queene.

Enter the Duke of SUFFOLKE *with the Queene, and they
take him for Duke* HUMPHREY, *and giues[2] him their
writings.*

    1. *Pet.* Oh we are vndone, this is the Duke of
Suffolke.
    Queene. Now good-fellowes, whom would you speak
withall?
    2. *Pet.* If it please your Maiestie, with my Lord
Protectors Grace.
    Queene. Are your sutes to his grace. Let vs see
them first,
Looke on them my Lord of Suffolke.
    Suf. A complaint against the Cardinals man.
What hath he done?
    2. *Pet.* Marry my Lord, he hath stole[3] away my wife,
And th' are gone togither, and I know not where to
finde them.
    Suf. Hath he stole thy wife, thats some iniury in-
deed.
But what say you?
    Peter Thump.[4] Marry sir I come to tel you that my
maister said, that the Duke of Yorke was true heire
vnto the Crowne,[5] and that the King was an vsurer.

---

    1 The two editions of 1600 read " That can get no succour,"
and the quarto of 1619 reads " They cannot get."
    2 Probably " giue."
    3 In this, and Suffolk's next speech, the two editions of 1600
read " stolne."
    4 Mr Collier calls him " Hump ;" but, if so written in the
early copies to which he has referred, it is an error ; for that
" Thumpe " is correct may be seen from the pun that Salisbury
makes on his name. Mr Collier's reading was probably occasioned by one of the prefixes of Gloster's speeches, as where
" Hump" occurs for " Humprey."
    5 The edition of 1619 reads, " true heire to the crown."

Queene. An vsurper thou woulds say.

Peter. I forsooth an vsurper.

Queene. Didst thou say the King was an vsurper?

Peter. No forsooth, I saide my maister[1] saide so, th' other day when we were scowring the Duke of Yorks Armour in our garret.

Suf. I marry this is something like, Whose within there?

Enter one or two.

Sirra take in this fellow[2] and keepe him close, And send out a Purseuant for his maister straight, Weele here more of this[3] before the king.

　　　　　　　　[Exet with the Armourers man.

Now sir what yours?[4]　Let me see it, Whats here?

A complaint against the Duke of Suffolke for enclosing the commons of long Melford.

How now sir knaue.

1. *Pet.* I beseech your grace to pardon me, me,[5] I am but a Messenger for the whole town-ship.

　　　　　　　　[He teares the papers.[6]

---

[1] The folio reads "mistress," with other alterations. Tyrwhitt's emendation of "master" is confirmed by this edition of the sketch. The error was probably occasioned by "master" having been denoted in the MS. from which the amended play was printed merely by the letter M.

[2] The two editions of 1600 read, "Sirra take this fellow."

[3] The edition of 1619 reads, "Weele heere more of this thing."

[4] The two editions of 1600 and the edition of 1619 read, "Now, sir, what's yours."

[5] This repetition is probably an error of the press. It does not occur in the edition of 1619.

[6] In the amended play this is as follows: "Teare the Supplication." Modern editors alter this; but it is a matter of very little consequence.

Suf. So now show your petitions[1] to Duke Hum-
    phrey.
Villaines get you gone[2] and come not neare the Court,
Dare the peasants write against me thus.·
                            [*Exet Petitioners.*
    Queene. My Lord of Suffolke, you may see by this,
The Commons loues[3] vnto that haughtie Duke,
That seekes to him more then to King Henry :
Whose eyes are alwaies poring on his booke,
And nere regards the honour of his name,
But still must be protected like a childe,
And gouerned by that ambitious Duke,
That scarse will moue his cap nor speake to vs,[4]
And his proud wife, high minded Elanor,
That ruffles it with such a troupe of Ladies,
As strangers in the Court takes her for the Queene.[5]
The other day she vanted to her maides,
That the very traine of her worst gowne,
Was worth more wealth then all my fathers lands,
Can any griefe of minde be like to this.
I tell thee Poull, when thou didst runne at Tilt,
And stolst away our Ladaies heart in France,
I thought King Henry had bene like to thee,
Or else thou hadst not brought me out of France.
    Suf. Madame content your selfe a little while,

---

[1] The two editions of 1600 read, " Show your petition."
The edition of 1619 follows our text.

[2] The two editions of 1600 read, " Villaines get *ye* gone," and
the same alteration occurs in other instances.

[3] Probably " loue," as we have " seekes " in the next line for
the verb.

[4] The edition of 1619 reads, " to speake to vs."

[5] The edition of 1619 reads, " take her for queene." The
same edition has the following line immediately following this,
which is not in the earlier copies—

    " She beares a dukes whole reuennewes on her backe ; "

which line, with the omission of the word " whole," occurs in
the amended play.

As I was the cause of your comming to England,[1]
So will I in England worke your full content :
And as for proud Duke Humphrey and his wife,
I haue set lime-twigs that will intangle them,
As that your grace ere long shall vnderstand.
But staie Madame, here comes the King.

Enter King HENRY, *and the Duke of* YORKE *and the
Duke of* SOMERSET *on both sides of the King,
whispering with him, and enter[2] Duke* HUMPHREY,
Dame ELNOR, *the Duke of* BUCKINGHAM, *the
Earle of* SALSBURY, *the Earle of* WARWICKE, *and
the Cardinall of* WINCHESTER.

Kin. My Lords I care not who be Regent in France,
or York, or Somerset, alls wonne to me.[3]

Yorke. My Lord, if Yorke haue ill demeande himselfe,
Let Somerset enioy his place and go to France.

Som. Then whom your grace thinke[4] worthie, let
him go,
And there be made Regent ouer the French.

War. Whom soeuer you account worthie,
Yorke is the worthiest.

Car. Pease Warwicke. Giue thy betters leaue to
speake.

War. The Cardinals not my better in the field.

Buc. All in this place are thy betters farre.

War. And Warwicke may liue to be the best of all,[5]

Queene. My Lord in mine opinion, it were best that
Somerset were Regent ouer France.

---

[1] The edition of 1619 reads, "your comming into England."
[2] The edition of 1619 reads, "then entereth."
[3] This of course means "all's one to me." This extraordinary instance of Henry's apathy and indifference is repeated in
the amended play.
[4] The edition of 1619 reads, "thinkes."
[5] The word "the" is omitted in the edition of 1619, but is
found in the amended play.

Hum. Madame onr King is old inough[1] himselfe,
To giue his answere without your consent.

Queene. If he be old inough, what needs your grace
To be Protector ouer him so long.

Hum. Madame I am but Protector ouer[2] the land,
And when it please his grace, I will resigne my charge.

Suf. Resigne it then, for since that thou wast king,[3]
As who is King but thee. The common state
Doth as we see, all wholly go to wracke,
And Millions of treasure hath bene spent,
And as for the Regentship of France.
I say Somerset is more worthie then Yorke.

Yorke. Ile tell thee Suffolke why I am not worthie,
Because I cannot flatter as thou canst.

War. And yet the worthie deeds that York hath
done,
Should make him worthie to be honoured here.

Suf. Peace headstrong Warwicke.

War. Image of pride, wherefore should I peace ?

Suf. Because here is a man accusde of Treason,
Pray God the Duke of Yorke do cleare himselfe.
Ho, bring hither the Armourer and his man.

---

[1] "Onr" is a misprint in the original for "our." The two
editions of 1600 read, "bold enough" instead of "old enoughe,"
which is a mistaken alteration. Hall thus describes the Queen's
impatience under the authority of the Protector : "This woman,
perceiving that her husband did not frankly rule as he would,
but did all things by the advice and counsel of Humphrey Duke
of Gloster, and that he passed not much on the authority and
governance of the realm, determined with herself to take upon
her the rule and regiment both of the king and his kingdom,
and to deprive and evict out of all rule and authority the said
duke, then called the lord protector of the realm : lest men
should say and report that she had neither wit nor stomach,
which would permit and suffer her husband, being of perfect
age and man's estate, like a young scolar or innocent pupil to be
governed by the disposition of another man."

[2] The edition of 1619 reads "ore."

[3] The edition of 1619 reads, "thou wast a king."

Enter the Armourer and his man.

If it please your grace, this fellow here, hath accused his maister of high Treason, And his words were these.

That the Duke of Yorke was lawfull heire vnto the Crowne, and that your grace was an vsurper.

Yorke. I beseech your grace let him haue what punishment the law will afford, for his villany.

Kin. Come hether fellow, didst thou speake these words?

Arm. Ant shall please your Maiestie, I neuer said any such matter, God is my witnesse, I am falsly accused by this villain here.

Peter. Tis no matter for that, you did say so.

Yorke. I beseech your grace, let him haue the law.

Arm. Alasse my Lord,[1] hang me if euer I spake[2] the words, my accuser is my prentise, & when I did correct him for his fault the other day, he did vow upon his knees that he would be euen with me, I haue good witnesse of this, and therefore I beseech your Maiestie[3] do not cast away an honest man for a villaines accusation.

Kin. Vncle Gloster, what do you thinke of this?

Hum. The law my Lord is this by case,[4] it rests suspitious,

That a day of combat be appointed,

And there to trie each others right or wrong,

Which shall be on the thirtith of this month,[5]

---

[1] The edition of 1600 reads, "master."

[2] The two editions of 1600 read, "If euer I spake these words." The edition of 1619 corresponds with our text.

[3] The edition of 1619 reads, "I beseech your worship."

[4] The comma ought to be inserted after "this," and left out after "case." The passage is obscure. Mr Knight reads "because," a sufficiently plausible conjecture.

[5] This line is entirely omitted in the edition of 1619 and by Mr Knight. The period of action of this and the first scene of

With Eben staues, and Standbags[1] combatting
In Smythfield, before your Royall Maiestie.
                              [*Exet* HUMPHREY.
   Arm. And I accept the Combat willingly.
   Peter. Alasse my Lord, I am not able to fight.[2]
   Suf. You must either fight sirra or else be hangde :
Go take them hence againe to prison.
                              [*Exet with them.*
      [*The Queene lets fall her gloue,*[3] *and hits the
            Duches of* GLOSTER *a boxe on the eare.*
   Queene. Giue me my gloue.   My Minion can you
      not see ?   [*She strikes her.*
I cry you mercy Madame, I did mistake,
I did not thinke it had bene you.
   Eln. Did you not proud French-woman.
Could I come neare ʃyour daintie vissage with my
      nayles,
Ide set my ten commandments[4] in your face.
   Kin. Be patient gentle Aunt.
It was against her will.
   Eln. Against her will.   Good King sheele dandle thee,

---

the amended play differ.   The month alluded to in the present
passage is April ; for when Gloster reads the agreement, he
says, "ere ſhe 30. of the next month," meaning May, as we
learn from the amended play.   The first three scenes of the
Second Part of Henry VI. are supposed to take place in March,
for King Henry, alluding to the same circumstance, says—

> "Away with them to prison ; and the day
> Of combat shall be *the last of the next month.*
> Come, Somerset, we'll see thee sent away."

   [1] Probably "sandbags."
   [2] The edition of 1619 reads, "I am not able for to fight."
The amended play reads, "I cannot fight."
   [3] In the amended play the Queen drops a *fan*, not a *glove*.
   [4] The nails.   So in "Westward Hoe," 1607, "your harpy has
set his ten commandments on my back."   Quoted by Steevens,
together with another quotation to the same effect.   The amended
play reads, "I could set," but modern editors adopt the reading
of our text.

If thou wilt alwaies thus be rulde by her.
But let it rest.   As sure as I do liue,
She shall not strike dame Elnor vnreuengde,

                    [Exet ELNOR.

  Kin. Beleeue me my loue, thou wart much to blame.
I would not for a thousand pounds of gold,
My noble vnckle had bene here in place.

Enter Duke HUMPHREY.

But see where he comes, I am glad he met her not.
Vnckle Gloster, what answer makes your grace
Concerning our Regent for the Realme of France,
Whom thinks your grace is meetest for to send.

  Hum. My gratious Lord, then this is my resolue,
For that these words the Armourer should speake,[1]
Doth breed suspition on the part of Yorke,
Let Somerset be Regent ouer[2] the French,
Till trialls made, and Yorke may cleare himselfe.

  Kin. Then be it so[3] my Lord of Somerset.
We make your grace Regent ouer the French,
And to defend our rights[4] gainst forraine foes,

---

[1] The two editions of 1600 read :

      "For that these words the Armourer doth speake."

[2] The edition of 1619 reads "ore."

[3] This and the next line are introduced by Theobald into the amended play, but unnecessarily. He says that, "without them, the king has not declared his assent to Gloster's opinion;" but the same may be said of the armourer's reply, which is introduced immediately afterwards from an earlier part of the old play. Mr Collier and Mr Knight reject Theobald's addition. Indeed, as Mr Knight justly observes, "the scene as it stands [in the amended play] is an exhibition of the almost kingly authority of Gloster immediately before his fall." Something, however, may be wanting, unless we suppose that Henry is treated even with less deference than usual. Malone supposes that Henry's assent might be expressed by a nod. See Collier's "Shakespeare," vol. v. p. 129.

[4] The edition of 1619 reads, "right."

And so do good vnto the Realme of France.
Make hast my Lord, tis time that you were gone,
The time of Truse I thinke is [1] full expirde,
   Som. I humbly thanke your royall Maiestie,
And take my leaue to poste with speed to France.
                  [*Exet* SOMERSET.
   Kin. Come vnckle Gloster, now lets haue our
    horse,
For we will to Saint Albones presently,
Madame your Hawke they say, is swift of flight,
And we will try how she will flie to day.
                     [*Exet omnes.*

Enter ELNOR, *with sir* IOIIN HUM, KOGER [2] BULLEN-
    BROKE *a Coniurer and* MARGERY IOURDAINE *a*
    Witch.

   Eln. Here sir Iohn, take this scrole of paper here,
Wherein is writ the questions you shall aske,
And I will stand vpon this Tower here,
And here the spirit what it saies to you,
And to my questions, write the answeres downe.
              [*She goes vp to the Tower.*
   Sir Iohn. Now sirs begin and cast your spels
    about,
And charme the fiendes for to obey your wils,
And tell Dame Elnor of the thing she askes.
   Witch. Then Roger Bullinbrooke about thy taske,
And frame a Cirkle here vpon the earth,
Whilst I thereon all prostrate on my face,
Do talke and whisper with the diuels be low,
And coniure them for to obey my will.
          She lies downe vpon her face.
      BULLENBROOKE *makes a Cirkle.*

---

[1] The edition of 1619 reads, "is I thinke."
[2] A mistake in the original copy for "Roger."

Bul. Darke Night, dread Night, the silence of the
    Night.[1]
Wherein the Furies maske in hellish troupes,
Send vp I charge you from Sosetus lake,[2]
The spirit Askalon to come to me,
To pierce the bowels of this Centricke earth,
And hither come in twinkling of an eye,
Askalon, Assenda, Assenda.[3]
    [*It thunders and lightens, and then the spirit
        riseth vp.*
Spirit. Now Bullenbrooke what wouldst thou haue
    me do?
Bul. First of the King, what shall become of
    him?
Spirit. The Duke yet liues that Henry shall de-
    pose,
But him out liue,[4] and dye a violent death.
    Bul. What fate awayt[5] the Duke of Suffolke.
    Spirit. By water shall he die[6] and take his ende.

---

[1] The amended play reads :
    "Deep night, dark night, the silent of the night ;"
in which place the word *silent* is a noun.   Fletcher, in the
"Faithfull Shepherdess," writes—
        "Through still silence of the night,
        Guided by the glow-worm's light."

[2] Sosetus, or rather Cocytus, is one of the rivers in the kingdom of his Satanic majesty.   In Nash's "Pierce Penilesse,"
the devil is called "Marquesse of Cocytus."   See Mr Collier's
edition, p. 13.
[3] The two editions of 1600 read "Askalon, ascenda, ascenda."
Ascalon is mentioned by Scott as one of the inferior devils.   It
may be a question whether these words are corruptions of Latin
or English.
[4] The two editions of 1600 read "Yet him out liue."
[5] The two editions of 1600 and that of 1619 read, "What
fate awaits."   The first folio reads, "What fates await."
[6] The two editions of 1600 read, "By water he shall die."

Bul. What shall betide the Duke of Somerset ?
Spirit. Let him shun Castles, safer shall he be
vpon the sandie plaines, then where Castles mounted
stand.[1]
Now question me no more, for I must hence againe.[2]
                      [He sinks downe againe.
Bul. Then downe I say, vnto the damned poule.
Where Pluto in his firie Waggon sits.
Ryding amidst the singde and parched smoakes,
The Rode of Dytas by the Riuer Stykes,[3]
There howle and burne for euer in those flames,
Rise Iordaine rise, and staie thy charming Spels.
Sonnes,[4] we are betraide.

Enter the Duke of YORKE, *and the Duke of* BUCKING-
HAM, *and others.*

Yorke. Come sirs, laie hands on them, and bind
    them sure,

---

[1] The word, "then," is omitted in the two editions of 1600, but restored in that of 1619. Steevens quotes, without reference, the following prophecy from an old chronicle, which is very similar to this :

    "Safer shall he be on sand,
    Than where castles mounted stand."

[2] It was anciently believed that spirits, who were raised by incantations, remained above ground only for a limited time, and answered questions with reluctance. In the amended play, the spirit says, after the same answer :

    "Have done, for more I hardly can endure."

The same observations may be made with regard to the prophecies told to Macbeth.

[3] *Dytas* is written by mistake for *Ditis*, the genitive case of *Dis*, which is occasionally used instead of the nominative by writers of the time. The genitive would, however, have been required in the Latin construction of the sentence. It is almost unnecessary to say that it means Pluto. So in Drant's Horace, 1567 :

    "Made manye soules lord *Ditis* hall to seeke."

[4] A mistake in the original copy for "sounes." It is corrected in the later impressions.

This time was well watcht.[1]   What Madame are you
    there ?
This will be great credit for your husband,
That you are [2] plotting Treasons[3] thus with Cun-
    iurers,
The King shall haue notice [4] of this thing.
                              [*Exet* ELNOR *aboue.*
    Buc. See here my Lord what the diuell hath
        writ.
    Yorke. Giue it me my Lord, Ile show it to the
        King.
Go sirs, see them fast lockt in prison.
                              [*Exet with them.*
    Buc. My Lord, I pray you let me go post vnto the
        King,
Vnto S. Albones, to tell this newes.
    Yorke. Content.   Away then, about straight.
    Buc. Farewell my Lord.   [*Exet* BUCKINGHAM.
    Yorke. Whose within there ?

                    Enter one.

    One. My Lord.
    Yorke. Sirrha, go will the Earles of Salsbury[5] and
Warwicke, to sup with me to night.   [*Exet* YORKE.
    One. I will my Lord.   [*Exet.*

---

   [1] A similar expression occurs in the "Merry Wives of Windsor," act v. sc. 5.
   [2] So in the original, but corrected in the later impressions to
"that you are."
   [3] The edition of 1619 reads, "Treason."
   [4] The two editions of 1600 read, "The King shall haue a
notice," which addition is omitted in the edition of 1619.
   [5] The two editions of 1600 read, "go will the Earle of Salsbury." I scarcely understand the meaning of the conversation
as it here stands, and think there is some error. Perhaps we
should read "invite" for "go will," or else we must suppose
the servant to understand an unusual phraseology.

Enter the King and Queene with her Hawke on her fist,[1]
and Duke HUMPHREY *and* SUFFOLKE, *and the*
Cardinall, as if they came from hawking.

Queene. My Lord, how did your grace like this
last flight ?
But as I cast her off the winde did rise,
And twas ten to one, old Ione had not gone
out.[2]
Kin. How wonderful the Lords workes are on
earth,
Euen in these silly creatures of his hands,
Vnckle Gloster, how hie your Hawke did sore
And on a sodaine soust the Partridge downe.
Suf. No maruell if it please your Maiestie
My Lord Protectors Hawke done towre so
well.[3]
He knowes his maister loues to be aloft.
Hum. Faith my Lord, it is but a base minde
That can sore no higher then a Falkons pitch.

---

[1] This minute stage direction, as Mr Collier observes, is omitted in the amended play. It shows the particularity with which such matters were sometimes attended to on our old stage, and as an ocular proof to the audience that the royal party were engaged in hawking. (Collier's "Shakespeare," vol. v. p. 133.)

[2] See Boswell's Malone, vol. xviii. p. 203. "Out of sight," I suppose, is understood ; but Percy explains it thus : "the wind was so high, it was ten to one that old Jone would not have taken her flight at the game."

[3] The two editions of 1600 and that of 1619 read, "doe towre so well." The amended play also agrees with this emendation. The three next lines are thus given in the edition of 1619.

> " They know their master sores a faulcon's pitch.
> *Hum.* Faith, my lord, it's but a base minde,
> That sores no higher than a bird can sore."

There seems to be some strange confusion in the differences between these two readings and the text of the amended play : but see the " Introduction " to this volume.

Car. I thought your grace would be aboue the
cloudes.[1]

Hum. I my Lord Cardinall, were it not good
Your grace could flie to heauen.

Car. Thy heauen is on earth, thy words and
thoughts beat on a Crowne,[2] proude Protector dangerous Peere, to smooth it thus with King and common-wealth.

Hum. How now my Lord, why this is more then
needs,
Church-men so hote. Good vnckle can you doate.[3]

Suf. Why not Hauing so good a quarrell & so bad
a cause.

Hum. As how, my Lord?

Suf. As you my Lord. And it like[4] your Lordly
Lords Protectorship.

Hum. Why Suffolke, England knowes thy insolence.

Queene. And thy ambition Gloster.

Kin. Cease gentle Queene, and whet not on these

---

[1] The first folio thus reads : " I thought as much, hee would
bee aboue the clouds." Modern editors generally read "he'd ;"
but Mr Knight restores the old reading.

[2] An image taken from falconry. A hawk was said to *beat*
when it fluttered with his wings. A similar phrase, without the
comparison, occurs in Lyly's " Maid's Metamorphosis," 1600, as
quoted by Steevens :

"With him whose restless thoughts do beat on thee."

The words, " bate " and " abate," as applied to this diversion,
are more particularly explained in "The Booke of Hawking,"
MS. Harl. 2340. In the "Tempest," act i. sc. 2, Miranda uses
a somewhat similar expression, and Prospero also in act v.
sc. 1.

[3] This is intelligible enough, though the edition of 1619 alters
"doate" to "do't," in which it is followed by Mr Knight.
See the notes of the commentators on the corresponding passage
of the amended play.

[4] The edition of 1619 reads, "and t'like."

furious Lordes [1] to wrath, for blessed are the peacemakers on earth. [2]

    Car. Let me be blessed for the peace I make,
Against this proud Protector with my sword.

    Hum. Faith holy vnckle, I would it were come to
that.

    Car. Euen when thou darest.

    Hum. Dare. I tell rhee [3] Priest, Plantagenets
could neuer brooke the dare.

    Car. I am Plantagenet as well as thou, and sonne
to Iohn of Gaunt.

    Hum. In Bastardie.

    Car. I scorne thy words.

    Hum. Make vp no factious numbers, but euen in
thine own person meete me at the East end of the
groue. [4]

    Car. Heres my hand, I will.

    Kin. Why how now my Lords?

    Car. Faith Cousin Gloster, had not your man cast

---

[1] This speech may be arranged as verse. The first folio of
the amended play reads :

> "I prythee peace, good queene,
> And whet not on these furious peeres,
> For blessed are the peace-makers on earth."

But the second folio of 1632 reads :

> "I prethee peace, good queene,
> And whet not on these too-too furious peeres,
> For blessed are the peace-makers on earth."

[2] See St Matthew, v. 9, "Blessed are the peacemakers, for
they shall be called the children of God."

[3] A mistake in the original copy for "thee." It is corrected
in the later impressions.

[4] In the amended play the place of meeting is first appointed
by the cardinal, and afterwards repeated by Gloucester. The
present passage shows that there is no necessity for Theobald's
emendation, who would give the repetition of the appointment
to the cardinal.

off so soone we had had more sport to day, Come
with thy swoord and buckler.

Hum. Faith Priest,[1] Ile shaue your Crowne.

Car. Protector, protect thy selfe well.

King. The wind growes high, so doth your chollour
Lords.

   Enter one crying, A miracle, a miracle.[2]

How now, now sirrha, what miracle is it ?

---

[1] The edition of 1619 reads, " God's mother, priest," which
agrees with the amended play. This is singular, these two
editions having been published after the prohibitory statute, and
the other before.

[2] This repetition does not occur in the two editions of 1600.
This scene is founded on the following story, related by Sir
Thomas More, and which he says was communicated to him
by his father : " I remember me that I have hard my father tell
of a begger that, in Kyng Henry his daies the sixt, cam with his
wife to saint Albonis. And there was walking about the towne
begging a five or six dayes before the kinges commynge thither,
saienge that he was borne blinde, and never sawe in hys lyfe.
And was warned in hys dreame that he shoulde come out of
Berwyke, where he said he had ever dwelled, to seek saynt
Albon, and that he had ben at his shryne, and had not bene
holpen. And therfore he woulde go seke hym at some other
place, for he had hard some say sins he came, that sainct
Albonys body shold be at Colon, and indede such a contencion
hath ther ben. But of troth, as I am surely informed, he lieth
here at Saint Albonis, saving some reliques of him, which thei
there shew shrined. But to tell you forth, whan the kyng was
comen, and the towne full, sodainly thys blind man at Saint
Albonis shrine had his sight agayne, and a myracle solemply
rongen, and *te Deum* songen, so that nothyng was talked of
in al the towne but this myracle. So happened it than that
Duke Humfry of Glocester, a great wyse man and very wel
lerned, having great joy to see such a myracle, called the pore
man unto hym. And first shewing himselfe joyouse of Goddes
glory as shewed in the gettinge of his sight, and exortinge hym
to mekenes, and to none ascribing of any part the worship to
himselfe, nor to be proved of the peoples prayse, which would
call hym a good and a godly man therby. At last he loked
well upon his eyen, and asked whyther he could never se nothing
at al in al his life before. And whan as well his wyfe as himself affermed falsely no, than he loked advisedly upon his eien

One. And it please your grace, there is a man that
came blinde to S. Albones, and hath receiued his sight
at his shrine.[1]

---

again, and said, I beleve you very wel, for me thinketh that ye
cannot se well yet. Yes, sir, quoth he, I thanke God and his
holy marter, I can se nowe as well as any man. Ye can, ·quoth
the duke ; what colour is my gowne? Than anone the begger
tolde him. What coloure, quoth he, is this mans gowne? He
told him also, and so forth, without any sticking, he told him
the names of al the colours that coulde bee shewed him. And
whan my lord saw that, he bad him walke faytoure, and made him
be set openly in the stockes. For though he could have sene
soudenly by miracle, the dyfference betweene divers colours,
yet coulde he not by the syght so sodenly tell the names of all
these colours, but if he had knowen them before, no more than
the names of al the men that he should sodenly se."—*The
Workes of Sir Thomas Moore,* 1557, p. 134. The similarity
between the last part of this account, and that in our text, will
be immediately perceived. The following account is given in
Grafton's " Chronicle," p. 597-8 : " In the time of King Henry
VI., as he rode in progress, there came to the towne of Saint
Albons a certain beggar with his wyfe, and there was walking
about the town, begging five or six days before the king's
coming, saying that he was borne blind, and never saw in all
his life ; and was warned in his dream that he should come out
of Berwicke, where, he said, that he had ever dwelled, to seke
Saint Albon. When the king was come, and the town full of
people, sodainly this blind man at Saint Albon's shryne had his
sight ; and the same was solemnly rung for a miracle, and *Te
Deum* songen ; so that nothing was talked of in all the towne
but this miracle. So happened it then, that Duke Humfrey,
Duke of Gloucester, a man no less wise than also well learned,
called the pore man up to him, and looked well upon his eyen,
and asked whether he could never see anything in all his life
before? and when, as well his wife as himselfe, affirmed fastly,
No, than he looked advisedly upon his eyen again, and sayde,
I believe you may well, for methinketh that ye cannot see well
yet. Yes, sir, quoth he ; I thank God and his holy martir, I
can see now as well as any man. Ye can, quod the duke, what
colour is this gowne? This anone the beggar told him. What
colour, quod he, is this man's gowne? He told him also, without staying or stumbling, and told him the names of all the
colours that could be shewed him. And when the Duke saw
that, he made him be set openly in the stocks." So much for
the plagiarisms of the sixteenth century !

[1] The edition of 1619 reads " at the shrine."

King. Goe fetch him hither, that wee may glorifye the Lord with him.

Enter the Maior of Saint Albones and his brethren with Musicke,[1] bearing the man that had bene blind, betweene two in a chaire.

King. Thou happie man, giue God eternall praise,
For he it is, that thus hath helped thee.
Hum. Where wast thou borne?[2]
Poore man. At Barwicke sir, in the North.
Hum. At Barwicke, and come thus far for helpe.
Poore man. I sir, it was told me in my sleepe,
That sweet saint Albones, should giue me my sight againe.
Hum. What are thou[3] lame too?
Poore man. I indeed sir, God helpe me.
Hum. How cam'st thou lame?
Poore man. With falling off on a plum-tree.[4]
Hum. Wart thou blind & wold clime plumtrees?
Poore man. Neuer but once sir in all my life,
My wife did long for plums.
Hum. But tell me, wart thou borne blinde?
Poore man. I truly sir.
Woman. I indeed sir, he was born blinde.
Hum. What art thou his mother?
Woman. His wife sir.
Hum. Hadst thou bene his mother,
Thou couldst haue better told.
Why let me see, I thinke thou cant not see yet.
Poore man. Yes truly maister, as cleare as day.

---

[1] This part of the stage direction is omitted in the amended ay.

[2] This line forms part of the king's speech in the edition of 1619, which also reads, " please your majesty " instead of " sir " in the following line. The context is in favour of the old arrangement.

[3] Omitted in the edition of 1619.

[4] The word " on " is omitted in the edition of 1619.

Hum. Saist thou so.   What colours his cloake?
Poore man. Why[1] red maister, as red as blood.
Hum. And his cloake?
Poore man. Why thats greene.
Hum. And what colours his hose?
Poore man. Yellow maister, yellow as gold.
Hum. And what colours my gowne?
Poore man. Black sir, as black as Ieat.
King. Then belike he knows what colour Ieat is on.
Suf. And yet I thinke Ieat did he neuer see.[2]
Hum. But cloakes and gownes ere this day many
   a one.
But tell me sirrha, whats my name?
Poore man. Alasse maister I know not.
Hum. What his name?
Poore man. I know not.
Hum. Nor his?
Poore man. No truly sir.
Hum. Nor his name?
Poore man. No indeed maister.
Hum. Whats thine owne name?
Poore man. Sander, and it please you maister.
   Hum. Then Sander sit there, the lyingest knaue in
Christendom.   If thou hadst bene born blind, thou
mightest aswell haue knowne all our names, as thus
to name the seuerall colours we doo weare.   Sight
may distinguish of colours,[3] but sodeinly to nominate.
them all, it is impossible.   My Lords, saint Albones
here hath done a Miracle, and would you not thinke
his cunning[4] to be great, that could restore this Cripple
to his legs againe.

---

[1] This word is omitted in the edition of 1619.
   [2] The word " yet " is omitted in the two editions of 1600, but
is found in that of 1619.
   [3] This speech is printed metrically in the amended play.   The
word " of " is omitted in the second folio.
   [4] This whole speech is adopted nearly verbatim in the amended
play.   The two first folios, however, read, " it cunning " instead of

Poore man. Oh maister I would you could.

Hum. My Maisters of saint Albones,
Haue you not Beadles in your Towne,
And things called whippes ?[1]

Mayor. Yes my Lord, if it please your grace.

Hum. Then send for one presently.

Mayor. Sirrha, go fetch the Beadle hither straight.
                                     [Exet one.

Hum. Now fetch me a stoole[2] hither by and by,
Now sirrha, If you meane to saue your selfe from
    whipping,
Leape me ouer this stoole and runne away.

Enter Beadle.

Poore man. Alasse maister I am not able to stand
    alone,
You go about to torture me in vaine.

Hum. Well sir, we must haue you finde your legges.
Sirrha Beadle, whip him till he leape ouer that sam
    stoole.

Beadle. I will my Lord, come on sirrha, off with
your doublet quickly,

"his cunning," which last reading is the right one. Rowe suggested
"that cunning," which has been followed by all modern editors.

[1] A humorous method of expression, occasionally used satiri-
cally at the present day. Armin, in his "Nest of Ninnies,"
1608, says : "Ther are, as Hamlet saies, *things cald whips* in
store." Now, according to Mr Collier, no such passage is to
be found in any edition of Shakespeare's Hamlet ; and he thinks
it unlikely that Armin refers to the old Hamlet which preceded
Shakespeare's, because he was an actor in the same theatre as
that for which Shakespeare wrote. It is not impossible that
Armin may have confused the two plays together, and wrote in-
correctly "as Hamlet saies," instead of "as Gloster saies."

[2] The second folio prints this, "New fetch me a stoole." I
mention this minute difference because it appears to confirm
Rowe's emendation of the well-known passage at the commencement of "A Midsummer Night's Dream," in opposition to the
opinion of Mr Collier.

Poore man. Alas maister what shall I do, I am not able to stand.

[*After the Beadle had hit him one girke, he leapes ouer the stoole and runnes away, and they run after him, crying, A miracle, a miracle.*

Hum. A miracle, a miracle, let him be taken againe, & whipt at euery Market Towne til he comes at Barwicke where he was borne.

Mayor. It shall be done my Lord.   [*Exet Mayor.*

Suf. My Lord Protector hath done wonders to day. He hath made the blinde to see, and halt to go.[1]

Hum. I but you did greater wonders, when you made whole Dukedomes flie in a day. Witnesse France.

King. Haue done I say, and let me here no more of that.

Enter the Duke of BUCKINGHAM.

What newes brings Duke Humprey of Buckingham?

Buck. Ill newes for some my Lord, and this it is, That proud dame Elnor our Protectors wife, Hath plotted Treasons gainst the King and Peeres By wichcrafts, sorceries, and cuniurings, Who by such meanes did raise a spirit vp, To tell her what hap should betide the state, But ere they had finisht their diuellish drift, By Yorke and my selfe they were all surprisde, And heres the answere the diuel did make to them.

King. First of the King, what shall become of him? (*Reads.*) The Duke yet liues, that Henry shal depose, Yet him out liue, and die a violent death. Gods will be done in all. What fate awaits the Duke of Suffolke? By water shall he die and take his end.

---

[1] The two editions of 1600 read " and the halt to go."

Suf. By water must the Duke of Suffolke die?
It must be so, or else the diuel doth lie.
　King. Let Somerset shun Castles,
For safer shall he be vpon the sandie plaines,
Then where Castles mounted stand.
　Car. Heres good stuffe, how now my Lord Protector.
This newes I thinke hath turnde your weapons point,
I am in doubt youle scarsly keepe your promise.
　Hum. Forbear ambitious Prelate to vrge my griefe,
And pardon me my gratious Soueraigne,
For here I sweare vnto your Maiestie,
That I am guiltlesse of these hainous crimes
Which my ambitious wife hath falsly done,
And for she would betraie her soueraigne Lord,
I here renounce her from my bed and boord,
And leaue her open for the law to iudge,
Vnlesse she cleare her selfe of this foule deed.
　King. Come my Lords this night weele lodge in S.
　　Albones,
And to morrow we will ride to London,
And trie the vtmost of these Treasons forth,
Come vnckle Gloster along with vs,
My mind doth tell me thou art innocent. [*Exet omnes.*

Enter the Duke of YORKE, *and the Earles of* SALSBURY
and WARWICKE.

　Yorke. My Lords our simple supper ended, thus,
Let me reueale vnto your honours here,
The right and title of the house of Yorke,[1]
To Englands Crowne by lineall desent.
　War. Then Yorke begin, and if thy claime be good,
The Neuils are thy subiects to command.

---

[1] The edition of 1619 gives the whole pedigree very differently
from this edition. It is necessary to transcribe the whole:

" Edward the third had seuen sonnes,
　The first was Edward the blacke prince,
　Prince of Wales.

Yorke. Then thus my Lords.
Edward the third had seuen sonnes,
The first was Edward the blacke Prince,
Prince of Wales.
The second was Edmund of Langly,
Duke of Yorke.
The third was Lyonell Duke of Clarence.
The fourth was Iohn of Gaunt,
The Duke of Lancaster.
The fifth was Roger Mortemor,[1] Earle of March.
The sixt was sir Thomas of Woodstocke.
William of Winsore was the seuenth and last.
Now, Edward the blacke Prince he died before his father,

> The second was William of Hatfield,
> Who dyed young.
> The third was Lyonell, duke of Clarence.
> The fourth was Iohn of Gaunt,
> The duke of Lancaster,
> The fit was Edmund of Langley,
> Duke of Yorke.
> The sixt was William of Windsore,
> Who dyed young.   .
> The seauenth and last was sir Thomas of Woodstocke, duke of Yorke.
> "Now Edward the blacke prince dyed before his father, leauing behinde
> him two sonnes ; Edward, borne at Angolesme, who died young, and Rich-
> ard, that was after crowned king by the name of Richard the second, who
> dyed without an heyre.
> "Lyonell, duke of Clarence, dyed, and left him one only daughter,
> named Phillip, who was married to Edmund Mortimer, earle of March and
> Ulster : and so by her I claime the crowne, as the true heire to Lyonell,
> duke of Clarence, third sonne to Edward the third. Now, sir, in time of
> Richard's reigne, Henry of Bullingbroke, sonne and heir to Iohn of Gaunt,
> the duke of Lancaster, fourth sonne to Edward the third, he claimed the
> crowne, deposd the merthfull king, and as both, you know, in Pomfret
> castle harmlesse Richard was shamefully murthered, and so by Richard's
> death came the house of Lancaster vnto the crowne."

The historical truth of these matters is of little importance in
the present question, which rather depends upon the chronicles
of the sixteenth century, notoriously inaccurate ; and history
must be made to accommodate itself to Shakespeare. The
differences in this instance between the impressions of 1600 and
1619, compared with the amended play, give us good arguments
for certain points connected with the history of the various editions, which the reader will find more fully investigated in the
introduction to the present play.

[1] This, as well as the name of Edward's second son, is an
error. Both mistakes are corrected in the amended play.

and left behinde him Richard, that afterwards was King, Crownde by the name of Richard the second, and he died without an heire.

Edmund of Langly, Duke of Yorke died, and left behind him two daughters, Anne and Elinor.

Lyonell Duke of Clarence died, and left behinde Alice, Anne, and Elinor, that was after married to my father, and by her I claime the Crowne, as the true heire to Lyonell Duke of Clarence, the thirde sonne to Edward the third. Now, sir. In the time of Richards raigne, Henry of Bullingbrooke, sonne and heire to Iohn of Gaunt, the Duke of Lancaster fourth soone to Edward the third, he claimde the Crowne, deposde the Merthfull King, and as both you know, in Pomphret Castle harmlesse Richard was shamefully murthered, and so by Richards death came the house of Lancaster vnto the Crowne.

Sal. Sauing your tale my Lord, as I haue heard, in the raigne of Bullenbrooke, the Duke of Yorke did claime the Crowne, and but for Owin Glendor, had bene King.

Yorke. True. But so it fortuned then, by meanes of that monstrous rebel Glendor, the noble Duke of York was done to death, and so euer since the heires of Gaunt have possessed the Crowne. But if the issue of the elder should succeed before the issue of the yonger, then am I lawfull heire vnto the kingdome.

War. What plaine proceedings can be more plaine, hee claimes it from Lyonel Duke of Clarence, the third sonne of Edward the third, and Henry from Iohn of Gaunt the fourth sonne. So that till Lyonels issue fails, his should not raigne. It fails not yet, but flourisheth in thee & in thy sons, braue slips of such a stock. Then noble father, kneele we both togither, and in this priuate place, be we the first to honor him with birthright to the Crown.

Both. Long liue Richard Englands royall King.

Yorke. I thanke you both. But Lords I am not your King, vntil this sword be sheathed euen in the hart blood of the house of Lancaster.

War. Then Yorke aduise thy selfe and take thy time, Claime thou the Crowne, and set thy standard vp, And in the same aduance the milke-white Rose, And then to gard it, will I rouse the Beare,[1] Inuiron'd with ten thousand Ragged-staues To aide and helpe thee for to win thy right, Maugre the proudest Lord [2] of Henries blood, That dares deny the right and claime of Yorke, For why my minde presageth I shall liue. To see the noble Duke of Yorke to be a king.

Yorke. Thanks noble Warwicke, and Yorke doth hope to see, The Earle of Warwicke liue, to be the greatest man in England, but the King. Come lets goe. *[Exet omnes.*

Enter King HENRY, *and the Queene, Duke* HUMPHREY, *the Duke of* SUFFOLKE, *and the Duke of* BUCKING-HAM, *the Cardinall, and Dame* ELNOR COBHAM, *led with the Officers, and then enter to them the Duke of* YORKE, *and the Earles of* SALSBURY *and* WARWICKE.

Kin. Stand foorth Dame Elnor Cobham [3] Duches of Gloster, and here the sentence pronounced against thee for these Treasons, that thou hast committed gainst [4] us, our States and Peeres.

---

[1] The two editions of 1600 read, "I wil rouse the Beare." The edition of 1619 agrees with our text.

[2] The two editions of 1600 read, "Maugre the proudest lords."

[3] This trial is an historical anachronism, having actually taken place some time before Henry's marriage. The same may, of course, be said of the angry scene between the queen and the Duchess of Gloster.

[4] The edition of 1619 reads, "against."

First for thy hainous crimes,[1] thou shalt two daies
in London do penance barefoote in the streetes, with
a white sheete about thy bodie, and a waxe Taper
burning in thy hand. That done, thou shalt be banished for euer into the Ile of Man, there to ende thy
daies, and this is our sentence erreuocable. Away
with her.

Eln. Euen to my death, for I have lived too long.
> [*Exet some with* ELNOR.

Kin. Greeue not noble vnckle, but be thou glad,
In that these Treasons thus are come to light,
Least God had pourde his vengeance on thy head,
For her offences that thou heldst so deare.

Hum. Oh gratious Henry, giue me leaue awhile,
To leave your grace, and to depart away,
For sorrowes teares hath gripte my aged heart,
And makes[2] the fountaines of mine eyes to swell,
And therefore good my Lord, let me depart.

Kin. With all my hart good vnkle, when you please,
Yet ere thou goest, Humphrey resigne thy staffe,
For Henry will be no more protected,
The Lord shall be my guide[3] both for my land and me.

Hum. My staffe, I noble Henry, my life and all.
My staffe, I yceld as willing to be thine,[4]
As erst thy noble father made it mine,[5]
And euen as willing at thy feete I leaue it,
As others would ambitiously receiue it,
And long hereafter when I am dead and gone,
May honourable peace attend thy throne.

---

[1] The edition of 1619 reads, " crime."
[2] Probably " make."
[3] Perhaps " guide."
[4] This line is inadvertently omitted in the two editions of 1600.
[5] The edition of 1619 reads,—
> " As ere thy noble father made it mine."

And this alteration, which is far from being either an improvement, or in any way necessary for the sense, is adopted by Mr
Knight.

Kin. Vncle Gloster, stand vp and go in peace,
No lesse beloued of vs, then when
Thou weart Protector ouer my land.[1] [*Exet* GLOSTER.
Queene. Take vp the staffe, for here it ought to stand,
Where should it be, but in King Henries hand?
Yorke. Please it your Maiestie, this is the day
That was appointed for the combating
Betweene the Armourer and his man, my Lord,
And they are readie when your grace doth please.
Kin. Then call them forth, that they may trie their
rightes.

*Enter at one doore the Armourer and his neighbours,
drinking to him so much that he is drunken,[2] and
he enters with a drum before him, and his staffe
with a sandbag fastened to it,[3] and at the other
doore, his man with a drum and sand-bagge and
Prentises drinking to him.*

1. *Neigh.* Here neighbor Hornor, I drink to you
in a cup of Sacke.
And feare not neighbor, you shall do well inough.

---

[1] The edition of 1619 reads " ouer this my land."

[2] " This year [1445] an armourer's servant in London appeled
his maister of treason, which offered to be tried by battle. At
the day assigned, the friends of the master brought him malmsye
and *aqua vitæ* to comfort him withall : for it was the cause of
his and their discomfort ; for he poured in so much, that when
he came into the place in Smithfielde where he should fight,
both his witte and strength failed him ; and so he being a tall
and hardy personage, overloaded with hote drink, was vanquished of his servant, being but a coward, and a wretch, whose
body was drawn to Tyburn, and he hanged and beheaded."—
Grafton's " Chronicle," p. 594.

[3] According to the old law of duels, persons of inferior rank
fought with an ebon staff or battoon, to the farther end of which
was fixed a bag crammed hard with sand. Butler alludes to
this when he says :—

> " Engag'd with money-bags, as bold
> As men with sand-bags did of old."

2. *Neigh.* And here, neighbor, heres a cup of Charneco.[1]

3. *Neigh.* Heres a pot of good double beere, neighbor drinke
And be merry, and feare not your man.

Arm. Let it come, yfaith ile pledge you all,
And a figge for Peter.

1. *Pren.* Here Peter I drinke to thee, and be not
affeard.

2. *Pren.* Here Peter, heres a pint of Claret-wine
for thee.

3. *Pren.* And heres a quart for me, and be merry
Peter,
And feare not thy maister, fight for credit of the Pren-
tises.

Peter. I thank you all, but ile drink no more,
Here Robin, and if I die, here I give thee my ham-
mer,
And Will, thou shalt haue my aperne, and here Tom,
Take all the mony that I haue.[2]

O Lord blesse me, I pray God, for I am neuer able

---

[1] A sweet wine ; so called from Charneco, a village near Lis-
bon, where it is made.   Allusions to it are common in writers of
the period.   In " The Discovery of a London Monster called the
Black Dog of Newgate," 1612, we have the following mention of
it amongst several other wines : " Room for a customer, quoth
I.   So in I went, where I found English, Scotish, Welch, Irish,
Dutch, and French, in several rooms : some drinking the neat
wine of Orleans, some the Gascony, some the Bourdeaux ; there
wanted neither sherry, sack, nor charnoco, maligo, nor peeter
seemine, amber-colour'd candy, nor liquorish Ipocras, brown
belov'd bastard, fat aligant, or any quick-spirited liquor that
might draw their wits into a circle to see the devil by imagination."   Part of this curious quotation is given in the variorum
Shakespeare under Warburton's name, but it was communicated
to him by Theobald.   See Nichol's " Illustrations of Literature," vol. ii. p. 437.

[2] The two editions of 1600 read, " Take all my money that I
have."   It may be worthy of observation, that the later editions
of our play read *Horner* instead of *Hornor*.

to deal with my maister, he hath learnt so much fence
alreadie.

Sal. Come leaue your drinking, and fall to blowes.
Sirrha, whats thy name?

Peter. Peter forsooth.¶

Sal. Peter, what more?

Peter. .Thumpe.

Sal. Thumpe, then see that thou thumpe thy
maister.

Arm. Heres to thee[1] neigbhbour, fill all the pots
againe, for before we fight, looke you, I will tell you
my minde, for I am come hither as it were of my
mans instigation,[2] to proue my selfe an honest man,
and Peter a knaue, and so haue at you Peter with
downright blowes, as Beuys of South-hampton fell
vpon Askapart.[3]

---

[1] The two editions of 1600 reads " Here to thee."

[2] The two editions of 1600 reads " as it were of man's instigation," while that of 1619 returns to our text, which is also followed by the amended play.

[3] This allusion to the well-known old romance is not in the
amended play, though frequently inserted from the sketch by
modern editors.   The giant alluded to is thus described :—

> " They had not ridden but a while,
>   Not the mountenance of a mile,
>   But they met with a giaunt,
>   With a full sorry semblant.
>   He was both mighty and strong ;
>   He was full thirtie feet long ;
>   He was bristeled like a sow,
>   A foot there was betweene each brow.
>   His lips wer great, they hanged aside,
>   His eies were hollow, his mouth wide.
>   He was lothly to looke on ;
>   He was lyker a devil than a man.
>   His staffe was a yong oake.
>   He would give a great stroke.
>   Bevis wondrod, I you plight,
>   And asked him what he hight ;
>   My name, sayde he, is Ascapart,
>   Sir Grassy sent me hetherward."

An account of the combat between Sir Bevis and this giant
follows the above, but I cannot find any allusion to the particular
method of striking mentioned in the text.   I quote from an

Peter. Law you now, I told you hees in his fence
alreadie.
[*Alarmes,*[1] *and* PETER *hits him on the head
and fels him.*
Arm. Hold Peter,[2] I confesse, Treason, treason,
[*He dies.*
Peter. O God I giue thee praise. [*He kneeles downe.*
Pren. Ho well done Peter. God saue the King.
Kin. Go take hence that Traitor from our sight,
For by his death we do perceiue his guilt,[3]
And God in iustice hath reuealde to vs,
The truth and innocence of this poore fellow,
Which he had thought to haue murthered wrongfully.
Come fellow, follow vs for thy reward. [*Exet omnis.*

Enter Duke HUMPHREY *and his men in mourning
cloakes.*
Hum. Sirrha, whats a clocke?

---

undated black-letter edition, "imprinted at London by Thomas
East, dwelling in Aldersgate streete, at the signe of the black
horse." According to Steevens, the figures of these combatants
are still preserved on the gates of Southampton ; and there certainly is some uncouth-looking sculpture that may perhaps have
its subject so interpreted.

[1] The word "and" is omitted in the edition of 1819.

[2] The real names of these combatants, says Douce, were John
Daveys and William Catour, as appears from the original pre-
cept to the sheriffs still remaining in the Exchequer, command-
ing them to prepare the barriers in Smithfield for the combat.
The names of the sheriffs were Godfrey Boloyne and Robert
Horne; and the latter, which occurs in the page of Fabian's
"Chronicle" that records the duel might have suggested the
name of *Horner* to Shakespeare. See more on this subject in
Douce's "Illustrations of Shakespeare," vol. ii. p. 8.

[3] According to the ancient opinion of duelling, the vanquished
person not only lost his life but his reputation, and his death
was always regarded as a certain evidence of his guilt. Bowle
adduces a similar instance in a duel in 1380, related by Muri-
muth, which concludes with the following apposite quotation :
"Magna fuit evidentia quod militis causa erat vera, ex quo mors
alterius sequebatur."

Seruing. Almost ten my Lord.

Hum. Then is that wofull houre hard at hand,
That my poor Lady should come by this way,
In shamefull penance wandring in the streetes,
Sweete Nell, ill can thy noble minde abrooke,
The abiect people gazing on thy face,
With enuious lookes laughing at thy shame,[1]
That earst did follow thy proud Chariot wheeles,
When thou didst ride in tryumph through the streetes.

Enter Dame ELNOR COBHAM *bare-foote, and a white
   sheete about her, with a waxe candle in her hand,
   and verses written on her backe and pind on,*[2] *and
   accompanied with the Sheriffes of London, and Sir*
   JOHN STANDLY, *and Officers with billes and hol-
   bards.*

Seruing. My gratious Lord, see where my Lady
     comes,
Please it your grace, weele take her from the Sheriffes?

---

[1] This was adopted without alteration in the first folio edition
of the amended play, but in the folio of 1632 we have, "*still*
laughing at thy shame," the reason of which interpolation is not
very obvious, nor does the addition appear necessary.   Mr
Knight follows Malone in his choice of the text of the second
folio, but Mr Collier has restored the reading of the first folio
and the old editions of the sketch.

[2] Modern editors generally put "with papers pinned upon her
back," as the above part of the stage direction is omitted in the
folio editions of the amended play.   Mr Collier says that modern
editors, by substituting "papers" for "verses," have left it
doubtful what kind of papers were fixed upon the dress of the
duchess, and he accordingly partially restores the old direction.
I say "partially," for Mr Collier inadvertently adds that no
existing authority states that they were *pinned on.*   It seems to
me that the stage direction of the first folio may remain with
propriety unaltered in any future edition of the amended play,
for the addition is no more required on account of the allusion
to the "papers" in the speech of the duchess, than another
interpolation is needed because she was "follow'd with a
rabble."   Such allusions cannot surely demand a stage direction
to assist the capacity of the reader.

Hum. I charge you for your liues stir not a foote,
Nor offer once to draw a weapon here,
But let them do their office as they should.

Eln. Come you my Lord to see my open shame?
Ah Gloster, now thou doest penance too,
See how the giddie people looke at thee,
Shaking their heads, and pointing at thee heere,
Go get thee gone, and hide thee from their sights,
And in thy pent vp studie rue thy shame,
And ban thine enemies. Ah mine and thine.

Hum. Ah Nell, sweet Nell, forget this extreme grief,
And bear it patiently to ease thy heart.

Eln. Ah Gloster teach me to forget my selfe,
For whilst I thinke I am thy wedded wife,
Then thought of this,[1] doth kill my wofull heart.
The ruthlesse flints doth cut my tender feete,
And when I start the cruell people laugh,
And bids[2] me aduised how I tread,
And thus with burning Tapor in my hand,
Malde vp in shame[3] with papers on my backe,
Ah, Gloster, can I endure this and liue.
Sometime ile say I am Duke Humphreys wife,
And he a Prince, Protector of the land,
But so he rulde, and such a Prince he was,
As he stood by, whilst I his forelorne Duches
Was led with shame, and was made a laughing stocke,
To euery idle rascald follower.[4]

---

[1] The edition of 1619 reads, "the thought of this."

[2] Perhaps "bid."

[3] The amended play reads, "mayl'd vp in shame," while modern editions have "mall'd up in shame;" but, from the spelling of the word in our text, it seems to be a question whether *maul'd* is not the true reading, at least of the old play. The emendation would perhaps express *wrapped up in a rough manner*, so that Johnson's explanation would still hold good. See Collier's "Shakespeare," vol. v. p. 148.

[4] The two editions of 1600 read, "To euery idle rascall follower," and the amended play adopts their reading. It was merely an older form of the word.

Hum. My louely Nell, what wouldst thou haue me
do?
Should I attempt to rescue thee from hence,
I shoulde incurre the danger of the law,
And thy disgrace would not be shadowed so.
　　Eln. Be thou milde, and stir not at my disgrace,[1]
Vntill the axe of death hang ouer[2] thy head,
As shortly it will be. For Suffolke he,
The new made Duke, that may do all in all
With her that loues him so, and hates vs all,
And impious Yorke and Bewford that false Priest,
Haue all lymde bushes to betraie thy wings,
And flie thee how thou can [3] they will intangle thee.

　　　　　Enter a Herald of Armes.

　　Mer. I summon your Grace, vnto his highnesse
Parlament holden at saint Edmunds-Bury, the first of
the next month.
　　Hum. A Parlament and our consent neuer craude
Therein before. This is sodeine.[4]
Well, we will be there.　　　　　[*Exet. Herald.*
Maister Sheriffe, I pray proceede no further against
　　my
Lady, then the course of law extendes.
　　Sher. Please it your grace, my office here doth
　　end,
And I must deliuer her to Sir Iohn Standly,
To be conducted into the Ile of Man.

---

　　[1] This is intended to be a question. According to Hall " the
duke of Gloucester toke all these thynges paciently, and sayd
litle."
　　[2] The edition of 1619 reads, " ore."
　　[3] The edition of 1619 reads, " canst," instead of " can."
　　[4] The word " sodeine " is omitted in the edition of 1619, and
this part of the speech breaks off suddenly. This astonishment
of Gloster is expressed apparently before he recollects he had
resigned " his staffe," or it would be inconsistent with the previous scene.

Hum. Must you sir Iohn conduct my Lady?

Stan. I my gratious Lord, for so it is decreede,
And I am so commanded by the King.

Hum. I pray you Sir Iohn, vse her neare the worse,
In that I intreat[1] you vse her well.
The world may smile againe[2] and I may liue,
To do you fauour if you do it her,
And so sir Iohn farewell.

Eln. What gone my Lord, and bid me not[3] farwell?

Hum. Witnesse my bleeding heart, I cannot stay
to speake.   [*Exet* HUMPHREY *and his men.*

Eln. Then is he gone, is noble Gloster gone,
And doth Duke Humphrey now forsake me too?
Then let me haste from out faire Englands boundes,
Come Standly come, and let vs haste away.

Stan. Madam lets go vnto some house hereby,
Where you may shift your selfe before we go.

Eln. Ah good sir Iohn my shame cannot be hid,
Nor put away with casting off my sheete:
But come let vs go, maister Sheriffe farewell,
Thou hast but done thy office as thou shouldst.

                                        [*Exet omnes.*

Enter to the Parlament.

Enter two Heralds before, then the Duke of BUCKING-
HAM, *and the Duke of* SUFFOLKE, *and then the
Duke of* YORKE, *and the Cardinall of* WINCHES-
TER, *and then the King and the Queene,*[4] *and then
the Earle of* SALISBURY, *and the Earle of* WAR-
WICKE.

Kin. I wonder our vnkle Gloster staies so long.

---

[1] This word is rather curiously transposed in the amended
play.

[2] In other words, as Johnson observes, the world may again
look favourably upon me.

[3] So also the amended play, but the edition of 1619 reads,
"and bid not me."

[4] The two editions of 1600 read "the king and queene."

Queene. Can you not see, or will you not per-
ceiue,
How that ambitious Duke doth vse himselfe?
The time hath bene, but now that time is past,[1]
That none so humble as Duke Humphrey was :
But now let one meete him euen in the morne,
When euery one will giue the time of day,
And he will neither moue [2] nor speake to vs.
See you not how the Commons follow him [3]
In troupes, crying, God saue the good Duke Hum-
phrey,
And with long life, Iesus preserue his grace,[4]
Honouring him as if he were their King.[5]
Gloster is no litle man in England,
And if he list to stir commotions,
Tys likely that the people will follow him.
My Lord, if you imagine there is no such thing,
Then let it passe, and call it a womans feare.
My Lord of Suffolke, Buckingham, and Yorke,
Disproue my Alligations if you can,
And by your speeches, if you can disproue me,
I will subscribe and say, I wronged the Duke.

---

[1] The edition of 1619 reads, "but now the time is past."
[2] The edition of 1619 reads, "Yet he will neither moue."
[3] The word "how" is omitted in the two editions of 1600.
[4] This line is entirely omitted in the edition of 1619, and accordingly we do not find it in Mr Knight's edition.
[5] The two editions of 1600 read "a king," instead of "their
king." Malone, who has collated his copy of the edition of
1600, "printed by W. W.," with a copy of the 1594 edition formerly in his possession, distinctly writes—

"*Thinking* him as if he were their king,"

as the reading of his copy of the first edition. If so, it must
have been a different copy from that now in the Bodleian, from
which the present text is reprinted, and another instance of the
curious variations in different copies of the same editions, which
were first discovered by Steevens (Boswell's "Malone," vol. x.
p. 73), and recently applied to good use by Mr Collier.

Suf. Well hath your grace foreseen into that Duke,
And if I had bene licenst first to speake,
I thinke I should haue told your graces tale.
Smooth runs the brooke whereas the streame is
    deepest.
No, no, my soueraigne, Gloster is a man
Vnsounded yet and full of deepe deceit.

Enter the Duke of SOMERSET.

Kin. Welcome Lord Somerset, what newes from
    France?
Som. Cold newes, my Lord, and this it is,
That all your holds and Townes within those Terri-
    tores
Is ouercome my Lord, all is lost.[1]
Kin. Cold newes indeed Lord Somerset,
But Gods will be done.
    Yorke. Cold newes for me,[2] for I had hope of
    France,
Euen as I haue of fertill England.

Enter Duke HUMPHREY.

Hum. Pardon my liege, that I haue staied so long.
Suf. Nay, Gloster know, that thou art come too
    soone,
Vnlesse thou proue more loyall then thou art,
We do arrest thee on high treason here.
    Hum. Why Suffolkes Duke thou shalt[3] not see me
    blush

---

[1] The two editions of 1600 read, "and all is lost."

[2] This and the next line are identically the same with the first two lines of York's former speech at p. 420 of this volume. The author of our play is apparently fond of the expression, "cold newes."

[3] The 1623 edition of the amended play reads, "Well, Suffolk, thou shalt," and the 1632 edition, "Well Suffolk, *yet* thou shalt." Malone and Knight read, "Well, Suffolk's duke, thou shalt;" while Collier follows the reading of the second folio.

Nor change mine countenance for thine arrest,
Whereof am I guiltie,[1] who are my accusers?
    Yorke. Tis thought my Lord, your grace tooke
    bribes from France,
And stopt the soldiers of their paie,
By which [2] his Maiestie hath lost all France.
    Hum. Is it but thought so, and who are they that
    thinke so?
So God helpe me,[3] as I haue watcht the night
Euer intending good for England still,
That penie that euer I tooke from France,
Be brought against me at the iudgement day.
I neuer robd the souldiers of their paie,
Many a pound of mine owne propper cost
Haue I sent ouer for the soldiers wants,
Because I would not racke the needie Commons.
    Car. In your Protectorship you did deuise
Strange torments for offenders, by which meanes
England hath bene defamde by tyrannie.
    Hum. Why tis wel knowne that whilst I was pro-
    tector
Pitie was all the fault that was in me,
A murtherer or foule felonous [4] theefe,
That robs and murthers silly passengers,
I tortord aboue the rate of common law.
    Suf. Tush my Lord, these be things of no account,
But greater matters are laid vnto your charge,
I do arrest thee on high treason here,
And commit thee to my good Lord Cardinall,
Vntil such time as thou canst cleare thy selfe.

---

[1] The edition of 1619 reads, "Whereof I am guilty," a change
for the worse, though retained by Mr Knight.
[2] The edition of 1619 reads, "Through which."
[3] The edition of 1619 reads, "So God me helpe."
[4] For "felonious," as in the two editions of 1600 and that of
1619. "Felonous" was the older form of the word, and occurs
in "Maundeville's Travels," edit. 1839, p. 291.

Kin. Good vncle obey to his arrest,
I haue no doubt but thou shalt cleare thy selfe,
My conscience tels me thou art innocent.

Hum. Ah gratious Henry these daies are dangerous
And would my death might end these miseries,
And staie their moodes for good King Henries sake,
But I am made the Prologue to their plaie,
And thousands more must follow after me,
That dreads[1] not yet their liues destruction.
Suffolkes hatefull tongue blabs his harts malice,
Bewfords firie eyes showes[2] his enuious minde,
Buckinghams proud lookes bewraies[3] his cruel thoughts,
And dogged Yorke that leuels at the Moone[4]
Whose ouerweening arme I haue held backe.
All you haue ioynd to betraie me thus :
And you my gratious Lady and soueraigne mistresse,
Causelesse haue laid complaints vpon my head,
I shall not want false witnesses inough,
That so amongst you, you may haue my life.
The Prouerbe no doubt will be well performde,[5]
A staffe is quickly found to beate a dog.

Suf. Doth he not twit our soueraigne Lady here,
As if that she with ignomious[6] wrong,

---

[1] Probably "dread."

[2] Probably "showe."

[3] Probably "bewraie."

[4] That is, *aims,* meaning to express York's great ambition. So in the "Tempest," act ii. sc. 1, Gonzalo says, "You are gentlemen of braue mettle ; you would lift the moon out of her sphere, if she would continue in it fiue weeks without changing." In Rider's Latin Dictionarie, 1640, we have "aime or levell." In "Titus Andronicus," act iv. sc. 3, Marcus says :

> "My Lord, I aim a mile beyond the moon ;
> Your letter is with Jupiter by this."

[5] The word "well" is omitted in the edition of 1619, though found in the amended play, which reads, "affected" for "performed."

[6] For "ignominious," as in the two editions of 1600, that of 1619, and the amended play.

Had sobornde or hired some to sweare against his
  life.
Queene. I but I can giue the loser leaue to speake.[1]
Hum. Far truer spoke than ment, I loose indeed,
Beshrow the winners hearts, they plaie me false.
Buc. Hele wrest the sence and keep vs here all day,
My Lord of Winchester, see him sent away.
Car. Who's within there? Take in Duke Humphrey,
And see him garded sure within my house.
Hum. O! thus King Henry casts away his crouch.
Before his legs can beare his bodie vp,
And puts his watchfull shepheard from his side,
Whilst wolues stand snarring who shall bite him first.
Farwell my soueraigne, long maist thou enjoy,
Thy fathers happie daies free from annoy.[2]
        [*Exet* HUMPHREY, *with the Cardinals men.*
Kin. My Lords, what to your wisdoms shal seem
  best,
Do and vndo as if our selfe were here.
Queene. What will your highnesse leaue the Parla-
  ment?
Kin. I Margaret. My heart is kild with griefe,
Where I may sit and sigh in endlesse mone,
For who's a Traitor, Gloster he is none.
        [*Exet King*, SALSBURY, *and* WARWICKE.
Queene. Then sit we downe againe my Lord Car-
  dinall,

---

[1] In Nash's " Pierce Penilesse," 1592, ed. Collier, p. 8, nearly
the same expression occurs : " I, I, well giue loosers leaue to
talke," so that it may perhaps be a proverb. It is repeated in
the amended play. It is almost unnecessary to observe that
"I" always stands for "ay" in works of this period. In the
editions of 1600 the "I" is changed to "Yea;" but that of
1619 generally retains the old form. The edition of 1619 here
omits the first "I."

[2] That is, *annoyance.* The older form of the word, occurring
also in " Piers Plowman." The still older word, *annuy,* occurs
in MS. Harl. 2277, fol. 46.

Suffolke, Buckingham, Yorke, and Somerset.
Let vs consult of proud Duke Humphries fall.
In mine opinion it were good he dide,
For safetie of our King and Common-wealth.

Suf. And so thinke I Madame, for as you know,
If our King Henry had shooke hands with death,
Duke Humphrey then would looke to be our King :
And it may be by pollicie he workes,
To bring to passe the thing which now we doubt,
The Foxe barkes not when he would steale the Lambe,
But if we take him ere he do the deed,
We should not question if that he should liue.
No.   Let him die, in that he is a Foxe,[1]
Least that in liuing he offend vs more.

Car. Then let him die before the Commons know,
For feare that they do rise in Armes for him.

Yorke. Then do it sodainly my Lords

Suf. Let that be my Lord Cardinals charge & mine.

Car. Agreed, for hee's already kept within my house.

Enter a Messenger.[2]

Queene. How now, sirrha, what news?

Mess. Madame, I bring you newes from Ireland,

---

[1] This and the next line are given to York in the edition of
1619 ; but, although this is sanctioned by the authority of Mr
Knight, the arrangement in our text seems the right one.   The
next speech that York makes does not lead the reader to suppose
that he had taken any part in the previous conversation ; and,
in the amended play, it will be found that the first line is in
Suffolk's speech.   The commentators are somewhat confused in
their explanations of the speech as it stands in the amended play ;
but, if they had carefully read the present sketch, no difficulties
would have been found.

[2] The first folio alters this to, "Enter a poste," which shows
that he was specially sent, and, as many of the directions do,
illustrates the next line :

"Great lords, from Ireland am I come amain."

Modern editors have unnecessarily returned to the older reading.

The wilde Onele my Lords, is vp in Armes,
With troupes of Irish Kernes that vncontrold,
Doth plant themselues[1] within the English pale.

    Queene. What redresse shal we haue for this my
      Lords?

    Yorke. Twere very good[2] that my Lord of Somerset
That fortunate Champion were sent ouer,
And burnes and spoiles the Country as they goe.[3]
To keepe in awe the stubborne Irishmen,
He did so much good when he was in France.

    Som. Had Yorke bene there with all his far fecht
Pollices, he might haue lost as much as I.

    Yorke. I, for Yorke would haue lost his liue before
That France[4] should haue reuolted from Englands
      rule.

    Som. I so thou might'st, and yet haue gouernd worst
      then I.

    York. What worse then nought, then a shame
      take all.

    Som. Shame on thy selfe, that wisheth shame.

    Queene. Somerset forbeare, good Yorke be patient,
And do thou take in hand to crosse the seas,
With troupes of Armed men to quell the pride
Of those ambitious Irish that rebell.

    Yorke. Well Madame sith your grace is so content,

---

[1] The two editions of 1600 read, " Do plant themselues."

[2] The edition of 1619 omits the word " very."

[3] This line is in the wrong place. It ought properly to be at the end of the messenger's speech, four lines above, and it is so arranged in the two editions of 1600, and in that of 1619. The end of that speech would then be as follows :

> " Doth plant themselues within the English pale,
> And burnes and spoiles the country as they goe."

We should of course read " burne and spoil," the bad grammar having probably crept in owing to its erroneous position in York's speech.

[4] "The word "France" is inadvertently omitted in the two editions of 1600, but supplied in that of 1619.

Let me haue some bands of chosen soldiers,
And Yorke shall trie his fortune against those
  kernes.[1]
Queene. Yorke thou shalt. My Lord of Buckingham
Let it be your charge to muster vp such souldiers
As shall suffise him in these needfull warres.
Buc. Madame I will, and leauie such a band
As soone shall ouercome those Irish Rebels,
But Yorke, where shall those soldiers staie for
  thee ?
Yorke. At Bristow, I wil[2] expect them ten daies
  hence.
Buc. Then thither shall they come, and so farewell.
         [Exet BUCKINGHAM.
Yorke. Adieu my Lord of Buckingham.
Queene. Suffolke remember what you haue to
  do.
And you Lord Cardinall concerning Duke Humphrey,
Twere good that you did see to it in time,
Come let vs go, that it may be performde.
       [Exit omnis, Manit YORKE.

---

[1] " Tertius ordo comprehendit alios etiam pedites, ac levis
armaturæ Machærophores, ab Hybernis *Karni* dicuntur—"
" Ricardi Stanihursti De rebus in Hibernia gestis liber," Antwerp,
1584, lib. i. p. 42. In a passage quoted by Bowle, from an early
English translation of the same book, we have the following
account : " The kerne is an ordinary souldier, using for weapon
his sword and target, and sometimes his peece, being commonly
good markmen. Kerne signifieth a shower of hell, because they
are taken for no better than for rake hells, or the deuils blacke-
garde." See also another description of them in Dymoke's
" Treatise on Ireland," in an Harleian MS., which I passed
through the press for the Irish Archæological Society, with
an introduction by Mr Butler. The two editions of 1600 read
"gainst those kernes," while in that of 1619 we have—

  " And Yorke shall trie his fortunes 'gainst those kernes."

[2] The edition of 1619 reads, " I'le."

York. Now Yorke bethink thy self and rowse thee
  vp,
Take time whilst it is offered thee so faire,
Least when thou wouldst, thou canst it not
  attaine,[1]
Twas men I lackt, and now they giue them me,
And now whilst I am busie in Ireland,
I haue seduste a headstrong Kentishman,
Iohn Cade of Ashford,
Vnder the title of Iohn Mortemer,[2]
To raise commotion, and by that meanes
I shall perceiue how the common people
Do affect the claime and house of Yorke,
Then if he haue successe in his affaires,
From Ireland then comes Yorke againe,
To reape the haruest which that coystrill sowed,
Now if he should be taken and condemd,
Heele nere confesse that I did set him on,
And therefore ere I go ile send him word,
To put in practise and to gather head,
That so soone as I am gone he may begin
To rise in Armes with troupes of country swaines,
To helpe him to performe this enterprise.
And then Duke Humphrey, he well made away,
None then can stop the light to Englands Crowne,
But Yorke can tame and headlong pull them downe.
                    [*Exet* YORKE.

---

[1] The two editions of 1600 read, " thou canst not it attaine."
[2] The two editions of 1600 read,

      "Vnder the title of Sir Iohn Mortimer,"

which addition does not agree with the scene where Cade
knights himself.   The edition of 1619 here adds the following
line :

      " For he is like him euery kinde of way,"

which is neither in the earlier editions, nor does it occur in the
amended play.   This of itself is nearly sufficient to show that
the edition of 1619 must have been printed from another copy.

Then the Curtaines being drawne,[1] *Duke* HUMPHREY
  *is discouered in his bed, and two men lying on his
  brest and smothering him in his bed. And then
  enter the Duke of* SUFFOLKE *to them.*

Suf. IIow now sirs, what haue you dispatcht him?
One. 1 my Lord, hees dead I warrant you.
Suf. Then see the cloathes laid smooth about him still,
That when the King comes, he may perceiue
No other, but that he dide of his owne accord.
  2. All things is hansome[2] now my Lord.
Suf. Then draw the Curtaines againe and get you
  gone,
And you shall haue your firme reward anon.
                                        [*Exet murtherers.*

Then enter[3] *the King and Queene, the Duke of* BUCK-
  INGHAM, *and the Duke of* SOMERSET, *and the
  Cardinall.*

King. My Lord of Suffolke go call our vnkle
  Gloster,

---

[1] In the simplicity of our old stage, the different apartments
were only separated by a curtain. See Collier's " Shakespeare,"
vol. v. p. 168. The curtain which hangs in the front of the present stage, drawn up by lines and pullies, which was the inven-
tion of Inigo Jones, and used in his masques, was an apparatus
not then known. At the time our play was acted, the curtains
opened in the middle, and were drawn backwards and forwards
on an iron rod. In " Lady Alimony," 1659, quoted by Malone's
"Be your stage-curtains artificially drawn, and so covertly
shrowded, that the squint-eyed groundling may not peep in."
There is also an old book, called " The Curtain-Drawer of the
World," 1612, which is in its very title an illustration of
Jacques's celebrated comparison. See also Boalstuau's " Theatre, or Rule of the World," translated by Alday, 1581.

[2] This bad English may have been intentionally put into the
mouth of the murderer ; but it is erroneously put in Suffolk's
speech in the first folio of the amended play. The second folio
corrects it.

[3] The word "then" is omitted in the edition of 1619.

Tell him this day we will that he do cleare himselfe.
   Suf. I will my Lord.   [*Exet* SUFFOLKE.
   King. And good my Lords proceed no further
      against our vnkle Gloster,[1]
Then by iust proofe you can affirme,
For as the sucking childe or harmlesse lambe,
So is he innocent of treason to our state.

Enter SUFFOLKE.

How now Suffolke, where's our unkle?
   Suf. Dead in his bed, my Lord Gloster is dead.[2]
              [*The King falles in a sound.*
   Queen. Ay—me, the King is dead : help, help, my
      Lords.
   Suf. Comfort my Lord, gratious Henry comfort.
   King. What doth mv Lord of Suffolk bid me com-
      fort?
Came he euen now to sing a Rauens note,
And thinkes he that the cherping of a Wren,
By crying comfort through a hollow voice,
Can satisfie my griefes, or ease my heart :
Thou balefull messenger out of my sight,
For euen in thine eye-bals[3] murther sits.
Yet do not goe.   Come Basaliske
And kill the silly gazer with thy lookes.[4]

---

   [1] The edition of 1619 reads, " proceed no further 'gainst our vnckle."
   [2] The two editions of 1600 punctuate this line rather differently :
          " Dead in his bed, my lord, Gloster is dead ;"
while the edition of 1619 reads, " My lord of Gloster's dead, which apparently confirms the punctuation of the first edition. Each of the three readings is perfectly consonant with sense and metre.
   [3] The two editions of 1600 read " thy " instead of thine."
   [4] The word " silly " is omitted in the edition of 1619, and also by Mr Knight. " Plinius sayth there is a wilde beast called Catobletas great noyeing to mankinde ; for all that see his eyen

Queene. Why do you rate my Lord of Suffolke thus,
As if that he had causde Duke Humphreys death?
The Duke and I too, you know were enemies,
And you had[1] best say that I did murther him.
    King. Ah woe is me, for wretched Glosters death.
    Queene. Be woe for me more wretched then he was,[2]
What doest thou turne away and hide thy face?
I am no loathsome leoper looke on me,
Was I for this nigh wrackt vpon the sea,
And thrise by aukward winds[3] driuen back from Eng-
    lands bounds,
What might it bode, but that well foretelling
Winds, said, seeke not a scorpions neast.

    Enter the Earles of WARWICKE *and* SALISBURY.

    War. My Lord, the Commons like an angrie hiue
    of bees,[4]

---

should dye anone, and the same kinde hath the cockatrice."—
"Bartholomæus de prop. rerum," lib. xviii. cap. 16. The same
property is also mentioned by Pliny of the basilisk. So, in
"Albion's England," as quoted by Reed,

> "As Æsculap an herdsman did espie,
> That did with easy sight enforce a *basilisk* to flye,
> Albeit naturally that beast doth murther with the eye."

[1] The edition of 1619 reads, 'and y'had."
[2] Johnson explains this, "Let not woe be to thee for Gloster,
but for me." The amended play reads "is" instead of "was;"
but our reading appears better, because the Queen is alluding to
the former misery of Gloster, which she now wishes the king to
believe has fallen upon herself on account of his death.
[3] Some editors have changed "aukward" to "adverse" in
the corresponding passage in the amended play, which reads
"twice" instead of "thrise." In "Cymbeline" we have the
expression, "rudest wind." Malone quotes the following apposite passage from Drayton :

> "And undertook to travaile dangerous waies,
> Driven by awkward winds and boisterous seas."

[4] The edition of 1619 reads, "an hungry hiue of bees," the
reading adopted by Mr Knight, though, perhaps, few readers
will think it an improvement.

Run vp and downe, caring not whom they sting,
For good Duke Humphreys death,[1] whom they report
To be murthered by Suffolke and the Cardinall
here.
   King. That he is dead good Warwick, is too true,
But how he died God knowes, not Henry.[2]
   War. Enter his priuie chamber my Lord and view
the bodie.
Good father staie you with the rude multitude, till I
returne.
   Salb. I will sonne.   *[Exet* SALBURY.
   [WARWICKE *drawes the curtaines and showes*
       Duke HUMPHREY *in his bed.*
   King. Ah vnkle Gloster, heauen receive thy soule.
Farewell poore Henries ioy, now thou art gone.
   War. Now by his soule that tooke our shape vpon
him,
To free vs from his fathers dreadfull curse,
I am resolu'd that violent hands were laid,
Vpon the life of this thrise famous Duke.[3]
   Suf. A dreadfull oth sworn with a solemne toong,
What instance giues Lord Warwicke for these words?
   War. Oft haue I seene a timely parted ghost,[4]

---

   [1] The word "duke" is omitted in the two editions of 1600.
   [2] Johnson says that "Henry" is here used as a word of three
syllables.
   [3] The word "thrise" is omitted in the two editions of 1600.
   [4] The following passage in Porter's "Two Angry Women of
Abingdon," 1599, appears almost a parody :

      "Oft have I heard a timely married girl
       That newly left to call her mother mam."

Timely-parted means *recently* in this instance, though some of
the commentators explain it by "in proper time." The commentators give us long notes on the incorrect application of the
word *ghost;* but it is again used in the same sense in this volume :

      "Sweet father, to thy *murdered ghost* I swear ;"

and it appears to have been used somewhat indiscriminately by
our early writers.

Of ashie semblance,[1] pale and bloodlesse,
But loe the blood is setled in his face,[2]
More better coloured then when he liu'd,
His well proportioned beard made rough and sterne,
His fingers spred abroad[3] as one that graspt for life,
Yet was by strength surprisde, the least of these are
  probable,
It cannot chuse but he was murthered.[4]
  Queene. Suffolke and the Cardinall had him in
  charge,
And they I trust sir, are no murtherers.
  War. I, but twas well knowne[5] they were not his
  friends,
And tis well seene he found some enemies.
  Car. But haue you[6] no greater proofes then these?
  War. Who sees a hefer dead and bleeding fresh,
And sees hard-by a butcher with an axe,
But will suspect twas he that made the slaughter?
Who findes the partridge in the puttocks[7] neast,

---

[1] So Spenser—

  " Ye pallid spirits, and ye ashy ghosts !"

[2] The two editions of 1600 read, "in the face."

[3] That is, widely distended. So in Peacham's "Complete
Gentleman," 1627 : " Herein was the Emperor Domitian so
cunning, that let a boy at a good distance off hold up his hand
and stretch his fingers *abroad*, he would shoot through the
spaces without touching the boy's hand, or any finger."—See
Malone's Shakespeare by Boswell, vol. xviii. 264.

[4] So in "A Midsummer Night's Dream," Hermia says to
Demetrius,

  " It cannot be but thou hast murder'd him."

The passage in the amended play (act iii. sc. 2) is very nearly
the same with the line just given :

  " It cannot be but he was murder'd here."

[5] The edition of 1619 reads, " but tis well knowne."

[6] The edition of 1619 reads " ye."

[7] A kite. See Bewick's "History of British Birds," edit.
1797, vol. i. p. 21. In a later edition of this work, the same
provincial expression is given to the buzzard.

But will imagine how the bird came there,
Although the kyte soare with vnbloodie beake ?[1]
Euen so suspitious is this Tragidie.

   Queene. Are you the kyte Bewford, where's your
     talants ?[2]
Is Suffolke the butcher, where's his knife ?

   Suf. I weare no knife to slaughter sleeping men,
But heres a vengefull sword rusted with case,[3]
That shall be scoured in his rankorous heart,
That slanders me with murthers crimson badge,
Say if thou dare, proud Lord of Warwickshire,
That I am guiltie in Duke Humphreys death.
                        [*Exet Cardinall.*

   War. What dares not Warwicke, if false Suffolke
     dare him ?

   Queene. He dares not calme his contumelious spirit,
Nor cease to be an arrogant controwler,
Though Suffolk dare him twentie hundreth times.

   War. Madame be still,[4] with reuerence may I say it,
That euery word you speake in his defence,
Is slaunder to your royall Maiestie.

   Suf. Blunt witted Lord, ignoble in thy words,
If euer Lady wronged her Lord so much,
Thy mother tooke vnto her blamefull bed,
Some sterne vntutred churle, and noble stocke
Was graft with crabtree slip, whose frute thou art,
And neuer of the Neuels noble race.

   War. But that the guilt of murther bucklers thee,
And I should rob the deaths man of his fee,
Quitting thee thereby of ten thousand shames,
And that my soueraignes presence makes me mute,
I would false murtherous coward on thy knees

---

  [1] The edition of 1619 reads, "with the vnbloody beake."
  [2] The edition of 1619 reads, "where's his talents."
  [3] The edition of 1619 reads, "Yet here's a." The word "case" is altered to "ease" in the three other editions.
  [4] The two editions of 1600 read, "Madame, be ye still."

Make thee craue pardon for thy passed speech,
And say it was thy mother that thou meants,
That thou thy selfe was borne in bastardie,
And after all this fearefull homage done,
Giue thee thy hire and send thy soule to 1ell,[1]
Pernitious blood-sucker of sleeping men.

    Suf. Thou shouldst be waking whilst I shead thy
    blood,
If from this presence thou dare go with me.

    War. Away euen now, or I will drag thee hence.
                  ⌊WARWICKE *puls him out.*

    [*Exet* WARWICKE *and* SUFFOLKE, *and then all the*
        Commons within, cries, downe with Suffolke, downe
        with Suffolk. And then enter againe, the Duke of
        SUFFOLKE *and* WARWICKE, *with their weapons*
        drawne.

    Kin. Why how now Lords ?
    Suf. The Traitorous Warwicke with the men of
    Berry,
Set all vpon me mightie soueraigne i [2]

    [*The commons againe cries,*[3] *downe with Suffolke, downe*
        with Suffolke. And then enter from them, the
        Earle of SALBURY.

    Sal. My Lord, the Commons made you word by me,
The vnlesse false Suffolke [4] here be done to death,

---

    [1] The edition of 1619 reads,

        "Giue thee thy hire, and send thee downe to hell ;"

which alteration implies a change of authorship, which the
reader will find more fully exemplified in the introduction to the
present play.

    [2] This last isolated letter is found in the original ; but, as it is
omitted in the later editions, it is most probably merely an error
of the press for a full stop.

    [3] This grammatical error is repeated several times.

    [4] The edition of 1619 more intelligibly reads, " That vnlesse
false Suffolke."

Or banished faire Englands Territories,
That they will erre from your highnesse person,
They say by him the good Duke Humphrey died,
They say by him they feare the ruine of the realme,
And therefore if you loue your subiects weale,
They wish you to banish him from foorth the land.
   Suf. Indeed tis like the Commons rude vnpolisht
    hinds
Would send such message to their soueraigne,
But you my Lord were glad to be imployd,
To trie how quaint an Orator you were,[1]
But all the honour Salsbury hath got,
Is, that he was the Lord Embassador
Sent from a sort of Tinkers to the King.[2]
   [*The Commons cries, an answere from the King,
        my Lord of Salsbury.*

   Kin. Good Salsbury go backe againe to them,
Tell them we thanke them all for their louing care,[3]
And had I not bene[4] cited thus by their meanes,
My selfe had done it.   Therefore here I sweare,
If Suffolke be found to breathe in any place,
Where I haue rule, but three daies more, he dies.
                  [*Exet* SALISBURY.
   Queene. Oh Henry, reuerse the doome of gentle
    Suffolkes banishment.
   Kin. Vngentle Queene to call him gentle Suffolke,
Speake not for him, for in England he shall not rest,

---

[1] It is, perhaps, necessary to observe that "quaint" here means *skilful, dexterous.* So Prospero says, "My quaint Ariel."
[2] A company or body of tinkers. So in "A Midsummer Night's Dream," act iii. sc. 2,
    "The shallowest thick-skin of that barren *sort*."
[3] The two editions of 1600 read,
    "Tell them we thanke them for all their louing care ;"
and the edition of 1619 reads "kind" instead of "louing."
[4] The two editions of 1600 read, "And had not I beene."

If I say, I may relent, but if I sweare, it is irreuocable.
Come good Warwicke [1] and go thou in with me,
For I haue great matters to impart to thee.

[Exet King and WARWICKE, *Manet Queene and* SUFFOLKE.

Queene. Hell fire and vengeance go along with
you,
Theres two of you, the diuell make the third.
Fie womanish man, canst thou not curse thy enemies?
Suf. A plague vpon them, wherefore should I curse
them?
Could curses kill as do the Mandrakes groanes,[2]
I would inuent as many bitter termes
Deliuered strongly through my fixed teeth,
With twise so many signes of deadly hate,
As leaue fast enuy[3] in her loathsome caue,
My toong should stumble in mine earnest words,
Mine eyes should sparkle like the beaten flint,

---

[1] The word "good" is omitted in the two editions of 1600.

[2] Bullein, speaking of Mandragora, says : "They doe affyrme that this herbe commeth of the seede of some convicted dead men ; and also without the death of some lyvinge thinge it cannot be drawen out of the earth to man's use. Therefore they did tie some dogge or some other lyving beast unto the roote thereof wyth a corde, and digged the earth in compass round about, and in the meane tyme stopped their own eares for feare of the terrible shriek and cry of this mandrack. In which cry it doth not onely dye itselfe, but the feare thereof kylleth the dogge or beast which pulleth it out of the earth."—"Bulwarke of Defence against Sickness," fol. 1579, p. 41. This quotation was first made by Reed, and has been inserted by most of the editors. The fabulous accounts, says Johnson, of the plant called a mandrake, give it an inferior degree of animal life, and relate that when it is torn from the ground it groans, and that this groan being fatal to the person who attempts the violence, the practice of those who gather them is to tie one end of a string to the plant, and the other to a dog, upon whom the fatal groan discharges its malignity.

[3] The three other editions read, " as leane facde enuy."

My haire be fixt on end,[1] as one distraught,
And euery ioynt should seeme to curse and ban,
And now me-thinks my burthened hart would breake,
Should I not curse them.   Poison be their drinke,[2]
Gall worse than gall, the daintiest thing they taste.[3]
Their sweetest shade a groue of sypris trees,
Their softest tuch as smart as lyzards stings.
Their musicke frightfull, like the serpents hys.
And boding scrike-oules make the comsort full.
All the foule terrors in darke seated hell.
   Queene. Inough sweete Suffolke, thou torments thy
   selfe.
   Suf. You bad me ban, and will you bid me sease?
Now by this ground that I am banisht from,
Well could I curse away a winters night,
And standing naked on a mountaine top,

---

[1] So the modern editors write, but the folios of the amended
play read, " Mine haire be fixt an end."

[2] Steevens has remarked that part of this speech has been
copied by Lee in his tragedy of " Cæsar Borgia, 4°. Lond. 1680.
As Steevens has not given the passage to which he refers, it may
be as well to insert it here :

> " *Mach.* Nay, since you urge, sir, my heart will break
> Unless I curse 'em !   Poyson be their drink.
>   *Borg.* Gall, gall and wormwood ! Hemlock ! hemlock ! quench 'em.
>   *Mach.* Their sweetest shade a dell of duskish adders.
>   *Borg.* Their fairest prospect, fields of basilisks ;
> Their softest touch, as smart as viper's teeth.
>   *Mach.* Their musick horrid as the hiss of dragons,
> All the foul terrours of dark-seated hell.
>   *Borg.* No more ; thou art one piece with me thyself :
> And now I take a pride in my revenge."

[3] The amended play reads, " the daintiest *that* they taste," and
Theobald wishes to read, " the dainties that," or " the daintiest
meat," because there is a substantive subjoined to every epithet
in the verses that follow.   See Nichols' " Illustrations of the
Literary History of the Eighteenth Century," vol. ii. p. 439,
where will be found a letter from Theobald to Warburton, sug-
gesting the above readings.   But surely, if any alteration is
necessary, it would be safer to return to the reading of the old
edition.

Where byting cold would neuer let grasse grow,
And thinke it but a minute spent in sport.
    Queene. No more. Sweete Suffolke hie thee hence
      to France,
Or liue where thou wilt within this worldes globe,
Ile haue an Irish [1] that shall finde thee out,
And long thou shalt not staie, but ile haue thee
    repelde,
Or venture to be banished my selfe.
Oh let this kisse be printed in thy hand,
That when thou seest it, thou maist think on me.
Away, I say, that I may feele my griefe,
For it is nothing whilst thou standest here.
    Suf. Thus is poore Suffolke ten times banished,
Once by the King, but three times thrise by thee.

Enter VAWSE.

    Queene. How now, whither goes Vawse so fast ?   [Sig. F.]
    Vawse. To signifie vnto his Maiestie,
That Cardinal Bewford is at point of death,
Sometimes he raues and cries as he were madde,
Sometimes he cals vpon Duke Humphries Ghost,
And whispers to his pillow as to him,
And sometime [2] he calles to speake vnto the King,
And I am going to certifie vnto his grace,
That euen now he cald aloude for him.
    Queene. Go then good Vawse and certifie the
      King.
                        [*Exet* VAWSE.
Oh what is worldly pompe, all men must die,
And woe am I for Bewfords heauie ende.
But why mourne I for him, whilst thou art here ?

---

    [1] *i.e.* Iris. See the amended play, act. iii. sc. 2, and Malone's
"Shakespeare" by Boswell, vol. xviij. p. 275. The edition of
1619 corrects "shall," which occurs in the same line, to "shalt."
    [2] The edition of 1619 reads, "sometimes."

Sweete Suffolke hie thee hence to France,
For if the King do come, thou sure must die.
　　Suf. And if I go I cannot liue: but here to
　　die,
What were it else but like a pleasant slumber
In thy lap?[1]
Here could I, could I,[2] breathe my soule into the
　　aire,
As milde and gentle as the new borne babe,
That dies with mothers dugge between his
　　lips,
Where from thy sight[3] I should be raging madde,
And call for thee to close mine eyes,
Or with thy lips to stop my dying soule,
That I might breathe it so into thy bodie,
And then it liu'd in sweete Elyziam,
By thee to die, were but to die in ieast,
From thee to die, were torment more then death,
O let me staie, befall, what may befall.
　　Queene. Oh mightst thou staie with safetie of thy
　　life,
Then shouldst thou staie, but heauens deny it,
And therefore go, but hope ere long to be repelde.
　　Suf. I goe.
　　Queene. And take my heart with thee.
　　　　　　　　　　　　　　　[She kisseth him.
　　Suf. A iewell lockt into the wofulst caske,
That euer yet containde a thing of woorth,
Thus like a splitted barke so sunder we.
This way fall I to deathe.　　*[Exet* SUFFOLKE.
　　Queene. This way for me.　　*[Exet Queene.*

---

[1] This line forms part of the previous one in the edition of
1619.
[2] This repetition does not occur in the edition of 1619.
[3] The edition of 1619 reads, " from my sight," which is clearly
an error.

Enter King and SALSBURY,[1] *and then the Curtaines be drawne, and the Cardinall is discouered in his bed, rauing and staring as if he were madde.*

Car. Oh death, if thou wilt let me liue [2] but one whole yeare,[3]
Ile giue thee as much gold as will purchase such another Iland.

Kin. O see my Lord of Salsbury how he is troubled,

---

[1] This stage direction is as follows in the amended play : "Enter the King, Salisbury, and Warwick, to the Cardinall in bed."

[2] This was probably suggested by the following account in Hall's "Chronicle" : "During these doynges, Henry Beaufford, byshop of Wynchester, and called the ryche Cardynall, departed out of this worlde, and was buried at Wynchester. This man was sonne to Jhon of Gaunte, duke of Lancaster, discended on an honorable lignage, but borne in Baste, more noble of bloud, then notable in learnyng, haut in stomacke, and hygh in countenaunce, ryche aboue measure of all men, and to fewe liberal, disdaynfull to his kynne, and dreadfull to his louers, preferrynge money before frendshippe, many thinges begynning, and nothing perfourmyng. His covetous insaciable, and hope of long lyfe, made hym bothe to forget God, his prynce, and hymselfe in his latter daies : for Doctor Jhon Baker, his pryvie counsailer, and hys chapellayn, wrote that he lyeng on his death bed, said these wordes : Why should I dye, hauing so much ryches, if the whole realme would saue my lyfe, I am able either by pollicie to get it, or by ryches to buy it. Fye, wyll not death be hyered, nor will money do nothyng? When my nephew of Bedford died, I thought myselfe halfe up the whele, but when I sawe myne other nephew of Gloucester disceased, then I thought myself able to be equale with kinges, and so thought to encrease my treasure in hoope to have worn a tryple crounc. But I se nowe the worlde fayleth me, and so I am deceyved, praying you all to pray for me."

[3] This is altered in the amended play to "and feel no pain." Theobald thinks the old edition supplies the best reading, as the Cardinal here labours more under the dreadful apprehensions in his mind of the result of approaching death than bodily pain. King Henry adds immediately afterwards, " how he is troubled," and wishes him to remember his Redeemer.

Lord   Cardinall, remember   Christ   must · saue thy
    soule.[1]
Car. Why died he not in his bed ?
What would you haue me to do then ?
Can I make men liue whether they will or no ? ?[2]
Sirra, go fetch me the strong poison[3] which the
    Pothicary sent me.
Oh see where Duke Humphreys ghoast doth stand,
And stares me in the face.   Looke, looke, coame
    downe his haire,
So now hees gone againe : Oh, oh, oh.
    Sal. See how the panges of death doth gripe his heart.
    Kin. Lord Cardinall, if thou diest assured of hea-
        uenly blisse,
Hold vp thy hand and make some signe to vs.[4]
                                    [*The Cardinall dies.*
Oh see he dies, and makes no signe at all.
Oh God forgiue his soule.
    Sal. So bad an ende did neuer none behold,
But as his death, so was his life in all.
    Kin. Forbeare to iudge, good Salsbury forbeare,
For God will iudge vs all.
Go take him hence, and see his funerals be performde.[5]
                                    [*Exet omnes.*

---

[1] The two editions of 1600 read —
        " Lord Cardinall, remember Christ must haue thy soule."
[2] So in " King John," act iv. sc. 2 :—
        " We cannot hold mortality's strong hand."
And again :—
            " Why do you bend such solemn brows on me ?
            Think you I bear the shears of destiny?
            Have I commandment on the pulse of life ? "
[3] The word " strong " is omitted in the edition of 1619.
[4] So in the old " King John," 1591, the legate says to the
dying sovereign :—
            " Lift up thy hand, that we may witnesse here,
            Thou diedst the servant of our Saviour Christ :—
            Now joy betide thy soule ! "
[5] The word " be " is omitted in the edition of 1619.

Alarmes [1] *within, and the chambers be discharged, like as it were a fight at sea. And then enter the Captaine of the ship* [2] *and the Maister, and the Maisters Mate, &ᵒ the Duke of* SUFFOLKE *disguised, and others with him, and* WATER WHICKMORE. [3]

Cap. Bring forward these prisoners that scorn'd to yeeld,
Vnlade their goods with speed and sincke their ship,
Here Maister, this prisoner I giue to you.
This other, the Maisters Mate shall haue,
And Water Whickmore thou shalt haue this man,
And let them paie their ransomes [4] ere they passe.
 Suf. Water!   *[He starteth.*
 Water. How now, what doest feare me? [5]
Thou shalt haue better cause anon.
 Suf. It is thy name affrights me, not thy selfe.
I do remember well, a cunning Wyssard told me,
That by Water I should die: [6]

---

[1] This word, so frequently occurring in old stage directions, and, having two distinct meanings, is frequently misinterpreted by the general reader. Perhaps the following is as good an explanation of the word as could be given. "*Classicum*, a trumpet for the warres, a sound or peale of trumpets or belles to call men together or to go to warre, alarme."—Rider's "Latin Dictionarie," 4º, London, 1640.

[2] In the amended play we have "Lieutenant" throughout the scene. Modern editors return to the old edition.

[3] In the two editions of 1600 his name is spelt "Walter Whickemore."

[4] The edition of 1619 reads, "ransome."

[5] The two editions of 1600 read, "what doest thou feare me." This appears to be a necessary addition, although the edition of 1619 follows our text.

[6] So, in Queen Margaret's letter to the duke, in Drayton's "Epistles," we have—

> "I pray thee, Poole, have care how thou dost pass,
> Never the sea yet half so dangerous was,
> And one foretold by *water* thou should'st die,
> Ah! foul befall that foul tongue's prophecy."

See Malone's "Shakespeare," by Boswell, vol. xviii. p. 283.

Yet let not that make thee bloudie minded.
Thy name being rightly sounded,
Is Gualter, not Water.

   Water. Gualter or Water, als one to me,
I am the man must bring thee to thy death.[1]

   Suf. I am a Gentleman looke on my Ring,
Ransome me at what thou wilt, it shal be paid.

   Water. I lost mine eye in boording of the ship,
And therefore ere I merchantlike sell blood for gold,
Then cast me headlong downe into the sea.

   2. *Pris.* But what shall our ransomes be?

   Mai. A hundred pounds a piece, either paie that
or die.

   2. *Pris.* Then saue our liues, it shall be paid.

   Water. Come sirrha, thy life shall be the ransome
I will haue.

This prophecy and its accomplishment are differently stated.
The note upon these lines is: "The witch of Eye receiv'd answer from her spirit, that the Duke of Suffolk should take heed
of *water*." The two editions of 1600 print *Walter* instead of
water, and it is probably one of those that Mr Collier refers to
in his edition of "Shakespeare," vol. v. p. 181.

[1] This scene is thus related in Hall's "Chronicle:" "But
fortune wold not that this flatigious person shoulde so escape;
for when he shipped in Suffolke, entendynge to be transported
into Fraunce, he was encontered with a shippe of warre apper-
teinyng to the Duke of Excester, the Constáble of the Towre of
London, called the Nicholas of the Towre. The capitayne of
the same barke with small fight entered into the duke's shippe,
and perceyving his person present, brought hym to Dover Rode,
and there on the one syde of a cocke bote, caused his head to
be stryken of, and left his body with the heade upon the sandes
of Dover, which corse was there founde by a chapelayne of his,
and conveyed to Wyngfelde College in Suffolke, and there
buried. This ende had William de la Pole, first duke of Suffolke,
as men iudge, by God's punyshment; for above all thinges he
was noted to be the very organ, engine, and devisor of the destruction of Humfrey the good duke of Gloucester, and so the
bloudde of the innocente man was with his dolorous death recom-
pensed and punished." See Holinshed's "Chronicle," p. 632,
and Grafton's "Chronicle," p. 610.

Suf. Staie villaine, thy prisoner is a Prince,
The Duke of Suffolke, William de la Poull.
   Cap. The Duke of Suffolke folded vp in rags.
   Suf. I sir, but these rags are no part of the Duke,
Ioue sometime went disguisde, and why not I?[1]
   Cap. I but Ioue was neuer slaine as thou shalt be.
   Suf. Base Iadie groome,[2] King Henries blood
The honourable blood of Lancaster,[3]
Cannot be shead by such a lowly swaine,
I am sent Ambassador for the Queene to France,
I charge thee waffe me crosse the channell safe.
   Cap. Ile waffe thee to thy death, go Water take him
   hence,
And on our long boates side, chop off his head.
   Suf. Thou darste not for thine owne.
   Cap. Yes Poull.
   Suf. Poull.[4]
   Cap. I Poull, puddle, kennell, sinke and durt,
Ile stop that yawning mouth of thine,
Those lips of thine that so oft haue kist the
Queene,[5] shall sweepe the ground, and thou that
Smildste at good Duke Humphreys death,
Shalt liue no longer to infect the earth.
   Suf. This villain being but Captain of a Pinnais,
Threatens more plagues then mightie Abradas,

---

[1] This line is omitted in the folio editions of the amended play, though completely necessary to the sense of what follows.

[2] A groom who attends upon inferior horses. Here, a term of reproach. See " Henry VIII," act. iii. sc. 2.

[3] Blakeway says that this is a mistake, and that Suffolk's great grandfather was a merchant at Hull. But we learn from Hall that Suffolk assumed a good ancestry, and therefore this line was a natural ebullition of his vanity.

[4] This and the next line are omitted in the folio editions of the amended play, but are introduced by modern editors as necessary to the sense.

[5] This word is placed at the end of the preceding line in the two editions of 1600.

The great Masadonian Pyrate,[1]
Thy words addes [2] fury and not remorse in me.
　Cap. I but my deeds shall staie thy fury soone.
　Suf. Has not thou waited at my Trencher,
When we haue feasted with Queene Margaret?
Hast not thou kist thy hand[3] and held my stirrope?
And barehead plodded by my footecloth Mule,
And thought thee happie when I smilde on thee?
This hand hath writ in thy defence,
Then shall I charme thee, hold thy lauish toong.
　　Cap. Away with him, Water, I say, and off with his
　　hed.
　　1. *Pris.* Good my Lord, intreat him mildly for your
　　life.
　　Suf. First let this necke stoupe to the axes edge,
Before this knee do bow to any,
Saue to the God of heauen and to my King :
Suffolkes imperiall toong cannot pleade
To such a Iadie groome.
　　Water. Come, come, why do we let him speake,
I long to haue his head for raunsome of mine eye.
　　Suf. A Swordar and bandeto slaue,
Murthered sweete Tully.

---

　[1] In the amended play we have—
　　　"Small things make base men proud ; this villain here,
　　　　Being captain of a pinnace, threatens more
　　　　Than Bargulus the strong Illyrian pirate."
Bargulus, or Βαρδυλλις, as Plutarch writes it in the life of Pyrrhus,
is mentioned by Cicero, *Bargulus Illyrius latro.* The change
was perhaps made for the sake of the metre, "Macedonian"
not well suiting the new construction of Suffolk's speech. Greene,
in "Penelope's Web" [1588], mentions "Abradas, the great
Macedonian pirat," who "thought euery one had a letter of
mart that bare sayles in the ocean." See Malone's "Shakespeare," by Boswell, vol. xviii. p. 289. The second folio reads,
"threats" instead of "threatens."
　[2] Probably "adde."
　[3] The two editions of 1600 read, "Hast not thou kist thine
hand."

Brutus bastard-hand stabde Iulius Cæsar,
And Suffolke dies by Pyrates on the seas.

       [*Exet* SUFFOLKE, *and* WATER.

 Cap. Off with his head, and send it to the Queene,
And ransomelesse this prisoner shall go free,
To see it saue deliuered vnto her.
Come lets goe   [*Exet omnes.*

   Enter two of the Rebels with long staues.

 George. Come away Nick, and put a long staffe in
thy pike, and prouide thy selfe, for I Can tell thee,
they haue bene vp this two daies.

 Nicke. Then they had more need to go to bed now.
But sirrha George whats the matter?

 George. Why sirrha, Iack Cake the Diar of Ashford
  here,
He meanes to turne this land, and set a new nap
  on it.

 Nicke. I marry he had need so, for tis growne threed-
  bare,
Twas neuer merry world with vs,[1] since these gentle
  men came vp.[2]

 George. I warrant thee, thou shalt neuer see a Lord
weare a leather aperne now a-daies.

 Nicke. But sirrha, who comes more[3] beside Iacke
  Cade?

 George. Why theres Dicke the Butcher, and Robin
the Sadler, and Will that came a wooing to our Nan

---

 [1] A proverbial expression. "Then stept forth the Duke of
Suffolke from the King, and spake with a hault countenance
these words: It was neuer merry in England, quoth hee, while
we had any Cardinals among us." Stowe's "Chronicles," by
Howes, fol. 1631, p. 546. See Malone's "Shakespeare," by
Boswell, vol. xviii. p. 294. The reading of the amended play
renders this quotation still more apposite.
 [2] The word "these" is judiciously omitted in the amended
play.
 [3] The edition of 1619 reads, "else."

last Sunday, and Harry and Tom, and Gregory that
should haue your Parnill, and a great sort more is
come from Rochester, and from Maydstone, and
Canterbury, and all the Townes here abouts, and we
must all be[1] Lords or squires, assoone as Iacke Cade
is King.

Nicke. Harke, harke, I here the Drum, they be
comming.

Enter IACKE CADE, DICKE *Butcher*, ROBIN, WILL,
TOM, HARRY, *and the rest, with long staues.*

Cade. Proclaime silence.

All. Silence.

Cade. I Iohn Cade so named for my valiancie.[2]

Dicke. Or rather for stealing of a Cade of Sprats.[3]

Cade. My father was a Mortemer.

Nicke. He was an honest man[4] and a good Brick-laier.

Cade. My mother came of the Brases.[5]

Will. She was a Pedlers daughter[6] indeed, and sold
many lases.

---

[1] The edition of 1619 reads, "be al."

[2] This passage is very obscure, unless he derives his name
from the Latin *cado*, which is partially confirmed by the amended
play, where he says, "our enemies shall *fall* before us." It
would appear that something is omitted.

[3] A measure less than a barrel. The quantity a cade should
contain is ascertained by Malone by the following extract from
the accounts of the celeress of the abbey of Berking: "Memo-
randum that a barrel of herryng shold contene a thousand her-
ryngs, and a cade of herryng six hundreth, six score to the
hundreth." Nash, in his "Lenten Stuffe," 1599, says, "the rebel
Jacke Cade was the first that devised to put redde herrings in
cades, and from him they have their name." Nash's account
was, perhaps, borrowed from this play.

[4] In the edition of 1619 and the amended play, this speech is
given to Dick Butcher.

[5] The edition of 1619 reads,

"My mother was come of the *Lacies.*"

[6] In the edition of 1619 this speech is given by Nicke.

Robin. And now being not able to occupie her furd
packe,[1]
She washeth buckes vp and downe the country.
Cade. Therefore I am honourably borne.[2]
Harry. I for [3] the field is honourable, for he was
borne
Vnder a hedge, for his father [4] had no house but the
Cage.
Cade. I am able to endure much.
George. Thats true, I know he can endure anything,
For I haue seen him whipt two market daies togither.
Cade. I feare neither sword nor fire.
Will. He need not feare the sword, for his coate is
of proofe.[5]
Dicke. But mee thinkes he should feare the fire, be-
ing so often burnt in the hand, for stealing of sheepe.
Cade. Therefore be braue, for your Captain is braue,
and vowes reformation : you shall haue seuen half-
penny loaues for a penny, and the three hoopt pot,
shall haue ten hoopes,[6] and it shall be felony to

---

[1] A wallet or knapsack of skin with the hair outward.   See
Malone's "Shakespeare," by Boswell, vol. xviii. p. 296.
· [2] The two editions of 1600 read, "Therefore I am honourable
borne."   Thus in the " Third Part of Henry VI.," edit. 1623,
p. 160, we have,
    " Widow, goe you along : Lords, vse her honourable."
This word "honourable" is altered to "honourably" in the
second edition of that play.
[3] The word "for" is omitted in the edition of 1619 and in
the amended play.
[4] The edition of 1619 reads, " because his father."
[5] Perhaps an exit ought to be marked here, as Will so soon
afterwards enters " with the Clarke of Chattam."
[6] The old drinking-pots, being of wood, were bound together,
as barrels are, with *hoops ;* and in " The Gul's Horn-Booke,"
1609, they are mentioned among other drinking-measures.   See
also Nash's " Pierce Penilesse," 1592, ed. Collier, p. 103.   Cade,
says Douce, promises that every can which now had three hoops
shall be increased in size so as to require ten.

drinke small beere, and if I be king,[1] as king I will
be.

All. God saue your maiestie.

Cade. I thanke you good people, you shall all eate
and drinke of my score, and go all in my liuerie, and
weele haue no writing, but the score & the Tally, and
there shalbe no lawes but such as comes[2] from my
mouth.

Dicke. We shall haue sore lawes then,[3] for he was
thrust into the mouth the other day.

George. I and stinking law too, for his breath stinks
so, that one cannot abide it.

Enter WILL *with the Clarke oj Chattam.*[4]

Will. Oh Captaine a pryze.

Cade. Whose that Will?

Will. The Clarke of Chattam, he can write and
reade and cast account, I tooke him setting of boyes
coppies, and hee has a booke in his pocket with red
letters.

Cade. Sonnes,[5] hees a coniurer bring him hither.
Now, sir, what your name?

Clarke. Emanuell sir, and it shall please you.

---

[1] The edition of 1619 leaves out the word "and," and the two
editions of 1600 read, "And if be the king."

[2] The edition of 1619 reads, "But such as come."

[3] Stephano makes a similar pun in the "Tempest," act. v. sc. 1.

[4] Ritson supposes him to have been Thomas Bayly, a necro-
mancer at Whitechapel, and formerly a bosom friend of Cade.
See W. Wyrcestre, p. 471. But Douce considers the character
to have been invented by the writer of the play, and there
certainly does not appear to be any evidence in favour of Ritson's conjecture.

[5] A misprint for "sounes." It is corrected in the later impressions.

Dicke. It will go hard with you, I can tell you,[1]
For they vse to write that oth top of letters.[2]

Cade. And what do you vse[3] to write your name?
Or do you as auncient forefathers haue done,
Vse the score and the Tally?

Clarke. Nay, true sir,[4] I praise God I haue bene so
well brought vp, that I can write mine owne name.

Cade. Oh hes confest,[5] go hang him with his penny-
inckhorne about his necke.

[*Exit one with the Clarke.*

Enter TOM.

Tom. Captaine. Newes, newes, sir Humphrey
Stafford and his brother are comming with the kings
power, and mean to kil vs all.

Cade. Let them come, hees but a knight is he?

Tom. No, no, hees but a knight.

Cade. Why then to equall him, ile make my selfe
knight.

Kneele downe Iohn Mortemer,
Rise vp sir Iohn Mortemer.
Is there any more of them that be Knights?

Tom. I his brother. [*He Knights* DICKE *Butcher.*[6]

Cade. Then kneele downe Dicke Butcher,

---

[1] The edition of 1619 reads, " I tell ye."

[2] Of letters missive, and public acts. In the " Famous Victories
of Henry V.," 1598, the Archbishop of Bruges says to King
Henry:

> "I beseech your grace to deliver mee your safe
> Conduct, under your broad seale *Emanuel.*"

The edition of 1619 reads, " ore the top of letters," and, in the
previous line, " I tell ye," instead of " I can tell you."

[3] The edition of 1619 reads, " What do ye vse."

[4] The edition of 1619 reads, " Nay, truly sir."

[5] The edition of 1619 has this speech as follows : " Oh he has
confest, go and hang him with his pen and inkehorne about his
necke."

[6] The edition of 1619 reads, " He knights him," and places
this direction at the end of the next line.

Rise vp sir Dicke Butcher.

[*Now sound vp the Drumme.*[1]

Enter sir HUMPHREY STAFFORD *and his brother, with Drumme and souldiers.*

Cade. As for these silken coated slaues I passe not a pinne,[2]
Tis to you good people that I speake.
Staf. Why country-men, what meane you thus in troopes,
To follow this rebellious Traitor Cade?
Why his father was but a Brick-laier.[3]
Cade. Well, and Adam was a Gardner,[4] what then?
But I come of the Mortemers.
Staf. I the Duke of Yorke hath taught you that.
Cade. The Duke of York, nay, I learnt it my selfe,
For looke you, Roger Mortemer the Earle of March,
Married the Duke of Clarence daughter.
Staf. Well, thats true : But what then ?
Cade. And by her he had two children at a birth.
Staf. Thats false.
Cade. I, but I say, tis true.
All. Why then tis true.
Cade. And one of them was stolne away by a begger-woman,
And that was my father,[5] and I am his sonne,
Deny it and you can.
Nicke. Nay looke you, I know twas true,[6]

---

[1] This forms part of Cade's speech in the edition of 1619.
[2] An idiomatic phrase of the time for I care not, or, I pay them no regard. "I care not a pin for you," is a common expression at the present day.
[3] The word "but" is omitted in the edition of 1619.
[4] The word "and" is omitted in the two editions of 1600.
[5] The word "that" is omitted in the two editions of 1600.
[6] The edition of 1619 reads, "I know was true," which Mr Knight has corrected to "I know 'tis true."

For his father built a chimney in my fathers house,
And the brickes are aliue at this day to testifie.[1]

Cade. But doest thou heare Stafford, tell the King,
that for his fathers sake, in whose time boyes plaide
at spanne-counter with Frenche Crownes,[2] I am content that he shall be King as long as he liues. Marry
alwaies prouded, ile be Protector ouer him.

Staf. O monstrous simplicite.

Cade. And tell him, weele have the Lord Sayes
head, and the Duke of Somersets, for deliuering vp
the Dukedomes of Anioy and Mayne, and selling
the Townes in France, by which meanes England

---

[1] The edition of 1619 reads " to testifye it."

[2] The amended play reads, "in whose time boys went to span-
counter for French crowns." The earlier commentators do not
give any note on the game of span-counter, which Strutt and
Nares suppose to have been thus played : one throws a counter,
or piece of money, which the other wins if he can throw another
so as to hit it, or lie within a span of it. It is alluded to by
Beaumont and Fletcher :

> " And what I now pull shall no more afflict me,
> Than if I play'd at span-counter."

Dr Simon Forman, and his companion and "bedfellowe," Henry
Gird, used to play at this game about 1570, as we learn from his
diary in MS. Ashm. 208 ; but this curious document does not
give us any information relative to the manner in which the
game was played. A few leaves onwards, in the same volume,
Forman gives us the following account, which is so good an
illustration of the fact of deer-stealing being a fashionable amuse-
ment in the time of Shakespeare, that I cannot resist the temp-
tation of inserting it here, especially, too, as it also affords an
example of the ancient method of styling members of the university by the title of "sir," already alluded to. Forman is speaking of his college life when he tells us : "Nowe ther were too
Bachelors of Arte that were too of his shife benefactors : the one
of them was Sir Thornbury, that after was bishope of Limerike,
and he was of Magdalen College ; the other was Sir Pinckney,
his cossine of St Mary Halle. Thes too lovyd hym [Forman]
nying welle, and many tymes wold make Simon to goo forth
tho Loes the keper of Shottofer for his houndes to go on huntinge
from morninge to nighte, and they never studied nor gave them-

hath bene maimde[1] euer since, and gone as it were
with a crouch, but that my puissance[2] held it vp.
And besides, they can speake French, and therefore
they are traitors.

Staf. As how I prethie?

Cade. Why the French men are our enemies be
they not? And then can hee that speakes with the
tongue of an enemy be a good subiect?
Answere me to that.

Staf. Well sirrha, wilt thou yeeld thy selfe vnto the
Kings mercy, and he will pardon thee and these, their
outrages and rebellious deeds?

Cade. Nay, bid the King come to me and he will,
and then ile pardon him, or otherwaies ile haue his
Crowne tell him, ere it be long.

Staf. Go Herald proclaime in all the Kings Townes.
That those that will forsake the Rebell Cade,
Shall haue free pardon from his Maiestie.

[*Exet* STAFFORD *and his men.*

Cade. Come sirs, saint George for vs and Kent.

[*Exet omnes.*

---

selves to their bockes, but to goe to scolles of defence, to the
dauncing scolles, *to steall dear and conyes*, and to hunte the hare
and to woinge of wenches ; to goe to Doctor Lawrence of Cowly,
for he had too fair daughters, Besse and Martha. Sir Thornbury
he woed Besse ; and Sir Pinckney he woed Martha, and in the
end he married her ; but Thornbury he deceyved Besse as the
mayor's daughter of Bracly, of which Ephues writes, deceyved
him. But ther was their ordinary haunt alwaies, and thethere
muste Symon rone with the bottell and the bage erly and late."
Thus if a bishop could steal deer when he was at college, surely
Shakespeare could do so in his early career without his respec-
tability being impeached by his editors, a sport then attended
with as little loss of reputation as stealing knockers would be at
the present day.

[1] The amended play reads, "main'd," so that this may be a
pun on the word "Mayne," in the previous line. Daniel has a
similar conceit in his "Civil Wars," 1595 :

"Anjou and Maine, the *maim* that foul appears."

[2] The two editions of 1600 read, "but that the puissance."

Alarums to the battaile, and sir HUMPHREY STAFFORD[1]
and his brother is slaine. Then enter IACKE CADE
againe and the rest.

Cade. Sir Dicke Butcher, thou hast fought to day
most valianly, And knockt them down as if thou
hadst bin in thy slaughter house. And thus I will
reward thee. The Lent shall be as long againe as it
was. Thou[2] shalt haue licence to kill for foure score
& one a week, Drumme strike vp, for now weele
march to London, for to morrow[3] I meane to sit in
the Kings seate at Westminster.   [*Exet omnes.*

*Enter the King reading of a Letter, and the Queene,
with the Duke of* SUFFOLKES *head, and the Lord*
SAY, *with others.*

Kin. Sir Humphrey Stamford and his brother is[
slaine,
And the Rebels march amaine to London,
Go back to them, and tell them thus from me,
Ile come and parley with their generall.
Reade.[4] Yet staie, ile reade the Letter one[5] againe.
Lord Say, Iacke Cade hath solemnely vowde to haue
thy head.

---

[1] "A detachment was made against Jack Cade under the
command of Sir Humphry and Sir William Stafford, to oppose
those of Cade's men that remained in a body, imagining that
most of them were retired to their several dwellings : but Cade
having placed his troops in ambuscade in the woods about
Sevenoke, the forces commanded by the Staffords were sur-
rounded, and most of them either killed or taken prisoners, the
two brothers who commanded them being killed on the spot."—
Hollinshed's "Chronicle, IIenry IV.," p. 364   The edition of
1619 reads, "where Sir Humfrey Stafford and his brother are
both slaine."

[2] The edition of 1619 reads, "and thou."
[3] The edition of 1619 reads, "and to morrow."
[4] This stage direction is omitted in the edition of 1619.
[5] Perhaps "once."

Say. I but I hope your highnesse shall haue his.

Kin. How now Madam, still lamenting and mourning for Suffolkes death, I feare my loue,[1] if I had bene dead, thou wouldst not haue mournde[2] so much for me.

Queene. No my loue, I should not mourne, but die for thee.

Enter a Messenger.

Mes. Oh flie my Lord, the Rebels are entered
Southwarke, and haue almost wonne the Bridge,
Calling your grace an vsurper,
And that monstrous Rebell Cade, hath sworne
To Crowne himselfe King in Westminster,
Therefore flie my Lord, and poste to Killingworth.[3]

Kin. Go bid Buckingham and Clifford, gather
An Army vp, and meete with the Rebels.
Come Madame, let vs haste to Killingworth.
Come on Lord Say, go thou along with vs,
For feare the Rebell Cade do find thee out.

Say. My innocence my Lord shall pleade for me.
And therefore with your highnesse leaue, ile staie behind.

Kin. Euen as thou wilt my Lord Say.
Come Madame, let vs go.   [*Exet omnes.*

---

[1] Malone prefers this reading to the "I fear me, love" of the folio editions of the amended play.   The difference is one which might easily occur in printing.

[2] The second folio reads, "Thou would'st not half have mourn'd."

[3] "The king and court were so terrified at the approach of these rebels to Blackheath, that they retired to Kenelworth Castle in Warwickshire."—Holinshed's "Chronicle," p. 366. Killingworth is the old name for Kenilworth, and Sir William Blackstone says it was the common pronunciation in his time. In Lancham's letter, we find "the castle hath name of Kyllelingworth ; but of truth, grounded upon faythfull story, Kenelwoorth."

Enter the Lord SKAYLES *vpon the Tower Walles walking.*
Enter three or foure Citizens below.[1]

Lord Scayles. How now, is Iacke Cade slaine?

1. *Cit.* No my Lord, nor likely to be slaine,
For they haue wonne the bridge,
Killing all those that withstand them.
The Lord Mayor craueth ayde of your honour from
the Tower,
To defend the Citie from the Rebels.

Lord Scayles. Such aide as I can spare, you shall
command,
But I am troubled here with them my selfe,
The Rebels haue attempted to win the Tower,
But get you to Smythfield[2] and gather head,
And thither I will[3] send you Mathew Goffe,
Fight for your King, your Country, and your liues.
And so farewell, for I must hence againe.

[*Exet omnes.*

Enter IACK CADE *and the rest, and strikes his sword*
upon London Stone.

Cade. Now is Mortemer Lord of this Citie,
And now sitting vpon London stone, We command,
That the first year of our raigne,
The pissing Cundit run nothing but red wine.
And now hence forward,[4] it shall be treason
For any that calles me any otherwise then
Lord Mortemer.

---

[1] This necessary stage direction is entirely omitted in the
edition of 1619.

[2] The second folio reads, " But get you into Smithfield."

[3] These words are transposed in the edition of 1619.

[4] This and the next line are thus given in the two editions of
1600 :—

> " And now henceforth, it shall be treason
> For any that calls me otherwise then."

The amended play agrees with our text.

Enter a souldier.

Sould. Iacke Cade, Iacke Cade.

Cade. Sounes, knocke him downe. [*They kill him.*

Dicke. My Lords,[1] theirs an Army gathered together
Into Smythfield.

Cade. Come then, lets go fight with them,
But first go on and set London Bridge a fire,[2]
And if you can, burne downe the Tower too.
Come lets away.   [*Exet omnes.*

Alarmes, and then MATHEW GOFFE *is slaine,[3] and all
the rest with him.   Then enter* IACK CADE *again,
and his company.*

Cade. So sirs, now go some and pull down the
Sauoy,[4]
Others to the Innes of the Court,[5] downe with them all.

Dicke. I haue a sute vnto your Lordship.

Cade. Be it a Lordship Dicke, and thou shalt haue it
For that word.

Dicke. That we burne all the Records,[6]

---

[1] The edition of 1619 reads, "My lord."

[2] The two editions of 1600 read, "set London Bridge on
fire." At that time the bridge was made of wood.

[3] This of course means in the course of the scene, and not necessarily before the arrival of Cade and his followers. He is described
by Holinshed, p. 635, as "a man of great wit and much experience in feats of chivalrie, the which in continuall warres had
spent his time in serving of the king and his father."

[4] The word "some" is omitted in the edition of 1619. According to Ritson, this trouble had been saved Cade's reformers
by his predecessor, Wat Tyler, and was not rebuilt till the time
of Henry VII.

[5] The word "the" is omitted in the edition of 1619.

[6] Reed says that a similar proposal was actually made in parliament in the time of the Commonwealth. But the objects
were different. In that instance it was to settle the nation on a
new foundation, whereas all Dicke appears to desire is the destruction of every thing connected with education and learning.

And that all writing may be put downe,
And nothing vsde but the score and the Tally.

Cade. Dicke it shall be so, and henceforward all
things[1] shall be in common, and in Cheapeside shall
my palphrey go to grasse.

Why ist not a miserable thing, that of the skin of
an innocent lamb should parchment[2] be made, & then
with a litle blotting ouer with inke, a man should
vndo himselfe.

Some saies tis the bees that sting, but I say, tis
their waxe, for I am sure I neuer scald to anything
but once, and I was neuer mine owne man since.[3]

Nicke. But when shall we take vp those commodities
Which you told vs of.

Cade. Marry he that will[4] lustily stand to it.
Shall go with me, and[5] take vp these commodities
    following :
Item, a gowne, a kirtle, a petticoate, and a smocke.

Enter GEORGE.

George. My Lord, a prize, a prize, heres the Lord
    Say,
Which sold the Townes in France.

Cade. Come hither thou Say, thou George, thou
    buckrum lord,[6]

---

[1] The edition of 1600, printed by W. W., reads, "al thing."
[2] These words are transposed in the edition of 1619. This
speech occurs in act iv. sc. 2, of the amended play. Here it is
act iv. sc. 7.
[3] The second folio reads, "my" for mine."
[4] This speech is printed as prose in the edition of 1619.
[5] These words are omitted in the edition of 1619.
[6] Cade here makes a pun on the word "say," which is explained by Minsheu to be a kind of woollen stuff. Spenser uses
the word—
> "All in a kirtle of discolour'd *say*
> He clothed was."

There seems also to be a play on the word George and *serge*, as
it is spelt in the amended drama.

What answere canst thou make vnto my mightinesse,
For deliuering vp the townes in France to Mounsier
    bus mine cue, the Dolphin of France ?
And more then so, thou hast most traitorously erected
a grammer schoole, to infect the youth of the realme,
and against the Kings Crowne and dignitie,[1] thou hast
built vp a paper-mill, nay it wil be saide to thy face,
that thou kepst men in thy house that daily reades[2] of
bookes with red letters, and talkes[3] of a Nowne and
a Verbe, and such abhominable words as no Christian
eare is able to endure it.   And besides all that,[4] thou
hast appointed certaine Iustises[5] of peace in euery
shire to hang honest men that steale for their liuing,
and because they could not reade, thou hast hung them
vp : Onely for which cause they were most worthy to
liue.   Thou ridest on a footcloth doest thou not ?[6]
    Say. Yes, what of that ?
    Cade. Marry I say, thou oughtest not to let thy
horse weare a cloake, when an honester man then thy
selfe, goes in his hose and doublet.
    Say. You men of Kent.
    All. Kent, what of Kent ?

---

[1] " Against the peace of the said lord the king, his crown, and
dignity," was the regular language of indictments.
[2] Perhaps " reade."
[3] Probably " talke."
[4] The edition of 1619 reads, " And besides all this."
[5] The edition of 1619 reads, " Iustices of the peace."
[6] This passage, though completely necessary for the sense, is
entirely omitted in the edition of 1619 and by Mr Knight.   This
shows the value of the old copies.   The first folio reads, " in a
footcloth," but the edition of 1632 restores the old reading.   A
footcloth was a kind of housing which covered the body of the
horse, and almost reached the ground.   It was sometimes made
of velvet, and bordered with gold lace.   Bulleyne, in his " Dialogue," 1564, says : "He gave me my mule also with a velvet
footcloth."   See "Richard III.," act iii. sc. 4 ; and " 2 Henry
VI.," act iv. sc. 1.

Say. Nothing but *bona, terra.*[1]
Cade. Bonum terum, sounds whats that?
Dicke. He speakes French.
Mill. No tis Dutch.
Nicke. No tis outtalian, I know it well inough.

Say. Kent, in the Commentaries Cæsar wrote,
Termde it the ciuel'st place of all this land,[2]
Then Noble country-men, heare me but speake,
I sold not France, I lost not[3] Normandie.

 Cade. But wherefore doest thou shake thy head
 so?

 Say. It is the palsie and not feare that makes me.[4]

---

[1] The edition of 1600, printed by W. W., reads, "Nothing but *terra bona.*"

[2] So all the editions. The amended play reads—

> "Kent, in the Commentaries Cæsar writ,
> Is term'd the civell'st place of all this isle ;
> Sweet is the country, because full of riches,
> The people liberal, valiant, active, wealthy,
> Which makes me hope thou art not void of pity."

The first folio reads, "you are." I have printed from the second edition of 1632. The passage, as given in our text, cannot be correct ; but Mr Knight reads,

> "Term'd *is* the civellest place of all this land."

I would rather read, "is term'd," the line running so much better, and transpositions frequently occur in these old copies. The passage in Cæsar which is referred to is as follows :—"Ex his omnibus longe sunt humanissimi qui Cantium incolunt."— "Comment de bello Gallico," v. 14. The passage is thus translated by Arthur Golding, 1565 : "Of all the inhabitants of this isle, the *civilest* are the Kentisfolke," a sentence which occurs nearly word for word in Lyly's "Euphues and his England," 1580 : "Of all the inhabitants of this isle the Kentish-men are the civilest." Shakespeare, or rather the author of the "Contention," had probably seen this last-mentioned book, the passage I have given being quoted by Malone. It may be mentioned that there was an edition of Golding's translation published in 1590, as Mr Collier does not seem to be aware of this. See his "Shakespeare," vol. v. p. 198.

[3] The edition of 1619 reads, "nor lost I."

[4] Peck thinks that this speech originates in a charm for an ague, which, however, I suspect he has altered to bring it

Cade. Nay thou nodst thy head, as who say,[1] thou
wilt be euen with me, if thou getst away, but ile
make the sure inough, now I haue thee.   Go take
him to the standerd in Cheapeside and chop of his
head, and then go to milende-greene, to sir Iames
Cromer his sonne in law, and cut off his head too,[2]
and bring them to me vpon two poles presently.
Away with him.

> [*Exet one or two with the Lord* SAY.

There shall not a noble man weare a head on his
  shoulders,
But he shall paie me tribute for it.
Nor there shal not a mayd be married, but he shal
  see[3] to me for her.
Maydenhead or else, ile haue it my selfe,

---

nearer the present passage. Blagrave, in his "Astrological
Practise of Physick," p. 135, prescribes a cure of agues by a
certain writing which the patient weareth, as follows : "When
Jesus went up to the cross to be crucified, the Jews asked him,
saying, 'Art thou afraid? or hast thou the ague?'   Jesus
answered, and said, ' I am not afraid, neither have I the ague.
All those which bear the name of Jesus about them shall not be
afraid, nor yet have the ague.'   Amen, sweet Jesus, amen, sweet
Jehovah, amen."—See Brand's " Popular Antiquities," by Hazlitt, iii. 236.

[1] The edition of 1619 reads,

   "Nay, thou noddst thy head at vs, as who wouldst say."

[2] " "Cade ordered the Lord Mayor and Aldermen to assemble
in Guildhall, in order to sit in judgement upon Lord Say ; but,
his lordship insisting to be tried by his peers, Cade hurried him
from the bar, and struck off his head at the Standard in Cheap-
side.   And afterwards meeting with Sir J. Cromer, who had
married Lord Say's daughter, he cut off his head, ordering that
and Lord Say's to be carried before him on spears."—Holinshed,
p. 364.   See also Grey's " Notes upon Shakespeare," vol. ii. p.
28.   According to the contemporary chronicles, it was William
Cromer whom Cade put to death.   Lord Say and he had been
previously sent to the Tower, and both, or at least the former,
convicted of treason at Cade's mock commission at Guildhall.

[3] Read " fee."

Marry I will that married men shall hold of me in
capitie,[1]
And that their wiues shalbe as free as hart can thinke,
or toong can tell.[2]

Enter Robin.

Robin. O Captaine, London bridge is a fire.

Cade. Runne to Billingsgate, and feche pitch and
flaxe and squench[3] it.

Enter DICKE *and a Sargiant.*

Sar. Iustice, Iustice, I pray you sir, let me haue
iustice of this fellow here.

Cade. Why what has he done?

Sar. Alasse sir he has rauisht my wife.

Dicke. Why my Lord he would haue rested me,
And I went and entred my Action in his wiues paper
house.

Cade. Dicke follow thy sute in her common place,
You horson villaine, you are a Sargiant youle,

---

[1] A tenure *in capite.* This is an equivoque on the preceding
line.

[2] There are several ancient grants from our early kings to
their subjects, written in rude verse, and empowering them to
enjoy their lands as "free as heart can wish or tongue can tell."
Nearly the precise words occur in the Year Book of Henry VII.
See Malone's "Shakespeare," by Boswell, vol. xviii. p. 321.
The disgusting custom of the *Mercheta Mulierum,* alluded to by
Cade, is thus described by Skene, and affords us a very apposite
illustration of the whole of this speech : "Marchequum significat
prisca Scotorum lingua : hinc deducta metaphora ab equitando,
Marcheta mulieris, dicitur virginalis pudicitæ prima violatio et
delibatio, quæ, ab Eveno rege, dominis capitalibus fuit impie
permissa de omnibus novis nuptis prima nuptiarum nocte ; sed
et pie a Malcomo tertio sublata fuit, et in hoc capite certo vac-
carum numero et quasi pretio redimitur." Dalrymple, however,
denies the existence of such a custom, and Blackstone is of
opinion that it never prevailed in England.

[3] The edition of 1619 reads, "quench." The other is still a
provincial expression, and the older form of the word.

Take any man by the throate for twelue pence,
And rest a man when hees [1] at dinner,
And haue him to prison ere the meate be out of his [2]
    mouth.
Go Dicke take him hence, cut out [3] his toong for cog-
    ging.
Hough him for running, and to conclude,
Brane [4] him with his own mace.

                    [*Exet with the Sargiant.*

Enter two with the Lord SAYES *head, and sir* IAMES
        CROMERS, *vpon two poles.*

So, come carry them before me, and at euery lanes
ende, let them kisse togither. [5]

Enter the Duke of BUCKINGHAM, *and Lord* CLIFFORD
        the Earle of COMBERLAND.

    Clif. Why country-men and warlike friends of
        Kent,
What meanes this mutinous rebellions, [6]
That you in troopes do muster thus your selues,
Vnder the conduct of this Traitor Cade ?
To rise against your soueraigne Lord and King,
Who mildly hath his pardon sent to you,

---

[1] The edition of 1619 reads, "he is."
[2] The edition of 1619 reads, "on's."
[3] The edition of 1619 reads, "and cut out."
[4] That is, "brain." The edition of 1619 reads "braue."
[5] "And as it were in a spite caused them in every street to kisse together."—Holinshed, p. 634. See also Hall's "Chronicles," sig. a. Farmer gives another parallel passage from the "Mirrour of Magistrates." Hall says, "to the great detestacion of all the beholders." See Malone's "Shakespeare," by Boswell, vol. xviii. p. 322.
[6] The edition of 1600, printed by W. W., reads,

        "What meanes this mutinous rebellion ?"

while the edition of 1619 reads,

        "What meanes these mutinous rebellions?"

If you forsake this monstrous Rebell here?
If honour be the marke whereat you aime,
Then hast to France that your forefathers wonne,
And winne againe that thing which now is lost,
And leaue to seeke your Countries ouerthrow.
    All. A Clifford, a Clifford.   [*They forsake Cade.*
    Cade. Why, how now, will you forsake your gene-
    rall,
And ancient freedome which you haue possest?
To bend your neckes vnder [1] their seruile yokes,
Who if you stir, will straightwaies [2] hang you vp,
But follow me, and you shall pull them downe,
And make them yeeld their liuings to your hands.
    All. A Cade, a Cade.
              [*They runne to Cade againe.*
    Clif. Braue warlike friends heare me but speak a
    word,[3]
Refuse not good whilst it is offered you,
The King is mercifull, then yeeld to him,
And I myself will go along with you,
To Winsore Castle whereas the King abides,
And on mine honour you shall haue no hurt.
    All. A Clifford, a Clifford, God saue the King.
    Cade. How like a feather is this rascall company
Blowne euery way,
But that they may see there want no valiancy [4] in
    me,
My staffe shall make way through the midst of you,
And so a poxe take you all.
    [*He runs through them with his staffe, and flies away.*[5]

---

[1] The edition of 1600, printed by W. W., reads "vnto" instead of "vnder."
[2] The edition of 1619 reads "straight way."
[3] These words are omitted in the edition of 1619.
[4] The edition printed by W. W. in 1600, and that of 1619,
read "there wants no valiancy."
[5] The edition of 1619 reads, "and then flies away."

Buc. Go some and make after him, and pro-
claime,
That those that bring the head of Cade,
Shall haue a thousand Crownes for his labour.
Come march away.   [*Exet omnes.*

Enter King HENRY *and the* QUEENE, *and* SOMERSET.

Kin. Lord Somerset, what newes here you of the
Rebell Cade?
Som. This, my gratious Lord, that the Lord Say is
don to death,
And the Citie is almost sackt.
Kin. Gods will be done, for as he hath decreede,
so must it be : [1]
And be it as he please,[2] to stop the pride of those
rebellious men.
Queene. Had the noble Duke of Suffolke bene
aliue,
The Rebell Cade had bene supprest ere this,
And all the rest that do take part with him.

Enter the Duke of BUCKINGHAM *and* CLIFFORD, *with
the Rebels, with halters about their necks.*

Clif. Long liue King Henry, Englands lawfull
King,
Loe here my Lord, these Rebels are subdude,
And offer their liues before your highnesse feete.
Kin. But tell me Clifford, is their Captaine here.
Clif. No, my gratious Lord, he is fled away, but
proclamations are sent forth, that he that can but
bring his head, shall haue a thousand crownes. But

---

[1] The edition printed by W. W. in 1600 reads, " so it must
be."

[2] The word " it " is omitted in the edition of 1619, and by
Mr Knight, though it seems necessary in the construction of the
sentence.

may it please your Maiestie, to pardon these their
faults, that by that traitors meanes [1] were thus misled.

Kin. Stand vp you simple men, and giue God
praise,
For you did take in hand you know not what,
And go in peace obedient to your King,
And liue as subiects, and you shall not want,
Whilst Henry liues, and weares the English
Crowne.

All. God saue the King, God saue the King.

Kin. Come let vs haste to London now with
speed,
That solemne prosessions may be sung,
In laud and honour of the God of heauen,
And triumphs of this happie victorie.

[*Exet omnes.*

Enter IACKE CADE *at one doore, and at the other maister* ALEXANDER EYDEN *and his men, and* IACKE
CADE *lies downe picking of hearbes and eating
them.*

Eyden. Good Lord how pleasant is this country
life,
This litle land my father left me here,
With my contented minde serues me as well,
As all the pleasures in the Court can yeeld,
Nor would I change this pleasure for the Court.

Cade. Sounes, heres the Lord of the soyle, Stand
villaine, thou wilt betraie mee to the King, and get a
thousand crownes for my head, but ere thou goest,
ile make thee eate yron like an Astridge,[2] and swallow
my sword like a great pinne.

---

[1] The edition of 1619 reads, "by these traitors meanes."
[2] It may be worth while to observe that the edition of 1610
reads "estridge," alluding of course to the old myth of ostriches
eating and digesting iron, concerning the truth of which Sir

Eyden. Why sawcy companion, why should I betray
   thee ?
Ist not inough that thou hast broke my hedges,
And enterd into my ground [1] without the leaue of me
   the owner,
But thou wilt braue me too.

Cade. Braue thee and beard thee too, by the best
blood of the Realme, looke on me well, I haue eate
no meate this fiue dayes, yet and I do not [2] leaue thee
and thy fiue men as dead as a doore nayle,[3] I pray
God I may neuer eate grasse more.

Eyden. Nay, it neuer shall [4] be saide whilst the
world doth stand,[5] that Alexander Eyden an Esquire
of Kent, tooke oddes to combat with a famisht man,
looke on me, my limmes are equall vnto thine, and
euery way as big, then hand to hand, ile combat thee.[6]
Sirrah fetch me weopons, and stand you all aside.

Cade. Now sword, if thou doest not hew [7] this burly-
bond churle into chines of beefe, I beseech God thou

Thomas Browne and Alexander Ross fought a [paper] battle
some two centuries ago. The word "estridge" occurs twice in
Shakespeare, "1 Henry IV.," act iv. sc. 1, and "Antony and
Cleopatra," act iii. sc. 2, meaning a kind of hawk ; while the
early editions of the amended play read "ostridge" in the corresponding passage to this. This affords an argument in favour
of the early composition of the old play, if difference of orthography is ever any argument in works of Shakespeare's time.

   [1] The edition printed by W. W. in 1600 reads, "into the
ground."

   [2] The edition of 1619 reads, "Yet if I do not."

   [3] This proverb is used by Pistol in "2 Henry VI.," act v. sc.
3. The *door nail* was the nail, on which, in ancient doors, the
knocker strikes. See Malone's "Shakespeare" by Boswell,
vol. xvii. p. 225.

   [4] The edition of 1619 reads, "it shall never."

   [5] The edition of 1619 reads, "whilst the world stands."

   [6] The edition of 1619 reads, "Ile combat with thee."

   [7] The edition printed by W. W. in 1600 reads, "if thou hewst
not."

maist fal¹ into some smiths hand,² and be turned to hob-nailes.

Eyden. Come on thy way.

[*They fight, and* CADE *fals downe.*

Cade. Oh villaine, thou hast slaine the floure of Kent for chiualrie, but it is famine & not thee that has done it, for come ten thousand diuels, and giue me but the ten meales that I wanted this fiue daies, and ile fight with you all, and so a poxe rot thee, for Iack Cade must die. [*He dies.*

Eyden. Iack Cade, & was it that monstrous Rebell³ which I haue slaine. Oh sword ile honour thee for this,⁴ and in my chamber shalt thou hang as a monument to after age, for this great seruice thou hast done to me. Ile drag him hence, and with my sword cut off his head, and beare it⁵ . . . . [*Exet.*

Enter the Duke of YORKE *with Drum and souldiers.*

Yorke. In Armes from Ireland comes Yorke amaine, Ring belles aloud, bonfires perfume the ayre,

---

¹ The edition of 1619 reads, "I would thou mightst fall," while the amended play has, "I beseech Jove." The difference between the editions of 1619 and 1594 was, perhaps, occasioned by the statute of 3 James I. ; but the alteration in the folio may have been intentional, and is judiciously restored by Mr Collier.

² The edition of 1619 reads, "into some smiths hands."

³ Hall gives the following account of Cade's death : "After a proclamacion made that whosoever could apprehende the saied Jac Cade should have for his pain a m. markes, many sought for hym, but few espied hym, til one Alexander Iden, esquire of Kent, found hym in a garden, and there in his defence manfully slewe the caitife Cade, and brought his ded body to London, whose hed was set on London bridge." The edition of 1619 reads, "was this that monstrous rebel."

⁴ The edition printed by W. W. in 1600 reads, "O sword I honor thee for this." The edition of 1619 prints this speech as verse.

⁵ The edition of 1619 reads, "and beare it to the king," these three words having dropped out in the Bodleian copy of our edition.

To entertaine faire Englands royall King.
Ah *Sancta Maiesta*,[1] who would not buy thee deare?

Enter the Duke of BUCKINGHAM.

But soft, who comes here Buckingham, what newes
    with him?
Buc. Yorke, if thou meane well, I greete thee so.
Yorke. Humphrey of Buckingham, welcome I sweare:
What comes thou in loue or as a Messenger?
    Buc. I come as a Messenger from our dread Lord
        and soueraign,
Henry. To know the reason of these Armes in peace?
Or that thou being a subject as I am,
Shouldst thus approach so neare with colours spred,
Whereas the person of the King doth keepe?
    Yorke. A subject as he is.
Oh how I hate these spitefull abiect termes,
But Yorke dissemble, till thou meete thy sonnes,
Who now in Armes expect their fathers sight,
And not farre hence I know they cannot be.[2]
Humphrey Duke of Buckingham, pardon me;
That I answearde not at first, my mind was troubled,
I came to remoue that monstrous Rebell Cade,
And heaue proud Somerset[3] from out the Court,
That basely yeelded vp the Townes in France.
    Buc. Why that was presumption on thy behalfe,
But if it be no otherwise but so,[4]

---

[1] For "majestas."

[2] The edition printed by W. W. in 1600 omits the word
"not;" and it will be at once seen that this omission is necessary for the sense of the passage, although again inserted in the
edition of 1619 and in Mr Knight's. This part of York's speech
is of course spoken aside.

[3] The same expression is used by Buckingham soon afterwards. In the amended play this line is altered, the other
remaining as it was.

[4] The edition of 1619 reads, "no otherwise then so."

The King doth pardon thee, and granst[1] to thy re-
    quest,
And Somerset is sent vnto the Tower.
   Yorke. Vpon thine honour is it so?
   Buc. Yorke, he is vpon mine honour.
   York. Then before thy face, I here dismisse my
    troopes,
Sirs, meete me to-morrow in saint Georges fields,
And there you shall receiue your paie of me.
                      [*Exet souldiers.*
   Buc. Come York, thou shalt go speake[2] vnto the
    King,
But see, his grace is comming to meete with vs.

Enter King HENRY.   [Sig. H.

   Kin. How now Buckingham, is Yorke friends with
    us,
That thus thou bringst him hand in hand with thee?
   Buc. He is my Lord, and hath dischargde his
    troopes
Which came with him, but as your grace did say,
To heaue the Duke of Somerset from hence,
And to subdue the Rebels that were vp.
   Kin. Then welcome cousin Yorke, giue me thy
    hand,
And thankes for thy great seruice done to vs,
Against those traitorous Irish that rebeld.

Enter maister EYDEN *with* IACKE CADES *head.*

   Eyden. Long liue Henry[3] in triumphant peace,
Lo here my Lord vpon my bended knees,

---

  [1] Perhaps, " grants."
  [2] Malone thinks that the omission of this line in the amended
play is an error, but the entrance of King Henry is an accidental
incident, and the scene does not require Buckingham's assump-
tion of authority.
  [3] The edition of 1619 reads, " Long liue King Henry."

I here present the traitorous head of Cade,
That hand to hand in single fight I slue.
    Kin. First thanks to heauen, & next to thee my
        friend,
That hast subdude that wicked traitor thus.
Oh let me see that head that in his life,
Did worke me and my land such cruell spight,
A visage sterne, cole blacke his curled locks,
Deepe trenched furrowes in his frowning brow,
Presageth warlike humors in his life.
Here take it hence and thou for thy reward,
Shalt be immediately created Knight.
Kneele downe my friend, and tell me whats thy name ?
    Eyden. Alexander Eyden, if it please your grace,
A poore Esquire of Kent.
    Kin. Then rise vp sir Alexander Eyden knight,
And for thy maintenance, I freely giue
A thousand markes a yeare to maintaine thee,[1]
Beside the firme reward that was proclaimde,
For those that could performe this worthie act,
And thou shalt waight vpon the person of the king.
    Eyden. I humbly thank your grace,[2] and I no
        longer liue,
Then I proue iust and loyall to the King.[3]   [*Exct.*

Enter the Queene with the Duke of SOMERSET.[4]

    Kin. O Buckingham see where Somerset comes,
Bid him go hide himselfe till Yorke be gone.

---

[1] The edition printed by W. W. in 1600 reads :—

"A thousand markes a yeere for to maintaine thee."

[2] This speech is rather ambiguously worded, but seems to imply Iden's ready acceptance of Henry's bounty.   The author, if this be the case, must have forgotten Iden's previous commendation of a country life, and his low idea of the value of court advantages.

[3] The edition printed by W. W. in 1600 reads :—

"Then I prooue iust and loyall vnto my king."

[4] This direction is found in the same place in the folio

Queene. He shall not hide himselfe for feare of Yorke,
But beard and braue him proudly to his face.

Yorke. Whose that, proud Somerset at libertie?
Base fearefull Henry that thou dishonor'st me,
By heauen, thou shalt not gouerne ouer me:
I cannot brooke that Traitors presence here,
Nor will I subiect be to such a King,
That knowes not how to gouerne nor to rule,
Resigne thy Crowne proud Lancaster to me,
That thou vsurped hast so long by force,
For now is Yorke resolu'd to claime his owne,
And rise aloft into faire Englands Throane.

Somer. Proud Traitor, I arest thee on high treason,
Against thy soueraigne Lord, yeeld thee false Yorke,
For here I sweare, thou shalt vnto the Tower,
For these proud words which thou hast giuen the king.

Yorke. Thou art deceiued, my sonnes shalbe my
baile,[1]
And send thee there in dispight of him.
Hoe, where are you boyes?

Queene. Call Clifford hither presently.

Enter the Duke of YORKES *sonnes,* EDWARD *the Earle
of* MARCH, *and crook-backe* RICHARD, *at the one
doore, with Drumme and soldiers, and at the other
doore, enter* CLIFFORD *and his sonne, with Drumme
and souldiers, and* CLIFFORD *kneeles to* HENRY,
and speakes.

Clif. Long liue my noble Lord, and soueraigne King.

---

editions of the amended play. Modern editors place it three
lines lower. The original position does not involve any ab-
surdity, for Somerset must at all events be within sight of the
king, and we have only to suppose him just entering a large
room.

[1] The second folio reads the corresponding passage as follows:

" Sirrah, call in my sonnes to be my baile:
I know ere they will let me goe to Ward,
They'l pawne their Swords for my infranchisement;"

Yorke. We thank thee Clifford.
Nay, do not affright vs [1] with thy lookes,
If thou didst mistake, we pardon thee, kneele
    againe.
  Clif. Why, I did no way mistake, this is my
    King.
What is he mad? to Bedlam with him.[2]
  Kin. I, a bedlam frantike humor driues him thus
To leauy Armes against his lawfull King.
  Clif. Why doth not[3] your grace send him to the
    Tower?
  Queene. He is arested, but will not obey,
His sonnes he saith, shall be his baile.[4]
  Yorke. How say you boyes, will you not?
  Ed. Yes noble father, if our words will serue.
  Rich. And if our words will not, our swords shall.
  Yorke. Call hither to the stake, my two rough
    beares.
  Kin. Call Buckingham, and bid him Arme him-
    selfe.
  Yorke. Call Buckingham and all the friends thou
    hast,
Both thou and they, shall curse this fatall houre.

---

which contains *three* variations from the first, and all improvements, though modern editors have only adopted two of them.
In the edition of 1619 this speech is erroneously given to the
king.

  [1] The second folio reads, "do not affright me," but York is
now speaking as a sovereign.

  [2] This is generally considered an anachronism, but Ritson
quotes Stowe to prove that there was "an hospitall for distracted
people" called St. Mary's of Bethlehem, as early as the
thirteenth century. See "Survey of London," 1598, p. 127,
and Malone's "Shakespeare," by Boswell, vol. xviii. p. 344.

  [3] The edition printed by W. W. in 1600 reads, "Why do
not."

  [4] The edition printed by W. W. in 1600 reads, "shall be his
suretie," an alteration which is partially adopted in the amended
play.

Enter at one doore, the Earles of SALSBURY *and* WAR-
WICKE, *with Drumme and souldiers. And at the
other,*[1] *the Duke of* BUCKINGHAM, *with Drumme
and souldiers.*

Clif. Are these thy beares ? weel bayte them soone,
Dispight of thee, and all the friends thou hast.
War. You had best go dreame againe,
To keepe you from the tempest of the field.
Clif. I am resolu'd to beare a greater storme,
Then any thou canst coniure vp to day,
And that ile write vpon thy Burgonet,[2]
Might I but know thee by thy household badge.[3]
War. Now by my fathers age,[4] old Neuels crest,
The Rampant Beare chained to the ragged staffe,
This day ile weare aloft my burgonet,
As on a mountaine top the Cædar showes,
That keepes his leaues in spight of any storme,
Euen to affright the with the view thereof.
Clif. And from thy burgonet will I rend the beare,
And tread him vnderfoote with all contempt,
Dispight the Beare-ward that protects him so.
Yoong Clif. And so renowmed soueraigne to Armes,[5]
To quell these Traitors and their compleases.

---

[1] The edition of 1619 reads, " and at the other doore."
[2] A helmet. See " Antony and Cleopatra," act i. sc. 5.
[3] The first folio reads " housed " and the second " house's "
instead of " household." The reading in our text is the correct
one. The speech is exactly the same in the amended play with
this exception. See Collier's " Shakespeare," vol. v. p. 216.
[4] Perhaps " badge," though the alteration does not seem to be
absolutely necessary.
[5] The first folio reads :—
" And so to armes victorious Father ;"
while the second folio has :—
" And so to Armes victorious noble Father."
This difference is not noticed by any of the earlier editors of
Shakespeare, although of some importance.

Rich. Fie, Charitie for shame, speake it not in spight,
For you shall sup with Iesus Christ to-night.
Yoong Clif. Foule Stigmaticke thou canst not tell.
Rich. No, for if not in heauen, youle surely sup in hell.   [*Exet omnes.*

Alarmes to the battaile, and then enter the Duke of SO-MERSET *and* RICHARD *fighting, and* RICHARD *kils him vnder the signe of the Castle in Saint Albones.*

Rich. So Lie thou there, and breathe thy last.[1]
Whats here, the signe of the Castle?
Then the prophesie is come to passe,[2]
For Somerset was forewarned of Castles,
The which he alwaies did obserue.
And now, behold, vnder a paltry Ale-house signe,
The Castle in saint Albones,
Somerset hath made the Wissard famous by his death.
                                           [*Exet.*

Alarme again, and enter the Earle of WARWICKE *alone.*

War. Clifford of Comberland, tis Warwicke calles,
And if thou doest not hide thee from the Beare.
Now whilst the angry Trompets sound Alarmes,
And dead mens cries do fill the emptie aire :
Clifford I say, come forth and fight with me,
Proud Northerne Lord, Clifford of Comberland,
Warwicke is hoarse with calling thee to Armes.
Clif. speakes within. Warwicke stand still, and view the way that Clifford hewes with his murthering Curtel-

---

[1] This is omitted in the amended play. The edition of 1619 inelegantly reads :—
    "So, lie thou there, and tumble in thy blood."
[2] "There died under the sygne of the Castle, Edmond duke of Somerset, who long before was warned to eschew all castles, and besyde hym lay Henry the Second erle of Northumberland, Humfrey erle of Stafford," &c.—Hall's "Chronicle."

axe, through the fainting troopes to finde thee out.
Warwicke stand still, and stir not till I come.

Enter YORKE.

War. How now my Lord, what a foote?
Who kild your horse?
    Yorke. The deadly hand of Clifford. Noble Lord,
Fiue horse this day slaine vnder me,
And yet braue Warwicke I remaine aliue,
But I did kill his horse he lou'd so well,
The bonniest gray that ere was bred in North.

Enter CLIFFORD, *and* WARWICKE *offers to fight
with him.*

Hold Warwicke, and seeke thee out some other chase,
My selfe will hunt this deare to death.
    War. Braue Lord, tis for a Crowne thou fights,
Clifford farewell, as I entend to prosper well to-day,
It grieues my soule to leaue thee vnassaild.
                    [Exet WARWICKE.
    Yorke. Now Clifford, since we are singled here
    alone,
Be this the day of doome to one of vs,
For now my heart hath sworne immortall hate
To thee, and all the house of Lancaster.
    Clif. And here I stand, and pitch my foot to thine,
Vowing neuer to stir, till thou or I be slaine.
For neuer shall my heart be safe at rest,
Till I haue spoyld the hatefull house of Yorke.
          [Alarmes, and they fight, and YORKE *kils*
             CLIFFORD.[1]
    Yorke. Now Lancaster sit sure, thy sinowes shrinke,

---

[1] This is a departure from the truth of history ; but it is very
remarkable that a different account should be given by the
author of "The True Tragedie," if both these plays were, as is
generally supposed, written by the same hand.

Come fearefull Henry grouelling on thy face,
Yeeld vp thy Crowne vnto the Prince of York.

> [*Exet* YORKE.
> [*Alarmes, then enter yoong* CLIFFORD *alone.*

Yoong Clifford. Father of Comberland,
Where may I[1] seeke my aged father forth?
O! dismall sight, see where he breathlesse lies,
All smeard and weltred in his luke-warme blood,
Ah, aged pillar of all Comberlands true house,
Sweete father, to thy murthred ghoast I sweare,
Immortall hate vnto the house of Yorke,
Nor neuer shall I sleepe secure one night,
Till I haue furiously reuengde thy death,
And left not one of them to breath on earth.

> [*He takes him vp on his backe.*

And thus as old Ankyses sonne did beare
His aged father on his manly backe,
And fought with him against the bloodie Greeks,
Euen so will I.   But staie, heres one of them,
To whom my soule hath sworne immortall hate.

Enter RICHARD, *and then* CLIFFORD *laies downe his
father, fights with him,[2] and* RICHARD *flies away
againe.*

Out crooktbacke villaine, get thee from my sight,
But I will after thee, and once againe
When I haue borne my father to his Tent,
Ile trie my fortune better with thee yet.[3]

> [*Exet yoong* CLIFFORD *with his father.*

*Alarmes againe, and then enter three or foure, bearing
the Duke of* BUCKINGHAM *wounded to his Tent.*

Alarmes still, and then enter the King and Queene.

Queene. Away my Lord, and flie to London straight,

---

[1] The edition of 1619 reads, "Where I may."
[2] The word "with" is omitted in the edition of 1619.
[3] The word "yet" is omitted in the edition printed by W.
W. in 1600, but it is found in the edition of 1619.

Make hast, for vengeance comes along with them,
Come stand not to expostulate, lets go.
  Kin. Come then faire Queene, to London let vs
    hast,
And sommon a Parlament[1] with speede,
To stop the fury of these dyre euents.
                    [*Exet King and Queene.*

*Alarmes, and then a flourish, and enter the Duke
    of* YORKE[2] *and* RICHARD.

  Yorke. How now boyes, fortunate this fight hath
    bene,
I hope to vs and ours, for Englands good,
And our great honour, that so long we lost,
Whilst faint-heart Henry did vsurpe our rights:
But did you see old Salsbury, since we
With bloodie mindes did buckle with the foe,
I would not for the losse of this right hand,
That ought but well betide that good old man.
  Rich. My Lord, I saw him in the thickest throng,
Charging his Lance with his old weary armes,
And thrise I saw him beaten from his horse,
And thrise this hand did set him vp againe,
And still he fought with courage gainst his foes,
The boldest sprited[3] man that ere mine eyes beheld.

Enter SALSBURY *and* WARWICKE.

  Ed. See noble father, where they both do come,
The onely props vnto the house of Yorke.
  Sal. Well hast thou fought this day, thou valiant
    Duke,

---

  [1] The edition of 1619 reads, "And summon vp a parliament."
  [2] The edition of 1619 adds " Edward."
  [3] The edition of 1619 reads, " spirited."

And thou braue bud of Yorkes encreasing house,
The small remainder of my weary life,
I hold for thee, for with thy warlike arme,
Three times this day thou hast preseru'd my life.
 Yorke. What say you Lords, the King is fled to
  London ?
There as I here to hold a Parlament.
What saies Lord Warwicke, shall we after them ?
 War. After them, nay before them if we can.
Now by my faith[1] Lords, twas a glorious day,
Saint Albones battaile wonne by famous Yorke,
Shall be eternest[2] in all age to come.
Sound Drummes and Trumpets,[3] and to London all,
And more such daies as these to vs befall.
        [Exet omnes.

---

 [1] The amended play reads, "by my hand."
 [2] This reading is peculiar to the present edition.   The other
reads, "eterniz'd," which is also found in the amended play.
 [3] The first folio of the amended play reads, "Sound Drumme
and Trumpets."